Domenico Sorrentino

A HUMAN ECONOMY

Economics in the Serivce of the Common Good

The Lesson and Prophecy of Giuseppe Toniolo

Vita e Pensiero

HISTORICAL STUDIES

Translated by Matthew Sherry

Our Sunday Visitor
Huntington, Indiana

Published in English by OSV, 2025

30 29 28 27 26 25 1 2 3 4 5 6 7 8 9

Our Sunday Visitor Publishing Division
Our Sunday Visitor, Inc.
200 Noll Plaza
Huntington, IN 46750
1-800-348-2440

ISBN: 978-1-63966-310-1 (Inventory No. T2960)
eISBN: 978-1-63966-311-8
LCCN: 2025944783

Cover and interior design: Amanda Falk
Cover art: AdobeStock

PRINTED IN THE UNITED STATES OF AMERICA

Table of Contents

Foreword

Can Giuseppe Toniolo, a forgotten economist almost never mentioned in the accounts of economic thought, who lived between the nineteenth and twentieth centuries (1845–1918), become relevant again, to the point of being considered an economist of the future? This is the thesis of this book, which I hope will prove stimulating even for "insiders." It is a thesis also supported by a distinguished Italian economist, Stefano Zamagni, who honors me with his preface, and who does not hesitate to call Toniolo "a marginalized economist because he was a visionary."

The English edition of this volume, published four years after the Italian one, emerges against the backdrop of a landscape already quite different from the one in which it was born. Published in 2021, I had developed it in the context of the years marked by the coronavirus pandemic and the corresponding global economic recession. The pandemic also highlighted what Pope Francis, in the encyclical *Evangelii Gaudium*, discussed as global "inequality," expressed in the vast income gap between the few who possess the bulk of the world's wealth and the many who lack it, all the way down to those who pay the highest price for this injustice, dying from hunger or disease. In the Church, these were the years in which Pope Francis was speaking out precisely for the "least" ones of society, calling for a global economic renewal, and moving the hearts of young economists (Message of May 1, 2019, the launch of "The Economy of Francesco").

The book is being published in the United States at a time when the world is experiencing dramatic and disastrous wars that are producing bloodshed and destruction (Ukraine, Israel, Palestine, Iran). Other wars, less well-known but no less deadly, are lurking behind hidden economic interests and new, emerging geopolitical reorganizations. It also comes out in English a few months after the death of Pope Francis, while the leadership of the Church is being taken over by an American pope, born in Chicago but trained as a pastor in a South American diocese of Peru. He has chosen the name Leo XIV, expressly following in the footsteps of another great pope of the same name, Leo XIII, known above all as the pope of *Rerum Novarum*, with whom Giuseppe Toniolo had a special connection, becoming a true apostle of his teaching.

By choosing the name Leo XIV, Robert Prevost not only inherited the legacy of his immediate predecessor, who was incisive on the social level with unequivocal words and gestures in favor of the poor. Pope Francis developed in two encyclicals, *Laudato Si'* and *Fratelli Tutti*, a coherent discourse on the themes of the protection of creation and universal brotherhood. He also aligned himself with the entire social doctrine of the Church, which developed organically from the social encyclicals of Leo XIII and were taken up, developed, and updated in the magisterium of subsequent popes, having its historical point of greatest ecclesial visibility in the pastoral constitution *Gaudium et Spes* (1965) of the Second Vatican Council.

The first moments of Pope Prevost's magisterium demonstrated this attention to the "social" and "economic," again denouncing war and calling for peace. The new pope also referred to the topic of information technology and artificial intelligence, which suggests further magisterial developments; it was to be expected from a pope born in the most technologically advanced country in the world.

This global and ecclesial landscape makes understanding the thought of Toniolo even more interesting, the only professor economist to have been declared a "Blessed" by the Church (April 29, 2012), as we await, hopefully, his canonization as a saint of the universal Church.

A professor at the universities of Padua, Modena, and Pisa, he was the recognized leader of social commitment among Italian Catholics of his time, and he paved the way for other great figures in the Italian social, economic, and political tradition, such as Luigi Sturzo and Alcide De Gasperi.

His approach to economic science, even as it received the appreciation of illustrious thinkers and politicians such as Messedaglia, Luzzatti, and Cossa, was nevertheless undervalued and "snubbed" by some economists who were popular at the time (Pareto, Pantaleoni, etc.), and who did not forgive him for having declared ethics an "intrinsic factor" of economic laws from the moment of his first university lecture, held in Padua in 1873. The adjective "intrinsic" was a challenge to the economic science of the time which, in its positivist structure and its autonomist claims, considered ethics at most as an extrinsic factor, as if to say, a boundary not to be crossed. Today, the reference to ethics is also being reevaluated in economics by thinkers (Sen, Zamagni, etc.) who reject the perspective of an a-valuative economy and support the need for a value-based "foundation" of economic science, in which Toniolo exposed a fundamental error and from which all the others descended — the "anthropological" error, which made us forget man as an organic unity whose articulations can be distinguished, not separated.

Given the principle of freedom as the defining characteristic of human beings, economic laws, Toniolo clarified, can only be "tendential laws," not comparable to the rigid laws of the physical world. Furthermore — and here is where the distance from the economists who opposed him became an abyss — Toniolo took this principle to its most logical conclusion, arguing that, while the ethical nature of economic laws must be recognized, an equal influence must be attributed to the religious dimension of human beings. True ethics cannot be emotional and changeable. It can direct human actions, including economic ones, to the extent that it presupposes moral "conscience" and the principle of "responsibility," which, ultimately, refers to God.

Economics, therefore, in Toniolo's view, needed to transcend the myth of the *homo oeconomicus*, to restore to humanity, and to ethically regulate humanity, the central place it deserves. Humanity is the subject and the purpose of economics. Hence his expression "human economy," to emphasize that humanity is the center of gravity, relative to the other factors (nature and capital) that characterize the economic act. In particular, capital, while indispensable as an aid to human activity in economics, can never replace it. Today, this applies not only to financial capital, but also to the latest generation of technological capital (internet, artificial intelligence): Toniolo, therefore, denounces a capitalist economy that overwhelms the human factor and no longer has any connection, especially in its financial aspect, with the real economy. On this basis, the concrete declination of his entire economic framework develops. Above all, in his "Treatise on Social Economy" (*Trattato di economia sociale*), unfortunately unfinished, Toniolo outlines the features of an economy at the service of humanity, a service rendered not in an abstract manner, but in the concreteness of a human condition which, in his time, that of the first and second industrial revolutions, already presented extremely critical characteristics.

Beginning with the human person, economic activity must be conducted with respect for the relational dynamics that distinguish the person, overcoming an individualistic, self-referential, and atomistic concept of the human being, which is instead intrinsically relational. This is particularly timely in the fragmented condition of society today, characterized by a confusion of values and increasingly "liquid" relationships (Baumann). From the first essential relationship, that of the family, the entire network of social groups develops — the so-called intermediate bodies, cherished by the social doctrine of the Church — and this ultimately extends to the entire fabric of society, organized into its various progressive and expansive elements, up to the nation, the state, and universal society.

At the heart of his economic thought was a concern for the most vulnerable, once represented by the great mass of the proletariat, the designated victims of a market not balanced by moral and institutional principles of solidarity (welfare state, welfare society). On the side of the most vulnerable in his time were the Church, with its social doctrine — Toniolo was consulted by Leo XIII for *Rerum Novarum* — and socialism, particularly in its Marxist version. Toniolo took a militant position in the first side (the "ethical-Christian" school), declaring, and in some ways prophesying, in his "Program of Catholics Confronting Socialism," that the Marxist vision of reality would produce, "under the guise of freedom, a more universal and cruel servitude." History proved him right. With the same prophetic acumen, coupled with practical commitment (legal protection of workers, support for the trade-union movement, promotion of cooperativism, etc.), Toniolo condemned bourgeois individualism as incapable of the solidarity that could have solved the social question at its root. His vision of "Christian democracy," emphasizing the common good achieved through the synergy of social classes, and not just through parliamentary methods, was distinguished by its particular attention to the defense of the neediest classes.

Toniolo deserves to be "known," in order to be "recognized," as an "economist of the future." Today, it has become difficult to discover him, partly due to the limited accessibility of his writings collected in the *Opera Omnia*. I am confident that the English edition will do its part. I humbly present it to the debate among economists. I am confident that, despite some undoubtedly outdated aspects, it is a vital and inspiring thought, one that the current crisis in economics and economic science can benefit from profitably. I hope that many economists in university training will also draw value from it, especially those young economists called by Pope Francis to join the movement "The Economy of Francesco," certainly also supported by Pope Leo XIV, committed to building "*a different economy, one that makes people live and does not kill, includes and does not exclude, humanizes and does not dehumanize, takes care of creation and does not plunder it.*"

Domenico Sorrentino
Assisi, July 1, 2025

Preface

I cannot help but admit that in introducing this work by Domenico Sorrentino I must try to keep in check the natural affection that is always felt toward a friend and a person of uncommon cultural breadth. But I cannot help but recognize that the author of this book is a scholar who is able to ally his vast open-mindedness with scholarly rigor and depth of analysis. As the reader will see, Archbishop Sorrentino understands that the economist is necessarily a bilingual figure, one who must be able to speak the language of *scientia* and that of *humanitas*. Hence the implication that the narrowest specialization must be matched with the broadest vision of the whole.

The great theme at the center of the work now brought for the reader's judgment is that of a systematic reconstruction of Giuseppe Toniolo's thought, with a twofold intention. For one, to revive the memory and renew the message of the economist Toniolo, who on account of having thought and written ahead of his time has never received due recognition from the profession to which he belonged. And for another, by analyzing Toniolo's thought and testimony Sorrentino lays bare the contradictions and omissions of the current economic mainstream, no longer capable of meeting the great challenges of our model of civilization. In this work of reconstruction, our author adopts Ludwig Wittgenstein's thesis according to which ideas, like words, are also actions, and therefore economic inquiry must not only illuminate, but also guide. It is to this second aim that I will turn my attention, albeit briefly, in what follows.

The goal of Sorrentino's presentation is to urge economists and policymakers to confront the pressing need to deal with the problem of the foundations. With explicit reference to Toniolo, Sorrentino writes: "The economic edifice (and not only it) is at risk of collapsing when it lacks solid foundations. This applies to economic practice as well as to science." And a little further on: "In offering this attempt at a summary I will limit myself to what I consider essential for the ends of economic discussion. I know well that Toniolo is a man of his time, and so there is no lack of dated aspects in his thinking, in some cases to be frankly considered obsolete" (p. 345). But this does not change the fact that the core of Toniolo's message retains, for the present day, all its freshness and ability to suggest plausible ways out of the great paradoxes that characterize our time.

The pages that Sorrentino dedicates to analyzing the state of health of economics as a discipline are stimulating and intriguing. The thesis he defends is that it is not possible for inquiry to confine itself to a sort of value-free limbo. It is necessary to take a position by choosing the observation point from which to examine reality. Otherwise, the discipline may continue to expand and increase its technical-analytical apparatus, but if it does not emerge from its self-referentiality it will be ever less capable of coming to grips with reality and so ever less capable of "being a guide for action." No one can deny that this is the real risk that the science of economics faces today. For fear of openly espousing a specific value, the preference is to hole up in analysis alone, dedicating growing intellectual resources to the use of increasingly refined logical-mathematical tools. But there can never be a trade-off between the formal rigor of economic discourse — which in any case is indispensable — and its ability to explain — that is, to interpret the facts. To put it another way, applied thought and theoretical thought must proceed at the same pace, just as Plato suggested in the famous parable in *Phaedrus*: "The furrow will be straight [and therefore the harvest will be plentiful] if the two horses pulling the plow advance abreast."

Indeed, the path of reductionism taken by the science of economics starting from the second half of the twentieth century has ended up disarming critical thinking, with results that are now plain for all to see. There is in this a specific responsibility on the part of the profession: For too long generations of young scholars have been led to believe that scientific rigor requires sterile conditions — that is, that inquiry, to be scientific, must be freed from any reference to value. The result is that axiological individualism — which is itself a value judgment — has acquired the status of a "natural" assumption that, as such, for one thing does not require any justification, and for another is set up as a benchmark against which every other hypothesis on the nature of man "must" be measured. So, it should come as no surprise if the hypothesis of individualism is alone granted, still today, the privilege of naturalness in official economic science.

No one can fail to see how the current crisis of meaning in economics depends largely on the circumstance that the decision, made over the last thirty years, to no longer deal with questions of value leaves the discipline particularly exposed to the ideological exploitation of its results. The invitation that Sorrentino courageously issues in this work is to consider the resumption of economic inquiry in which intellectual interest and civic engagement come back into reciprocity, just as Toniolo's testimony has laid out for us. This is necessary if one wishes to understand that the assumption of a world occupied only by *homines oeconomici* ("economic people"), who relate to each other only in forms of trade and consumption, inevitably entails a destiny of exclusion. The anthropological reductionism dominant today is unable to understand that the human being is an essentially relational entity, and that otherness is at the origin of personal identity, not vice versa.

The extraordinary initiative presented in Assisi, Italy, in November 2020 (*The Economy of Francesco*), to which Archbishop Sorrentino made a contribution of central importance, takes up not a few of the Tonioliian arguments revisited in this volume. The challenge that is posed to economists, business owners, and politicians is to work with courage to find the means, which do exist, to transform from within and surpass the market-economy model that has been consolidated during the present era. The end to be pursued is that of asking the market not only to produce wealth and ensure sustainable growth, but also to place itself at the service of integral human development — that is, a development that tends to keep in harmony the three human dimensions: the material, the socio-relational, and the spiritual. The present-day market, while it ensures progress in the first dimension, that of growth — and Pope Francis explicitly recognized this — certainly does not improve things with respect to the other two dimensions. One could think of the worrying increase in the social costs of growth. On the altar of efficiency, erected as a new myth of the second modernity, nonnegotiable values like (substantive) democracy, distributive justice, positive freedom, ecological sustainability, and still others have been sacrificed. One must be careful not to confuse the ideas: The market discussed here is certainly compatible with commutative justice and negative freedom (the freedom to act), but not with distributive justice or positive freedom (the freedom to achieve). Likewise, it can go arm in arm — as has, in fact, happened — with dictatorial political structures, whereas this is not compatible with the vision of the market advocated by the civil economy paradigm.

The social doctrine of the Church has always insisted on the point of principle that the mechanism of the market is not an ethically neutral one, the outcomes of which, if deemed unacceptable according to some standard of distributive justice, can always be corrected after the fact by the state (or by another public agency). One should pay heed that it is precisely this position — which refers to John Stuart Mills' distinction between the "laws of production" and the "laws of distribution" of wealth — that has legitimized the well-known dichotomous model of the social order, by which the state is identified as the place of solidarity and the market as the place of privatism, whose sole end is that of maximum allocative efficiency. That such a model is no longer sustainable is known to all. Although the present market economy postulates, *ex ante*, equality among those who intend to take part in it, it generates, *ex post*, inequalities in the results. And when equality in being diverges too much from equality in having, it is the very rationale of the market that is called into question. It is in this precise sense that Pope Francis's suggestion is to be interpreted: If the intention is to "save" the order of the market, this must be restored as an economic institution that tends toward inclusion. Inclusive prosperity is the goal. If it is true that a prosperity that does not tend to include everyone is immoral, an inclusivity divorced from prosperity is likewise unacceptable, given that what is not produced cannot be distributed.

Sorrentino reminds us of the reason why, despite the quality of the intellectual forces in the field, a credible solution to that trade-off has not yet been reached. It is because something has been forgotten: that a human society is unsustainable when the sense of fraternity is extinguished and everything is reduced on the one hand to improving transactions based on the exchange of equivalents and on the other to increasing the transfers implemented by structures of public assistance. There is no future for a society in which the principle of fraternity is dissolved; there is no happiness for a society in which there is only "giving to get" or "giving out of duty." This is why neither the liberal-individualist vision of the world, in which everything (or almost everything) is exchange, nor the state-centric vision of society, in which everything (or almost everything) is duty, is a sure guide for getting us out of the shallows in which the second great transformation in the sense of Karl Polanyi is putting the stability of our civilizational model to the test.

There is a specific reason to take satisfaction in this book by Sorrentino. It comes down to this: Why is it that so much of today's social thought, however refined and elegant, is sterile, incapable of grasping reality and therefore incapable of suggesting guidelines for action aimed at the common good? The main reason is that, from the time in which globalization and the Third Industrial Revolution began to give the economy a completely new direction, the separation between the economic sphere and the social sphere was consummated, assigning to the former the task of producing wealth (without excessive concerns about the way in which this might take place, thus making ethics a useless, indeed harmful burden), and to the latter the task of ensuring its redistribution.

This led to the belief that a society could progress along the path of integral human development while keeping a division between the code of efficiency, which along with a well-defined set of rules would be enough to make the market work well, and the code of solidarity, which under the vigilant guidance of the state would guarantee distributive justice. Hence the paradox that afflicts our societies: On the one hand, many are taking positions on behalf of those who for various reasons are left behind by market competition or even excluded from it. On the other hand, the entire system of values (one could think of the criteria for evaluating individual action, lifestyle, education, etc.) is centered on efficiency.

So, is it any wonder that social inequalities are increasing even amid a global increase in wealth? And that the indicators that measure public happiness register continuous decreases after per capita income has exceeded a certain threshold? And that the principle of merit is clumsily confused with meritocracy, as if they were synonymous? And that reciprocity is confused with altruism or philanthropy? And that common goods (water, air, land, knowledge, etc.) are taken and treated as if they were public goods?

The heartfelt appeal that the author of this dense work addresses to us, taking up Toniolo's thought with critical acumen, is to put the principle of gift as gratuitousness — donation is not sufficient — back in the public sphere. Sorrentino tells us that the culture of giving is one of the indispensable prerequisites for the state and the market to function well for the common good. Without extensive practices of giving, it may be possible to build an efficient market and an authoritative (and even just) state, but it will never be possible to overcome those "discontents of civilization" of which Sigmund Freud speaks. In fact, there are two categories of goods that we cannot do without: goods of justice and goods of gratuitousness. The former — one could think of the goods provided by the welfare state — establish a specific *duty* on the part of a subject — typically the public agencies — to ensure that citizens' rights to those goods are satisfied. Goods of gratuitousness, instead, look to an *obligation* that stems from the bond that unites us to each other. In fact, it is the recognition of a mutual *ligatio* between people that the *ob-ligatio* is established. And so, while in order to defend a right one can, and must, resort to the law, an obligation is fulfilled through reciprocating gratuitousness. No law can ever impose reciprocity, and no incentive can ever favor gratuitousness. Yet no one fails to see how important goods of gratuitousness are for the need for happiness that every man carries within himself. Efficiency and justice, even if united, are not enough to make us happy.

The twentieth century wiped out the third pillar in its constructivist fury. Everything had to be traced back either to the capitalist market or to the state, or at most to a mix of these two basic institutions, depending on the ideological and political sympathies of the various social actors. Today there is the awareness that the bipolar state/market paradigm has run its historical course and is giving way to a tripolar model of the social order: state, market, community — that is, public, private, civic. Modernity was based on two pillars: the principle of equality, guaranteed and legitimized by the state, and the principle of freedom, made possible by the market. Postmodernity has brought out the need for a third pillar: reciprocity, which translates the principle of brotherhood into practice.

This is why the book in the reader's hands is to be given welcome and its diffusion encouraged, so that other scholars and researchers, retracing its steps, may add new links to a chain that, over time, can only grow longer and stronger. Antoine de Saint-Exupéry wrote that "perfection is achieved, not when there is nothing more to add, but when there is nothing more to take away." For this book — in which there is nothing to take away — I wish the success, in terms of both reading and criticism, that it richly deserves.

Stefano Zamagni

Abbreviations

Opera Omnia di Giuseppe Toniolo

CS: *Capitalismo e socialismo*, preface by S. Majerotto (Vatican City, 1947).

DC I–II: *Democrazia cristiana. Concetti e indirizzi*, I–II, preface by A. De Gasperi (Vatican City, 1949).

DC III–IV: *Democrazia cristiana. Istituti e forme*, I–II, preface by A. Ardigo (Vatican City, 1951; DC III corresponds to vol. I, DC IV to vol. II).

IC: *Iniziative culturali e di azione cattolica*, preface by G. Dalla Torre (Vatican City, 1949).

LL I–II–III: *Lettere, vol. I (1871–95), vol. II (1896–1903), vol. III (1904–18)*, collected by G. Anichini, organized and annotated by N. Vian (Vatican City, 1952–53).

OPS: *L'odierno problema sociologico. Studio storico-critico*, preface by A. Fanfani (Vatican City, 1947).

RF: *Dei remoti fattori della potenza economica di Firenze nel Medio Evo e scritti storici*, preface by S. Majerotto (Vatican City, 1952).

SEST I–II: *Storia dell'economia sociale in Toscana nel Medio Evo, vol. I, La vita civile-politica, vol. II, La vita economica*, preface by M. Romani (Vatican City, 1948).

SS I–II: *Scritti spirituali, religiosi, familiari e vari, I–II*, preface by F. Costa (Vatican City, 1952).

TES: *Trattato di economia sociale e scritti economici, IV*, preface by F. Vito (Vatican City, 1949–52).

NOTE
Each of the volumes indicated above will be cited in full the first time, subsequently in abbreviation, according to the list just presented. In places, to assist the reader, the full citation will be reproduced. Considering that in some volumes of the *Opera Omnia*, in addition to the fundamental text that gives the volume its title there are also articles, essays, reviews, etc., when these are cited repeatedly or with particular frequency we will hold to the following list of abbreviations, adding the abbreviation of the volume title as indicated above. If the work by Toniolo cited is the one that gives the volume its title, the abbreviation will follow immediately; otherwise it will be preceded by "in."

Articles and essays cited from the Opera Omnia *of Toniolo*

Criteri direttivi: "*Criteri direttivi sull'ordinamento degli istituti bancari esclusi i banchi di emissione*," in *Atti e documenti del XIV Congresso cattolico italiano* (Venice, 1897), pt. I, 186–94; now in TES V, 537–50.
Criteri scientifici: "*Criteri scientifici etico-economici intorno al credito dal punto di vista cristiano*," in *Atti del II Congresso cattolico italiano degli studiosi di scienze sociali*, Padua, August 26–28, 1896 (Padua, 1898), 194–209; now in TES V, 485–523.

Democrazia cristiana: *La democrazia cristiana* (Rome: Società cattolica italiana di cultura, 1900); now in DC I, 15–174.

Elemento etico: *Dell'elemento etico quale fattore intrinseco delle leggi economiche. Prelezione al corso di economia politica nell'Università di Padova, 5 dicembre 1873* (Padua: Ed. Sacchetto, 1874); now in TES II, 266–92.

Genesi storica: "La genesi storica dell'odierna crisi sociale economica," in *Rivista internazionale di scienze sociali e discipline ausiliarie* [hereafter RISS], 1893, vol. I, 39–68 and 223–53; now in CS, 103–98.

Indirizzi e concetti: Indirizzi e concetti sociali all'esordire del sec. XX (Pisa: Mariotti, 1900); now in DC II, 1–282.

Lezioni distribuzione: Sulla distribuzione della ricchezza. Lezioni (Verona-Padua: Drucker e Tedeschi, 1878); now in TES IV, 103–213.

Linee e quesiti: Alcune linee e quesiti di un programma di economia sociale cristiana (Bergamo: S. Alessandro, 1886); now in TES II, 367–91.

Passato e futuro: "Passato e futuro dell'azione economica fra i cattolici d'Italia," in *Azione sociale*, December 1906, 1–10; now in DC II, 285–300.

Problema sociologico: Il supremo quesito della sociologia e i doveri della scienza nell'ora presente (Rome: Un. Typ. Coop. Ed., 1903; from articles published in the RISS: 1903, vol. XXXII, 169–96, vol. XXXIII, 18–47; 1904, vol. XXXV, 161–77, 321–45, and 481–509), reworked and republished two years later with the title *L'odierno problema sociologico. Studio storico-critico* (Florence: Libreria editrice fiorentina, 1905). It is this edition that is used, with the same title, with a preface by Amintore Fanfani and the addition of a study on Spencer in the appendix, in *Opera Omnia di G. Toniolo* (Vatican City, 1947).

Problemi ed ammaestramenti: *Problemi ed ammaestramenti sociali dell'età costantiniana*, in RISS, 1913, vol. LXII, 23–43, vol. LXIII, 3–20 and 330–

54; now in CS, 1–102.

Programma scientifico: L'Unione cattolica per gli studi sociali in Italia. Intendimenti, costituzione, operato e programma scientifico (Padua: Tipografia del Seminario, 1903); now in IC, 75–133.

Provvedimenti sociali: Provvedimenti sociali popolari (Rome: Società cattolica italiana di cultura, 1902); now in DC III, 1–201.

Riforme tributarie: Riforme del sistema tributario, in *Atti del II Congresso cattolico italiano degli studiosi di scienze sociali*, Padua, August 26–28, 1896 (Padua: Tipografia del Seminario, 1898), 194–209; now in TES V, 524–36.

Salario: "*Il salario. Saggio di una esposizione sistematica delle sue leggi,*" in *Giornale degli economisti,* 1878, vol. VII, 261–80 and 343–64, vol. VIII, 267–89; now in TES IV, 214–91.

Socialismo: Il socialismo nella storia della civiltà. Linee direttive (Florence: Libreria Editrice Fiorentina, 1903); now in CS, 267–446. This is a book resulting from various articles published in the RISS: 1899, vol. XX, 3–16, with the title "*Cenni sulle crisi sociali e sulle corrispondenti dottrine socialistiche,*" and the subtitles "*L'ordine e il disordine sociale,*" "*Le crisi sociali*"; 1899, vol. XXI, 537–56, with the title "*Cenni sulle dottrine socialistiche nella storia,*" and the subtitles "*Nella cultura classica pagana,*" "*Nella cultura cristiana medioevale*"; 1900, vol. XXII, 34–49 and 161–76, with the title "*Il socialismo nella cultura moderna,*" and the subtitles "*La preparazione del socialismo teorico moderno,*" "*Lo sviluppo del socialismo teoretico moderno (1517–1800)*"; 1900, vol. XXIII, 49–69 and 169–80, with the title "*Il socialismo nella cultura moderna,*" and the subtitles "*La maturazione sistematica del socialismo,*" "*La elaborazione scientifica idealistica (1804–1848),*" "*La elaborazione scientifica positiva (1848–1870)*"; 1901, vol. XXV, 69–87 and 353–71, with the title "*Il socialismo nella cultura moderna,*" and the subtitle "*La diffusione universale del socialismo teoretico dal 1870 ad oggi*"; 1902, vol. XXVIII, 87–102 and 349–64, with the title "*Il socia-*

lismo nella cultura moderna," and the subtitles "*L'universalizzazione del socialismo pratico dal 1870 ad oggi,*" "*L'atteggiamento odierno del socialismo,*" "*Ammaestramenti finali.*"

Sperimento sociale: "*Un grande sperimento sociale. Storia, giudizi, ammaestramenti,*" in RISS, 1897, vol. XV, 202–19 and 481–89; now in DC III, 255–323.

Trattato: Trattato di economia sociale, in TES IV.

Other frequent abbreviations

Attualità del pensiero: M. L. Fornaciari Davoli, G. Russo, eds., *Attualità del pensiero di Giuseppe Toniolo* (Milan: FrancoAngeli, 1982).

Chiesa nella storia: D. Sorrentino, *Giuseppe Toniolo. Una Chiesa nella storia* (Milan: Vita e Pensiero, 2012).

Contributi alla conoscenza: Various authors, *Contributi alla conoscenza del pensiero di Giuseppe Toniolo* (Pisa: Pacini, 1984), proceedings of the conference "Economy and Society in the Crisis of the Modern State: The Thought of Giuseppe Toniolo," Pisa, December 18–19, 1981,

DEC: L. Bruni, S. Zamagni, eds., *Dizionario di economia civile* (Rome: Città Nuova, 2009).

Economia e società: D. Bodega, A. Carera, eds., *Economia e società per il bene comune. La lezione di Giuseppe Toniolo (1918–2018)* (Milan: Vita e Pensiero, 2020), conference proceedings, Catholic University of the Sacred Heart, November 24, 2018.

Economista di Dio: D. Sorrentino, *L'economista di Dio. Giuseppe Toniolo,* preface by F. Miano (Rome: AVE, 2012).

Profilo di storia: E. Screpanti, S. Zamagni, *Profilo di storia del pensiero*

economico, I, Dalle origini a Keynes, II, Gli sviluppi contemporanei (Rome: Carocci, 2004; 6th edition, 2017).

RISS: *Rivista internazionale di scienze sociali e discipline ausiliarie L'uomo come fine:* A. Carera, ed., *Giuseppe Toniolo. L'uomo come fine. Con saggi sulla storia dell'Istituto Giuseppe Toniolo di Studi Superiori* (Milan: Vita e Pensiero, 2014; conference proceedings, Catholic University of the Sacred Heart, March 21–23, 2012).

Introduction

Catholics ask "that a capitalist economy epitomized by the lending of capital to the enterpriser be replaced with a human economy par excellence, so that capital may become a follower and ally of the industrious man."[1]

This quote from Giuseppe Toniolo, dated 1896, is situated in the context of a heated debate (which we will get a chance to examine). For now, let it suffice to justify this systematic rereading of his economic thought. With it I complete, in a conceptual trilogy, two other works, one of a biographical[2] and the other of a theological[3] character. The present work presupposes both and often refers to them.

On April 29, 2012, Toniolo was declared blessed: the first economist — in the academic sense — to be raised to the honors of the altar. Spanning 1845 to 1918, his life was intense and multifaceted. He had a leading role in inspiring cultural and social engagement among Italian Catholics. Catholic Action numbered him among its prominent representatives, and the Catholic University of the Sacred Heart among its precursors. He can therefore be approached from multiple points of view.[4]

The fact remains that his intellectual and academic efforts had the economic sphere as their center of gravity. When he was called "professor," "of economics" was understood. He boldly moved into this field with the lecture he gave at the University of Padua in 1873, titled "On the ethical element as an intrinsic factor of economic laws": This would be the common thread of his economic thought, systematically presented in the *Trattato di economia sociale* ("Treatise on Social Economics"; hereafter *Trattato*).

His economic theory, even in the Catholic world, ended in the shadows,[5] which did not allow it to express its rich potential. The need for that potential today — this is the thesis of the present author — ranks high among those of the renewal of economics that many are hoping for. There is, in Toniolo's pages, a scholarly lesson, but also an authentic store of prophecy, in the double sense of a somehow inspired message and a certain predictiveness visible in the light of the course of history.

Unfortunately, Toniolo the economist is unknown, or known mainly to the handful of specialists in his thought.[6] The reason? In historical terms, several can be conjectured.[7] Decisive today is the limited availability of his texts,[8] a shortcoming that must be remedied.

To this it should be added that his thought — extremely broad in its perspectives amid the religious, social, economic — never deliberately separates the economic dimension from all the other dimensions of society. So it can happen — and does happen — that economists view him more as a sociologist than as an economist.[9] It must be recognized, as a mitigating factor, that one who takes in hand the *Trattato* with its large preparatory volume, comparing it with the current treatises on economics crammed with graphs and equations, gets the impression more of a sociological than of an economic treatise.[10] The more strictly economic discussion, in a technical sense, begins with the subsequent volume. But who says that all discussion of economics must begin with numbers, money, and finance? Isn't it true that the word *economy*, with its root *oikos* ("house"), refers first to the family and only after that to the market?[11] But words have their own destiny. From time to time we need to rediscover them starting with their DNA.

The present writer is not an economist.[12] So he writes about economics with fear and trembling, leaving the debate on the more specific aspects to the experts.[13] But what drives me to this adventure is the fact that for decades I have been acquainting myself with Toniolo's works, including those in the field of economics. I therefore consider myself qualified to correctly present his thought, referring to his texts and trying to put them in their context. I will refer to the five volumes of the *Trattato*, but not only to those. None of the volumes of the *Opera Omnia* will be overlooked. It will be an exhibit full of quotations, making plenty of room for Toniolo's texts (almost like an anthology), to allow readers to approach his thought as directly as possible, and also his language, albeit a bit redundant, with terms that in the meantime have become obsolete.[14]

I believe it is time — after a long season of rediscovery in writings and conferences[15] — to set out an overview and guide to a systematic rereading of Toniolo the economist. In this way I hope to provide a service for beginners who would like to know more, and a stimulus for experts in the field to take an interest in him. The conference on Toniolo held in Milan, Italy, in November 2018, a century after his death, showed how, also in the domain of economics, he is anything but a shadow of the past.[16]

I also hope that the timing is right: the renewal of economics is an urgent matter that cannot be postponed. The COVID-19 pandemic — the setting in which this work was born — has laid bare the fragility of the global system. The deficit of solidarity appears evident, with an uneven economic landscape showing an ever-widening split between the few who hold the bulk of the world's wealth and the very great number of poor people. The condemnation that Pope Leo XIII's *Rerum Novarum* made, against the backdrop of the First Industrial Revolution, pointing to the immense number of proletarians forced into a condition "little better than that of slavery itself," still seems — despite an undoubted global growth of the economy — to be relevant. Pope Francis's initiative to involve young people in rethinking the economy (Economy of Francesco[17]) speaks volumes.

Toniolo was the "prophet" of *Rerum Novarum*. His system of economics is in full harmony with the principles of the social doctrine of the Church. Naturally, much has changed since his death — including in economic matters — in the panorama of facts and theories. Social doctrine itself has developed. A compendium presents this in an organic manner,[18] but the documents of Benedict XVI and Francis have enriched it and are pushing it toward new frontiers.[19] Pope Leo XIV, taking the name of the pope of *Rerum Novarum*, may well signal continuity in this direction. So, recovering Toniolo's thought under the present circumstances does not mean that this can be proposed again in its entirety. It will be necessary to distinguish relevance and irrelevance, light and shadow. But the fundamental structure of his thought remains — in my view — solid and fertile. There are flowers that rapidly bloom into beauty but soon wither. There are trees that take time to grow, but then defy the centuries. I believe that Toniolo the economist belongs to the latter category.

Chapter I
The Motives of Economic Action

What sort of economics?

University of Padua, December 5, 1873. Giuseppe Toniolo, twenty-eight years old, is a professor nervously beginning his academic career with a pre-lecture that will determine his freedom to teach political economy. The topic: "On the ethical element as an intrinsic factor of economic laws." He is speaking to an audience of experts that includes the professors Angelo Messedaglia[1] and Luigi Luzzatti,[2] his former teachers, whom he venerates as masters. The fact that they are listening to him is enough to make him feel both honored and anxious. Will he live up to their expectations? In the end, he resolves the mental strain by appealing to a "solemn judgment" he heard a few days before from one of them: "To the humble is reserved not only the supernal kingdom, but also that of science."[3] Translation: Science cannot be conducted except in the recognition of "not knowing" (ancient Socratic wisdom!), and so relying on the humility of the seeker. This also applies to economics: "A science to which the finest minds of every nation have been applying themselves for over a century, yet whose conclusions are today called into question."[4]

In entering the grand arena of economics, Toniolo carefully selects his field. The science to which he refers as having been born more than a century before bears the names of Adam Smith and David Ricardo, of what is called the "Manchester," or "classical," school. This is prevalent in his time, but he firmly keeps his distance from it. His preference goes to a school established in Germany[5] but with no shortage of adherents in Italy. Indeed, he emphasizes "for love of truth and devotion to country" that in Italy it has a long history of like-minded men, if not actual precursors, from Genovesi[6] to Verri,[7] from Ricci[8] to Carli,[9] from Gioja[10] to Minghetti.[11] These are names that express, in his view, the "Italian genius," which "shuns all that smacks of excess or exclusivity and is distinguished by a certain sense of proportion and harmony":[12] "We love to contemplate in its real unity, connection, and harmony what others like to analyze separately."[13]

So, the young professor will speak about economics. But right away he opts for a school alternative to the dominant one, and rebels against the current impression of economic science as a "doctrine of balance sheets of debit and credit."[14] In short, talking about economics doesn't mean immediately thinking about money!

So, what are we talking about?

"Nomos" and "ethos"

The word *eco-nomy* is clearly of Greek coinage (a work attributed to Aristotle bears this very name). It brings together *oikos* ("house") and *nomos* ("law") — that is, literally, laws of the house, or, if preferred, care of the household. An etymology rediscovered today, in an ecological vein, in the encyclical *Laudato Si'* by Pope Francis, which urges us to safeguard creation as "our common home." With regard to wealth — understood as the whole of what constitutes the "house" and, in the plural, all of the "houses" that make up the social organism — economics indicates the laws that govern its management and increase.

One would have expected Toniolo to mention this etymology at the beginning of the *Trattato* (he will touch on it instead in speaking of the family[15]). He does not do so, unlike one textbook he admired, that of Luigi Cossa,[16] preferring to get right into the "scientific" definition. To him the etymology probably seems more appropriate in reference to "individual, private economics" as distinct from "social economics,"[17] which he characterizes with the following definition:

> Social economics (others say "political"), according to a summary concept, is the *science of the social order of wealth.* In other words, it studies how the activity of peoples *normally* originates and unfolds in achieving material well-being, in service of the higher goals of civilization.[18]

The pre-lecture of 1873, which we are dealing with as a distant prelude to the *Trattato*, goes, so to speak, to the fountainhead of economic activity, to what constitutes its soul: its motives, dynamics, interests. It is a contribution to the definition of economic laws. The question the young professor aims to answer is: Where does the economy come from? What are the impulses and components that make up its laws?

Let's go back for a moment to the definition in the *Trattato*, to focus on that "normally," which the author highlights in italics. Behind that adverb there is a dimension of his thought that he had focused on the previous year, publishing what is the second overall title of his bibliography — namely, an essay read at the Padua Academy of Science, Letters, and the Arts on the topic "On physical and social facts with regard to the inductive method."[19] It was a study that was admired by the prince of Italian economists — Francesco Ferrara[20] — even as he was attacking our author, together with others, for his "Germanism," his adherence to the German historical school. In that essay, following Minghetti[21] and J. S. Mill,[22] Toniolo had emphasized the human character of economic laws. By virtue of this character, the study of economics must certainly rest on facts — and therefore on statistics and historical events — with a fundamentally inductive method (moving from facts to principles). But since it is still a question of human actions, and hence not of purely physical, but of moral facts imbued with freedom, the laws that economics establishes do not have the rigidity of physical laws: They are rather laws of tendency. Toniolo's thought is thus, programmatically, anchored between history and statistics — the latter discipline was also a subject he taught[23]

— and the synthesis of values, in which the "first principles," dictated a priori, marry with the "laws of tendency," established through the analysis of facts.

Let's get back to the Padua lecture. Taking a position in the ongoing debate, the young academic aims to demonstrate "the efficacy that the most noble needs of the human spirit have on economic facts and laws: that is, to use the phrase under consideration today, *of the ethical element as a factor intrinsic to the laws themselves*."[24]

Anyone who wants to understand Toniolo must start here. The thesis he presents is not, to tell the truth, his trademark. He borrows it from the aforementioned historical school of economics, to which "in this" (and therefore not in everything!) he adheres.

The prevailing English view of his time is characterized, in his judgment, by the fact that it sees personal (or rather individual) interest as the motive of human activity, and so "the dynamic principle in the mechanism of economic society."[25] Toniolo recognizes an indisputable but partial truth in this thesis. This theoretical deficit undermines, in his eyes, the entire system of political economy in the most accepted version (today one would say "mainstream").

We reiterate that, for him, too, the reference to personal interest is essential. This interest is even "the gravitational force of the moral world, of which indeed it is not only a condition and means of equilibrium, but also one of the elements and factors of progress; not only a principle of preservation, but also of incessant renewal."[26]

Having admitted this, what Toniolo contests is the one-sidedness and exclusivism of this view. Personal interest — our author maintains — is not the sole engine, the exclusive foundation, of economic life. This is an error that he blames on the founder of modern economic science, Smith, and his *Inquiry into the Nature and Causes of the Wealth of Nations*[27] (recognizing however that he expressed a more comprehensive and balanced view in *The Theory of Moral Sentiments*).[28] This error would produce severe damage in conjunction with that liberal individualism which had its political-subversive translation in the French Revolution and, on the specifically economic side, in the social question. Predictable results of a view of the economy that, "too easily presupposing the spontaneous harmony of private and public interest," exalts the activity of the individual and posits abstention (laisser-faire, laisser-passer) as the sole canon of economic policy, resulting in a growth of selfishness and materialism, and the harshening of social conflict.[29]

The complex nature of man

The diagnosis is clear: the Smithian vision rests on a "defective analysis of human nature."[30] We are faced with an anthropological error that leads to an economic error. In fact, the economy is a human activity. If man is mutilated, the economy is mutilated. To understand the economy, and indeed all social life, it is necessary to consider "how all of man, and so also his ideas, his opinions, the sentiments and passions of the human heart, must necessarily find their place in the overall formula of social life."[31]

The analysis continues with a focus on the various aspects that make up the "complex nature of man."[32] First, alongside the principle of utility, there is the principle of "the good, child of the spontaneous recognition of a prevailing moral law."[33] The reference here is to ethics in the strict sense, an ethics that is fused with many other aspects of human nature: the religious spirit, the sense of honesty and fairness, cultivation of the true and the beautiful, the habit of temperance, the virtue of sacrifice. And more: the awareness of one's own moral dignity, the love of personal independence and freedom, the sense of honor, the love of glory, familial affection, love of country, the sense of nationality, of benevolence and universal brotherhood, liberality, compassion, and "all the multiple impulses by which the most noble need for sociality is nourished and spread among men."[34]

We cannot give a detailed presentation of Toniolo's examples, aimed at showing how only the consideration of this complexity also explains the different profiles of the various societies and cultures, with evident effects on the economic side. If anything, it should be underlined how ethics in the strict sense (the moral law perceived by conscience) is joined with ethos — that is, the manner in which various societies express themselves in a shared course of thought and practice.

In particular, Toniolo highlights the role, also social and economic, of the "religious principle."[35] He then insists on sociality, placing it "among the most innate, efficacious, and expansive needs of man; it materializes in the family and in the state; it is reflected in love of country, rises to the spirit of nationality and broadens to that of universal solidarity." And he continues:

> This sentiment, reacting to that of selfishness, has the task of drawing man out of himself and making him live, so to speak, in his fellow men. And indeed, from the moment man founds a family the reason for his existence no longer ends with himself, but continues in his children; his personal aims are subordinated to those of other beings over whom his responsibility extends, and so from that moment on the sense of personal benefit no longer reigns supreme in him, but that of the good of others also sits as moderator of his actions. What holds true for the moral bonds of the family also applies to all other forms of human association, whereby man gradually coordinates his existence for the ends of the whole of humanity, so that the efficacy of this need for sociality can be said to be bound up with the entire process of civilization.[36]

Family and relationships

A key point of his analysis is the emphasis on the "family spirit." This animates not only microeconomics, but also macroeconomics, and Toniolo identifies it in the economic profiles of the various nations. "Moreover, the family spirit is so efficacious in the economy of nations that, emerging from the circle of domestic coexistence, it enlivens and maintains all of the social institutions that are informed by it."[37]

He gives an example:

> For many centuries industry took its life and nourishment from domestic virtues and traditions, and still today the changes in the technical and economic conditions of production are not enough to explain the progressive disappearance of small industries, without admitting a significant role for the slackening of the family spirit among the members of the same and in the relationships between master craftsman, journeymen, and apprentices.[38]

A family spirit that is also developed in the love of country, with the sense of nationality that tempers purely material interests. Moreover, the universalistic surmounting of economic boundaries itself cannot be explained by recourse to economic interests alone, without taking into account the "sense of universal solidarity":

> What largely prepared the way for free trade was this innate sense of human brotherhood, promoted by the philosophical doctrines of certain humanitarian schools and by the political and social events of the last century.[39]

The whole man

Ultimately, one cannot understand the meaning of economics unless one understands that *homo oeconomicus* is first of all *homo*, and so economics is the science of specific human actions:

> Man is the first and greatest efficient cause of social and economic laws. And therefore *man in association as producer, distributor, consumer* of wealth is the proper object of political economy, which must be based primarily on the factual knowledge of his nature, considering him in his essence, his varieties, and the degree of civilization that he has reached, and taking him with his sense of personal interest but also without self-interest and with others more excellent, and also with all of his irremovable imperfections, just as in his life in society, when taken in the aggregate he appears neither entirely *selfish* nor entirely a *hero*: in fact the whole man, with every one of his moral elements, none excluded, in keeping with the expression of Terence: "I am a man; I regard nothing human as alien to me."[40]

This integral anthropology is the foundation for the edifice of an integral economics. In it, ethics is not only, as Minghetti had already underlined, an extrinsic element[41] — that is, ethical "fence posts" placed at the borders of economic activity — but rather something that lies within the laws of economics:

> But after it was demonstrated that morality is thus one of the *extrinsic factors*, however important, of economic laws, it remained to be clarified how within the spirit of man there exist impulses and tendencies that, in harmony with the overarching moral law, drive him to recognize it, accept it, and translate it into action: ethical–psychological needs which, inseparably accompanying us in all the manifestations of our individual and collective industriousness, truly become *intrinsic factors* of the economic laws themselves.[42]

What is the upshot of this? What is the difference between the theorists of the dominant school of Smithian derivation and the new school to which Toniolo ascribes? The young professor summarizes this in a concluding passage that is like the finale of a symphony, in which the theoretical synthesis is embroidered with images and overflowing with passion:

> These construct a political economy that is the result of a single selfish force, an arithmetical and mechanical economics, a system of cold and inflexible formulas; we and the new school with us, without presuming to overthrow everything, ask only that this *dry osteology* take on viscera and flesh and color and warmth, a human face and features; that, clinging to the anthropology and history of civilization, it may live and walk with thinking and working humanity, and at the same time may contribute more effectively to the solution of the great problem of our age, which is that of reconciling the new industrial systems and the new economic life that are the basis of the rationale of the *useful*, respecting and renewing the ethical sentiments on which the destinies, the decorum, and the peace of society depend.[43]

In this summary, almost a manifesto, is the whole future course of Giuseppe Toniolo's thought and action.

The problematic intersection of ethics and economics

A misunderstanding remains to be dispelled, which years later Toniolo would get a chance to shed light on in reviewing Cossa's *Primi elementi di economia politica* (*First Elements of Political Economy*). This author had proclaimed — and it cut Toniolo to the quick — that the "vaunted importance of the ethical, juridical, and political elements in the field of pure economics does not ennoble it, but throws it into confusion." Toniolo replies by defusing the controversy, even declaring himself in agreement if by this statement his esteemed interlocutor intended to affirm only the autonomy, but not the separation, of ethics and economics: their integration, in fact, does not imply the confusion of levels, but rather presupposes their distinction,[44] a distinction nonetheless — our author specifies — within a hierarchical coordination (in which the higher level, it goes without saying, belongs to ethics). He would return to the same theme more extensively in 1893, presenting, in the first volume of the debut of *Rivista internazionale di scienze sociali e discipline ausiliarie* (*International Journal of Social Sciences and Auxiliary Disciplines*), another successful volume by the same author, *Introduzione allo studio dell'economia politica* (*Introduction to the Study of Political Economy*).[45] Cossa, Toniolo points out, recognized the importance of ethics for economics, but placed it on the level of art, not science, invoking it in economic policy but excluding it from "pure economic science." What to make of this? It is a clarification that is worth repeating in full:

> The distinction of the respective fields is beyond question, and no one today would seriously affirm (except perhaps due to imprecision of language) that economics is a branch of ethics. Even when the same human act is the object of ethics and of economics, the autonomous existence of the two sciences is ensured by their different task and point of view, the one examining the lawfulness of the act itself, the other its utility. The economist will never pronounce on the basis of his expertise whether an act is honest and rightful or not, but will have to receive this judgment from the superior science of ethics, limiting himself to considering only the utilitarian aspect. But is it true that when the scholar examines the laws of economics within his own field, if he should wish to conduct pure science he must ignore the rules of ethics and take

> them into account only in the field of that art? If each order of truths, composing a distinct science, enjoys its own autonomy, it cannot be denied that among the different orders of truth there is a hierarchy that cannot be denied without contradicting the encyclopedic unity of science and the respective relations and subordinations, such that every doctrine must start from the postulates of higher doctrines. And this cannot be a matter of indifference for the best theoretical treatment of each science. In the concrete case, starting from the canons of economic morality serves as a guide for seeking out and defining the laws of economic utility, at least in the same way that the hypotheses of the physical sciences facilitate the seeking out of laws that are subsequently positively demonstrated. For this purpose it is enough to clearly establish this criterion, that all that is honest is converted at least remotely and mediately into the useful. So the one who is in possession of a moral law is already on the way to finding the economic law. This is more evident when it comes to the laws of the distribution or consumption of wealth, whose substantial content is ethical and legal; if this is disregarded, the formulation of laws of pure utility is almost impossible due to the indefinite complication of the factors involved, or rather it appears to be an extrinsic, constantly variable result of a mechanical conflict of forces between those in society who struggle to achieve their own utility as opposed to that of others. Similarly, the analysis of utility in its subordination to the doctrines of ethics helps to formulate the limits of economic laws, these stopping at the border beyond which would lie the illicit, in the full certainty that every injustice compromises or eliminates utility.[46]

All clear, then? Shall we call it a draw? In reality, the dominant economic science would long continue to pursue a de facto separation on the basis of distinction. Perhaps nobly rebelling against the accusation of amorality, Vilfredo Pareto argues: Should the geometer, perhaps, because he is interested in the laws of geometry, be reproached for neglecting the laws of chemistry?[47] A specious consideration, Toniolo would reply. The laws of economics are laws not external to man, but based on his consciousness and psychology,[48] where every appraisal inevitably comes about through the influence of a plurality of elements, so that the search for utility proper to economic evaluation does not exist except in conjunction with other appraisals, not least that of the moral norm. In considering economic laws without this awareness, one would run the risk of playing a purely theoretical game, tacitly linked to the condition: "If there existed a man who had only and exclusively a purely economic interest ..." But this man does not exist. Hence the intrinsic character of ethics in economic laws, according to Toniolo's realistic perspective, which takes nothing away from the specificity of ethics in its objective definition.

Toniolo would return to this theme, within the broader landscape of the science–faith relationship, exploring it above all in the context of the activities of the *Unione cattolica per gli studi sociali* (Catholic Union for Social Studies) and then of the *Società cattolica italiana per gli studi scientifici* (Italian Catholic Society for Scientific Studies).[49] He would then further specify the needs of the "encyclopedia of knowledge," the various branches of which have their autonomy but also their interdependence, with a structural subordination to the philosophical–theological principles concerning the ultimate meaning of all reality, and so of the sciences themselves that deal with it under various profiles. No confusion, but also no separation:

> So we are at the opposite pole from that methodical theory of liberal economists which, presuming to prepare I don't know what social reform, begins in science and then in practice to separate the doctrine and applications of economic-social utility from morality and from the philosophical principles from which this is derived, and even more so from the heights of the supernatural to which it is remotely connected.[50]

Following in Viktor Cathrein's footsteps, he includes the thesis of the subordination of economics to ethics in a more general principle:

> One cannot fully judge a being in its nature and ends except by

> considering it in the place it holds in the universal order of beings, and analogously, a doctrine cannot be assessed except in relation to the universal order of truth — that is, in the encyclopedia of human knowledge.[51]

From irrelevance to relevance

This initial approach to Toniolo the economist, in an essential kernel of his thought, already suggests a re-evaluative hypothesis that will accompany our entire journey of rereading this authentic master of Italian Catholics in the social field. Students of economics may not find his name in their textbooks for a long time yet. Economists may continue to ignore him, due in part to that interpretative inertia which often presides over the phenomena of academic and cultural success, decided with the classic labeling of "major" and "minor." But the originality of his thought will perhaps assert itself by the very force of pressing historical challenges and bring light to the new season of economics. If Adam Smith will be remembered for the "invisible hand," and Karl Marx for the *Communist Manifesto,* Giuseppe Toniolo will reemerge as a forerunner of the synthesis of ethics and economics, for having considered ethics as an intrinsic, and therefore indispensable, element of economic activity: Without ethics, economics is diseconomics! In the transition between the 1800s and 1900s, in comparison with his colleagues upon whom greater fame smiled, he appears to be a marginal thinker out of step with his time. That "irrelevance" of his may be turning into relevance today, or even into historical urgency.

Chapter II
Economics as a Science

The historical background

To go from the pre-lecture of 1873 to the *Trattato* is to make a leap not only in space, from Padua to Pisa, where Toniolo had been a full professor for quite a while,[1] but also in time, dealing with a span of more than thirty years. In fact, Toniolo published it in 1907 (with a second edition, revised and expanded, in 1915: almost the last testament of his teaching, given that he would die three years later). From the point of view of his thought, the *Trattato* is a work of maturity.

For him, this period of time had been a great workshop. Toniolo was not purely an academic. His "papers" exude history. This was demanded, even on the theoretical level, by the structure of his thought, according to which there could be no science without starting from life and looking at life. Knowing is, he loved to say, "a means to acting."[2] In his essays on economic history (in particular on the medieval economy in Florence[3] and, more broadly, in Tuscany[4]), he was concerned with identifying in lived history the context in which economic laws come true, showing their perennial aspects and their contingent variations.

He was educated in this, as we have seen, by training in the historical school of economics embodied above all by Wilhelm Roscher.[5] So can he be called a "historical economist"?[6] If so, it must be emphasized that his thought shows a theoretical-historical-practical balance that goes beyond the boundaries of the historical school, as well as of other schools, and guarantees its own unique features. His interest in history and practice was certainly driven by his lay spirituality, marked by what one might call mystical impulses, always translated into historical prophecy, in the vision of a Christianity that, despite the ups and downs of its not always glorious two millennia, was a candidate in his eyes — without fear of being gainsaid — to be the future of civilization (for this reason he loved to speak of "*incivilimento*," meaning, by this the process, toward full civilization).

It is impossible to read the *Trattato* without this background. If he failed to complete it, this was precisely because he never dedicated himself exclusively to the "desk." His was the temperament of an animator, on both ecclesiastical and social fronts. His economic vision was refined in the school of the facts. And in this period, there were many of these.

Social facts, first: He had begun his academic journey a few years after the *commune de Paris* (1871), where socialist preaching had unleashed a revolutionary experiment that had thrown Europe into dismay. The specter announced by the *Communist Manifesto* of Marx and Friedrich Engels (1848) had shown its most disturbing face in Paris (Marx saw in the *commune* "the glorious harbinger of a new society"[7]), providing a gauge — for one not wishing to close his eyes to reality — of the gravity of the social question.

On another front, the previous year the national question had arisen forcefully in Italy. The breach of Porta Pia (September 20, 1870) had on the one hand unified Italy and brought to completion the efforts of the Risorgimento (Italian unification), but on the other, by wiping the Papal States off the map with a bunch of weapons, it had produced a wound in the Church, making Pope Pius IX — not satisfied with the unilateral reassurances of the Law of Guarantees — take on the appearance of a prisoner pope. The more zealous laypeople joined in his defense in the "Catholic movement." Along a different line, others, pastors and laypeople — no less Catholic but of a more patriotic bent (the young Toniolo was also affected by this climate[8]) — hoped for a conciliation between the new state and the Church: diehards and appeasers, in constant tension.

Toniolo took his place among the diehards, perhaps more out of love of discipline than by natural inclination, but he stood out among them for his personality and originality. His gaze went beyond the earthquakes on the surface, focusing on the invisible fault that produced them, which in his eyes was, for one thing, the crisis of thought, due to the rationalist atmosphere that was corroding the fabric of Christian culture, and for another the irruption of socialism, which in the name of an admittedly just defense of the proletariat advocated a revolution that undermined the social order itself at the root. The confrontation with socialism was during those years one of the biggest points of his theoretical and practical effort.

The volume *Socialismo e capitalismo* (*Socialism and Capitalism*) is crucial for understanding his thought and his economic theory itself, bent on defining the pathology and physiology of the social order. His essays on Christian democracy, in its principles and institutions, provided the arsenal of remedies for the crisis. While he explored the theoretical aspects, he remained alert to the concrete economic and social crises that were developing before his eyes.[9] The Italy of his time was in a largely underdeveloped situation on the economic-social level compared with other European economies:

> In the traumatic decade that elapsed between 1888 — the year following the disastrous battle of Dogali and the entry into force of an openly protectionist general customs tariff — and 1898 — the year of the riots due to the high price of bread, which shook the country from Milan to Puglia for weeks — it seemed more than once that the trajectory of a country that had recently risen to political unity and independence — and as if turned in on itself after an intense first constructive effort — was about to reach a catastrophic turning point.[10]

This was a challenge for Catholics, whom the Pisan professor felt obliged to push toward generous social action as a persuasive antidote to socialism while clearly opposing the revolutionary movement. On the other hand, his work as an intellectual, economist, and animator would be equally influenced by the subsequent phase, which registered a sort of miracle of industrialization (at least in the north) linked to the development of finance, with new social phenomena between crises of the family, cultural reactions (intra-ecclesial modernism, aggressive secularism), and social reactions of opposing character between nationalistic euphoria and socialist agitation (agrarian crises) in a context of technological-cultural enthusiasm (*la belle époque*), and at the same time of precariousness of international alliances and blocs that would tragically lead to the First World War.[11]

The Leonine climate

Between the pre-lecture of 1873 and the *Trattato* of 1907 not only society but also the ecclesial panorama had changed. The decisive transition was from the pontificate of Pius IX, characterized by the *Syllabus of Errors* and the psychology of an offended papacy, to the pontificate of Leo XIII, the pope of *Rerum Novarum* and of the Church's renewed attention to social issues. Toniolo had a spontaneous rapport with Pope Leo.[12] At the pope's direct encouragement and that of his secretary of state, Cardinal Mariano Rampolla del Tindaro, he began intensive efforts to motivate Italian Catholics to combine the program of papal defense with that of a new presence in society.

In the social sphere it was necessary to move past purely charitable, beneficent activities and toward what today we would call "political charity" (although this adjective was taboo at the time, due to the *non expedit,* the Holy See's ban on Italian Catholic participation in political life on account of the Roman question). The result was the Catholic Union for Social Studies, founded by Toniolo in 1889, the *International Journal of Social Sciences and Auxiliary Disciplines* (1893), and finally a true social agenda that took shape in the "Milan Program" (1894), later taken up by what could be called the "Turin Program" (1899);[13] all a presence that was enriched by academically minded ambition in the Italian Catholic Society for Scientific Studies,[14] the seed of the future Catholic University.[15] This would be summarized in the program — still social but preparatory to politics — of "Christian democracy": a manifesto that kindled flames of enthusiasm in the young members of the *Opera dei Congressi* (Work of the Congress), but also aroused peevish resistance in the old (President Paganuzzi and others).

The scuffles between the two fronts — with Toniolo at the center of a difficult mediation — became increasingly lively with problems that, especially with the precursors of modernist theology, crossed the boundaries of ecclesial and doctrinal communion, pushing a new pope, Pius X, to dissolve the *Opera dei Congressi*. Toniolo came away worn out, but did not leave the stage. He gained further appreciation through the revival of Catholic Action, contributing to the drafting of the new statutes and assuming the presidency of the People's Union. But the atmosphere of social fervor of the Leonine era was by now a thing of the past. With difficulty the professor attempted to resurrect it with the Social Weeks, the first celebrated in Pistoia in 1907. In this climate his *Trattato* came to light, the fruit of a long incubation. In November of the same year he sent it to the pope, asking him for a few lines of encouragement to help promote it in ecclesial circles, convinced as he was that "the false studies of positivist sociology have prepared the way for many of today's philosophical and religious aberrations, which have also made inroads among young laypeople and clerics."[16]

The "project" of 1886

Judging by its substantial identity with the lecture notes for the 1888–89 academic year, Amleto Spicciani observes that the *Trattato* could have come to light about twenty years earlier.[17] Why so long and, what's more, without finishing the work? In addition to Toniolo's activism in the 1890s, which cut into his time for study, perhaps the desire to elaborate a thought that would be as complete as possible and rigorously subjected to the scrutiny of scientific progress also played a role. Most pressing of all was the painstaking task of reframing all of economic thought — including that which he himself had presented until 1878 — within the demands of Christian truth that Leo XIII was progressively developing in an organic magisterium (*Inscrutabili Dei Consilio,* 1878, on the relationships between faith and civilization; *Quod Apostolici Muneris,* 1878, against socialism; *Aeterni Patris*, 1879, on Christian philosophy; *Diutur-*

num, 1881, on civil power; *Immortale Dei*, 1885, on the Christian constitution of states). The encyclical on the social question (*Rerum Novarum*, 1891) had not yet arrived, but it was, so to speak, in the air,[18] and in all probability, Toniolo read the text in advance.[19]

This systematic revival of Christian social thought proposed at the highest magisterial level had to be translated for the Catholic culture, including a stringent examination of the different disciplinary fields with the perspectives of faith. Could economics have failed to answer the call? Toniolo, signing himself X,[20], had already written about this for *Movimento Cattolico* (Catholic Movement), the official bulletin of the *Opera dei Congressi*, beginning in 1880.[21] In the same magazine he picked up the thread at the end of 1886 with a wide-ranging article, also unsigned ("On the contemporary course of the social-economic sciences and the corresponding duties of Catholic scholars"[22]). In the same year, the second section of the *Opera dei Congressi* adopted Toniolo's concrete project of economic science in a twenty-four-page booklet: *Alcune linee e quesiti di un programma di economia sociale cristiana* (*Some Guidelines and Questions for a Program of Christian Social Economics*).[23] It is a sort of programmatic index, woven out of questions ("To happily resolve a debated topic, it is often enough to pose the question appropriately."[24]). The contribution had been requested by Count Stanislao Medolago Albani, head of the second section of the *Opera*, which, set up as a charity section, had broadened its horizon to social economics.[25]

What Toniolo was proposing to Catholics constituted the soul, or embryo, of his future *Trattato*, based on a clear inspiring principle — that is, to reestablish the organic relationship between science and faith:

> In order to satisfy, in the first place, the aim of bringing social economics — namely, the science of material utility — under the rule of Catholic faith and morality, it would not suffice to make an isolated demonstration of some truth or a partial illustration of some economic question under the guidance of that superior light, but it is indispensably necessary that all economics truths and the related problems of application, as a whole, be shown as dependent on and supported by those principles of moral phi-

> losophy. In other words, it is necessary that this subordination of the reasons of utility to Christian ethics be traced back to a *scientific system* as *rigorous and complete* as possible.[26]

This theoretical foundation was then to be followed by positive verification: "Ethical-economic doctrines must be concretely defined and proven with *statistical and historical facts*."[27] By adopting this deductive-inductive method, the entire subject of economics is developed in its various parts on the foundation of an introductory part aimed at presenting "the general principles surrounding the *social order* in general, in its normal constitution, in its laws, in its ends of civilization,"[28], and a concluding part "in which is defined the action that economic life exerts on social order and life, and so the influence of the proximate end in the economy, which is the moral well-being in conjunction with otherworldly happiness, in which civilization essentially consists."[29]

Within these two parts, as between a foundation and a peak, runs the "real and proper treatment of the economic order in the various *phases* in which its activity manifests itself":

a. the production of wealth;
b. the exchange of economic goods, or circulation of wealth;
c. the exchange of economic services, or distribution of wealth;
d. the consumption or use of wealth;
e. the overall law of the economic order and of the consequent material well-being of society.[30]

This was a demanding program in which he would only partially succeed. Despite the ponderousness of the five volumes of the *Opera Omnia*, which include the *Trattato* and other economic writings, Toniolo's economic thought is like an unfinished symphony. But what he has left to us allows us to imagine the whole in some way.

The "program" of the nineties

So between 1888 and 1893, like an arc of thought and action that immediately prepares the way for and then follows *Rerum Novarum*, Toniolo draws up a program of principles for Christian economics and sets up two instruments for promoting it: the *Unione cattolica per gli studi sociali,* inaugurated in the bishopric of Padua under the auspices of Bishop Giuseppe Callegari on December 29, 1889 (he did his all to make sure that the birth of the new creature took place, as an alternative sign, during the centenary of the French Revolution[31]); and, a few years later, in 1893, the *Rivista internazionale di scienze sociali e discipline ausiliarie* (RISS), directed by the neo-Thomist Salvatore Talamo.[32]

The first step in this strategy is the publication, between 1888 and 1889, of two studies that are not found in the *Opera Omnia*, simply because they would be included in the program of the *Unione cattolica per gli studi sociali,*[33] in its turn taken up and completed in the program of the aforementioned magazine. This is now the program on which all his scientific activity and social action would focus. Even on first comparison with established economists of his time — let's take Maffeo Pantaleoni or Pareto, openly hostile to him, but also others closer to him, like Cossa, Valenti, Supino, Graziani — the difference leaps out.

Toniolo's is an "integral" economics. This is his constant fascination: the social order of wealth — which for him is the specific object of economic science — is not established except on the basis of the primary elements that constitute society and its institutions, beginning with the human person in his individual dignity; proceeding to his familial and more broadly social relations (up to classes, the nation, global interdependence), securing private property as an institution at the service of the dignity of the person but emphasizing its social function; then moving on to the state, brought onto the field in the name of the common good and with an integrative and subsidiary function; and up to the global perspective of the need for the recognition of a moral agency to promote and guarantee the universal ethical norm: an agency that for Toniolo can be no other than the Church, as the historical expression of the revelation that deepens and completes rational morality. The dynamics that generally draw attention when talking about economics (production, circulation, profits, money, etc.) are operational aspects whose solidity depends on the integrity of the constitutive order. An economy is healthy to the extent that it is integral. Guarding this integrity is the true answer to the social crisis. Let's hear from him:

> Gather into a bundle the entire harmonious system of the fundamental institutions of society, rooted in nature, perfected by Christianity, consecrated by history, and it will emerge on its own that this system in its wholeness and unity is the *sovereign remedy* for the *modern social crisis* itself. It is such a remedy that (to use an image) without omitting the necessary loving care for the diseased leaves and branches of the great tree of society, this must however be applied mainly to the *trunk* and indeed to the root. Metaphor aside, today it is necessary first of all to raise up and protect the moral and religious dignity of the individual, and of the worker in particular; to strengthen and reconsecrate the family with a broad patriarchal basis; to legitimize property by reiterating its duties and beneficial social function; to recompose class organisms; to reaffirm the economic autonomy of the nation, corresponding to its political independence; to revive the function of the law as guardian and that of the state as supporter and unifier; to forge lasting, harmonious international relations for supreme and universal social interests; and to reinforce it all with tradition, continuous and progressive at the same time. And moving from the concrete order to the abstract one of principles, it is urgent that *faith,* emerging from the depths of conscience, govern and sanctify anew the whole of society; that *justice* again rule over all the functions of the social body from bottom to top; and that *charity,* penetrating every part of it, circulate copiously and vivifyingly through all its veins and almost overrun and transform it.[34]

This was the scientific program that the first issue of the Rivista Internazionale di Scienze Sociali would set — with lyrical accents — under the banner of Christian civilization:

> Nothing more comprehensive and higher than this idea. ... Nothing more practical. ... Nothing more universal. ... Nothing more

> perennial. … Nothing more Italian. … No other idea, therefore, can better express in powerful summary the supreme remedy for the social needs of the times.[35]

As for specific interests in the economic field, the magazine undertook to advocate:

> The remedy for the economic crisis that today universally and profoundly afflicts all classes, and the multitudes of workers the most, ought to be proposed indeed not in a disconnected individualism or an all-consuming statolatry [worship of the state], but rather in the harmonious restoration of all of the economic-social institutions that the Catholic Church historically introduced, regenerated, and propagated, with the methods required by the scientific and civic advances of the modern age, but in all their substantial wholeness, and with all their fruitful spirit of justice, equity, and charity.[36]

The "polyhedron of truth"

This is — from a bird's eye view — Toniolo's economic vision. It is also the framework of his *Trattato*. Looking at things in the light of how the developments of the economy and economic science have unfolded over time, we have no trouble understanding why, in economic history, it has been little studied and appreciated. Toniolo goes decisively against the tide. Hundreds of pages of the introductory first volume are dedicated to a meticulous definition of the scientific identity of social economics. It is like the construction of a mosaic, which he puts together with the love of a scientist, and I would say even of an artist, tile by tile. The underlying concern is to react to one of the typical tendencies of modern science, which becomes ever more the science of the tile and moves ever further away from being the science of the mosaic (the example is mine, but does not stray far from Toniolo, who prefers to speak of the "polyhedron of truth"):

> One cannot fully analyze a single aspect of science without em-

> bracing in a comprehensive view all of the faces of the great polyhedron of truth. This is the source of the great syntheses that discover the *one* in the *many* also in the immense domain of thought.[37]

So where should social or political economics be situated if we adopt this logic of the whole? We have seen that he defines it as "the science of the social order of wealth,"[38] underlining its character as a science and not as a simple scientific discipline descriptive of contingent facts and relationships,[39] a science as a "doctrine of *demonstrated laws* and so of *absolutely* or *relatively* necessary relationships,"[40] a science that is both theoretical and practical: It is interested in the laws of what is, but also in the laws of what must be. For Toniolo, this practical aspect should also be classified as science, and not simply art, as many economists of his time would have preferred. Economic science is, for Toniolo, theoretical and practical.

As for its specific character within the framework of the sciences, it seems clear to Toniolo that it should be characterized first of all as a "moral science," having "as its object the being and activity of man, a rational and free being,"[41] then as a "social science," with its specific place among the sciences "that study the makeup and life of human society through its overall ends,"[42] and finally as a "hedonic science, or of utility," in that it revolves "around the means suitable for achieving a final result."[43]

Such a definition was far from being a foregone conclusion for the economists of his time, as Cossa clearly demonstrates in a detailed report on the *status quaestionis* and the different solutions.[44] But even for those who found themselves close to the Toniolian option (and Cossa was fairly close[45]) on these three aspects — moral, social, hedonic — the problem was that of coming to an understanding of their contents. The most evident one is undoubtedly the hedonic aspect, expressed by the law of the minimum means to obtain desired ends: a principle of rationality and psychic instinct, which we can all experience. But on the moral aspect, how many different possibilities there are! Shouldn't these have been left to the domain of "art," rather than presuming to attribute them to "science"? Pareto would maintain this with bold strokes in his *Manuale* (*Textbook*), in almost open controversy with Toniolo.[46]

The social aspect presents no less a hermeneutic complexity, if consideration is given to the two opposing views of individualism and socialism: on the one hand, a concept of society understood atomistically — that is, as a juxtaposition of unconnected individuals — with the consequence of an individualistic economy; on the other, a concept of mass society, devoid of or poor in stable relationships, in intermediate bodies, in organic freedoms, which will be easy prey for power, and this concept of society will tend to correspond to a socialist or even statolatrous economy. As a "social science," Toniolo emphasizes, economics can only be based on a correct view of society:

> From here arise those notions that attribute an *organic* character to *social economics* — that is, those that lead to the consideration of society not indeed as an assemblage of individuals grouped together on a single level (according to a concept of society called *atomistic*), but rather as a system of natural and historical groups, hierarchically superimposed and coordinated into unity. The errors of an *individualistic* (liberal) *economics* start precisely from a false scientific premise regarding the nature of society, as if it were nothing other than a sum of individuals. The other and opposite errors of *socialism* are likewise a logical consequence of an incorrect concept regarding this organism, which fails to grasp its essentially unalterable nature, capable of modification and improvement only in its accidents. *Political-sociological economics* (or of social policy), with its statolatry, in turn starts from the error that society is a concrete entity with a life of its own, independent of the individuals who compose it.[47]

Economics and sociology

So it is necessary for a good framing of economics to start from sociology — the great flag of 1800s positivism between the Comtes and the Spencers — or at least coordinate it with sociology (in this, I believe, Pareto would have agreed with him[48]), but striking out its errors and restoring it to the truth of man and of the social order. The sociology that Toniolo has in mind is far from being a purely descriptive science.[49] The collection of psychic data and the analysis of social processes are certainly an aspect of it. But without a vision that offers the point of reference and the conceptual horizon, the data will never provide enough elements to penetrate the nature of society. Sociology as a science must therefore be distinguished from the auxiliary disciplines that serve it precisely by collecting useful data (history, statistics, ethnology, geography, etc.).[50]

But where to place the point of reference? In the edifice of the sciences — with a perspective that Toniolo borrows from scholastic philosophy and from theology — one cannot grasp the foundation of society if one does not look in a coordinated way at ethics, philosophy, and theology. It is here that Toniolo and Pareto part ways. Could there have been room for dialogue between the two? I don't know. The fact is that while Toniolo, although keeping his distance, cited Pareto with respect,[51] recognizing the "originality" of his mathematical method,[52] Pareto completely snubs — as we have seen from correspondence with Pantaleoni — Toniolo's "metaphysical drivel." Perhaps there could have been a point of dialogue between the two where Pareto admits that his *homo oeconomicus* is, overtly and with good reason, a mental abstraction, which is not, however, intended to exclude the *homo ethicus* and the complex man of actual reality.[53] The first *homo,* the *oeconomicus,* is outlined by abstraction as a function of pure science; the second, made of flesh and bone, is to be traced back to the level of art, of the ethics of experience, to which Pareto himself is not insensitive.[54] But Paretian science, proclaiming itself pure, Toniolo would reply, is in reality nothing other than positivistic science, founded on the postulate — characterized by a precise epistemological reduction — of the verifiability of logical statements solely with physical-experimental reality, alone quantifiable and therefore translatable into mathematical language. But can reality be reduced to the physical?

Pareto and Toniolo: two worlds. Their points of view become irreconcilable on the point of the radical crisis of today's sociological culture and of economics itself: the exclusion of the ethical-theological reference. This is not just a problem of economics, but of contemporary culture as a whole. Having lost the metaphysical, ethical, and transcendent compass, thought on humanity and society, including economics, apart from the more technical aspects of each discipline, navigates without a route and without a destination. On the contrary, according to Toniolo, only by recovering the ethical-transcendent principle, which for him ultimately coincides with the Christian vision, is it possible to develop a well-founded conception of society and the economy, respecting and consolidating their physiology, correcting their pathologies, and orienting their path toward the final goal of civilization.

With this choice, both theoretical and practical, and, I would say, strategic, Toniolo distances himself from the tendency of much of the science contemporary to him, which claims — illusorily — to be "science without premises."[55] This was a position that, in the positivist landscape, was greatly in vogue, but that afterward, in the same philosophical-scientific debate, was gradually scaled down. Is a science without premises possible? One can, of course, and must, make every effort to be objective in the analysis of reality, on pain of remaining trapped in comfortable ideologies. But man inevitably brings with him, when he approaches any research project, a world of premises that are the basis on which all other achievements rest, and without which all achievements would lack an anchor, ending up in the quicksand of relativism and skepticism. So it is better to play with cards exposed, confessing the starting premises and proceeding in scientific debate with mutual corrections based on the serene comparison with reality.

Using this logic, Toniolo examines the various directions of sociology between 1800 and 1900, reaching the conclusion that the cycle of sociology of a positivist, materialist, evolutionist, and Marxist stamp is in a phase of obsolescence, while a new cycle of a sociology based on neo-spiritualism appears on the horizon, capable of recognizing the positive role of religion in the history of civilization. Authors whom he studies in support of his thesis are Gabriel Tarde, Ludwig Stein, and Benjamin Kidd.[56] The publication that resulted from this took shape between 1903 and 1905. Introducing it for the *Opera Omnia,* Amintore Fanfani would observe that it is precisely from this text that the *Trattato* "may appear to develop and apply methods and directive criteria to the narrower field of economics."[57] In effect, the journey of science toward a new encyclopedia that would put God back at the top of the pyramid of the sciences, driven in part by the social crisis and the emerging need of the laboring masses to shake off their servile yoke, also helps to understand the meaning of economics. By recovering a finalistic view of man and the cosmos, one comes to understand "that man is not a mechanical accounting device (*homo oeconomicus*), nor the civil consortium a business society, nor the social problem a simple matter of the stomach (*Magenfrage*)."[58]

The integral method

An economic science thus conceived must be matched with an adequate method:

> Method signifies the path of the mind in seeking the truth and communicating it to others, and so resolves itself in the *logical process for the formation of* science *and for its exposition.*[59]

Put that way, everything is obvious. But in Toniolo's pages, a complex disquisition opens up that shows to what extent, in modern culture, the question of method has become entangled in fundamental problems that concern the very possibility of the human mind to draw upon the truth. On this theme philosophy, moving away from the balance of medieval thought, has increasingly developed to the detriment of the certainty that is proper to science, swinging between the extremes of a certainty confined to thought (idealism) that neglects the data of reality, and a certainty relying only on experimental data (positivism) that neglects the principles of the intellect, almost inevitably resulting in skepticism:

> In this "anti-metaphysical period par excellence" it is seen that whichever starting point is taken in the search for truth, either idealism or empiricism, through intermediate attitudes of thought ranging from a conception of the universe (of the knowable) that is either exaggeratedly spiritualistic or grossly materialistic, one always and inexorably descends, as a final result and in spite of the almost dogmatic affirmations of doctrinaire scientists, into a systematic skepticism that annihilates or

> minimizes the breadth, the functions, the value of science.[60]

It would take too long to follow here the examination that Toniolo carries out to bring this conclusion to light. He calls upon an extensive series of thinkers to show the reemergence in his time of the need for what he calls the integral method, in which deduction from principles and induction from facts find their point of meeting and balance, thus helping the mind, also in social and economic research, "to discover the necessary in beings and therefore the absolute in truth." A conquest, or reconquest, in which he sees the special contribution of Catholic thinkers, above all thanks to Leo XIII's revival of that "comprehensive philosophy" (Thomism and, more generally, scholasticism) which has always constituted a main road of Christian thought.[61] And this is stated not only based on a priori principles, but also of historical evidence:

> So to bring *economic* laws back to the ideal and positive type of *Christian civilization*, in order to definitively judge their legitimacy, is to set for oneself a final criterion of evaluation that is indeed not arbitrary but flows and arises from the center of the real and historical life of humanity.[62]

One interesting final note here is that which emerges, almost furtively, not from the *Trattato*, but from a review that Toniolo made in 1891 of Luigi Cossa's book *Introduzione allo studio dell'economia politica*.[63] Admiring it for the precision of its concepts, Toniolo finds an opportunity to observe that economics, too, has become increasingly scientific, and therefore inclined to take advantage of mathematical precision:

> It is in this sense that the effort of what is called the *mathematical* school in economics and the other called the *exact positive* school has value, in that they accustom one to the strict discipline of thought, and indeed not because the tool of mathematics turns out to be widely applicable to economic facts, or a more or less subtle analysis of the hedonic element decisive in more complex problems. This tendency toward scientific precision, so

> compelling for at least some economists, seems to us to be a return (may the reference be legitimate as an honorary title) to the approach of scholasticism, indeed so despised for the inexorable rigor of its definitions, its method, and its technical language, and now copied unconsciously for the needs of the advancing knowledge of the sciences even more remote from philosophy.[64]

This is a doubly significant recognition of the mathematical method in economics, if one considers that, in all of Toniolo's writings, we will not find a single diagram, and at most will come across a few statistical or exemplifying numbers. Here even the mathematical method is allied with the precision of scholasticism!

Chapter III
Economics in History

Why history matters

Judging from the volumes dedicated to the "remote factors of the economic power of Florence in the Middle Ages" and the "history of social economics in Tuscany in the Middle Ages," the Pisan professor appears to be a historian of economics[1] at least as much as he is a political economist.[2]

In reality the two aspects are intimately connected. Precisely his conception of economics, as we have seen, led him to keep his feet firmly on the ground of facts, not only of his time but also of those gone by. Concerning facts and doctrines, a complex and organic history in which facts influence theories, theories influence facts, and the importance of historical analysis needs to be considered.[3] Meanwhile, upstream, a precise philosophical and theological vision: a conception of the relationship between God and the world, between Providence and freedom, based on the principle of the Incarnation, according to which the presence of God among men, with its culmination in Jesus of Nazareth and its development in the Church, projected toward the eschatological goal, is the fulcrum of history.[4] Also presupposed is a conception of history as teacher of life and as an "auxiliary discipline of the social sciences."[5]

This explains why the first volume of the *Trattato*, preparatory to the whole, devoted a fair section to a survey of the development of economic facts and theories over time. This is divided into three parts: a first phase that covers developments up to the Middle Ages, in which economic knowledge emerges in an incidental or fragmentary form; a second that moves forward to the mid-eighteenth century, in which an autonomous-empirical treatment is outlined; and a third that encompasses the second half of the eighteenth century to the author's day, and is the time of rational-systematic treatment.[6]

The civilizations of the ancient Orient

The view that Toniolo presents of economic antiquity, set beside an informative textbook of our time such as that of Larry Neal and Rondo Cameron,[7] but even merely beside Fanfani's *Storia economica* (*Economic History*),[8] immediately brings out not only how much the data has grown over the span of a century but also the distance of perspectives that divides his pre-evolutionist and providentialist world from that of a contemporary historian. We will limit ourselves to a few highlights.

Toniolo first takes a look at the economy that developed against the background of Oriental culture, from China to India, from the Babylonians to the Persians to the Egyptians, highlighting how these civilizations were capable of imposing works from the economic point of view. Phoenicia stands out, representing "the highest level of economic evolution in all of antiquity,"[9] a panorama before which Toniolo is struck with admiration. At the same time, he wonders how this cycle of civilization, including in terms of economics, it went into a process of decadence. To explain this, he does not limit himself to empirical reasons but draws on the criteria of the philosophy of history: While the grandiose beginnings are explained by the closeness of those peoples and times to the original revelation of God, which favored a more interior and precise perception of transcendence, decadence would be linked to the perversion of the religious sense. Here one of the characteristic principles of his historical hermeneutics emerges:

> But in the long run, once the best religious and civil laws and doctrines had been perverted or at least stripped of their author-

> ity in the public conscience, the *economic energy* of those Oriental populations finally found itself either drowned forever in the shameful sensual materialism of Babylon, the Phoenicians, and ultimately the Egyptians, or rigidified in the Chinese skepticism of Lao Tzu and Confucius, or exhausted by the ascetic pessimism of the Brahmins or the Buddhist nirvana.[10]

That's debatable. This view, in any case, reiterates how for Toniolo the economy was anything but a distant or secondary theme with respect to the religious universe; on the contrary, he saw them as intimately connected.

The Greco-Roman world

His gaze then shifts to the Greco-Roman world. Here, in general, wealth "did not mount so high nor last so long as in the Asian Orient."[11] This was the case in Greece, where the elevated level of thought was not matched by the political and economic order. Likewise in Rome, where the transition from a primordial agrarian economy to a capitalist economy and then to a pantheistic state economy, reaching its peak with Diocletian,[12] resulted in a situation in which

> all individual freedom is dissolved in imperial regulationism and arbitrariness, and centralized wealth extends the servile landed estate into the provinces and accustoms the dominant *Urbs* to living in wasteful and rapacious luxury, at the expense of the tributary universe.[13]

On the cultural level, Toniolo notes that the philosophical and moral ideas of the Greco-Roman world were not favorable "to the esteem of wealth."[14] In particular:

> Industrial and mercantile work appear incompatible with the mission of peoples who had a profound awareness of their intellectual primacy in civilization, like the Greeks, or of their fated calling to dominate the world, like the Romans. Classical culture is saturated with these concepts.[15]

However, it does not escape our author that, despite this unfavorable climate, the classical world saw some theoretical development in the economic field, even if one only thinks of Plato's communist utopia, refuted by Aristotle. Above all, the "inclusion of economics, together with ethics and politics, as distinct parts of moral philosophy"[16] remained a significant legacy of thought. As for the Romans, their legal genius was not as fruitful on the economic side: "On the whole, Roman law in itself and in its subsequent applications always remained the symbol of an individualistic economy, with its counterweight in state absolutism."[17]

The pre-Christian biblical world

Moving on to the pre-Christian biblical world, Toniolo notes how it, from a historical-genealogical point of view, sinks its roots into the ancient Orient (Chaldea), finding itself, in its Palestinian settlement, constantly up against Assyria and Egypt. Despite this background in common with the ancient civilizations, the Old Testament shows a specificity that is explained well by divine revelation and, on the social-economic side, in which it appears as "a true link between two immense civilizations."[18] Analyzing its economic-social system, Toniolo summarizes the informative principles as follows:

- The balance between the individual element and that of family and nobility. This is clearly visible if one examines the dimensions of "domestic society," characterized by solidity, authority, genealogical continuity, economic stability (guaranteed by the non-dispersion of familial assets).
- The coordination of private interests for social preservation, especially of the lower classes. One's thoughts run to the social trilogy of the Sabbath rest, the seventh-year rest (suspension of work in the fields, leaving their spontaneous fruits for the poor), and the jubilee (which provided for the remission of debts every fifty years).
- The subordination of material and civil life to higher spiritual ends.

Everything, he concludes, instills and sculpts the conviction that external life, including economics, must serve the ethical one in its internal and final dimension.[19]

Christianity

"Christianity represents, also in subordinate social-economic respects, the greatest event in history."[20] Toniolo intends to affirm this not only as a believer, but as a historian. To demonstrate it, he recalls a few principles that characterize the Christian message and its cultural impact:

a. the vindication of individual autonomy through the doctrine of the supernatural ends of the soul and the moral equality of every human person, with the consequence that the human person and society are understood as the beginning and end of wealth;
b. monogamous and indissoluble marriage, which reconstitutes the organism of the family, the "first cell of the social economy and prototype of every association";[21]
c. the doctrine of self-denial in the use of material goods, as an instrument for spiritual ends, which legitimizes and regulates the consumption of wealth;
d. the precepts of justice and charity, which regulate the circulation and fair distribution of goods, linking progress to the "growing moral and material elevation of the humble, poor, and industrious multitudes."[22]

Christianity thus places "on its true foundations the very science of the constitution and economic life of the peoples."

In the order of facts, this was a true "rebirth of civilization." The pantheism[23] of the pagan state gives way to the emancipation of the personality, in the name of equality of all men before God. Set free, individuality expands in associations of every kind: familial, religious, civil, economic. The set of intermediate organisms between the individual and the state is born. The new state germinates in the municipality and from here develops into the great state, never absolute, often elective, always tempered by participation. Above is the Church, distinct and independent from the state, guardian of the humble, representative of the unity and universality of the human race.[24] A real *novus ordo* animated by an ideal *novus ordo*. Of course, there is no lack of obstacles, and indeed they are mighty. It is not a fairy-tale landscape. "Incessant struggles between races and classes, arrogance, corruption, brutal passions, material greed"[25] must be taken into account, but the new course, in spite of it all, asserts itself.

Wealth also benefits from this new socio-political-ecclesial horizon. Progressively, the state economy inherited from the Roman Empire adapted to Germanic customs and new concepts of Christian duty. From the fifth to the twelfth century, a fundamentally agrarian land-based economy was consolidated. From the thirteenth century, under the municipal regime, the industrial and mercantile economy was born. Alongside and within these economic processes, a thought develops that, from the Fathers of the Church to Scholasticism, is structured in an increasingly organic way, also moving into the area of economics with topics such as a just price, condemnation of usury, the theory of value, the social meaning of property, and integrating commutative justice (to each his own) with distributive justice (the fair social distribution of wealth). It is the time of the Christian Middle Ages, in which there is established "a human economy par excellence, whose theories are based on man (and not on the instrument, as in the capitalist economy); not solely individualistic, but social; not bent only on material utility, but civil, that is, coordinated with spiritual civilization."[26]

The pages of ethical-civil and economic history that Toniolo wrote on Tuscany in the Middle Ages, almost as a field test in a particularly representative region, move in this direction.[27] He had no doubt that he would find there an archetype to reproduce: that of a society in which cooperation between the classes, expressed by the flourishing of the arts and crafts guilds, would produce both well-being for workers and social democracy, in a harmonious *polis* impregnated with Christian culture. An idealization of Florentine society in the 1300s? It can be suspected. In any case, if it is true that this archetype as such could hardly be proposed in today's social conditions, still stimulating are the ideas he gathered from it on the free association of workers (the idea of the guild, with a libertarian slant), on the connection between work and the capital subordinated to it, on the concepts of usury and the subsidiary function of capital, and on the relationship between economy, society, and civilization within the landscape of a democracy inspired by ethics and Christianity.

Modernity: Progress or regression?

"One of the most difficult tasks of historical criticism," Toniolo wrote in 1905, "is that of detecting in the ideas as well as in the life of peoples, in a word, in civilization, *regressions in the guise of progress*."[28] Approaching this chapter of Toniolo's economic thought — and not only the economic — requires a good dose of interior freedom. In our sensibility and even in our language, being modern has become almost second nature (despite all the insistence — but this is still a philosophical-critical discussion remote from the current culture — on the category of the "postmodern"). We say we are modern to say that we are up-to-date, *à la page,* with the times. Who among us would not suffer to be described as backward, a man of the past? If we remain stuck in this psychology, Toniolo's pages on this theme will be indigestible a priori. In fact, Toniolo has a much less optimistic concept of modernity than we do, just as, on the contrary, he has a much more optimistic concept of the Christian Middle Ages. On the other hand, Toniolo's anti-modern position cannot be exploited for a reactionary purpose. Our author developed his analysis of modernity not as a traditionalist incapable of opening up to progress, but as a man of the future, a progressive. Put that way, we are faced with a puzzle. Calm, critical discernment is needed, while not making allowances for our initial prejudices or Toniolo's systematic-ideological tendency.[29]

In reality, what to us — with the label of modernity — seems like progress, to Toniolo appears to be regression. And not because he fails to see the positive innovations that emerged with humanism and the Renaissance, in which the beginning of modernity is usually identified (although there is no lack of those who trace its precursors back a few centuries earlier). But Toniolo knew well that alongside the Renaissance of pagan tonalities, which won out, there was also a humanism and a Renaissance of Christian stylings.

He finds a positive innovation in the history of economic science itself, which in this period begins to register treatments of economics no longer merely occasionally, but *ex professo*, with an approach that presents a certain specificity and autonomy while remaining on empirical ground: at first empirical-monographic (from the sixteenth century) and then empirical-systematic (from the seventeenth century).

This interest was driven by several facts that mark the transition from the Middle Ages to the modern age: in the political field, the process of state expansion with the tendency toward absolutist centralism and the foundation of political colonies on other continents; in the economic field, the development of international trade, with the influx of precious metals, the rise in prices, the exacerbation of usury and poverty for the lower classes; on the financial level, the ever-increasing expenses of the states, especially to fund standing armies and prolonged wars. All these things contribute to the ferment of the economic situation, arousing the interest of scholars and prompting specific examination.[30]

The latter remained empirical, dedicated to one phenomenon or another. However, the overall economic logic remained unexplored. And this was due in part, Toniolo notes, to the cultural-philosophical climate far removed from the medieval system's characteristic flair for organic knowledge.

Against this vision of the whole, paradoxically, a return to pagan culture and the Protestant Reformation found themselves allied. The former proved to be a "fatal setback of ideas and sentiments."[31] Begun on the literary level, it made its way into politics, inducing the ruling classes to prefer the economic-political models of pagan civilization to those of Christian inspiration. The Lutheran Reformation, for its part, "by breaking the harmonious connection between reason and faith, with the dispersion of the unity of thought in the peoples, hastened the dissolution of the civil social order that until then had revolved around supernatural ethics."[32] The Christian Middle Ages thus found itself undermined by two enemies that, for opposite reasons, ended up playing the same game.

Utilitarianism in power

The euphoria of humanism and of the Renaissance with its creative streak, rebellious against systems and covetous of freedom, thus finds itself having to reckon with a dynamism of an economic, social, and political nature that more than ever needed guidance inspired by an overall vision, precisely at a time when this was becoming increasingly problematic and almost impossible. Devastating effects were produced in customs and in historical-economic processes:

> Bursting forth in the sentiments and practices of peoples and governments of *utilitarianism* [were] three characteristic forms: *economic utilitarianism,* by this time poorly contained by the precepts of religious morality, became greed for sensual enjoyment among the enriched classes of the old nations (Italy) and for material accumulation among the acquisitive bourgeois classes of young nations (England, Holland, etc.), and this to the detriment of the multitudes, hence the conflict with the upper classes; *ethical utilitarianism*, no longer tempered by the concept of universality typical of the Middle Ages, transformed the national consciousness (fueled by the prosperity, throughout the fifteenth century, of the growing peoples: Bavaria, the countries of the Rhine, Flanders, England) into a *jealous competition of selfish interests* of commerce, preparing immense international conflicts. Finally, supported by the need for greater unity and firmness in the face of vaster horizons of external conquests and internal struggles, came the rise of *political utilitarianism*, which, no longer restrained by higher spiritual powers (the Church), but transformed into personal and dynastic despotism by the name of *reasons of state*, justified oppressive violence within and aggressive violence without.[33]

This was in a way a return to the prototype of the ancient societies, "built for millennia on the privilege of a few with the immolation of the many."[34]

All economic and civic concepts and relationships were toppled. Toniolo's fresco is devoid of shadings, a merciless picture of a historical process that sees work and merit as the source of wealth replaced with

> usurpation (of the goods of the Church, of the pious works, of

> the people), capitalist usury, the discovery of gold, emoluments of state and court. … No more concern for equality under the law, for the protection of the weak, for the uplifting of the people, but the restoration of the Germanic, English, and Spanish fideicommissum in favor of a new courtly aristocracy; industrial privileges for the growing bourgeoisie in Germany and England; monopolies of mercantile companies in the new colonies. And on top of that, to the detriment of the multitudes, the artisan guilds everywhere were closed and enslaved to finance; in England they were suppressed and their assets confiscated; the peasant's emancipation from the German princes was halted; the servitude of the worker in the countryside and in the industries was reproduced by the laws of Elizabeth; the Irish landowners were dispossessed en masse by Cromwell; Spain, Holland, England reproduced black slavery in America.[35]

National unity itself ended up being torn apart by civil-religious struggles, by commercial conflicts, by enormous international wars instrumental to the balance between the states, and by the predominance, first of France, then of Spain, and finally of Austria, with the rule of material force inside and out:

> It was the reappearance of pagan civilization. With it the best achievements of Christian civilization were crippled or scattered, and the distant future was compromised. In fact, modern capitalism, the proletariat, and socialism originated in that period and then matured in the nineteenth century.[36]

In this way the conditions were put in place for the belated violent reaction of the French Revolution.

The idol of money

In this regressive framework, in the universal empire of utilitarianism, one understands how economic studies would also tend to confine themselves to the perimeter of an empiricism that, renouncing grand visions, focuses on emerging individual themes. There is certainly no lack of Christian thinkers who keep the tradition of Scholasticism alive (a second Scholasticism). Our author evokes a few representatives in passing: Francisco de Vitoria and his successors, Melchior Cano, Domingo de Soto, Bartolomé de Medina, Francisco Suàrez, "vindicators of Christian social ethics"[37]; followed by theologians and philosophers like Thomas de Vio (Cardinal Cajetan), Nicholas of Cusa, etc., who take on individual issues of economic morality "with ever broader views, especially in the controversies over the legitimacy of the usurious loan, already advocated by some Protestants."[38] But they do not suffice to "rekindle the past vigor in economics."[39]

By this time interests are mainly focused on money, trade, colonies, and economic policy. And when it comes to placing these partial studies in a set of ordered doctrines, the preference goes, Toniolo emphasizes, not to the founding perspective of social economics, but to the operational one of economic policy. This is the case with the "mercantile system or mercantilism." Here the philosophical principles remain implicit; even more, they are taken out of play. Definitions are given, in an axiomatic way, for a few guidelines that are now more the consecration of reality than its critical examination. The principle that social life, including economic life, depends on the directives of the state is thus taken for granted: a true reversal of the relationship that Christian civilization established between society and the state, the former having by its nature a primacy to which the state must bend, and not vice versa. In particular, then, a norm is made — we would say an idol — of a "presumed economic principle" — that is:

> Money is the maximum means of enrichment of a people, and therefore sets the measure of its wealth, in the sense that money is the backbone, the blood, the soul of economic activity and therefore the principle from which wealth is generated and continuously enlivened, so that as long as there is money all else follows of its own accord, and indeed public wealth in general is proportional to the amount of money circulating in the state.[40]

Toniolo amply exemplifies the consequences of this approach, with its disastrous effects:

> The fetishism of money diverted some nations (Spain) from productive work and engulfed others in banking capitalism and financial market speculation (Holland, England); in almost all of them regulation diluted individual private energy and initiative, and, by virtue of the economic jealousies and struggles between nations, in the long run it depleted or exhausted the wealth of a large part of the European peoples, finally provoking a great movement of reaction.[41]

Chapter IV
Between Science and Revolution

System and systems

Between 1750 and the end of the nineteenth century, economic doctrine reached a level of scientific maturity, taking on the form of a "rational system," and that is, as our author explains it, "a harmonious set of truths under the guidance of several *principles of reason* that all of those illustrate and validate."[1] At the beginning — with the physiocratic system — this still happens in an "indeterminate" form due to the confusion of economics with the other social sciences. Subsequently, with Adam Smith's treatise *The Wealth of Nations* (1776), a precise determination makes economics the science of wealth. The rational perspective asserts itself over the empiricism of the mercantile system:

> Now there is sought in the *very nature of the individual*, amid that supposed jumble of clashing atoms held in check only by the force of the state, another *bond of stability and continuity*, and this is identified in the innate demands of the *reasonable spirit* of man himself, and thus it aims at the scientific construction of a *social*

> *economic order* that is the product of *psychological laws*, which are in turn natural, almost instinctive, and fatal (deterministic).[2]

Physiocratic system

The age of the Enlightenment, with its famous compendium of the *Encyclopedie*, was wedded to an economic approach that, from the Greek word *physis* (nature), was called "physiocratic." The fundamental principles: There is a natural order of relationships that, by divine will, governs the world and forms a sort of eternal and universal code based on the nature of men and things, and so is essentially good. Freedom, property, and authority are the foundation of this order, in which *individual utility* necessarily coincides with general utility and with justice. This produces the supreme canon of policy: to let it be done, to let it pass (*laisser faire, laisser passer*). The utmost freedom, therefore: The state limits itself to blocking the violation of this principle of freedom.

In keeping with the rediscovery of nature, on the specifically economic level of physical nature, the earth, understood as cultivated land, is reassessed as the mainstay of wealth. State favors are reserved for agriculture and other industries only insofar as they are instrumental to agriculture. Among the exponents of this school is A. R. Turgot (1727–81), finance minister to King Louis XVI and author of the first systematic treatise on economics (*Reflections on the Formation and Distribution of Wealth*). The one-sidedness and optimism of this approach would be miserably refuted by revolutions, the French foremost. Toniolo has a field day in observing that human freedom has a heavy influence on action according to nature, and that the unjust outcomes of the economy demonstrate well how it is not utility that automatically generates justice, but, if anything, the contrary. So individual freedom needs to be counterbalanced by positive action on the part of the state.[3] And if the optimism over an indefinite progress is belied by the facts, on the specifically economic side the basing of wealth on physical nature is likewise incomplete, given that

> the primary source of wealth is *man* with his work, and nature is instead a coordinate factor, albeit very important; not just nature in the form of land, but rather in all forms: the vegetative force

> of the soil is *nature*, as is the expansive force of steam or the illuminating and dynamic force of electricity, so that nature enters into all industries.[4]

So, if all industries are productive, they all require proportionate protection and favor from the state.[5]

Physiocracy found favor in revolutionary France and had followers in Italy, inspiring the economic reforms of Peter Leopold in Tuscany. In reality, the Italian thinkers of this period were characterized by what Toniolo calls *economic eclecticism* — a mixture of physiocratic and mercantilist doctrines — and notable among them were the Neapolitans Ferdinando Galiani[6] and Antonio Genovsi,[7] the Milanese Cesare Beccaria[8] and Pietro Verri,[9], and the Venetian G. M. Ortes.[10]

Adam Smith and the industrial system

With *An Inquiry into the Nature and Causes of the Wealth of Nations,* Smith sets a milestone whereby he is considered the founder of modern economics. In the background is a set of typically English facts: an increase in industry and trade; a political context in which, with respect to state centralism, old elements of freedom had been recovered on the level of private autonomy (*habeas corpus*) and local autonomy (*self-government*); a utilitarian spirit of capitalist stamp, which drives the separation of economics from ethics. On the ideological level there is the influence of the Scottish philosophical "school of good sense" or of "common sense," in which morality was identified with mental sentiments, thus removing the sentiment of utility from subordination to higher ethical norms.[11] The political liberalism of David Hume exercises a notable influence.

In this atmosphere, Smith designs the pillars of his system: Wealth is the complex of useful material things produced by man's industry, supported by nature and capital. The motive of work is individual interest or utility, "through which the struggle of particular interests, moderated by competition, produces general well-being (individualism)."[12] The condition for the advancement of wealth is the maximum freedom of production and circulation, the role of the state being limited to the legal protection of people, property, and common security, with the exception of works of public utility superior to private interest. Toniolo's judgment on this approach is, to say the least, severe:

> While the physiocrats did indeed admit a remote dependence of the economy on an *eternal moral law*, intuited by human reason, A. Smith philosophically disavows the superior authority of *ethics*, making morality a product of human sentiment on a par with *utility* and so equating it with this, hence the spirit of *utilitarianism* (in the *economic* order, all from utility and for utility). Indeed, for him general well-being arises from the *utility of individuals*, and thus he implicitly affirms that society results from a sum of individuals, without any *hierarchical organization by class*, hence a prevalent *individualism* or atomism (all from the individual and for the individual). And similarly he views the very function of the state in a predominantly *material* sense: to ensure the development of wealth without coordinating it for higher spiritual and civil purposes (all for material well-being). Finally, this *individualistic and material utilitarianism*, which he derives from human nature without regard for historical national entities, imprints on his economics a character of diluted cosmopolitanism (all for universal humanity).[13]

Smith had great scientific influence. J. B. Say accentuates his optimistic physiognomy, which, idealizing individual freedom and infinite progress, asserts the spontaneous concord of individual and general interests, according to Frederic Bastiat in *Harmonies of Political Economy,* published in 1850; a perspective balanced by the "pessimistic" stance of Thomas Malthus (theory of the population developing more rapidly than resources) and David Ricardo (theory of income rising along with food prices), down to the *Principles of Political Economy* (1848) by J. S. Mill, in which the realism of the struggle of interests prevails, with a vision of "intrinsic and fated opposition between the wealthy classes and the have-nots."[14]

Also, on the practical level, the efficacy of the Smithian or classical system was profound and universal. The economic-liberal criteria informed codes, administrative laws, political provisions, and international treaties. The spirit of enterprise was stimulated, especially in the middle and bourgeois classes, also fostered by scientific and technological applications in every branch of production. A success, however, that was anything but triumphal, with the experience of the disappointments of an individualistic economy, pessimistic forecasts gained the upper hand:

> In fact, Smith's system with its logical developments constituted a theory that proved the most suitable yet for deeply instilling the spirit of *material greed*, especially in the dominant classes, ingraining the consideration of *man* as a means to wealth and not vice versa, and this especially to the detriment of the working classes; lifting up the powerful in unbridled and universal competition and pushing down the weak, thus increasing *capitalism* in the bourgeois classes and spreading wage earning among the working class; favoring *cosmopolitical interests* and on top of that sacrificing the economic autonomy of the individual nations. On the whole, Smithian *classical* economics pushed the indefinite industrial production of wealth (industrialism) at the expense of *fair distribution*; it precipitated economic progress, endangering social *preservation*; and it thus became not least the author of a *social crisis.*[15]

Sociological economics

A reaction was to be expected and was not long in coming, inspiring alternative systems that were no longer based on the individual, but on society. The causes, in Toniolo's judgment, were multiple, in the facts and in the theories.

In the facts, it is the time of the development of large industries, vast properties, world trade, and universal competition: capitalism imposes itself and inequalities are accentuated. Politically, parliamentarism and universal suffrage express broad and popular forms of government, at least in principle, since they are "in the effective exercise of power exploited by the doctrinaire and acquisitive middle classes"[16] — in short, democracy more in name than in fact. At the same time the ethical and religious crisis is growing, "giving way to indifferentism and in short order to denial."[17] The outcome of these transformations on the civil level is a complex and lasting malaise, a true social crisis, which coincides with the practical organization of socialism.[18]

This transition from the individualistic perspective to the sociological-socialist also gets a contribution from thought, with the shift from the philosophical influence of Immanuel Kant to that of George Wilhelm Friedrich Hegel:

> According to the dominant concept of Hegelian philosophy, what generates and governs every civil social relationship is the *collective idea,* resulting from the most contrary individual ideas and superior to them; an idea that, necessarily developing from the awareness of the populations, incessantly transforms social institutions, and this through the state, which concretely embodies public awareness and is its guardian and authoritative and unlimited organ.[19]

Three pillars of this view enter the conventional wisdom:

- the directive force of humanity is situated in society and not in the individual;
- everything, in thought as in fact, is changeable and relative;
- the state possesses the fullness of all authority.

Thus a system develops in a subsequent iteration of schools within the same framework of sociological economics.

The first is the *historical school* of economics (List, Roscher, Hildebrand, Knies),[20] parallel to the historical school of law. This is a reaction to the abstract doctrinairism of the French Revolution, through the recovery of national institutions. Like a pendulum, the canons of this view swing to the exact opposite of the Smithian school: one cannot speak of human-social economics because economic institutions and laws are never fixed and universal, but only specific to each nation. Hence the method is marked by historical relativism.

There follows the *social-political school.* It is born under the impact of the social crisis, influenced scientifically on the one hand by the development of positivist sociology (Auguste Comte), and on the other by the formation of socialist doctrines (see Friedrich Engels, Johann Karl Rodbertus, and Marx). The phenomena of wealth are addressed, taking into account the organic constitution of society, in the light of a scale of ethical values, advocating state intervention for the reform of economic relations. This approach increasingly asserts itself starting with J. S. Mill's "conversion" to it in 1869 (the year of the economic crisis), finding its main exponents in Germany (Schäffle, Schmoller, Wagner).[21] Also in this rank are the young economists who in 1872 met in Eisenach to develop social-economic reforms aimed at alleviating the social crisis and preventing the socialist revolution.

Meanwhile, the *biological-positive school* takes shape — between Herbert Spencer and Albert Schäffle, in the wake of Darwin's evolutionary thought and of the paradoxical encounter between materialism and the Hegelian vision — arriving at Ernst Haeckel's universal monism.

Toniolo makes an intense and forceful critique of these multiple directions of sociological economics. Let this conclusion suffice:

> Arising at first in reaction to the consequences of an intemperate cosmopolitanism, it harshened, with the concept of solely national economies, the economic jealousies between peoples. Later on, eager to correct the sinister effects of a deceptive liberalism, it restored nothing less than authoritarian economic arbitrariness. And finally, intent on preventing or containing the intrusive claims of socialism, it encouraged and justified the socialist program with the dual doctrine of the evolution of every economic institution and of statolatry, in the name and service of the fated and ill-defined *becoming* of civilization. All this for having accepted the compromising guidance of an evolutionary human morality.[22]

What about Marxist socialism?

One who reads Toniolo's *Trattato* with the eyes of today, but having been born in the last century, when the world was that of the Cold War and socialism, in its Marxist version, was a concrete economic and political system that governed Eastern Europe, China, and other countries with an iron fist, at this point finds himself perplexed. It seems to him that the *Trattato* is missing some pages, precisely those that he would expect to be dedicated to Marxism. Is it possible that the few almost incidental notes on this topic offered in the general framework of sociological economics were enough for Toniolo? This would be an inexplicable and unjustifiable oversight.

In reality, one volume of the *Opera Omnia* — *Capitalismo e socialismo*[23] — is dedicated entirely to socialism. We will make this a specific object of consideration. So why the low profile of the topic in the *Trattato*? In the years straddling the 1800s and 1900s Toniolo had dealt extensively with socialism as a broad phenomenon, inclusive of Marxism. In a certain way the thought, indeed the specter, of socialism constitutes the nightmare that generates much of his social and economic thought. Paradoxically, the excessive ideological way with which he reads socialism — Paolo Pecorari spoke of a "holistic interpretation of socialism"[24] — suggests to him that he not dedicate to it, in the *Trattato*, more than a few notes. For him, in fact, the term "socialism" has a meaning that goes far beyond the economic domain, identifying itself with the pathology of the social order itself. So, he traces the socialist tendencies in history as a factor of crisis that accompanies the path of civilization, at home above all in pagan civilization, peeping out — but under full control — in particular critical moments of the Christian Middle Ages, and then reappearing in the modern age as a subversive threat to the social order due precisely to the pagan revival to which this bowed down. Hence the interpretation he makes of the socialism of his time, in the various spirits that characterize it — the "pantheistic statist," with a Marxist slant, and the "anarcho-individualist" — and in the various times of maturation, until arriving at that moment of self-criticism which appears to our author as the very crisis of the system, now forced by events to take on a moderate reformist tone. The Russian Revolution, reproposing Marxism as not only an ideological but a concretely subversive factor, would explode as his life was at its end Finally, it must be noted that the *Trattato* was published in years in which the historical-political triumph of Marxism was not at all a given — at least in the form that subsequent history has shown us — and the theory had entered a phase of heated discussion among the Marxists themselves.[25] All this ultimately explains why Toniolo devotes marginal attention in the *Trattato* to a specifically economic analysis of Marx's theses. Above all, he was interested in the sociological and political soul of the system.

Neoclassical reaction

A century after Smith, it was Carl Menger's turn, with his research on the method of the social sciences (1882), to bring the balance of the scientific scale back to the side of individual utility as a universal principle, reacting, with the pamphlet on historicism (1883), to the abuse of history in economics. There is a return to studying fundamental economic motivation (in Italy, with Pantaleoni, Pareto, and Enrico Barone). The theme of the relationship between economics and morality also returns (Sidgwick[26] and Marshall[27]). It is certainly a recovery of balance, but for Toniolo it is still insufficient, given that

> despite these happy tendencies, the guarantees of scientific legitimacy are still incomplete; others, too rigidly distinguishing pure economics from applied, and in that splitting hairs around the analysis of the sense of utility (of *homo oeconomicus*), risk reawakening doctrines of an abstract and incorrect utilitarianism; others, while tempering it with morality, present this as consisting of subjective sentiment (and therefore changeable and uncertain), without the character of prevailing law, or accept it only in applied economics and not indeed as informative of theoretical economics itself, thus diminishing the intrinsic rational authority of the first principles and the practical efficacy of the restorative virtue of the social order of civilization.[28]

So ends this look at the schools that have had, more or less, good fortune in the textbooks and histories of economics. A critical look, with which Toniolo spares little or nothing, is being repaid with the same coin when he sets up the idea of an alternative school, the ethical-juridical one that has its touchstone in Christianity. With rare exceptions,[29] we will look in vain for mention of him among the authors of mainstream economic culture. But the ethical-juridical-Christian school is for Toniolo the school of the future. Whom will history, in the long run, prove right?

Chapter V
The Christian Economy

"Christian" economics?

The adjective "Christian" as applied to economics — to today's sensibility, including the ecclesial — sounds inappropriate, like the similar designation, also dear to Toniolo, of "Christian" science. In fact, the thought comes spontaneously that the treatment of economics, like that of science, should have no connotation other than adherence to reality (*adaequatio rei et intellectus*, to use the classic scholastic definition of truth), and hence should be above all party flags. There was discussion on this topic during our author's time. Toniolo recognized that, in principle, the truth is the truth, and that's it. Therefore science — including economic science — is science, and that's it. But he noted that words have their own historical weight, and applied the adjective Christian to science at a time when, for many, the "scientific" was something that a priori ruled out a relationship with faith. The First Vatican Council proclaimed that there is a harmonious relationship between science and faith, which are not in opposition: If faith is authentic and science is honest, they can support and even encourage each other.[1]

Toniolo succeeds easily — after all that he has illustrated on the historical level — in showing how the changes in the economic schools are the result of poor anchoring to something that may provide foundation and stability. This, for him, cannot be other than a higher ethical norm, a norm all the surer if confirmed by divine revelation, which precisely characterizes "Christian" economics.

The professor speaks about this, outlining a path that has become, over time, increasingly complex. He depicts a tree that sinks its roots into biblical culture, slowly growing over the centuries, blossoming abundantly in the nineteenth century, in reaction to secularist tendencies aimed at putting the Church out of the social game. He attributes to thinkers like Chateaubriand, Joseph de Maistre, Edmund Burke, Friedrich Schlegel the merit of having raised the fortunes of the faith in the culture. He acknowledges writers like Cesare Balbo (*Meditazioni storiche — Historical Meditations*) or Cesare Cantù (*Storia universale — Universal History*) for having relaunched a philosophy of history "whereby faith in Christ becomes the cornerstone of history."[2] With this foundation in place, the early 1800s registers a flourishing of studies to illustrate the social value of Christianity, redeeming the Middle Ages from ostracism and putting it back in a positive light. The effects could not help but spill over into the social sphere, bringing about a genuine school.

The forerunners of the ethical-social school

The school takes shape gradually. At first, in reaction to the French Revolution, comes what are called the "feudal politicians," with their concern for freeing society from the absolute state. This is the case with Adam Müller in his *Elemente der Staatskunst* (*The Elements of Statecraft*, 1810) or with Villeneuve de Bargemont in *Economie politique chretienne* (*Christian Political Economy*, 1834) and *Histoire de l'économie politique* (*History of Political Economy*). They are followed by Charles de Coux, professor of political economy at the Catholic University of Louvain, with his *Essais d'économie politique* (*Essays on Political Economy*, 1836), and especially his successor Charles Périn, with the first economic treatise of this school, *De la richesse dans les sociétés chrétiennes* (*On Wealth in Christian Societies*, 1861). They get a helping hand from the statistical research of Frédéric Le Play with *Les ouvriers des deux mondes* (*The Workers of the Two Worlds*, 1855) and then *La réforme sociale en France* (*The Social Reform in France*, 1864):

> In this Le Play, after dealing the first hatchet blow to what are called the "principles of 1789" — that is, of rationalist and leveling individualism — advocates the need to rebuild the social order on religion, on the continuity of the familial nucleus, thanks to the testamentary freedom of the progenitor, on solidarity between the upper and lower classes through patronage, on the freedom of work and association; all cemented by the observance of the Decalogue and Christian custom.[3]

The school in maturity

It is in the last three decades of the nineteenth century that, according to Toniolo,

> a reconstructive work unfolds for this school, both polemical and practical, which hastens its maturity, and this (note well) under the friction of the *decisive triple crisis,* which sculpts the contemporary scientific period (from the beginning of the twentieth century): that of liberal economic individualism; of collectivism, both catastrophic-revolutionary (of K. Marx) and reformist (of Bernstein); and finally of positive sociology (Kantian and Spencerian): a triple crisis summarized by the failure of materialism, represented by neo-Kantian subjectivism and resurgent neo-Hegelian idealism.[4]

The forerunner was Wilhelm Emmanuel Ketteler, bishop of Mainz (*Die Arbeitfrage und das Christenthum — The Labor Question and Christianity*, 1864), who was followed by a whole series of writers and thinkers in various European nations: in France (de Mun, La Tour du Pin, Lorin), in Germany (Moufang, Hitze, Hertling), in Austria (Vogelsang), in Belgium (Woeste, Verhaegen), in Holland (Schaepman), in Spain (Rodriguez de Cepeda), in Switzerland (Decurtins), in Italy (Medolago Albani). It is a movement that, in 1884, converged in Switzerland, in Fribourg, under the leadership of Cardinal Gaspard Mermillod and with the collaboration of theologians like Augustinus Lehmkuhl in the International Union of Social Studies (Fribourg Union).[5] It is a great fresco that, many years later,

Alcide De Gasperi would revive in the memory of Italian Catholics as they prepared to return to politics after the dramatic parenthesis of fascism.[6]

The culmination of this reconstructive movement is the magisterium of Leo XIII, with his extensive statements on social themes, and above all with *Rerum Novarum.*[7] Under Toniolo's pen there unfolds a landscape of names and trends in Catholic studies[8] that put the conditions in place for a sociology understood as the general doctrine of society and civilization, finally reconciled with Catholic traditions. In this framework the *social economics of the ethical school* is outlined, "which subordinates the rational-positive legitimacy of the utilitarian (hedonic) laws of wealth to their correspondence with the spiritual ends of civilization and with human destinies in the higher supernatural life."[9]

One school, two approaches

It is a school that has a common basis but knows internal differences, which the professor interprets as two souls of the same organism — different but complementary accents.

What are the common aspects? In the negative, the two tendencies agree in identifying their adversaries: liberalism and socialism.

> The whole *ethical-Christian school* among Catholics arose and was maintained in *opposition to liberal individualism, to pantheistic socialism* (collectivist), and, even more so, to *anarchic individualist socialism*, and to the respective utilitarian-materialist, and therefore anti-religious, spirit.[10]

If the "no" is important, more important is the "yes," the prescriptive proposal of the different schools, which Toniolo summarizes this way:

> They all base the system of *economic relations* on *the fundamental institutions of society*, as a collective moral entity — that is, on personal autonomy, on the family, on class hierarchy — both relations and institutions under the guarantee of natural law, in its turn the reflection of the eternal moral law, of which positive law is an application. They all invoke the recomposition (with-

> out offense to personal equality and civil freedom) of society in *juridically constituted classes,* as an intermediate organ between individuality and the state, to prevent the atomistic dissolution or centralizing political absorption of collective being and life. They all agree that the social order and the economic order itself must contribute to the *essentially spiritual ends of civilization* and be coordinated with the *supernatural life* of which the Church is teacher and guide.[11]

In this shared framework, two groups can be distinguished: the *social conservatives* (Périn, Claudio Jannet, etc., followed by others of the aforementioned Fribourg Union), who prefer, "in the contemporary organic social crisis, to rely on the spontaneous justice and charity of the upper classes toward the lower, and so on *patronage* or *mixed professional unions*, having recourse by preference to the *normal institutions* of society."[12] The other tendency is that of the *social reformers* (Christian democrats), who,

> more concerned with the *workers' social struggle* and the urgency of its remedies, while accepting these fundamental approaches and measures, appeal above them to a more intense intervention of the *juridical action* of the state, to regulate the relations between the classes in conflict, thanks to three series of provisions: the *labor contract* or rather the wage contract, the *social legislation* protecting and promoting the elevation of the working multitudes, and the *autonomous professional unions* of capitalists and workers, linked by mixed committees.[13]

Toniolo clearly fits into this latter tendency. His whole *Trattato*, which exhausts its historical reconstruction here, is meant to be an expression of this school in general, and of its reformist-democratic tendency in particular.

A posthumous judgment

At this point the systematic part begins. Will Toniolo be able to give his

Trattato, through and through, this character of a school? Will he be able to reform economics and economic science with these conceptual premises?

A Catholic economist of his school, Francesco Vito, in the introduction to the *Trattato*, observes with realism: "There are in this work, as well as in the remaining essays on political economy, chapters or paragraphs or pages so faithful to the dominant approach that they could stand, without any conflict, in any work of classical economists."[14] Yet Vito forgets that at least some of the pages with an "approved" flavor were inserted into the *Trattato* by the editors, to complete what the professor had not managed to elaborate. I think of the discussion on distribution, a substantial re-presentation of the lectures of 1878 which Toniolo himself considered a youthful and in some aspects outdated phase of his thought, not yet measuring up to Christian economics.[15] Vito's consideration is accompanied by an important annotation on the method of the Pisan master: his scientific honesty was such — one would say to the point of scruple! — as to be revealed also

> in the extreme reserve with which he seeks to assert his scientific views until sufficient meditation and careful elaboration have given him the awareness of having done as much as humanly possible to discover the truth. This moral sensibility is so lively in him that it leads him to the singular conduct of continuing to give credit to and even teach, despite having distanced himself from them, certain prevalent doctrines, for fear that the incompleteness of the scientific edifice he was aiming to build would harm young people in the initial stage of training in the scientific method.[16]

A consideration that testifies to the extreme moral reliability of Toniolo the scientist, but at the same time helps one to grasp the *Trattato* as an unfinished work, and so to be completed in line with its founding intuitions. If, however, the reception of Toniolo's work in his time "was the least favorable that could be imagined,"[17] what Vito himself wrote is even more valid today:

> To one who is familiar with the difficulties and distress in which traditional economic science finds itself in the face of the formidable problems of contemporary reality, it appears all the more necessary to get back to the balanced vision of knowledge, of the relationships between facts and principles, between the order of means and the order of ends, outlined by Toniolo. The significance of his contribution is great, because today we can invoke his ideas for the solution of problems he did not know of or even glimpse. So profound, fruitful, and lasting is their content! It is difficult to find more eloquent proof of the vitality and fruitfulness of a master's teaching. But what is sure is that much, very much, in a certain sense everything, remains to be done. Toniolo has mapped out the way: the journey beckons."[18]

Words of an economist from over half a century ago, but that seem to be written today and for today, and impel us to continue with confidence the effort of revisiting Toniolo's work.

Chapter VI
The Logic of Economics

The economic order

After the long historical part, Toniolo finally enters into the systematic. As a good architect of the edifice he is preparing to build, he lays its foundations. These are the premises, which he summarizes as follows:

> The premises of *social economics* consist of: positive notions around a few *first facts,* which are man, the population, the cosmos; other *derivative* facts, which are the essential elementary institutions of society, for example, the family, classes, nations, etc.; all of this dominated by a few general (speculative) concepts or principles, which reveal the nature and fundamental relationships of those facts themselves.[1]

So where to begin? Toniolo has no doubts: from the principles! The first revolves around the concept of order. There exists "an order endowed with the character of utility, that is, conducive to material well-being,"[2] with its specific role in the broader social framework:

> The economic order is *a lower aspect of the higher*, more complex

> and elevated *social order*, that is, of that harmonious system of human relationships conducive to achieving, in obedience to a supreme ethical law, the common good, that is, to providing that mutual aid with which all members (individuals and families) may better bring about their own improvement (physical, intellectual, moral), in coordination with the ultimate otherworldly end. So, the ethical-human society serves the domestic society (individuals and families), and the common good serves the private good.[3]

This framing of the economic order within the context of the social order allows Toniolo to reiterate its character as moral — and therefore dependent on human freedom — and at the same time as natural, in that it is engraved by a "divine orderer" in the very nature of man. He is quick to point out that this understanding, in the history of thought, had its travails[4] before finally being clarified by Christianity.

Ethical principles

The moral law "is the first and remote factor of the social order."[5] This has specific consequences with respect to the social order of wealth, such as its relationship with all human beings, without exception, but with particular reference to the weakest, and so with a "proportional gradation" of each one's duties. This is a view that remains relevant in the face of the economic inequalities that continue to characterize the world:

> This obligatory ethical law is prescribed for all and for the advantage of all, because men are substantially equal in their nature and moral end; hence an *essential equality for them in duty*, from which no one is exempt. But since in men there is still an accidental gradation of faculties and corresponding limitations (deficiencies), in social coexistence aimed at the common good the ethical law is expressed with the *proportional gradation of duty*, so that in mutual relationships or services aimed at the common good the duty falls on individuals in proportion to their respective aptitudes or faculties (personal and real) and is exercised toward others in pro-

> portion to their respective deficiencies, and therefore their need to make use of the collective services. In this regard, *he who has more owes* [*more*], *and he who has less receives more.*[6]

It is the criterion with which Toniolo interprets the crisis of his time, but which can be applied in full force to the crisis of our time:

> Social crises (and the very one that afflicts us) have their first origin in the forgetting or open violation of this law of the *proportional duty* of the haves toward the have-nots, or otherwise of those better endowed with any superiority (physical, moral, economic, civil) toward those less favored by nature and human contingencies.[7]

We won't dwell on the rereading that our author does of this relationship between ethics and economics in various cultures — from India to China, from Greece to Rome — with summary observations that could lend themselves to debate, above all where there emerges too clearly the ideological postulate of the problematic or unsuccessful outcome of those economies, compared with the progressive effect of the economy developed in the light of the Christian vision. Of the latter, Toniolo offers a few intense biblical brushstrokes. We will limit ourselves to presenting the overall judgment:

> While the pagan societies in fact saw their wealth disappear amid the sense of irreparable ruin, on the contrary the manifold flourishing of economic activity and the indefinite increase in wealth occurred historically only after twenty centuries, among the peoples of Western civilization, under the radiance of Christian morality.[8]

It would be interesting to have a discussion on this thesis, a century after its enunciation, between historians of individual economies and experts on the current global economy. According to recent literature on the topic, this question is neither strange nor devoid of foundation.[9] It is, at the least, difficult to dispute, in the Toniolian vision, the notion that — from the point of view of principles and ideals, if not of concrete realization — with Christianity an ethical-social principle favorable to the poorest has been introduced into history that is not to be found, at least in such decisive terms, in the fundamental inspirations of other cultures and religions. Christianity effects, or at least continually promotes, an overturning of the social pyramid. The statement is strong:

> For millennia the pyramid of the wealthy, privileged few was built on the enslavement and poverty of the multitudes; from now on, economic-social progress would begin to be measured by the growing emancipation and well-being of the working classes.[10]

It is a value of principle, which for the Pisan professor is expressed above all in the centuries of the Christian Middle Ages in which the Church had free rein, while quite a different story begins when modern culture distances itself from Christian principles: then the conditions are put in place for what in the nineteenth century becomes *liberal optimism*, certainly not advantageous for the poor, to end up in *socialist pessimism*, "represented by catastrophic collectivism and nihilistic anarchy," and therefore also far from resolving the cause of the poor.[11]

Legal principles

What Toniolo states about the social order from the legal point of view is exemplary for its consistency:

> Given human society, that is, the ethical-civil order, whose end is to endow the common (general) *good* with moral, physical, intellectual improvement and the relative economic increase for all members (individuals in families), thanks to *a system of reciprocal relations or services,* the juridical-political society arises, with its own end of bestowing "security and external coercive efficacy" on the ethical-civil order itself so as to make it "inviolable," that is, to guarantee it, thanks to positive prescriptions and provisions admissive of coercion.[12]

After centuries of legal culture that possessed a chiefly state-centric accent, it is not easy for us to accept this Toniolian view of the relationship between what is primary and what is secondary in the social order, which also leads to the affirmation that, by the very nature of things, primacy does not go to the state, but, in the first instance, to the human person and his relationships, in the second instance to society as a whole, and only afterward does the state come into play in service of the two preceding instances.

> On the elementary basis of the domestic societies (individuals in families) is thus erected the ethical-civil society, but then the political society or state guarantees and integrates it. … So, the juridical-political society serves the ethical-civil society, as this serves the domestic society, that is, individuals and families. The political society or state is therefore distinct from the ethical-civil society, but not separate; indeed, it is a special form of organization of the latter, *for a particular and coordinated purpose.*[13]

So, the state, far from identifying itself with society and totalizing it, is an instrument and function of it,[14] which does not detract from its importance. On the contrary, Toniolo dwells at length on the characteristics and tasks of the state, distinguishing its legal function (in the three parts of juridical-constituent, juridical-guardian, juridical-unifier) and its social-civil one, aimed at assisting human-social progress — the whole of it always directed to the common good.[15] This is not without a precise economic consequence:

> Every mistaken concept about the nature and ends of the state itself, or any incorrect action by it, must have sinister repercussions on the economy of the peoples. The schools forget all of this, alternately throughout history and still today tending toward nihilism or state pantheism.[16]

Toniolo examines each of the functions of the state in relation to the economy. I will limit myself to pointing out, because of its special importance, the analysis that he dedicates to the juridical-guardian function by which the state, with the force of law, protects "the integrity of that complex organic entity which is society with its classes (collective entities) and with its elements (private entities)."[17] Maintaining the right balance in this function is vital. It is worth rereading one of his dense pages in its entirety:

> This legal protection in particular (directed to the end of the common good) has *as its object* in the first place the *compositional elements* of human coexistence, that is, individuals in families (private entities). In fact, they are the truly *real living entities* with their own obligatory moral end, while ethical-civil society is nothing but a conceptual entity, *resulting* from a system of mutual relations between these. So in defining and guaranteeing the *existence, faculties*, and *sphere of action*, in keeping with the nature of these private entities, the law is not entering into particular interests, but rather providing for the *common good*, since it is in the interest of all without distinction that the integrity of their being and ends be recognized, under the rule of the moral law, in relations with both the state and other citizens. Hence the *equality of all under the law*, that is, in the faculty of not being hindered and of being assisted (negative and positive aspect of law) by others in the achievement of the obligatory ethical ends. Hence also that first and fundamental right of *personal freedom* or rather *autonomy*, of being recognized as moral entities *having their own ends that cannot be renounced*, which is the source of every other civil freedom and distinguishes private life from public, whose *jealous delimitation sets* Christian law apart from pagan, and especially that of the modern age. But hence moreover the right of noninterference in themselves and in their development of private economic institutions, for-profit companies, the faculty of negotiation and trade, respect for particular property, etc. ...
>
> The legal protection of the state further extends to the organisms of the social body (collective entities) that are a development of individual private ones, like classes, permanent as-

> sociations, collective property, institutions of public utility. The state must recognize their existence in the fullness of their faculties with regard to social ends. So, it cannot refuse to grant legal personality to collective entities answering honest and permanent ends of society, like foundations (*universitates rerum*) and corporations (*universitates personarum*), and so, for example, public charity institutions, professional unions (of class), groups for civil purposes, and the like. …
>
> Respect for the autonomy of private and collective entities moreover entails the free exercise of their faculties, that is, the freedom of individual and social activity and its results, as long as it unfolds in the immense domain of the honest. Thus it is spontaneous industriousness that prepares material for the law, and not vice versa, as is manifested in all the expressions of life, but especially in economic activity. This erupts more each day from the depths of human energies in the various forms of industrial work, mercantile trade, sharing of profits, consumption and uses of wealth, always knitting complex new mutual moral-utilitarian bonds that the law then regulates and sanctions, transforming them into legal ones. Woe if the law does not second the flexibility and expansion of economic life, and worse if it compresses its spring, which is free individual and collective industriousness.[18]

It's an important page. In addition to this function of the state, which has a "necessary and principal" character, "because without it the external benefit of the security of order, which is the state's very reason for being, would not be achieved,"[19] Toniolo also attributes to the state as "secondary and accidental" a social-civil function. It is a function of "assistance and integration" (here the social doctrine of the Church has built up the concept of "subsidiarity"), with respect to those activities that invoke first of all the rights and duties of the primary bodies of society:

> If the juridical function of the state is predominantly *conservative* (of the external order), the social-civil function is predomi-

> nantly and immediately *assistive of the progress* of humanity, but in this capacity it is quintessentially *supplemental*, that is, called to supplement, through those higher degrees of perfection, the insufficiency of spontaneous individual and collective energies.[20]

Woe, Toniolo warns, if the right balance is not kept in this area, ending up in state socialism:

> State intervention for the economic progress of society is legitimate whenever the insufficiency of spontaneous individual and collective (social) energies is experienced (it is a notion of fact).[21]

And yet there is plenty of room for this subsidiary action of the state. Precisely, Toniolo's openness to subsidiarity distinguishes, as we have seen in the panorama of Catholic social positions, his position as a democratic reformer. Understandably, however, he uses great caution in underlining the integrative-subsidiary character of this state function. Already in his time there were complaints of cultural miseducation regarding the correct relationship and balance between civil society and the state, in favor of a tendency to identify the state with society, according to a continuous stream of modern political philosophy that, with this center of gravity in the state, finds liberalism and socialism converging. It is thus understandable why Toniolo, while opting for judicious state action in the social field, especially in favor of the most disadvantaged social classes, should conclude with the following truly solemn warning (almost a premonition of even more serious perversions in a time like ours, in which the state presumes to legislate on the most intimate elements of the ethics of life, of the identity of the human person, of sexuality, of the family, as if moral truth could be established with parliamentary majorities):

> But there always remains the impassable *absolute limit* of the action of the public powers (with their laws and their provisions) marked by the *general good*. The state does not enter the sphere of the private good, that is, within the sacred confines of individual and family life, as long as this in no way impinges on the

> common good. Here the state has only to recognize, respect, and protect this citadel of personal freedom, which is also the first vital cell of the economy. This is an absolute limit that lies, so to speak, below the *general good* open to public action. There is another no less absolute limit above. Law is an indisputable *moral faculty* made inviolable with coercion. So every positive law of the state that is manifestly contrary to the *ethical, rational, divine* law (and therefore to the natural law), from which the law derives its reason for being as a means for ensuring the moral good in civil consortium, is intrinsically invalid. If the power of the state is halted there, it is annihilated here. This supreme limit safeguards the integrity of the primary energies and cardinal institutions of the vital economic order, and if it is crossed, the law degenerates into tyranny, destroying economic life itself at the root.[22]

Toniolo's analysis continues — according to his characteristic attitude of scientific concreteness based on historical experience and, at the same time, always accompanied by an apologetic-religious interest — with a long digression on the law in history, to show how medieval Christian culture provided for this balance, while since the beginning of the modern era it has increasingly collapsed in favor of a political or state utilitarianism, generating a neo-pagan absolutism that then became — from the French Revolution until the middle of the nineteenth century — an individualistic utilitarianism that the state embodies coercively, "atomizing society and abandoning capitalism and the proletariat to their struggle, in the midst of which the immense edifice of modern wealth teeters on the precipice."[23] The situation turns, in the last part of the nineteenth century, to what our author calls "social utilitarianism" (solidarism):

> Both for reasons of the salvation of society in the face of the inherent crisis (reformist social legislation), and due to the doctrinal preconception that it belongs to the state, as the supreme pantheistic organism, to provide by means of laws for the indefinite evolution of civilization (what is called the *state of culture*),

according to the concepts of Hegel, Bluntschli, Treitschke, Wagner. In it the state economy, towering over the private, becomes an organ of transformation, not always justified, often invasive (public enterprises, state monopolies and government-granted monopolies, absorbing regulationism, state property, prohibitive regime) of economic institutions and material relations. In this latter form the law, in the service of collective utilitarianism, equating the legal and social functions of the state and putting itself in the place of morality, enthrones its omnipotence also in the domain of wealth (Cathrein, Weiss, Pesch).[24]

Economic principles

This brings the discussion to the third premise, concerning economic life more directly: life based on three fundamental "facts" — man, cosmos, and society — in which several "speculative economic principles" are manifested, which Toniolo illustrates with the guidance of a constellation of authors who have dealt with them with a variety of approaches:[25] among his Italian contemporaries, Pantaleoni and Pareto, adherents of Menger's psychological-exact school. These speculative principles revolve around the following concepts:

a. Utility

   A concept that applies to all reality and all sciences, wherever there is a relationship between means and end: a means that accords with a result is useful, one that does not is useless. We are within the doctrine of (hedonic) utility from which economics also draws inspiration. For the economist, utility "is the aptitude of material things to serve human ends and so to satisfy the corresponding needs."[26]

b. Economic activity

   "This is the exercise of the human faculties deployed on material things, to apply them to the satisfaction of human needs."[27] Economic activity is realized in the relationship between two elements: the utility of things and the effort (or sacrifice) that man must face in order to procure them. Effort that can stem either from the state in which matter is found or from the limitation of the things available.

c. Wealth

"The entirety of useful material things accessible to human social activity."[28] In order to talk about this in the economic sense, useful things, along with their material and external character — underlined to distinguish them from spiritual wealth — must also have the character of limited things: Climate is a very important thing, but what farmer, Toniolo asks, would make an entry for it in his ledger? (A century later, and in the face of the current dramatic environmental urgencies, the question arises as to whether the example would have been formulated in the same way today). Another economic trait of things is their fungibility: goods can be exchanged, determining trade. Toniolo points out that the economic character of goods is also expressed in their quality as "final goods" or "instrumental goods." The former are necessary to satisfy primary needs (bread, clothing, etc.); the latter are instrumental to the former (producing them or allowing them to circulate). The change in the concrete relationship between these different goods also influences economic activity.

d. Value

In the concept of value, "the previous concepts are almost summarized,"[29] so it is no coincidence that immense scientific reflection flows into it. In general, from the economic point of view, "value is the appraisal of a material thing in the dual regard of its utility and of the limitation of the utility itself."[30] Utility is an essential element, so much so that it is customary to say of a useless thing that it has no value. But the limitation of a thing, albeit secondarily, integrates, from the economic point of view, the concept of value: A very useful thing like air has no economic value (at least as long as there is plenty of it and it is good air!). The value changes when there is little of a useful thing, and so a sacrifice must be made to procure it. With respect to economic interest, therefore, "value arises as soon as the utility inherent in things is limited in quantity,"[31] either because such useful things are rare (value of rarity), or because they must be produced from things in a rawer state (value of production). Ultimately, the concept of value "goes back to the value of the costly human services aimed at procuring them, precisely with a view to utility."[32]

The judgment of value on a certain thing is also elaborated in relation to the intentions: "use value" is one thing (a thing is desired that it may be consumed); "exchange value" is another (a thing is desired with the intent of trading it for others in the possession of others). The judgment on exchange value is more complex than that on use value, since it is built not on just one thing, but on "all those that are to be exchanged, compared with each other to determine their degree of equality of appraisal." Exchange value is thus the aptitude of multiple things to be traded for each other, or the capacity of a thing to purchase other things in exchange. However, Toniolo rightly observes that exchange value is connected to use value and depends on it. In fact, if there is an interest in exchanging things, it is precisely because they are assigned a certain use value. The two values refer to each other. This can happen on the individual and the social level:

> For example, a nation is rich by joint reason of the quantity of useful things possessed and their exchange value or purchasing capacity, and therefore its wealth increases when, while the things possessed remain the same, their value has increased, so that by selling them abroad it can purchase a greater quantity of things in exchange.[33]

This picture explains how the value of things can vary, depending on the judgment made of them. The subjective element is decisive and has repercussions on all manifestations of economic activity:

> If *use* value increases or decreases in the subjective judgment of things, the personal activity to make use of the things themselves is also raised or lowered; if *exchange* value rises, consumption shrinks, circulation slows down, and finally production diminishes and stops; vice versa, if the value decreases, consumption increases, trade expands, and finally production is elicited; and these fluctuations in value are then reflected in the rewards of human activity, and therefore in the apportionment of useful goods and consumption.[34]

This brings in the theory of *marginal utility*, in which Toniolo simply makes the prevailing formulation his own. The reasoning is built on the comprehension of the relationship between the satisfaction that a good provides (which is necessarily decreasing) and the effort required to procure it (which is necessarily increasing). There is a point at which the descending line of satisfaction and the ascending line of effort cross: at the point that good subjectively ceases to have value, because it is no longer worth making the effort to procure it. Economic engagement thus halts at the margin of satisfaction which is higher than the effort, and therefore justifies it. If one were to continue, absurdly, to make efforts to obtain something that he no longer enjoys, he would be performing an economically irrational act.

What applies to each thing (unitary value) also applies to them as a whole (total value). We will skip over the details of this explanation (economists of Toniolo's time and especially after him would have used graphic-mathematical models here, which are foreign to the sensibility of our author). Instead, the conclusion seems more important, which is once again linked to the general horizon of values, showing how the value of each thing or of them as a whole is in reality quite far from being calculable in a mathematical and deterministic way. Here one could proclaim, interpreting the Toniolian view: Tell me what kind of man you are, and I will tell you the value you attribute to things. Around this principle, civilizations rise and fall, and in either case differentiate themselves. At this point, Toniolo could have given the example of the famous gesture performed by the young Francis of Assisi when he stripped himself, to the point of nakedness, of all the possessions of his father, Pietro di Bernardone. Even from the point of view of the judgment of economic value, that gesture was not an antieconomic act, but simply an act of a different appraisal of marginal utility (and, ultimately, for this very reason, a founding act of a more elevated economy: *the economy of Francesco*!). His new ideal now gave a very different value to things like money, which until recently had been at the center of his life. Toniolo sums it up well:

> Thus it is definitively the *appraisal of life* that from each time to the next determines the instances of the appraisal of goods, and it is through this alternating ebullience and torpor of need that the general law of use value (both unitary and total) is implemented in history.[35]

e. Price and money

Intimately connected with the concept of value is that of price, "that is, of *value expressed in money*, this being understood as a product destined to serve as a general means of exchange."[36] Toniolo illustrates the birth of money by showing its instrumental value for the facilitation of exchange: it is nothing other than a thing — ordinarily a more or less precious metal — useful as a tool for valuation and purchase, to allow that, by assigning a certain value to money, with it one can also *count* the value of other things that otherwise could only be exchanged physically (barter) and with great difficulty in estimating their comparative value. But since money, too, as an object is something that has a certain value, similar to that of all other things according to the previous concepts relative to value, the different attribution of value to this instrument of comparison, intended for exchange, necessarily also influences the price of the things exchanged.

The introduction of money Toniolo observes was of great utility for the extension and multiplication of commerce. But it also contributed to "the development of distinct classes among which this is carried out, and to the diversification and improvement of the fundamental system of production and consumption, and so by these means to giving a decisive predominance to *exchange value*."[37]

f. Hedonic law

We thus come to the last of the economic principles: the law of utility, or hedonic law (from the Greek word ἡδονή, pleasure). This law

> expresses the norm according to which economic activity, that is, the static and dynamic order of wealth, is established and expressed in its final emanation, and can be designated as that regulating principle which aims to achieve the maximum useful effect with the minimum use of costly means (either real, of materials and forces, or personal, of sacrifices) for man.[38]

Toniolo observes that this coincides with the concept of order, which is precisely the proportion of means to end, and is reproduced in all the great manifestations or moments of economic life: production, distribution, consumption.[39] Economic progress revolves around this law,

> which is translated into concrete reality, thanks to the constant tendency to increase wealth and therefore satisfaction indefinitely, because of the corresponding pleasure, and at the same time to decrease indefinitely the efforts and therefore the sacrifices to achieve them, because of the corresponding pain.[40]

Only in God, our author observes, is the useful effect or well-being infinite, while the effort or sacrifice is zero, given that he creates from nothing. To man it is given only to gradually modify this relationship, such that

> the establishment of an increasingly favorable relationship between these two terms by which the useful effect, namely enjoyment, is increasingly expanded thanks to wealth, while the expenditure of forces, namely hardship, is increasingly restricted thanks to human intelligence and energy, marks the degrees of economic progress in history.[41]

Chapter VII
Foundations of Social Economics

The theme we are about to focus on is, in Toniolo's thought, among the most decisive. Toniolo speaks of it in terms of "first facts," which are at the basis of the entire economic edifice: man, cosmos, population. Without these first facts the economy simply would not exist.

Man

As in the great pre-lecture of 1873 on ethics and economic laws, so in the *Trattato*, the center around which the economic discourse revolves is the human person. The "whole" man, Toniolo emphasizes, in the fullness of his dimensions, starting from his conscience, sculpts him as an autonomous being with a specific end (his "own good") to be pursued in freedom and responsibility. From the economic point of view, Toniolo highlights:

> It is noteworthy how in the common judgment wealth should be esteemed more and more as a means to spiritual ends, and man as its beginning and end, and economic laws as quintessentially human.[1]

This humanistic concept of the economy also explains how the greater or lesser perception of human dignity always ends up influencing economic life:

> And so the solidity and vigor of economic society itself is held in relation with the dominant concept of man, of the nobility of his destinies and of his power as the forger of his own fate, and is therefore measured by the value of the individuals who compose it. This is the root of the inferiority of most ancient nations, including Greece and Rome, in which what was esteemed was the citizen, and indeed not man in all his dignity as an autonomous moral being. This was the intimate upheaval introduced by Christianity, which, affirming the freedom and sublimity of the human soul, generated a new society and in it opened an inexhaustible source of economic energies. This is the reason for the economic superiority of the contemporary Anglo-Saxons, because among them, together with the growth of the sense of solidarity, the sense of individuality is more vigorous and its autonomy more respected.[2]

Once again it is possible to debate the historical considerations that Toniolo develops to illustrate the impact of the humanistic principle on the economy (he continues by comparing, between the negative and the positive, respectively, "the Indian who has lost every virtue of industriousness" and "the exuberant vigor of the work of free citizens in the medieval Christian municipalities"[3]). What remains is the principled affirmation of human centrality in the economic process.

For economic purposes, the human person must be considered, he continues, not only in his dignity and conscience, but also in his needs, both individual and social. At this point the analysis pushes into the rough terrain of the development of needs, of their rhythms and processes, of the conditions that determine them. In any case, in the expansion of needs there is not a continuous and progressive evolution. There can be progress and regression, to the point that it could come about, Toniolo notes, following Hippolyte Taine, that "to the progenitors of the French

Revolution the worker in the field scarcely preserved the figure of man."[4] The influencing causes might be countless. But still "the primary cause of the cycle of needs lies in the *idea of the ends of life* and of its subsequent elevation."[5]

Needs are "the internal and immediate motives, the impetus of man's economic industriousness."[6] The extensibility or elasticity of needs is the measure of economic progress. Not all needs are equally extensible: individual needs are less so than social ones, and needs aimed at present satisfaction are less so than those that look to the future:

> There comes a time when what is commonly called superfluous becomes the best portion of human joys.[7] … Thus, behind the prevalence of spiritual impulses, economic life in turn becomes *spiritualized* in its objects.[8]

But be careful, Toniolo warns, this must take into account, even from the strictly economic point of view, the ethical-rational limits, since

> all needs, even mistaken ones, become an opportunity and stimulus for economic industriousness, but only those that are rational and honest determine a normal and progressive development.[9]

In addition to needs, another human element that influences the economy is that of faculties, whether physical or psychological. The individual psyche is the "flamelet of all social life,"[10] although, in turn, conditioned by it. Faculties vary greatly in individuals and peoples, a source of renewal. The possibility of developing specific faculties, especially the spiritual, drives an indefinite progress (this does not mean infinite, "as contrived by the doctrinarians of the French Revolution, or certain recent followers of evolutionism, or the utopianists of all times"[11]). The economy, Toniolo concludes, participates in all this dynamism.

Cosmos

The relations of the cosmos with humanity "do not concern only the physical life of the human generations, nor their economy, but the whole of the social constitution and civilization."[12] Of course, for his part, man also affects the cosmos. It is a bond of mutual influence: The economy lies in the interplay of this relationship.

The first influence is territory, with its geological and morphological constitution. This affects the corporeal makeup, the intellectual temperament, and the moral habits of populations. The great human races are also explained in relation to the environment:

> And it seems to be an ethnological law that the races better disposed to civilization are those that are tempered by more varied telluric influences, as well as by greater admixtures of blood; this would explain the primacy of the Aryan race of Iran, whose descendants inhabited India, Persia, and the whole of Europe.[13]

Primacy of the Aryan race? I don't know if Toniolo, if he lived during the Holocaust, would have used this same terminology, which for us reechoes the unhappy period of racial laws. But what he ultimately wants to show is the relationship between the environment and human development. Is there any denying this? Even if in hindsight everything advises against racial evaluations that, starting from purely factual analyses of physio-psycho-intellectual qualities, end up lowering, in the common sensibility, the fundamental value of dignity that is the same for all and must be respected with equal intensity for every human race.[14]

Toniolo gives similar consideration to space. At the beginning of humanity's history this appears as a place of exploration, conquest, and diffusion of the human species, until a level of stabilization arrives with the occupation of various territories:

> This is a great fact in the interest of civilization, whereby the age-old period of nomadic populations ends, and their stable settlement begins and is consolidated. The surface of the earth thus prepares the landscape ... growing territorial circles, for the various groups of human coexistence.[15]

Geographical locations, in turn, "generate the sense of homeland and nationality" in which "love of country forms a step toward love of humanity."[16] The sea and the climate exercise a specific influence. Maritime populations dwelling on the shores find themselves in readier contact with other peoples, thanks to seafaring, while climate is also decisive to the extent that it awakens or lulls human activity.[17]

Influenced by the external world, man does not remain passive: "He modifies it and adapts it to his own service."[18] Hence two complementary movements, from the cosmos toward man, and from man toward the cosmos. In the first aspect:

> By means of all the cosmic-telluric agents, Providence has prepared with predisposing action the elementary conditions of life, the occasions and impulses extrinsic to the industriousness of the human race, anticipating from geological eras immemorial the existence and work of man, and with concomitant action marking and sculpting on the earth's crust for man himself the main and permanent lines of his conduct. In these respects humanity is reconnected with the cosmos and its laws, which it can direct to its ends but not set aside without destroying itself and annihilating its own kingdom.[19]

This must be emphasized: Lack of respect for nature is suicide for humanity. One cannot think of exploiting nature indefinitely; there is a law "of decreasing productivity" in the territorial industries (of the soil and subsoil) and of repercussions to some extent on the others (manufacturing, trade, etc.). "Nature, at the same time that it contributes as a necessary and powerful factor in production, makes its action gradually felt as limiting its progress."[20]

Toniolo, as we have said, lives in a time when the ecological disaster is yet to come. If he were rewriting the *Trattato* today, perhaps he would discuss the environment at great length. Still, in his considerations there is no lack of elements that foreshadow today's mindset of respect for the common home:

> Rather, man continually tries to escape these tendencies, the exhaustion of an increasingly reluctant nature, with ingenuity and enterprise, seeking new and untapped reservoirs of materials and forces and making more effective use of the old ones, and so the natural law of productivity and diminishing returns is often blocked or overturned. However, with incessant recurrence, at the end of each historical cycle of progress the cosmic tendency toward deterioration always reemerges and nature makes its relatively limiting action felt, almost as if to warn us, like the Roman slave who reminded the general riding in triumph that he was a man, that even amid the advancements of wealth, which are victories of the spirit, we are always chained to the world of matter.[21]

Population

A third foundational fact of the economy is population — that is, the organic complex of people — as an extension of the individual in time and space:

> By means of the population, which is a continuation of God's creative work, man is able to attribute a certain perenniality and universality to his existence, to obtain assistance that increases his operative power indefinitely, to discern ends that transcend the selfishness of the present and broaden to altruism in a distant future; hence the first move toward that ever higher, broader good, which initiates civil moral progress (Schäffle, Kidd). Now the root of these virtues of progress is concealed in the vital demographic organism, so that every deviation from it, like every continuation of its normal structure, has repercussions, through indirect means, on the course of civilization, and therefore on the economy.[22]

In this framework, the first significant element is the differentiation of the sexes:

> The sound social order rests in the first place on the balance of the sexes, from which marriage and the family are the rudiments

> of civil life. This division into two groups, male and female, is the fundamental form of specification of human-social functions, which for woman are centered on domestic life and its internal ends, while for man they radiate from here to external collective life.[23]

Reading this statement with the eyes of our time, when sexual identity itself today is problematized, gives a bit of a jolt. And yet, at least in the essential, it is a fundamental truth, as Toniolo qualifies it, given that it would be difficult to refute the notion that the two sexes, precisely in their distinction, reciprocity, and complementarity, should carry out a vital function in the social and economic order. What appears dated, instead, is the operative characterization of the sexes, if we think of the progressive rediscovery of the female role also in extra-domestic work (except for balances to be sought between man and woman to guarantee the family its vocation).[24] It seems to me that in this Toniolo had a certain openness, but always marked by his concern over a mechanical equalization that in fact, especially in the industrial world of his time, ended up being hardly respectful of female dignity, and in any case a problem for familial balance.[25]

Alongside the differentiation of the sexes, the relationship between the different personal statuses of married, single, and widowed influences the economy. The interpretation that Toniolo gives of this landscape makes the whole distance of a century palpable. I nonetheless believe that it is reasonable not to let go altogether of the thought that a certain balance between all these states of life also contribute to the good of society and the economy. Who does not see today, in an era of declining birth rates and little propensity for marriage, how in the long run this also poses serious problems for the economy? Toniolo dwells on a comparative analysis of the social contribution of the married, single, and widowed:

> Each group unfolds a new function of civilization: The married represent the energy of social preservation and continuity; the single (in their early years) the individual forces in preparation, and later (in permanent single life) the free energies available

> for innovative initiatives and common progress (in the life of study, the armed forces, government, charity); and the widowed depict, in the freedom of the senses, almost a rebirth of spiritualizing virtues in life's twilight; all this with repercussions on the economy.[26]

These words may sound naive today, but they prompt reflection, at least for one able to critically distance himself from his own time and from the politically correct. If not true in every aspect, they have the soul of truth that is worth the trouble to preserve. They at least underline the incontrovertible fact that each group has its own vocation with respect to social well-being:

> The ideal, which tends to be transmuted into bracing reality only in honest, progressive, and vigorous peoples, is that all three age groups should grow proportionately, renewing themselves with ever more youthful offspring, who should then endure until old age, maintaining their center of balance in a powerful adult class.[27]

In this logic of positive analysis, always in relation to a vision of the economy never dissociated from ethics, the *Trattato* brings itself to bear on population dynamics, with its essential manifestations of marriages, births, and deaths. Marriage, first and foremost. On this Toniolo has firm words of warning:

> Marriage in the permanent monogamous form, the only natural and perfect relationship between the sexes that deserves this name, the normal state for man, the seed of social life, a school of moral education, more than any other comparable fact presents itself as a *product* and at the same time a *factor* of civilization.[28]
> At the other extreme, the most alarming symptom of dying civilized peoples is the discrediting and perversion of marriages, few in number, barren of offspring, poisoned by adultery and divorce. Greek and Roman decadence constitutes the classic period of these devouring ailments.[29]

Our author gives many examples, running through the centuries up to the present (of his time, of course), to affirm the principle that if on the one hand a certain well-being is a condition for establishing a family, on the other

> all the causes and circumstances that bring offense, discredit, or slackness to familial ties and to their ends must have a sinister impact on the economic power of a country, which points to the family as the cell of the production and consumption of wealth.[30]

Toniolo applies a similar examination to the birthrate, pointing out the unfortunate results of the Malthusian theory that undermines it.[31] The statement is peremptory: "Life is a good for oneself and for society, in the present and in the future."[32] Where love for life diminishes, a period of disintegration begins, also in the economy. The persistence of a very high mortality rate marks backward populations, such that "the mortality rate is the most direct index of the degree of civilization."[33] A high mortality rate

> is the great enemy of both civil and economic progress, which can only take place with continued regularity when mortality as compared with births has taken on a progressively tempered course, giving rise to a normal surplus of births over deaths.[34]

Toniolo substantiates this thesis with ample historical evidence. His summary expression for all of the biological demographic elements is *the increase in the vital energy* of the populations, which if for one thing it concerns time, with the species' rise in numbers as it multiplies from generation to generation, for another concerns space, with growing local distribution across the globe.[35] We will skip past the analysis that Toniolo conducts on the first aspect (relationship between average lifespan, demographic density, etc., in reference to economic aspects[36]). Let his conclusion suffice:

> In the continuity of the centuries, the increase in population appears irregular and very slow, like the uncertain and contested

> conquests of a real struggle for physical life, simultaneous with that for attainments in economy and culture. But on top of that the efficacy of the biological-demographic system on the economy does not unfold in all its fullness except in vigorous and adult populations, which did not come to be until the mature period of Western Christian civilization. Without today's large populations it would not be possible to sustain the enormous modern economy and keep it growing.[37]

In writing this, on the demography/wealth/Christianity relationship, Toniolo had before his eyes the European Industrial Revolution and the not so flourishing economic situation of other continents, like Asia and Africa. What should we say today, if we look at the global horizon, which registers an economic growth of Eastern peoples of non-Christian religion and culture? A discussion, therefore, that requires discernment of its essential elements and questionable applications, in the applications that Toniolo makes, keeping always before his eyes, as an ideal-type, Christian civilization.

One last look at this extensive chapter that the *Trattato* dedicates to demographic expansion in space:

> Human existences not only intensify (average lifespan) and multiply over time (reproductive development), but they spread in space with relocational movement.[38] It is a movement "that unfolds in history in *three* successive *forms*: *transmigration, colonization,* and *migration*."[39]

The first form implies an immense flow of races moving along entire historical eras, which ceases with stable settlement in a territory. Yet Toniolo does not fail to point out some value dynamics in the motivations that encourage or discourage movement. In this too, he underlines, with a different tendency in the pagan and Christian eras. In the former

> racial selfishness or pride succeeded in lulling and often extinguishing this sense of cosmopolitan migration. … In all of pa-

> ganism the national political idea (reaffirmed by national religions) arrested the movement of universal humanity.[40]

On the contrary, Christianity, by placing the accent on the divine fatherhood and redemption, "hence the sublimation of the dignity of humanity, which restored its sovereignty over the whole earth,"[41] gave a new stimulus to migratory movement. Toniolo situates the Crusades themselves (a topic that today is at least embarrassing for other reasons) within this attitude toward the movement of Christian peoples, an attitude that was developed with colonization:

> Once the immense fact of the transmigration of races had largely ceased, and these had been constituted into political nations with fixed territories, the colonization of the new era came to mean the establishment abroad (therefore no longer internal colonization), with demographic elements of the mother country, of autonomous circles of political social existence, in varying degrees of dependence on that country.[42]

This colonization became transoceanic, a dynamic that our author considers positive for the ends of the economy and of civilization, but not without critically noting the excesses and abuses, and certainly not dependent on Christianity as such, since it is rather the "fetishism of a neo-pagan state" that explains "the despoiling and destruction of those indigenous people and the political subjugation of those territories,"[43] as well as slavery, later determining the reactions that lead to the emancipation of the colonies.

At that point the phase of *political-industrial* (*capitalist*) *colonization* begins, as well as the modern form of emigration entirely linked to economic processes that push people to seek more favorable living conditions in other regions of the world. A migratory movement that develops largely from Europe and specifically from Italy, and that Toniolo evaluates positively (this should be remembered, as the immigration movement has reversed, and migrants are now knocking on our doors just as in the past we knocked on the doors of others):

> For one thing, emigration extends all the types of human relationships, and with them universal solidarity, and for another, due to the variety and competition of bloodlines, vocations, and cultures, it keeps emulation alive between lineages and nations; hence a twofold impulse to progress for humanity. Just as the Aryan transmigrations into Europe began the fruitful conflict with the ancient world millennia ago, so emigration to the continent of Columbus still fuels the competition between Europeans and Americans in all civil experiments, and now the migratory currents toward Manchuria, Korea, and Australia arouse the simultaneous competition of Asia, Europe, and America in the civilizing conquest of the immense Pacific. Social life would stagnate in national selfishness or continental traditionalism without the migratory currents that bring missionaries, merchants, workers where weapons and science have not yet reached.[44]

Toniolo's view on emigration, it seems to me, is decidedly too optimistic, sometimes even disappointing if, adopting that fraternal gaze of solidarity which the blessed economist did indeed share, one examines things not only from the point of view of a cold economic process, but also and above all from the point of view of the people involved, who in those processes were (and today still are!) more victims than heroes. Here the missionary tension gets out of hand, and perhaps with too much naivety he judges the Anglo-Saxons of his time as "present-day Romans" engaged in a great work of civilization. His Eurocentric perspective is greatly obsolete where he notes:

> Europe, until recently the only continent that does not receive but sends its emigrants to all the others, boasting of having spread a good 130 million people of European origin to the other continents since the end of the Middle Ages, can well glory in being the standard-bearer of Christian civilization throughout the world.[45]

What would our author say in the face of the current phenomenon of boats of African migrants heading for the European coasts as the place of their hopes? I believe that as a sensitive Christian he would first engage with their human point of view: They deserve no less respect than the Italian migrants scattered around the world. Then, perhaps, considering some social and cultural effects of destabilization of the Christian culture of our territories, I suppose he would add — in his typical vision of historical cycles, rotating (positively or negatively) around the axis of Christian civilization — that Europe is getting what it deserves, after having cast its Christian tradition behind it, becoming a continent poor in life, family, and faith.

But with these reflections we are on the shaky ground of interpretative hypotheses, inevitably influenced by our scenario. The quite different perspective in which Toniolo was immersed led him to conclude:

> On the whole, while emigration forms the vanguard of the army proceeding to the subjugation of the land for the purposes of the economy, it serves in this a twofold function of balance and propulsion, and has thus become an indispensable therapeutic means in the social question and a necessary condition for the global progress of wealth. What would become of the Europe threatened by socialism without the safety valve of emigration? And would it suffice today for the powerful cosmopolitan economy to plant military flags on the two hemispheres, without the immense floods of our emigrants?[46]

Nowhere as in this chapter does Toniolo show himself to be a man of his time. It is the destiny of thought that must yield to the current of history. But with the necessary critical precautions, in this broad treatment of the fundamental facts of economic life — man, cosmos, population — Toniolo's *Trattato* offers stimulating points of view.

Chapter VIII
Economics and the Social Order

The higher factors of the social order

> On the three elementary facts — man, cosmos, population — is erected the derivative fact of the *social order*, which is a system of *relationships* (performances, services) *between men, intuited, desired, implemented by the human spirit,* and therefore moral.[1]

This summary outlook opens the second volume of the *Trattato*, second only in terms of the division of the *Opera Omnia*, given that for more than two hundred pages this volume continues the train of thought of the last part of the first volume, the one that Toniolo considers preparatory.[2] This breadth (which, in the meticulousness of the clarifications, often presents repetitions), says much about the importance that Toniolo attributes to the principles. It is the consequence of his belief that "facts rest on ideas."[3]

Causes of the social order

The first focus on the social order concerns its causes: the psychological (the human spirit always aims at ends, for which it chooses proportionate means) and the spiritual-supernatural (under the different particular ends is concealed the ultimate end, the final good that coincides with God himself). "Thus *authority*, and supernatural authority first of all, together with freedom reveals itself as the greatest factor of the social order,"[4] a principle that our author illustrates with examples drawn from the history of the influence of religion in society (India, China, Greece, Rome, the Christian era). Also added is the "psychological-moral cause," grasped on both the individual and the social level:

> *Moral conscience* is the main engine and moderator of practical action and of custom, the *proximate efficient cause* of order, in proportion to the rectitude, intensity, and breadth of the sense of duty, sanctioned by the good or evil that follows.[5]

Conscience is influenced by language, religion, civil traditions:

> Thanks to these factors of culture, religion, and civil history, alongside the *conscience of the individual person, the conscience of the social personality* is formed and grows.[6]

This whole process has specific implications for the economy, starting with "economic technology" — namely, the "sum of knowledge regarding the substances, processes, and material tools of wealth itself,"[7] technology to which Toniolo dedicates an extensive historical survey, deriving from it the "law of civilization":

> The higher the vision of the internal ends of humanity ("Weltanschauung"), the better the predisposition to invent the external means that serve as a ladder.[8]

A doubly thought-provoking conclusion, reading it today, as amazing technology tends to become technocracy[9] in the global context of a profound moral crisis. Compared with our time, Toniolo's still had a certain balance. Yet the fact remains, based on the history of humanity and of religion, that religion and moral rectitude are not in themselves adverse to technological development; on the contrary, they foster it, while at the same time keeping it grounded in humanity. Toniolo arrived in time to see the negative results of a technology not governed by the moral sense:

> That which is most manifest in contemporary technology, the effect of which was to shatter and disperse the organized and *autonomous artisan class* of previous centuries and to transform it into an individual, disintegrated, precarious proletariat, in the face of the industrial and mercantile bourgeoisie that has moreover become the *capitalist ruling class.*[10]

By comparison, he explains, the Christian Middle Ages is the opposite:

> If the manual technology of our municipalities in that time aroused the spirit of association and class among the people, modern *capitalist technology* nourished, together with enterprise, the greedy spirit of social and political dominance among the acquisitive bourgeoisie, while the marvelous system of rail and naval transport throughout the world not only unified the universal market but was sometimes able to contrast the sentiment of a hybrid cosmopolitanism and humanitarianism with love for one's birthplace. But there is more: The present technological revolution was followed not only by the social question, but also by a profound mutation, not yet well defined, around the concepts and ideals of a future *incivilimento.*[11]

Here, in a prophetic flash, Toniolo catches hold of our time. What sociologist in the know today would be able to examine social processes in the light of an ideal? In the time of all-out relativism (Benedict XVI spoke of a "dictatorship of relativism"), one gropes around in empirical observation, in search of dominant tendencies that often defy decisive measurement and significant predictability, since by their nature they vary with time, culture, psychologies, conditioning, virtue and vice, and so on. One can thus read with interest a perceptive and honest book on the social order like Jon Elster's,[12] with its many graphs on the options that lead to social cohesion or disintegration, with the risk of arriving at a very skeptical conclusion on the predictability of social behaviors. Interesting, of course, as a mental game and a stimulus to further research in the field. But one is led to wonder: Is it worth the trouble? Toniolo does not shirk the empirical observation of reality, but he performs this by opting for a value-based analysis, whose underlying hypothesis is the objective existence of a moral order and the presence, in each individual, of a moral conscience. Considering this reality, all the possible and contrasting choices nonetheless remain pinned, in the depths of each person and so in culture and society, to value judgments. It is a crossroads before which social science itself is divided.

Religion and the distribution of wealth

For Toniolo there is no doubt: If intelligence, becoming science and technology, influences economic progress, a specific influence comes from religion. This is, in his eyes, a fact not only assertable a priori but deducible from history: a historical fact. He deduces this, for example, by looking at the phenomenon of the distribution of goods, with respect to which two "historical types" are compared. One is that of the ancient pagan societies as a whole:

> Almost overwhelmed by fate, the ancient societies saw the economic order in their midst turn ever more to the profit of the strong, the powerful, the princes, progressively concentrating wealth and triumph in them with the contrasting degradation, despoliation, immolation of the enslaved and bleeding multitudes. … The most hateful and provocative formulas of the contemporary criticism of domineering socialism, like the struggle for the conquest of power, the prevalence of the strong over the weak, the triumph of the ever richer rich over the ever more exhausted poor, are for that age historically true. They find real and terrible embodiment throughout paganism's reign of more than five thousand years.[13]

Far different is the historical type of Christian civilization: "Jesus Christ halted and reversed this fatal cycle in the field of wealth itself"[14] and shifted "the center of gravity of the economic order in favor of the more populous classes."[15] The result was the uplifting of all the weak, "whom paganism mocked, rejected, oppressed."[16] This is the case with children or women. The latter, "for all previous centuries victims of masculine brutality and domineering at home, of public scorn outside, crushed under the burden of toil,"[17] met with entirely different treatment in Christianity:

> Through Christianity, women found themselves spiritually equal to men, queens of their heart, sublimated in their virginity, honored in motherhood; educators of the growing generations and so arbiters of custom, which count more than law; participants in the general culture with Catherine of Alexandria, with Paula and Eustochium (biblical and philosophical studies), in social reforms with Melania (abolition of slavery), in civil political reforms with Matilda, with Joan of Arc, with Catherine of Siena, with Isabella of Castile; and for the sake of their defense and dignity the civil *ius* (dowry, inheritance) is corrected, constitutional law is modified (succession to the throne), and the wonderful institution of chivalry is propagated.[18]

The current rather laborious course of enhancing the female role within the Church — compared with the insistence of feminist culture — could lead to the objection that there is still much to be done in this direction. Toniolo, perhaps, would not deny this, but would point out that it is with Christianity that the direction of female redemption is traced. A similar reversal of fate occurred for the poor, who "became an object of veneration, since it was taught that in the poor Christ himself is to be seen.[19] And a true revolution for workers:

> A people who never existed before or outside of Christianity, except under the opprobrious names of slave, menial, plebeian, and in whom work in its personal source and social function

> was always degraded and disrespected. … But for the worker in the new era, almost a springtime opened up for the disinherited people after that age-old winter: asserted first was the freedom of the soul, then the dignity of work (the two arguments for the abolition of slavery), and work, especially manual work, sanctified by a God, a worker in the craftsman's shop, by the apostles, by monks.[20]

Workers whom Christian culture organizes with the strength of associations (the medieval guilds were of this type) and protects with laws of tutelage, generating a process whereby, "*from the bosom of the humblest and most populous classes the true human social ascensions begin*, which, continuously renewing the upper classes from the roots … promise vitality and indefinite development for the social order."[21]

The result is an overall picture that Toniolo depicts as a historical fact and, at the same time, an ideal to which Christianity cannot fail to aspire:

> The pyramid of the economic order of the pagan era, which, resting on the permanent sacrifice of the servile and impoverished multitudes, always erected its apex to the exclusive and unjust advantage of the wealthy classes, gives way in the Christian era to a pyramid (to continue the metaphor) built on the base of free and industrious multitudes, in which the dynamic system of all the forces coming from above and below converges more and more in the growing elevation of the multitudes themselves. In it the economic hierarchy is not leveled, but the helps and incentives for the many are multiplied, that they may legitimately raise themselves up its tiers with the fulcrum of meritorious work.[22]

The tone, it must be acknowledged, is somewhat triumphalistic, if one observes reality in all its twists and turns, certainly not all of them luminous. Toniolo, for his part, is not blind. He admits that this process "suffers resistance and setbacks."[23] Yet he is convinced that, in Christian civilization, the last word goes to the course correction that continually puts Christianity back in line with the ideal goal. A principle of conversion that appears active to him also in his time:

> Thus one can recognize how after the restriction of the economic orders in hatred of the people (in the sixteenth–eighteenth centuries) in the neo-pagan Renaissance (which even reproduced slavery in America) and in the Protestant Reformation, and after the centralization of wealth through the utilitarian capitalism of the nineteenth century, the bursting forth of a socialist democracy, which today simmers and threatens, prepares broader and more normal foundations for an industrial democracy (Webb), which then, having regard for its traditions, will probably be a new expansion of Christian democracy (Leo XIII).[24]

Prophecy unfulfilled? One should not overlook that "probably" which attenuates the forecast by subjecting it to precise conditions. Enraptured by the vision of the Christian future, Toniolo does not forget that this is not a fated goal (as, for example, Marx imagined the future classless society), having to come to grips with the complex and unpredictable dynamics of Providence and freedom.[25]

Harmonious proportion

Our author points out one typical factor of influence on economic processes in "economic consciousness," defined as follows: "a set of concepts, sentiments, purposes, in which populations participate around their material interests."[26] A consciousness not separated from other forms of consciousness, in search of a "proportional balance" of the different elements. In this consciousness "utilitarian" sentiments have their part, but also legal, civil, religious, and moral ones:

> If the harmonious proportion between utilitarian and ethical factors is altered, the normal course of wealth is also disrupted. If for example the equilibrium is broken in favor of a religious consciousness exalted to the point of mysticism, the economy is suffocated, as among the heirs of Brahminical transcendental-

> ism in India or in Tibet under the Great Lama, or it languishes and is extinguished amid the disputes of a theologizing people as in Byzantium. But woe, vice versa, if the religious and ethical consciousness weakens to the point of skeptical indifferentism: Then the greedy sentiments of material interest for revenge become sharpened to the point of domineering, and then the world of work groans under the tyranny of utilitarianism, as happened throughout the nineteenth century in Europe and America.[27]

It's a sure bet that Toniolo sees this balance achieved in the Christian Middle Ages:

> Whatever may have been written of Christianity in this respect, accused of "withering the flower of life" (Hegel, Bebel, and in part Harnack) by virtue of a demanded asceticism, historically there is no doubt that it alone could boast of having instilled in the peoples, in just harmony, the most robust and elevated moral consciousness, and at the same time the most industrious economic consciousness. The Middle Ages, especially at the height of power for the municipality, was the age of faith in its most sublime manifestations to the point of asceticism, and of the ideals of art, freedom, democracy, to the point of enthusiasm. But in it the populations deeply felt all the realities of life with its dignity, its joys, its sufferings, its hopes; they lived an intense life like the Americans today, and their very passions or faults attested to the exuberance, not the exhaustion, of energy.[28]

Hence the importance — also as a task of the economist and the statesman — of contributing to the formation of a correct social-economic consciousness. Here is the secret of the solution to the social crisis:

> And if today the poor distribution of income to the detriment of workers promises to be corrected, this is happening not so much due to the assaults of socialism, but because around the legitimacy of certain reforms to relieve the proletariat a more

> upright popular consciousness is forming somewhere, validated by the acquiescence of the capitalist classes, by the messages of moralists and philanthropists, and by a better concept of the social duty of governments.[29]

With a finale imbued with Christian optimism, Toniolo concludes, "Let us be certain that still tomorrow the quality and direction of consciousness will inform the economic order."[30]

Between individualism and collectivism

The multiple economic models that history registers are ultimately arranged around two "foci," corresponding to the two directive centers of individual consciousness and collective consciousness. In reality, Toniolo explains, between the two foci there are relationships of coexistence and exchange: The individual economic consciousness tends to expand in the collective economic consciousness, and this reacts on the individual consciousness. The result is a continuous dynamism between accents that go toward one pole or the other, in the continuous search for balance, a balance that is achieved with the concept of "solidary order," determined by the awareness of solidarity:

> [The] awareness that the most extensive and complete particular good of individuals is obtained through the general good of society, and so by subordinating one's own good to the good of others, in homage to a higher moral law, in which both rediscover their ultimate reason and their sanction.[31]

Which is not easy, Toniolo warns. One's own good (on an individual basis) does not always and spontaneously coincide with the good of others:

> Sentiments of utility are not enough to nourish a full, lasting, effective awareness of solidarity without their being strengthened and integrated by motives of the moral and precisely religious law.[32]

History is full of testimonies of this continuous conflict between individuality and sociality, of *private selfishness* and *public selfishness*. Christianity created the conditions for integration between the two poles, generating the awareness of solidarity in the common good between individuals and collectives. A balance put in crisis by modernity:

> The Renaissance and the Reformation brought back in the fifteenth–seventeenth centuries the absorbing pantheism of pagan antiquity, including in the economic field, just as the nineteenth century saw the reproduction of the example of the atomizing individualism of society, with the perversion of the rational and Christian traditions of solidarity. But today, through the ethical school, solidarism meets with opposition from the main lines of this solidarity, promising vast future applications.[33]

One should not overlook the contrast between solidarity, entirely of Christian inspiration, and solidarism, a pathological expression of solidarity as found in the socialist ideologies. The awareness of solidarity upheld and imparted by Christianity has an intrinsic universal character; "it is meant to spread across space to all nations."[34]

Organs, institutions, and laws

The social order is made up of organs and institutions. The term *organ*, Toniolo cautions, is to be understood in a sense that is quite far from the abuses of naturalistic-morphological sociology. Organs are to be understand here as "forms of human association and coexistence, each distinguished by its own specific end and corresponding functions, and so having an autonomous existence with respect to the comprehensive existence of the society with which they cooperate."[35] This conception of autonomous social organs was practically unknown in pre-Christian antiquity, an era in which, sooner or later, "the social constitution found itself entirely absorbed by the state."[36] It comes as no surprise that, in this statist logic, antiquity should incline toward forms of communism such as in Crete, Megara, Sparta, and that Plato himself should propose an aprioristically egalitarian plan of coexistence:[37]

> Before this desolate spectacle, like the announcement of an unexpected dawn comes the maxim of Saint Paul, which likens the new society of Christians gathered in the Church to *a mystical body* in which the life that circulates in its *individual and distinct parts* flows back into the *common perfection*. A mystical concept indeed, but one that is a prelude to an *organic* renewal of social coexistence, through which from that day onward history has us witness an even newer process, which in breaking or rather dissolving that monstrous political pantheism arrives at first distinguishing the *family*, the integration of individuality, from every other species of human association, as a seed that comes before and nourishes every other, and later *the whole social being* from the *political* — namely, *society* from the s*tate* — with the exception that by hierarchical degrees it reconnects these distinct autonomous circles with universal humanity through the Church.[38]

A work of social reorganization that resembles a birth, a rebirth (Toniolo loves to speak of palingenesis). "With the organic concept of society, the only true social order had sprouted."[39] A process that takes place gradually, starting from the recognition of the individual in terms of his moral and spiritual dignity, with the consequence of the gradual liberation of private and social life from the political domination of the empire, which the invasions of the Germanic races, "with their individualism," contributed to breaking apart, driving the shattered society under the protection of the Church, "which in the dioceses, monasteries, ecclesiastical territories undertakes to protect, gather together, and unify."[40]

An economic consequence of all this: The fate of wealth is no longer chained to the state, but develops in three great "autonomous circles" of economic life:

> A *private economy*, true generator of wealth, with its colossal enterprises, its manifold associations, its powerful technology; a *social economy*, with its monies, its banks, its railways, its commerce, international, transmitter of the private economy; and a

> robust and complex *state economy*, which derives its political-financial power from the private and social economic spheres, and exercises over them only an integrating and coordinating function.[41]

Family, nations, universal society

In relation to this grand design, Toniolo distinguishes the "extensive social organs," developed horizontally in space, and the "intensive," developed vertically in the social hierarchy. To the former belongs, first of all, the family, the "vital cell of society," "private social organ," whose evolution Toniolo follows here (we will skip over his extensive and meticulous reconstruction), starting from its patriarchal stage flourishing in antiquity.[42] It was in this type of family that humanity served its apprenticeship and found the stimulus for the formation of property (which for a long time was domestic and aristocratic):

> And this was the first and most constant school of the orderly management and use of material goods, so that *oikos* (house) is the root of the word *economy*.[43]

The patriarchal family ran out of time, under blows of an economic nature but also due to the perversion of customs, to give way to the "normal family," reconstructed by Christianity with its specific ethical character upheld in the face of the state.[44] Also on the economic level, with this new familial phase, a truly autonomous private economy was born:

> The whole social economy of the Middle Ages, of this youth of the Christian social order, rested on the broad base of domestic clusters, that is, on large families, supported by entities that were their luxuriant but distinct offshoots: the rural leagues, the noble coteries, the Colleges of the Arts.[45]

How ideal that medieval model was in Toniolo's eyes is clearly visible by contrasting it with his grim description of the contemporary crisis:

> In the present day the intensity of the social crisis in Europe and America can be traced back to the first roots of the private family economy. Indeed, the monetary concerns that stifle the formative moral virtues of bourgeois families; the stagnation, the exploitation, the disappearance of in-home work, the women and children dispersed in the factories, the precariousness and dispersion of the daily earnings in working-class families; the individualism that breaks up domestic unity and harmony in all classes … shattered the vigorous and solid nucleus of the contemporary family. Which no longer puts up any virtue of resistance or exercises any moderating function in the face of the vortex of a social economy that engulfs everything, including itself, and may be preparing a socialistic economy in which goods would be leveled and assimilated on a par with families.[46]

From the womb of the family the "social organs" are born, which develop in terms of noble alliances, lineages, nations, universal society. Toniolo dedicates specific attention to each of these realities, which, although of considerable interest, we believe we can skip here so as not to get bogged down.[47] We will limit ourselves to a brief mention of the concept of "national economy," which expresses itself "in the real formation of a system of relationships of material interest, whose prominent characteristics distinguish it from those of other peoples."[48] For Toniolo, the nation is "the social organ par excellence, with which humanity, with a variety of concrete forms and active virtues, takes part in bringing about civilization."[49] From the economic point of view, the nation "is suited to bringing its power of production to the highest degree,"[50] both due to the convergence of many favorable elements of a social, traditional, and moral nature, and also because the nation represents the

> nearest and most secure market for its own trade. Woe to a people that produces almost exclusively for other nations and lives almost entirely on external trade, quite remote and therefore uncertain and wavering, without this solid basis of operation. This is the justification at certain times for protectionist doctrines,

> because without intensifying wealth at home, expansion abroad would not be possible. ... Thus the nation is the natural and historical ladder for mounting to universal human relations.[51]

Regarding universal society, Toniolo warns against the conception that it is the fruit of the individualistic Enlightenment. So where does it come from?

> Universal society does not result from relationships between individuals (or private associations) and the human race in the world. This is the false conception of the eighteenth-century encyclopedia and of nineteenth-century individualism. Universal society itself is a *world organism*, whose constituent parts are the *races* and *nations*, which, with varieties of aptitudes and indefinite degrees of development, coexist on the globe, so that *variety* and *gradation* are also integral elements here.[52]

The result is a precise economic principle: "It can be stated that an international economy is destined to be always unstable and perhaps harmful if it does not rest on a series of robust and mature national economies. This is the contemporary trend."[53]

Yet it does not escape Toniolo that the theme of the nation, revisited in the light of the tragic experience of the war — the first world conflict, which so embittered his last years and struck his own family[54] — in the landscape of nationalist passions and conflicting interests shows its most problematic side when "the specific historical mission of each individual nationality, in contributing in different ways to the common advances, turns into closed-off nationalism, which violently opposes and absorbs all the other races and nations."[55]

Chapter IX
Hierarchy as *Diakonia*

Social classes and economy

With the concept of class, to which Toniolo dedicates the last part of the introduction to social economics, we come to the sphere of "intensive" social organs, "which represent a top-to-bottom gradation of the population into hierarchical groups."[1]

Hearing of social hierarchy in terms of "higher" and "lower" organs prompts an instinctive revulsion in today's reader. We feel ourselves — albeit in different ways and with different approaches (Toniolo also referred to this, but in an overtly Christian sense) — as children of the *liberté-égalité-fraternité* triad of the French Revolution. To understand the Toniolian sense of hierarchy, it helps to clear away some misunderstandings and a certain degree of hypocrisy latent in today's politically correct jargon.

Between misunderstandings and hypocrisy

The misunderstanding: Toniolo, speaking of classes — or the set of a certain category of people — and emphasizing their hierarchical positions, does not intend in the least to undermine the principle of the equal dignity of every human being. On the contrary, he vindicates this principle as one of the imperishable achievements of Christian civilization, as compared with that of paganism, in which man was not considered as himself, but rather in his social position as free or slave.

Christianity abolishes this distinction. More precisely, the egalitarian vision of humanity allows Christianity to welcome with truth the accidental differences that make each person something absolutely original. Personal and social differences assert themselves, but they must be grasped in a harmonious vision, with a view to mutual service and common benefit.[2] If they drive the natural formation of groups, these must avoid closing groups off (castes), adjusting themselves as open groups that can be accessed little by little as their conditions are met. The factual reality often contradicts all this, but in principle it is so.

The foundation of all this variety is the incontrovertible fact of the diversity of talents and situations in which each human person finds himself. We all perceive and recognize that there are social, cultural, organizational positions that play a directive role: the adjective higher, according to Toniolo, is to be understood in this sense — not in the ontological-personal sense (at this level we are all perfectly equal), but in the functional sense, with regard to a specific assessment of personal qualities and consequent responsibilities. It concerns not what we are, but what we do. In this sense there are "higher classes," with directive responsibility in the social body. A scientist, in terms of dignity, is no different from an illiterate. But it is clear that the latter, grappling with a technical-scientific problem, will rely on the scientist. Something of the sort applies to the other directive classes. It would be mocking the weakest to insist on equality where differences are evident. Populism, the forerunner of dictatorship, conceals this hypocritical and demagogic betrayal on the part of the ruling classes.[3] Of course, it can happen, and may happen more than one suspects, that the illiterate, with his practical and spiritual wisdom may give points to the presumptuous intellectual, but becoming aware of the diversity of "talents" in terms of responsibility, and therefore of service, is vital precisely to guarantee, safeguard, and serve universal equality. A hierarchy understood in Christian terms — in the Church and in society — is necessarily *diakonia* (service).

The directive classes (or higher, in Toniolian jargon) must answer for their faculties. Superiority does not add anything to their dignity, but much to their responsibility. A contemporary economist who fights for equality, Thomas Piketty, states, "Inequality is not necessarily bad in itself: The central question is to find out whether it is justified, whether there are reasons for it."[4] In reading Toniolo's analysis we will have to keep these preliminary considerations in mind.

The genesis of classes

From where do classes arise? "The *first origins* lie in the variety and accidental gradation of human *physical-mental faculties*, from person to person."[5] Historical materialism (Marx, Loria, Sombart) is wrong, Toniolo emphasizes, in tracing class differences back to economic-material causes alone. The latter can provide a further element, but do not have exclusivity. Sometimes economic success is the consequence of social advancement due to other factors (as in the case of the military, religious, administrative classes, etc.). All throughout history one finds the formation of these classes, which, when it comes to the "higher moral classes," attests to "the rational and positive necessity of certain directive functions of collective living."[6]

Christianity made its original contribution to class dynamics. For one thing, "by reconsecrating and spiritualizing the ends of society and the state, as well as the principle of authority in God, it legitimized the hierarchy of the moral-civil classes as organs for the realization of superior goods in human coexistence, which from this gained vigor and prestige";[7] for another, "its greatest originality, as against the pagan times, was that of having given a legitimate, permanent, and endlessly extensible basis to the economic classes properly so called, founded on activity productive of wealth. It was the result, legitimate in the social order, of the religion of work, through which a second social hierarchy was formed, which from then on drew its immediate origin not from an authoritative act from above, but from personal energies rising from below."[8]

Among the elements that influence the genesis of classes is class consciousness:

> The modern capitalist classes, also in a regime of freedom, owe their predominance to the common adherence to several prin-

ciples of social and political conduct that ensured their predominance. And masses of workers who share the same happy and sad conditions of work become a class only on the day when they acquire the conviction of their own special importance in the social body — that is, when the awareness of special duties, rights, and interests is formed in them. Educating those classes in the right awareness is indeed the problem of the future.[9]

Emulation or struggle?

Classes have their own tendencies, or temptations. One is artificial rigidification within the social hierarchy. The other is a tendency to transform mutual emulation, competitiveness, or conflict of interests into class struggle. With a view to the solution of violent or destructive conflictual dynamics, Christianity offers a remedy, outlining a precise ethics of social hierarchy. First, it bases this on God's plan, and therefore regulates the relations between classes in such a way as to guarantee unity and diversity:

> Men (already in Ecclesiastes) are equal before God, but in the depth of his wisdom the Lord *has separated them and distinguished their ways*. So, consecrating a law of nature, the formation and function of classes rested on the duty of each one (and thus of each social group) to contribute with free and meritorious activities, in proportion to the type and degree of his aptitudes, to the realization of this social order for the common good.[10]

Another element accentuated by Christianity is freedom, and therefore personal merit:

> The highest qualification of individual and collective elevation became not so much authority from above, but personal merit: the virtues and talent that raise the lowest commoner to the highest levels of ecclesiastical dignity; the civil merits that with new elements rejuvenate the English nobility; the economic initiative, that alredy in our municipalities, in just a few generations, took the country bumpkin to the top of the fat bourgeoisie with

> the Peruzzi, with the Alberti, with the Medici; and that today in Europe and America, with a dizzying spiral from bottom to top, drives the expansive life of the social hierarchy.[11]

Of course, Toniolo admits, "class conflict and strife"[12] also marked the Christian era, from the Middle Ages (see the Ciompi Revolt, 1378) up to the systematic struggle of the proletariat against the capitalism of the nineteenth century. But under the influence of Christianity, the sense of duty of all the classes, especially of the upper classes toward society, was not entirely lost:

> And today the reconstruction of the proletariat as a class is indeed announced not as the probable result of a *catastrophic struggle* to the detriment of capitalism, but as the fruit of a *workers' legislation* that may reproduce the ancient Christian harmony of the upper and lower classes, on the basis of the recognition of the respective classes' autonomy.[13]

Making a general assessment of the importance of the "class hierarchy," Toniolo concludes:

> Class is the necessary organ of the social constitution. It can be stripped of legal recognition and of pathological accretions, but not destroyed. The contemporary era took every privilege away from the classes and believed it had abolished them; instead, it finds itself grappling with the fact of two gigantic classes: the empire of the capitalist class and the convulsive gestation of the working class. The classes, with their hierarchical system, are the normal means of ensuring the improvement of social life. It is on the shoulders of their class that the best individuals most readily strengthen and elevate themselves, and from there they can effectively redound to the general good. The more varied and freer the exchange between these, the more active civil progress will be. The economic division of labor has its first origin in the social division of the classes, and both benefit from mutual sup-

> port. The static type and dynamic energy of the economy of a people take root in the constitution, interweaving, and vitality of its social classes.[14]

Countryside and city

To describe the varied world of the social economy, Toniolo also dedicates pages of analysis to the configuration of the relationship between countryside and city. What he says about the different social, cultural, and economic vocation of the two realities is significant. "In history, the city has a function of initiative and of the diffusion of progress in all forms.[15] The countryside

> continues to represent, with the isolation of families or of collective groups, the sense of the solidity of the elementary organisms of society; the essential and permanent interests of humanity, like those of the soil in which it is rooted; devotion to customs and traditions under the protection of the ruling authority. In a word, it has the office of physical, moral, and political preservation.[16]

From this complementarity of vocations stems the principle that "the proportion between civil and rural populations determines the structure and spirit of a nation."[17]

The tribe, the state, the Church

It is interesting that only in this part, near the conclusion of his preparatory volume, after having focused on the private and social dynamics of the social order, should Toniolo come to show an interest in public institutions — namely, associations that, like the tribe, the state, and the Church, are distinguished from the others by having, in different degrees, a "juridical-authoritative character."[18]

As for the tribe, this is born from below, from the patriarchal family, which gradually becomes a "noble society" settled in various village communities, which converge into the tribe, "the first organic kernel of public life in this ontogenetic process of the state."[19] In the tribal assemblies, in which all of the free with private and public rights participate, political interests, wars, peace, migrations, punitive justice are decided. It is the first stage in the formation of the state. The latter takes shape according to either the centralizing Oriental type of state (even Rome ultimately gave in to this), or the organic state, in which the political order emerges concretely from the bosom of social forces and fashions itself on them, bringing together the organization of political classes, the constitution of local autonomies (municipalities, provinces), and the increase of central power.[20] Historically,

> Christian society found itself accompanied from the beginning by the new factor, almost inadvertently grown within its bosom, of a *priestly hierarchy* equipped with the fullness of dogmatic and moral authority, which for one thing is not restricted to caste but remains open to all, nor is it transmitted by inheritance, and for another, due to its spiritual, distinct, and independent ends, is not confused with the state.[21]

This leads to finally delineating itself as an organ of public, but not strictly political, law.

Toniolo outlines this development. In his assessment the role this class plays in society is significant, even when, with modernity, the political organization of the clergy declined:

> Yet with only *political potentiality* enduring in it, and normally limiting itself to the simple mediating action of consecrating, inspiring, informing the life of the state with its religious moral influence, the ecclesiastical hierarchy always continued to be an integrating factor of this. Indeed, for all time the clerical class stands with its reminder that the legitimacy and authority of the state stem primarily not from force but from a moral principle.[22]

Nobility, people, local autonomies

Toniolo also recognizes a social-economic role for the nobility, a theme that today sounds strongly dated, since in the span of a century it has increasingly vanished from social and cultural consciousness and just a few traces of it remain in nostalgic groups. But the 1800s still had a living and thriving noble class before its eyes. Toniolo traces it back to its origins, recognizing in feudalism a time in which the nobility takes on a "complete, autonomous, and lasting (hereditary) hierarchical organization,"[23] up to the point at which

> the body of the nobility detaches itself from the rest of the constitution of the state, and with its own privileges (negative and positive) acquires legal-political autonomy in the face of royal power itself, and it finally matures thanks to the passing down of offices and the corresponding feudal assets from father to son.[24]

When in the modern age the absolute princes transformed the feudal aristocracy, as a political class, into *court nobility*, the conditions were put in place for its decay.

Distinct from these classes is the people: a term used here in a specific sense at the level of juridical-political organization, not referring to the population as a whole, but only to that part of it made up of the middle and lower economic classes, organized in guilds. The people, thus understood, had a long gestation process, but in the end

> the juridical-political order of the popular middle classes was not inferior, but rather superior, due to profound and lasting influences, to that of the nobility.[25]

The regulations of the guilds led to the formation of commercial law and the first attempts

> at an economic-social policy in favor of the working classes, so that the entry of the industrious bourgeoisie into the parliaments of Europe since the Middle Ages became in our day a pledge of the possible advent of the more select working classes in government.[26]

Another constitutive element of the social organism is that of local autonomies, (understood as the faculty and right of the various territorial centers to govern certain public interests on their own). These gradually developed "in multiple concentric circles (parishes, municipalities, provinces, regions) everywhere, becoming a hearth of vitality enduring until the French Revolution."[27]

This medieval landscape is not devoid of the central power of the state, acting as a unifying element, but it is a power applied lightly:

> Royal power in the Christian era (*rex,* from *regere*) resembles a *magistracy,* which is exercised under its own moral and sometimes juridical-political responsibility, a trait that pervaded the whole hierarchy of officials of the Middle Ages, especially of our municipalities, with the institution of the *sindacato.*[28]

Something quite different developed between the fifteenth and sixteenth centuries, when the climate of resurgent paganism gave the state the character of a centralizing absolutism:

> [The result was] a historical period of social and economic perversion whose effects persist today. This explains the terrible ideological and positivist reaction from the French Revolution of the eighteenth century up to our time against the privileges of the noble class and the absolutism of the throne together; the formation of an anti-popular capitalism, lording over the whole economy; and the contemporary proletariat, invoking the despoliation of landed and movable wealth together. All writers recognize in the period of monarchical absolutism the origin of the social crisis and of the present socialism (Mayer, Sombart, Loria).[29]

But here we are at the level of degeneration, which makes appear, even more sharply, "the genesis of the state in Western civilization, on the triple pedestal of classes, local autonomy, and coordinating central power."[30] And it shows even more clearly the "ordering and integrating" function of the Church, which historically carried out a task of consecration and at the same time of limitation of the powers of the state. "It faced and solved on its own the social problem in the Middle Ages; it presents itself as a counselor and assistant in the solution of it even today."[31]

Freedom, association, property

> The whole social organism with its public institutions definitively aims to equip with the protection of the law the three fundamental private institutions of *personal freedom,* of *association,* and of *property.*[32]

As for freedom, comparing this with slavery in its various phases, from antiquity to the modern era,[33] Toniolo highlights it as the first and greatest private institution. It is

> the legal recognition of the human person — that is, of those essential qualities of *man's* nature by which he is distinguished from all other beings; qualities of an autonomous moral being with his own spiritual ends (and others coordinated with them), which according to higher ethical law he has the duty to achieve with his *free and responsible mental energy*, and in the exercise of which, therefore, everyone in society has the right not to be hindered (negative *freedom*), but rather assisted (positive *freedom*) by his peers, and, for this purpose, to be protected and integrated by the authority of the state.[34]

Efficacious — in this context — are the brushstrokes that our author dedicates to slavery throughout its historical process, starting from pre-Christian antiquity, characterized by a genuine "slave economy" recognized as legitimate and natural by men of genius like Aristotle and Plato.[35] The progress of the Christian spirit put the conditions in place for overcoming this, albeit with hesitation and resistance destined to be gradually overcome,[36] while the perversion of these principles caused an authentic retrogression that in the modern era saw slavery reproduced on the coasts of Africa, with the trading of blacks, and in America, where it aroused reactions that eventually led to its abolition. The same happened with the legal suppression of servitude and forced labor in the climate of the French Revolution, due to the abolition of noble privileges on August 4, 1789:

> Thus the most shameful of all the setbacks of the first three centuries of the modern era, that of personal freedom, was repaired, and the greatest *human* regeneration was accomplished in the law of Western civilization.[37]

We will leave the details aside. The conclusion is that with Christianity, established or recovered after the always lurking neo-pagan regurgitations, "*personal freedom* became the cornerstone of the new social order, which was no longer based on the privileged quality of citizen imparted by the state, but on the unalterable and inalienable nature of man and humanity."[38]

As an expansion of free individuality, the right to association arises, from the necessary associations, mainly the family, to the voluntary, to which were added legal moral entities like foundations, pious works, guilds, etc.

If association is a projection of the person in the human world, particular property is the "projection of the objectified personality in the material world."[39] Property, like sociality, is one with the person, with his dignity and his rights; of course, if it be conceived correctly (in Christian terms!) with its indispensably "social function," which distinguishes it from the right to use and abuse (*ius utendi* and *abutendi*) of the ancient conception and protects it from the naturist or socialist accusations of modernity (one could think of Rousseau[40] or Proudhon[41]). It is, in reality,

> the legal recognition of the exclusive reservation for or belonging to the human person (individual or collective) of useful material things, through an act of mental and physical energy that connects them to himself for all the legitimate ends of man in society, and so for the particular good coordinated with the general good.[42]

Note specifically "legitimate ends" and "general good." Property is a means and not an end: "the means most natural (of reason) and at the same time most efficacious (of utility) to achieve the *good of individuals and of all.*"[43] Therefore, nothing arbitrary or selfish. It is needed by a mature personality, as "personal property," and by a mature society, as the property of "collective entities," intermediate between person and state: two forms of property called to exist in a proportionate manner.[44]

Freedom, association, property, our author concludes, journey together, responding to the same logic:

> Without an understanding of the rational and historical course of constitution and development of these three great private institutions — that is, personal freedom, association, and particular property — it would not be possible to solve any sociological and economic problem, because they are the center of gravity for all of the social institutions composing the foundation stone of the entire order of society in civilization, and especially of the economy.[45]

Chapter X
Principles in Action

Economic laws under the scrutiny of reality

With this chapter we come to the second volume of the *Trattato* (corresponding to the third of the *Opera Omnia*).[1] Toniolo sends it off to the press in December 1909. He begins with a lucid introductory page that summarizes his overall vision, emphasizing first of all the systematic character of his *Trattato*, which now moves from the premises of the economy to the economy in action, in its two phases of the production and circulation of wealth. Then comes the clarification that if the whole introductory volume concerned the "great speculative premises and de facto components of the *constitutive order* of wealth,"[2] now, with the discussion on production and circulation, the focus shifts to the *operative order*. Finally, he underlines that, precisely by moving to the practical level, he has been able to put his conception of economic laws under the scrutiny of reality, scientifically engaging with the different schools of his time: from J. S. Mill (individualist school) to Roscher and Schmoller (historical school), from Wagner (social political school) to Minghetti, Baudrillart (ethical-juridical school) to Brants, Antoine, Pesch (Christian school), "and recently with the addition of talented economists and colleagues from Italy, from Lampertico to Cognetti and to Ricca-Salerno, to

Pareto, Graziani, Supino."[3]

In dialogue with these schools of thought, Toniolo fully confirms the nature of the laws of economics as outlined in the introductory volume, underlining their rational-positive character:

> The laws (or rather procedures of economic activity), daughters of the intelligent and free energies of man and therefore essentially psychological-moral, all find themselves guided *by the single eminently rational hedonic principle* of achieving the maximum useful effect with the minimum expenditure of means, and are expressed as the ray of white light refracting in many colors and with graduated intensity through the prism, thanks to those various and changeable accidental modalities and that degree of development which are occasioned *by the eminently positive* or de facto *circumstances* of time, space, and civilization, in the midst of which that principle itself receives its concrete and progressive actualization, so that these laws find their scientific justification precisely in the fact that the opposite of those procedures considered in their definitive tendency would be repugnant at once to the reasonable demands of the mind and to the most constant experiences of humanity.[4]

Addressing the themes of production and distribution with "patient and objective" analysis, Toniolo intends to test the validity of those laws. What is the outcome of this experiment? He voices, with the enthusiastic sensation of Archimedes's "eureka," the perception of a universal order in which the economy is also situated:

> And it seemed to me that what leaped forth clear and chiseled was, for one thing, the universal and immutable *unity* of that *primary* hedonic *law*, which responds in utilitarian terms to the nature of men and things, and for another that the subordinate *multiplicity of secondary laws*, to put it in Bacon's parlance, revealed the connection that in its development economic activity maintains with the fundamental facts of the physical and social world.[5]

It is also confirmed that

> the observance of the higher imperatives of ethics and law, including positive laws and the political action of the state in utilitarian relations, appears to be indeed not a superimposition, but rather a *necessary condition* for the full useful efficacy and normal development of the economic laws themselves.[6]

The operative economic order

Toniolo lays out the division of the various parts of the economy, adding to production and circulation, already mentioned, distribution and consumption. We will leave aside the discussion on how these ought to be organized. The importance that Toniolo ascribes to the question of distribution is significant: "The measure of economic progress is provided mainly by the goodness of the system of distribution."[7] And in any case he underlines that, in each of these parts, it is always the fundamental hedonic law (maximum effect with minimum means) that emerges:

> So, production defines how the maximum wealth or product may be achieved with the minimum sacrifice of productive factors (means). Circulation has in view the greatest possible useful efficiency of exchange with the minimum use of circulatory instruments. Distribution investigates how the most useful and widespread division of national net income may be carried out among the producing classes, without diminishing their productive power. This similarly applies to consumption, which indicates how the most complete and progressive satisfaction of needs (personal and social) may be provided with the minimum dispersion of present and future wealth.[8]

What it means to produce

Production is to be understood as "the series of common human procedures with which the utility of material things is made effective or increased."[9] It is an activity that includes three factors: the man who works; nature, understood as the complex of substances and forces of the external world (cosmos); and capital — namely, a product intended to assist production. The three elements stand in a precise hierarchy: one, the center is man, the real and proper factor of production, while "the other two are nothing but supports, the one primordial, the other derivative. Man lords over them and makes them serve his own ends, and so production is a quintessentially human fact."[10]

Before going into the details, Toniolo provides a survey of industry as a concrete order of production resulting from "a set of various factors (nature, capital, labor) converted to obtain a particular product."[11] Worthy of note is the emphasis on the "material" character of the industries considered from the economic perspective. They all

> arrange themselves around matter or material goods, external to man precisely as the characteristics of wealth are. So there falls away of its own accord the ancient conception (although perpetuated today by some) of immaterial industries or (liberal) professions, which transcend the field of economic production as much as they may influence it, because the result of these professions is not material and often is even within man.[12]

"Immaterial," for example, are the professions of judge, teacher, lawyer, doctor. It should be noted that Toniolo does not maintain that people in these categories do not work in the common sense of the term, but that in these cases it is not a matter of work productive of wealth "that could become part of anyone's assets or commerce,"[13] much less that it could give rise to an industry. It is a precise semantic choice. A choice that would be difficult to uphold in a time like ours, in which not only the classic liberal professions, but much of industrial work, has become digital, increasingly taking on an "immaterial" appearance.

Beyond the various forms that production assumes, our author confirms in it the emergence of the supreme law of economics, the realization of the maximum product with the minimum expenditure of productive means. And this with a view to utility, which is certainly individual utility, but also social, and in any case a utility "amended, completed, and contained by the ethical law of duty."[14] To produce is a duty: toward

God, toward ourselves, toward others.[15] A duty, however, proportional "to the variety and gradations of individual aptitudes":[16]

> [And] limited by the harmonious coexistence of other superior duties in relation to the hierarchy of human-social ends. For individual social classes, the duty of material production ceases if it is incompatible with the exercise of other functions that are higher and more obligatory because they are more directly connected with moral-civil ends — for example, for the classes serving religious offices, liberal professions, political functions, etc.[17]

Finally, Toniolo adds, the duty of production also lies within the guarantee of private and public law.[18]

Work

Work is defined as "the exercise of human faculties aimed directly at the production of wealth." The "material" semantics returns, which our author reiterates by noting that "the exercise of human energies that aims at a goal other than wealth (e.g., the discovery of truth, the maintenance of order, ethical perfection), will be a more excellent activity, but is not work in the economic sense."[19]

Entering into the analysis, it is highlighted that in work all the faculties of man — the whole man — are involved; indeed, with the progress of civilization the intellectual element grows. It is up to the working human person to conceive the final idea, what he wants to produce, coordinate the corresponding means to realize it, and then materially execute the product. On the basis of these functions, two classes of workers are distinguished:

> [Those] superior, and they are (in economic language) the *enterprisers* who carry out the organization and management, and the *workers* who see to the *execution* of the work. They are two functions of the same act, and so two classes (both working) that complement each other. Woe if the *progress* of one does not proceed parallel to that of the other. … And woe if, as today in Eu-

> rope, antipathies and conflicts will persist between enterprisers and laborers in the performance of work; both classes of workers (higher and lower) will suffer equally.[20]

On the subject of the efficacy of work, Toniolo identifies the causes that differentiate it: individual causes (special aptitudes that distinguish workers of different nations, according to a sort of ethnography of work), historical causes linked to human conditions and events — for example, nutrition, hygiene, education — and above all causes linked to the influence of religious and philosophical doctrines. Examples help to get this across:

> The mysticism of Brahma, considering work as the punishment of a life destined to extinguish itself in pain, stifled the zest for work among the Indians under the weight of pessimism. The whole spirit of the pagan societies of Greece and Rome was unfavorable to work. … Christianity in this respect has incomparable merits.[21]

It was, in fact, Christianity that

> thoroughly innovated the concept of work, thus carrying out an unexpected and immense revaluation against the age-old prejudices of paganism. Maturing the doctrines of Judaism (Bible), it declared work a *duty*: as a normal way of providing for one's own preservation and improvement with regard to spiritual ends, as a means of *expiation* for guilt and as a school of *virtue* — that is, of moral improvement and therefore of social-civil elevation. It similarly considered the worker as a continuer of the divine work of creation, thus endowed with high *dignity*, in the exercise of both the directive work of the mind and the operative work of the arm.[22]

All of this is confirmed by the example of Jesus Christ, who became a worker, by a whole series of historical expressions — for example, the Benedictines — and by the ecclesial magisterium, so that the lofty concept of work is the "trait that distinguishes Western Christian civilization, eminently active, from the passive one of the Oriental peoples."[23] It likewise distinguishes it from the Muslim religion, of which our author, following an oversimplifying and in any case inadmissible stereotype in the contemporary multireligious and multicultural context of dialogue, says that "it sanctifies war and fanaticism, persecuted work and educated the populations to idleness."[24] However, within the Christian world itself the return of paganism in modernity favored the oppression of the working classes:

> Greedy materialism led industrialists to push laborers' work to the point of paroxysm as a means of exploitative earnings, while workers suffer this only as a necessity and despise it as a mark of new servitude. And in the meantime, the productive function and educational virtue of work are fearfully compromised by the convulsion of socialism.[25]

Civil institutions, laws, and politics influence the power of work. When the laws protect the worker, his dignity, his rights, the efficacy of production also benefits:

> The worker (as proven recently) remunerated fairly or generously repays with interest, with the intensity and diligence of his work, the enterpriser with higher wages, while the poorly paid worker takes revenge with slow, interrupted, and imperfect work (theory of high wages).[26]

Finally, the efficacy of work is affected by social causes, like the demographic composition of the workers (men, women, children, etc.).[27]

Nature

Understood as a productive factor, this is "the complex of materials and forces from the external world serving production."[28] Toniolo is quick to point out:

> The function of nature is not primary, but only *integral,* because although it has its own power to produce (e.g., the grass of natural pastures), it does not ordinarily contribute to production unless it is subordinated to the rational function of human work.[29]

So once again the primacy of man returns; which does not mean that nature is of little importance. Toniolo dedicates pages to portraying it in its varieties, recalling how it contributes to production with a range of possibilities that must be carefully evaluated. For example, it is no small thing that, when it comes to localized and nontransferable forces, as in the case of the soil of a given farm, which by its nature cannot be displaced and accumulated at will (as instead the calories and power of steam can be, in a factory), the contribution of nature occurs in a *decreasing* manner — that is, in an ever lessening measure, until complete exhaustion.[30] Characteristics of this type — which make the manufacturing industry profoundly different from the agricultural — are anything but a matter of indifference for economic logic. Much less are they a matter of indifference for social logic, since they impact the culture of the peoples, and become distinctive of the "economic autonomy of each nation."[31]

Capital

Contrary to the commonplace approach that considers "capital" to refer first of all to money, Toniolo adopts the definition of capital as "a product destined to assist production."[32] So this concept includes any product set aside from consumption to be destined for further production.[33] This is a concept, moreover, that was consolidated in the textbooks of the time.[34]

As for the relationship between man and nature, so for the relationship between man and capital Toniolo reiterates the hierarchy of values: capital "is a purely *subsidiary* and *instrumental* factor, and therefore not fundamental but subordinate."[35] This leads to a decisive consequence in the field of the distribution of wealth: The value of capital in increasing the revenue of production must be recognized, but given that it

> does not operate except by virtue of new human activity that puts and keeps it in use in industry, it is declared that the reve-

> nue from it does not belong to the one who owns it by the sole qualification of having prepared and possessing it, but rather by the qualification of participating in its use in production (profit of the capitalist).[36]

Capital is divided into immobile and mobile. Immobile, for example, is the capital of the mining industries (shafts, elevators, scaffolding), that of arable land (tillage, drainage, irrigation, granaries, cellars), of industry (factories, buildings), etc. Mobile capital, on the other hand, is that which can be relocated and mobilized (tools, machines, cargo vehicles, ships, etc.). It is also distinguished as fixed or circulating, "depending on whether it performs its role in production continuously, serving multiple technical production cycles, or instantaneously serving only one production cycle."[37] The distinction is significant when it comes to calculating its value. And it is also evident that the progress of the economy in general stands "in relation to the absolute increase in circulating capital and at the same time to the relative decrease in fixed capital."[38]

It is only at this point that, after having clarified well the meaning of "effective capital," Toniolo introduces monetary capital, "which can be called *representative*, precisely because money represents all economic goods in their value."[39] As such, the monetary stock has the "character of an *instrumental good* more than any other similar good, with the only difference that, while the other goods are immediate means of production, this is an immediate means of circulation of wealth."[40] From the point of view of the private economy:

> The first portion of money, usually destined for the purchase of products for personal need, *represents* a fund or means of consumption and *is not capital*. The second portion, destined for the purchase of tools or means of production, represents the effective capital into which it is converted and so is capital itself, which by this means bears fruit.[41]

With these clarifications, the different ways of employing capital can be distinguished, and therefore the different figures of the owners of capital, the capitalists:

> The one who, being the owner of capital, himself applies it in industry at his own risk and for his own profit, or the one who provides his capital to the industrialist, sharing with him, if not in the management, at least to some degree in the economic-legal risk (hazard) of capital and its revenue, is *an enterprising capitalist.* A distinction is made between the capitalist director and the capitalist shareholders or partners, but both are enterprisers. Those instead who provide capital to industry without participating either in the managerial activity or in the risks of production are simple *lending capitalists.* They are not enterprisers. The qualification of compensation for the former is the merit of production *personally effected* (profit), for the latter the merit of production *materially assisted* (interest). Meanwhile, it is understood that the economic power of national industries depends mostly on the former, not so much on the latter. Those are the worthy authors of production; these can become its parasites.[42]

This is a very weighty and also very timely assessment. Almost prophetic, then, with respect to what we are experiencing in contemporary capitalism, is this statement:

> The excess of mobile mercantile capital, which, disdainful of stable application, clutters the banks, or fattens itself on usury, or runs wild in the financial markets, or stagnates in public debt, deprives all the industries of direct and valuable support, disturbs and exhausts them. It is one of the pathological forms of modern capitalism.[43]

Primacy of the factor of labor

Looking at the three factors, Toniolo establishes their hierarchical relationship: "*They are hierarchically coordinated into unity*, under the rule of the factor of labor."[44] A conclusion that he establishes not only for a priori moral reasons, but also by observing history, which shows how, progressively, man has dominated nature. Today, to tell the truth, we are worried about this domination of man due to the ecological disasters that it can entail. Furthermore, Toniolo himself warns, with Bacon, that *natura non nisi parendo vincitur*: nature can be commanded only by obeying it![45]

As for capital, Toniolo recognizes its importance. It is a child of man, of his ability, even of his virtues. Indeed, in this our author sees a difference between paganism and Christianity:

> The ancient nations were epicurean consumers of wealth, often acquired iniquitously with slavish sweat, with usury, with oppressive tributes, and they extinguished themselves in a frenzy of delights amid the exhaustion of all their wealth. Christian *self-denial*, which taught detachment from any disordered affection for possessions, for the first time restrained in the peoples their voracious consumption in the present, accustoming them to saving their surplus for the future, and thus capital was formed in the medieval populations. And when these were at risk of becoming corrupted in the inebriation of the first riches gained in Levantine trade in the first Crusades, the apostolate of Saint Francis in honor of *poverty* kept them from dissipatory luxury, and capital accumulated even more.[46]

This reference to Saint Francis in a historical sketch of the rise of capitalism is surprising. In fact, at first glance, who is more anticapitalist than Francis of Assisi? The famous gesture with which he cast off money and clothing in front of his father and the bishop, leaving himself naked, seems an image not only of anticapitalism, but even of anti-economy. Where is the economic rationale in that gesture, the hedonic principle of maximum result with minimum effort? Everything seems irrational. And yet, it suffices to ask oneself what was the "maximum" that the young convert intended for himself — that is, an existence full of God, of freedom, of love, to see that this gesture was his "coin" for acquiring it, the minimum means for the maximum result, a gesture that was at first glance irrational and yet full of reasonableness, which precisely in its antieconomic appearance became the manifesto of an alternative economy, one that does not make money an idol, but rather puts man at the center. Along this path, his thoughts and practices would develop the Franciscan school of economics, rediscovered today.[47] Paradoxically, if Max Weber traced modern capitalism back to the Calvinist spirit, Toniolo goes back not only to the Middle Ages, but even to Saint Francis! So, the progress of capital emerges as the fruit of Christian culture, as a positive and meritorious element of production, but on the condition that it remain firmly under human control:

> Regarding the relationships between the factors of production and their comparative development, it can be concluded that if work progressively dominates nature by means of capital, it is always man who triumphs, so that economic production is human par excellence, even when due to the enormous employment and instrumental use of the capital factor one speaks of a *capitalist economy par excellence.*[48]

"Human economy"

How near to heart this anthropocentric vision of the economy was for our author emerges from the tug-of-war that he entered into in 1896 during a congress of the *Unione cattolica per gli studi sociali.*[49] He had given a talk on credit (to which we will return),[50] expressing his hope that "a *capitalist economy* epitomized by the lending of capital to the enterpriser be replaced with a *human economy* par excellence, so that capital may become a follower and ally of the industrious *man*."[51] It seemed to some that he was hardly open to the new reality of the capitalist economy, almost a prisoner of the traditional Catholic view of the fruitless character of lending and therefore of the illicitness of interest. He had to explain himself further, distinguishing the lending of the capitalist who becomes an enterpriser or at least associates himself with the risks of the business, and so has the right to his share of compensation, and that of the capitalist who limits himself to lending, demanding a return regardless of the risks of the business. In the latter case he is entitled, according to Toniolo, to no more than an indemnity for the fact that the capital on loan has undergone damage for a certain time due to "loss of profit." However, nothing is owed to him in terms of that actual compensation or profit which only work can claim. In short, capital cannot be equated with labor; on the contrary, it must be subordinated to it. The debate was heated. In the final motion it was asked that it be said that capital must be "coordinated" with labor. Toniolo accepted this on the condition that coordination meant "subordination."[52] He really wasn't willing to give in. It was his take-no-prisoners fight for a "human economy" against the capitalist degeneration of his time, and perhaps even more so of ours.

The business: Cell of the economic organism

With his systematic mind, Toniolo brings himself to the production of wealth, highlighting its "special organic constitution," starting from those elementary organisms that we call businesses. These are like families in society and cells in the human body. The business is "the elementary body of a particular private economy."[53]

In its essential composition it presents a staff (a boss or enterpriser with a certain number of coworkers), a material made up of a gathering of forces and substances of nature, and an order instrumental for achieving the purpose.[54]

The enterpriser is fundamental, with his various offices of establishment and organization of the business, with technical, economic, and legal responsibility before the public and the state. This can be a physical or moral person. In any case, the business risk falls on the enterpriser — that is, the risk that the necessary advancement of a certain expenditure of energies could lead to an unfortunate outcome.

The *product* or useful effect of production is

> a *complex of new costly goods or riches* whose value at the end of the production cycle must provide the *reintegration* of the original value of the material (substances, forces of nature, and capital) and the *remuneration* of the value of the personnel's services (work). This overall value of the result of production makes up the gross *total revenue* of the company. Which, taking into account the two portions and destinations from which it results — that is, the basis of reintegration and remuneration — gives rise to the notion of *net revenue.*[55]

In this key, we can also understand the concept of *cost* and *profit*. The latter, from the enterpriser's point of view, is "that uncertain and variable (random) value which he perceives as compensation for his own exclusive functions."[56] When the business is a partnership of capitalists, the profit "is reduced only to the random compensation for the investment of capital in production, compensation that, due to its apportionment among partners, is called a dividend."[57] This type of partnership, Toniolo cautions, has been arrived at through a long historical journey that goes from the family business to the partnership company, with various profiles of moral entities. Finally, state enterprises are also born. But the prototype of the business is the private, in which a triple phase of development is clearly visible: the business that produces for ongoing consumption, that which produces to order, and finally the business of anticipation, stockpiling, speculation, called so because it produces not in response to consumer demand but in some manner awaiting it, "speculating on sales at times of higher prices and positioning itself to make a profit."[58]

Industry and enterprisers

An industry is the set of homogeneous businesses in a country for each branch of production. "The vital formation of distinct branches of industry in a population is the daughter of its historical circumstances."[59] National production is born from this, in which factors of lineage and nationality have their influence, but in which the economic policy of the state is also a coefficient of assimilation. The decisive value is still the value of the producing classes. Toniolo dedicates a particularly intense page to enterprisers, appealing that they be trained and educated. They can be "the ministers of the civilization or the decadence of a people":[60]

> The training and education of a class of enterprisers is a historical result that cannot be improvised. More than on extensive manpower or on improved machinery, the civil respectability of a nation depends on the acquired talent and traditional virtues of these captains of industry and commerce, as can be said of the bourgeoisie of our free medieval municipalities, especially

> Florence. Their abuses, however, can become a cause of scandal and public perversion, as happened for the capitalist classes of Holland, England, and Germany at the time of the Reformation, and as is lamentably seen to some extent in nations today, hence the severity of the Church and of canon law in combating and correcting the abuses of the capitalists at the head of industry and commerce, as well as the harsh criticisms and popular enmities against them in the most recent times.[61]

"May the saint of Assisi rise again!"

Who wouldn't think such an exclamation came from Toniolo? In reality, he simply makes it his own, many years after the lectures on distribution that we are following here, copying to the letter[62] the inspired words of his "master" Luigi Luzzatti, an economist and politician who returned to the university chair in Perugia after a long period dedicated to politics. The words of Luzzatti are imbued with pessimism about the fate of the society and economic science of his time. The professor-statesman sees the future in bleak colors. But speaking to the Umbrians from the Perugian chair he waxes rhapsodic:

> The *Perugian method*, the one used by St. Francis of Assisi amid so much opposition of classes, parties, interests, will always be the most fruitful! When, across the marvelous swells of your *seraphic* hills, he preached peace between the countryside and the cities, he softened the hearts of the powerful toward the humble, untangled with his inexhaustible treasures of goodness the gloomy enigmas of suffering in the Middle Ages, and, reasoning on equal terms with the sultan, worked the miracle by which Christianity and Mohammedanism, accustomed to destroying each other, for a moment came together on the human level; how much wisdom, judging by the effects, was contained in that sublime, ignorant little friar! How he recalls those other exalted ignorants of Galilee, who in their humility prevailed over the learned Pharisaism of Jerusalem, the philosophical splendors of Athens, the civil wisdom of Rome, and prepared the glories of

> the renewed age! And even today, while some are intensifying the class struggles and holding them up as fated by history, while those born of the same land, the children of the same redemption, are divided into adverse camps, the reprisals of labor clashing with those of capital, and while perils beset the moral unity of the homeland, which dissolves into hatred (the dominant note of our century), may the saint of Assisi rise again! May his shadow return, which has departed, return to console the Italy widowed of his light!"[63]

A soaring page, which resembles other pages from Toniolo's own pen.[64] Voiced by Luzzatti — a non-Catholic of Jewish origin — to Toniolo, it appears as a solemn confirmation, above suspicion, of his entire spiritual and scientific journey, but not without adding the warning:

> The contemporary salvation of society will not come from a vague contemplation of a Christian ideal, however attractive, yet still vaporous and abstract. This could be just the beginning of an individual and social regeneration, certainly not the end. The final end is found only in that organism of Christianity, simultaneously supernatural and historical, positive and vital, which has its head in the Roman pontificate. Precisely from this height, the peoples in the hour of darkness and desolation await the light that illuminates and the virtue that redeems.[65]

Chapter XI
Laws of Productivity

Openness to science and technology

Although drawn to the Middle Ages, Toniolo is immersed in modernity. A critical immersion, certainly, aware of the lights and shadows. He admires modernity for its progress in science and technology. To the great discoveries that have led to a qualitative leap in the economy he dedicates pages that are enthusiastic to say the least,[1] underlining the greatness of the historical fact

> by which empirical production has finally become scientific in our day. Perhaps, in terms of material structure and of technological-economic processes, this is the greatest upheaval the world has ever seen.[2]

What would he have said about the internet era and the digital economy? In his vision as a believer, it is a fact that "bears the imprint of a providential disposition that imparts wonder and gratitude."[3] Yet he does not fail to observe that this development, too, lies within the great cycle of Christian civilization, having found its condition of possibility "in the human social fact of the emancipation, education, and ordering of the producing classes" achieved in the Christian Middle Ages, to which is added "the 'cosmic social fact' of the geographical discoveries," and finally "the present technological social situation. … The contemporary technological-scientific transformation thus completes a historical cycle of a good eight centuries."[4]

Nonetheless, his enthusiasm for the technological development of the economy does not make him lose sight of the painful consequences that this process implies on the human level, a page that remains urgently relevant:

> Every *technological innovation* of progressive science necessarily brings with it a *modification of relationships of interests* already established, with the aftermath of inevitable sufferings. To some extent it uproots labor, makes invested capital useless, displaces industrial sites, and thus temporarily diminishes production benefits. Finally, every technological-scientific transformation *tends to centralize industries*. The adoption of those scientific-industrial inventions requires great intelligence and culture, as well as ever new capital, thus bringing production and its rewards to the most enlightened and richest people, who are always few, to the detriment of those mediocre in mind and wealth, but in the meantime production is affected by the rise and establishment of a class of cultured and powerful enterprisers who outstrip the medium and small ones, who decline and disappear among the wage earners, attributing a capitalist imprint to industry. These are the characteristics of the modern economy and of every age of great scientific advances in production, which make felt the need for other virtues to accompany their progress.[5]

The moral-civil education of producers

One of the most edifying pages of the *Trattato* arises from this, the one that presents as the second cause of progress in production "the improvement of the ethical conscience, which regulates industrial relations in society."[6] It is important that Toniolo should arrive at this consideration not only for ethical but also for practical reasons, in the name of the interests of production itself:

> It may well be doubted whether the progress of material production, under the guidance of positive and utilitarian science, outside of the reasons of *duty* and *high social ends,* may remain *continuous* and *regular*, or rather whether that progress itself *may be generated* vigorously.[7]

This is not difficult for him to exemplify in an analysis that deserves to come before the eyes of every economist or enterpriser:

> An enlightened greed can drive the industrialist along the road of colossal undertakings, but once enriched, to selfishly enjoy his gains he will close the factories, halting production to the detriment of the nation. The fever of quick profits gives a convulsive movement to the speculations of a businessman, who then in one day will squander and ruin the normal sources of his own and others' wealth. … Indeed, it can be said that in the absence of these [economic-industrious virtues] the increase of positive knowledge in itself does not ensure material progress. That technical knowledge has only the quality of a *means*, which also increases the power of good or evil depending on the use made of it. And so notions of *product knowledge* further suggested the sophistication and adulteration of merchandise, just as the art of the subtle devices of commerce made the frauds of the mercantile companies and financial markets easier. And in this way the actual progress of wealth, in spite of the science, remains suppressed.[8]

Is there a remedy for all this? Toniolo is convinced that there is, and even establishes what might be considered a law of the good economy: "*All material scientific progress requires a proportionate elevation of morality in the producing classes.*"[9] It is worth rereading the long, ardent page in which he illustrates this law, showing its concrete implications:

If, due to scientific progress, which increases the power of production, this takes on an ever more social character, the result is a *growth of responsibility* for the enterpriser, and so the duty to coordinate his actions for the general good. If, through his own fault, a tradesman is forced to close his small store and workshop, the social damage is almost unnoticed, but if imprudent or scandalous speculations bring down an industrial establishment that has enormous investment capital, thousands of workers, trade in the millions, debit and credit relationships with mercantile firms, banks, and financial exchanges at home and abroad, doesn't that failure become a public disaster, perhaps turning into a national economic crisis? So individual whims in productive progress must meet with growing restraint from the enterpriser's sense of *social justice.*

Likewise, if scientific industrial progress temporarily upsets, harms, sacrifices the interests of many, generating new problems of transition, this requires a higher sense of *social equity* to facilitate the arduous *process of the adjustment or establishment of better economic relations.* The mechanized plant kills the manual industries of the same trade, and would it not be fair that those who benefit most from progress should alleviate the suffering of those who are its victims? The large modern factory crowds wage earners together and pushes them down; is it not appropriate that other and more advantageous forms of collective labor contracts should be devised?

If in all technological-scientific progress the first to benefit are the privileged who are able to keep up with the growth of knowledge and capital, thus creating a centralization of industries; nothing but the *love of the good* on behalf of the multitudes can determine a movement of decentralization — that is, the distribution of those advances of civilization to the humblest and most numerous. The big industrialists take advantage of the tremendous capital of joint-stock companies through the simple *calculation of their own utility.* But only out of disinterested *love for others* do philanthropists succeed in spreading production

> cooperatives and credit unions among the mediocre and the small. Hence the need for *diffusive charity*.
>
> Without a progressive elevation of social justice, equity, and charity among producers there can be no fulfillment of the law of *incivilimento*, which is the proportional participation of all in the same benefit of *productive* activity, enhanced by science. Most people will remain excluded from this scientific industry and its triumphs, which so honor the genius, dignity, and power of man, or, with this being made the endowment of the few, the many will also be dominated and kept down in civil terms, as happened with the modern wage earner. And so, with wealth increased but the *value of man* generally diminished, has not the ultimate aim of material progress failed? And in the long run, will not this very progress in production be compromised in its primary source, which is no other than man (Vincenzo Gioberti)? Hence the corresponding historical law: Every material advance hides the seed of its own destruction if it is not accompanied by a more than proportional progress in the morality of the peoples and of the analogous civil institutions. This is the enormous danger that looms over the marvel of modern production.[10]

An inspiring page also for today, perhaps more than ever. Toniolo proceeds to show how this law has unfolded over time, moving from the medieval scenario to that of modernity. One may be more or less in agreement on some of his historical applications; the essential message remains intact.

The role of the state in the economy

Alongside the first two causes, Toniolo underlines the importance of laws, to the extent that they apply to the great institutions of freedom, association, and property, and in general to the function of the state, including its industrial policy.

As for freedom, on the economic terrain this concerns the faculty of choosing one's profession or industry, the technical methods of its exercise, the related contracts, trade, compensation, the respective location and relocation:

> These are individual economic freedoms, which together with the various regimes of ownership find guarantee and fulfillment in *industrial legislation* and *policy*, whose organs are the *class corporations* and the state.[11]

Here follows a long excursus on the historical development of the organization of class,[12] starting from the artisans' colleges or guilds, which were the backbone of the medieval economy. These were institutions that were born according to a regime of autonomy and freedom that was progressively restricted with the formation of absolute states. Contributions to this process came from

> those social-political causes characteristic of the transition from the Middle Ages to the modern age, which achieved a *centralization of royal power* in vaster territorial states, and economically the *system of mercantilism*. But to these were added, in particular with regard to the state's duty relative to *national production,* connected with the previous guild structure, three causes in particular: moral, with the degeneration and languishing of the religious and charitable spirit among the members of the guilds, the sharpening in them of petty class selfishness, infesting common solidarity; social, with the expansion of companies and at the same time of wage earning, both incompatible with the old artisan mercantile statutes; political, with the need for broader and more robust coercive state provisions, to put a brake on the decline of industry in the ancient nations and a lever to the growth of production by new peoples. Such state legislation is informed by the concept, opposed to the Christian one that prevailed until this time, that the faculty to found and operate a trade does not arise from natural law under the immediate aegis of autonomous class associations, but stems from a "concession" of the prince (charter), who is therefore responsible for coercive-

> ly disciplining its exercise in the general, economic, and political interest, subjecting the pre-existing guild system to the purpose of a restrictive regime, or gradually taking its place.[13]

It is clear that, for Toniolo, this is a deviation. When in Italy, in the fascist era, the talk would turn to corporatism, and some would think that with this lexicon the totalitarian state was coming close to the thinking of our author, a great semantic and political misunderstanding would arise: Toniolian corporatism is the opposite of the fascist, presenting itself as a balancing of any absolutism or even dominance on the part of the state, and as a remedy for modernity's tendency to disintegrate intermediate bodies. Toniolo's assessment is a full-blown condemnation:

> From the sixteenth century the interest of national production, to be achieved coercively by the state with the immolation of freedom, became the cornerstone of domestic and foreign policy for three centuries. True political-economic materialism.[14]

No less disastrous was the liberal reaction of laissez-faire, laissez-passer, transferred not only into government policies, but also into the first scientific definition of economics with Adam Smith:

> For the first time in the economic history of Christian civilization, the development of economic activity proceeded almost absolutely untethered from any special disciplinary rules dictated by the general interest.[15]

It was the opposite excess, and excesses come at a price. Here, in fact, is what sprang from it:

> Production got a very vigorous universal impetus from this, such as had never occurred in the history of the world. But at the same time (heed well), in this regime of freedom without restraint of law or conscience, that *legal predominance* of the proprietary and enterprising classes, burdening the workers for

> three centuries with their privileges and coercions, was replaced by the *de facto preponderance,* often no less unjust and cruel, that the speculative capitalist classes, equipped with the power of modern knowledge and capital, made to weigh on the present industrial and agricultural proletariat, which was crushed by it, to prepare in misery and class hatred, within the resurrected trade unions, the vendetta against society and the state. Never before had so many forces ready to produce wealth found themselves faced with so many forces conspiring to destroy it. Then the idea resurfaced that freedom itself can enslave, and law instead become liberating.[16]

Hence the Toniolian encapsulation of the "state's function of regulation and promotion, as an organ of the progress of wealth," developed as follows:

- To guarantee "the faculty of all citizens and foreigners to establish any business, and to exercise it with every technical-economic modality, with every support of association, without limits on trade, domestic and foreign, ensuring the mutual obligations freely contracted for this purpose."[17]
- "To safeguard the higher personal rights that might be compromised in production (safety, hygiene, morality)."[18]
- To regulate "industrial practices within the limits of the general interest, reserving to itself, if such interest should require it, the establishment of a public or state enterprise (a plant, an arms factory, the mint, the postal service, the railways), either in competition with citizens or in the form of monopoly (municipalization or nationalization of public services)."[19]
- To provide "for the industrial education of the nation, with training, technical schools, exhibitions, awards, and, if necessary on a temporary basis, with a protectionist customs regime, adapting it to the needs of the national economy and the international market."[20]

Toniolo had the opportunity to deal with this last situation at a critical moment in the Italian economy, tested in its agricultural industry by American competition in the grain market. We are in 1894. The economic schools and political parties are faced with opposing stances, between the pure liberal demand and the protectionist reaction. Toniolo weighed in with a truly masterful article,[21] taking a position in favor of a temporary protective duty measure, showing however that this should not be the normal option. International free trade remains the ideal, not only for the balancing function that competition exercises, but also because it highlights "the brotherhood and solidarity of interests among all the peoples."[22] Universalism, however, cannot be achieved at the expense of the organic constitution of humanity, which also finds its vital expression in nations:

> Universality may come about to some extent in the grain trade itself, but cosmopolitical uniformity will never impose itself on the organic and historical constitution of individual agricultural regions and populations. Here truly the universe will never absorb the homeland![23]

Law of coordination

> With the support of the three coefficients of industrial science, the education of producers, and promotion by the state, comes the development of the normal laws of progress, which consists in the increasingly complete achievement of the maximum product with the minimum expenditure of factors.[24]

Having said this, however, there still remains the concrete question of how to delineate the elements that make up each individual business, and then the ensemble of businesses in the industry. Here Toniolo borrows the *law of defined proportions* from the mathematical school of economics (Marshall, Valenti). The metaphorical term of comparison is that of the various chemical agents that make up a body. A business is healthy and grows to the extent that its elements are carefully chosen, in a proportionate manner, with respect to its specific ends,

> through a selection and application of those types of work, capital, natural forces, and materials that offer the highest degree of useful efficacy, responding to the nature of the business itself.[25]

The results of production are in relation with a certain quantitative and qualitative combination of its elements or factors:

> It is up to the genius and experience of each enterpriser, according to the nature of each type of production (agriculture, mining, manufacturing), to grasp and define in the particular situation, with the help of the applied sciences, this relative maximum.[26]

But that's not enough. Beyond the proportion between the elements, a business that wants a certain return must also see to its organization or management. In relation to this, Toniolo points out a series of laws that lead to progress in production, developing on the threefold level of the technical order (manual/artificial), the personal order (division of labor), and the legal order (individual/social).

Law of technological progress

History is clear: There is a tendency for human work to use ever more factors (of nature and capital), and these ever more artificially elaborated. From the first tools to the complex machines of our time, "technology is making progress that can be said to be socially profound and infinite."[27] As compared with manual production, production enhanced by technology achieves results that can be astonishing. Technology increases productive power, allows continuity of production (which human fatigue would hinder), and increases the perfection of the product, ensuring the regularity, homogeneity, and uniformity of the work. Ultimately, production comes out more abundant, more complete, with a better market (due to the reduction in production costs). In a certain sense,

> in the *mental order*, machines spiritualize work, removing man

> from the most burdensome and servile part of it — that is, from the office of organic motor and executor — to reserve for him the predominantly intellectual task of invention, construction, direction, supervision of the machine itself, thus raising his personal value.[28]

Interesting, I would say daring, is this spiritualizing qualification of technology. The discussion applies in a particular way in our time, with the developments of that industry which is generally called 4.0 (the Fourth Industrial Revolution), based on digital technology. There are some today who wonder, "Should we be optimists or catastrophists, imagining a world in which, freed from work, we will carry out only works of art, or foreseeing brutalized societies of men without work, on the margins of production systems dominated by machines?"[29] Toniolo had before his eyes the First and Second Industrial Revolution, and he analyzes it without anguish. He is, in this sense, a modern economist who looks to the future. But he is anything but a technology fanatic, the risks of which he understands well:

> Machines (it is said), replacing the worker in whole or in part, deprive him of work, hence mass unemployment, impoverished proletariat, exhausted populations; the machine, far from lightening and spiritualizing human work, weighs it down, enslaving it with the overwhelming power of natural forces, and with the uniformity of the mechanical process it rigidifies the intellect, erases meritorious personal initiative and with it the virtue of work, hence working classes wearied in body and soul; the mechanical system causes immoderate production with its crises and gives preponderance to the selfish interests of enterprisers at the sacrifice of the workers, hence the disorders of modern social production and distribution.[30]

These are realistic considerations; the historical reactions to what today we would call technocracy are a fact. Toniolo recalls the violent destruction of machines that began in Nottingham in 1811 with the workers' revolution of the Luddites (from the name of one of the leaders), brought from England to the Continent, the systematic socialism of Marx (manifesto of 1848), the criticisms against machines (Sismondi) and industrialism (Romagnosi), down to the criticism brought against the modern capitalist economy as a whole (Engels):

> The criticisms are not entirely unfounded, but to respond to them it is necessary to distinctly define the *effects of machines on production* and on the connected relationships.[31]

It is true, for example, that the introduction of machines puts a certain number of workers in hardship, but at the same time, with the multiplication of consumer products at a reduced price, there is a final benefit for everyone, not excluding the workers.[32] As far as employment is concerned, it cannot be concealed that, with mechanization, jobs are lost — this is the immediate effect — but then, due to a sort of law of compensation, the products themselves, becoming more abundant and decreasing in price,

> cause the expansion of demand for them, for the satisfaction of which new industries arise and multiply, which end up calling back not only the workers initially dismissed but a greater number of them, ultimately determining a growth of the working class and its well-being.[33]

Moreover, the stimulating effect on employment also comes "from the need to erect alongside the *machine-based* industries a second series of industries *manufacturing the machines* to serve them."[34] So, everything resolved? All good? Is it possible to reason, with the worker's neck on the line, in such an abstract way? Isn't this the temptation of an economy that, Pope Francis would say, discards many people with the consoling thought that tomorrow, progressively, it will go better for them, too? What poor person would accept this solely futuristic consolation?

Toniolo comes back down to earth and to his Christian spirit when he admits:

> Certain *transitory* effects to the detriment of workers are equally

> undeniable. Every transformation of the *wage fund* (of a mechanical industry) inevitably excludes a number of workers, and the *law of compensation,* which then calls them back to work in a proportion equal to or greater than before, is implemented with a slow *historical process,* gradually, as consumption expands and new businesses arise (Graziani, Supino). And in the interim workers find themselves inactivated and populations impoverished. Much worse if the mechanical transformation occurs *rapidly and simultaneously* in many branches of industry, so that workers rejected from one factory find jobs already reduced in others.[35]

And moreover, our author continues, the conditions of the law of compensation do not always present themselves or do so only in part. For example, if jobs have disappeared in the cotton industry and have arisen in the metallurgical industry, workers cannot easily transfer due to lack of training. And if disappearing in one nation they arise in another, workers will not always be able to move:

> In all these cases, mechanical industrial transformations can turn into a true workers' social crisis. And so it really was for Great Britain from 1770 to 1830, and for the other Continental nations later.[36]

On the psychological consequences, one cannot generalize. So, it cannot be said that mechanical work automatically afflicts the worker physically and spiritually. Indeed, there are undoubted advantages: Is it better to unload a ship on the backs of porters, or using a crane? One example among many. As for the monotony of operations that impoverishes muscular and mental exercise, this is an evident fact. But, at the same time,

> the contact with improved mechanisms, the need to follow their movements, increases intelligence, the spirit of observation, the rapidity of movements, so that the worker ends up dominating the scientific instrument, elevating his own value.[37]

The specialized worker, a skilled working class, is born. Compared with the manual trades of the past, Toniolo observes, based on statistics of the time, there is a disappearance of age-old professional ailments, while the average lifespan is lengthened and physical hygiene and intellectual energy are elevated.

And what about industrial crises? They are a fact. But they cannot be blamed on the spread of mechanization; on the contrary, this can put the brakes on them, "since the enterpriser who has a million invested in machines is very careful not to cause a suspension of production that would leave an enormous capital unprofitable even for a few days."[38]

Ultimately, between advantages and risks, there arises the problem of guarantees and correctives. Some are within the system itself. And here Toniolo seems to intuit some scenarios of our digital age:

> When machinery everywhere should reach the perfection of the *automated system* (in which the mechanism does everything by itself), human work, relieved of every servile exercise and reduced to supervision, would be truly *spiritualized*.[39]

Correctives are the responsibility of *social action* and the *state* (compensation for accidents at work and provisions aimed at preventing them, exceptional measures for times of rapid technological transformations temporarily detrimental to employment, etc.):

> *Industrialists, associations*, and *government* must contribute to alleviating the fate of the *ranks of the unemployed* with temporary aid, with placement offices, with facilitating new training, if need be, by assisting emigration.[40]

Finally, it is important that the progress of mechanical inventions remain within the horizon of the "ends of civilization":

> Undoubtedly, in the designs of Providence, the industrial applications of machines, which wonderfully increase the power and speed of production, are intended to attenuate man's need, espe-

> cially for the manual worker, of excessive and absorbing material occupations, and to grant him more leisure and time for the life of the spirit. To work, yes (as J. S. Mill wrote), but for purely material-economic goals, as few months of the year as possible, and with as little strain on life as may be compatible with the duty to procure the economic means of existence, and this to preserve as best as can be the culture of the mind, the intimacy of the family, civil social functions, moral education, and religious improvement.[41]

A great ideal that, of a society truly happy, to use a word rediscovered today in the economic field.[42] This ideal was cultivated "by the hardworking classes of the ordinary Christians of the Middle Ages,"[43] quite unlike what Toniolo condemned in looking at his own time:

> In our day, on the contrary, the facility of the machinery in modern factories has served to prolong work by day and night, to exclude Sunday and holiday rest, to displace women and adolescents from beneath the domestic roof, to make the worker forgetful, under the burden of work, of his dignity and duties as a father, as a citizen, as a Christian, and to materialize his existence. But all this was not a fated consequence of machines, but rather an enormous human abuse of their benefits, to the detriment of civilization.[44]

Law of the division of labor

For the best functioning of a business, another important law is the division of labor. Among human beings, alongside the one nature there are accidental variations that imply particular aptitudes and vocations. Specializing people according to their vocation is profitable. "Every operation that goes against fit or aptitude involves inertia or the dispersion of forces, and on the contrary, *a man in his place is worth two*."[45] The entire history of the economy confirms this, registering a progressive specialization within the world of work at the professional, functional, and technical level. One decisive stage was when the functions of execution and management were distinguished into two hierarchical classes. With what consequences? In the first place, the improvement of the manufacturer itself. This also saves time, raw materials, and tools:

> The *overall result* resolves itself in *more copious, more perfect, less expensive production*, and so in a realization of the law of maximum useful effect with minimum sacrifice of means.[46]

The moral-social advantages are not lacking:

> The division of labor (also in its internal application within businesses), by educating and improving everyone's faculties in relation to a special productive task, raises the *value of individuality*. Conversely, by restricting the activity of individuals to an increasingly limited object it makes the need for mutual cooperation in society more keenly felt and thus increases the value of sociality. In this way, by taking the place in the world assigned to him by Providence for carrying out his specific mission, man achieves his *own personal good*, and at the same time contributes to the *universal good* and fulfills the law of solidarity, whereby the various individual ends merge into the sole and common general end.[47]

Here, too, Toniolo's balanced analysis does not fail to look at the other side of the coin. "What glory for a man to have spent his whole life putting the head on a pin?"[48] Always repeating the same movement, as if he were a machine, brutalizes the worker. Then there is the risk of precariousness, given that in the event of a factory closing those who know how to do that thing, and only that, will have a hard time finding work elsewhere. All true! But this, Toniolo replies, depends on the fact that this law also has its limits and so needs to be applied with balance:

> The operations of the spinning, weaving, and dyeing of cloth, which mostly form distinct businesses, today sometimes tend to be carried out in a single factory, to relieve for example the weav-

> ing industry from artificial fluctuations in the price of yarns purchased elsewhere.[49]

As for individual persons, attention must be paid to *human unity*:

> A certain alternating variety of related and connected acts left to the worker supports the physical forces, broadens ingenuity, nourishes the love of work, whereas excessive simplicity, uniformity, monotony in actions exhausts the human faculties and diminishes man.[50]

Limits may then arise from the general framework of social responsibility with respect to its overall needs.

The law of progress from the individual to the collective

This is the great theme of association or cooperation applied to the business for the ends of production. If the division of labor has its foundation in the variety of human characteristics, cooperation is suggested by the limitation of individual forces. Following Genovesi, Toniolo recalls that in association two plus two do not make four, but five.[51] Association releases a quantity of forces that would remain latent in individuals, and this through emulation, through discipline, through mutual oversight. The forces of the one are integrated with those of the other, and in this way they multiply. Association "ensures continuity in space and time for businesses and their economic functions."[52]

Beyond productivity, association also has undoubted ethical-civil advantages:

> [It] binds men together with contributions of material interest, which reaffirm those of duty, right, and brotherhood; thus it is a means of social cohesion. It is the necessary complement of *individuality*, which remedies its own weakness with the strength of others, ensuring personal autonomy (freedom) in the face of the dangers of absorption — for example on the part of a pantheistic state — and at the same time it is the corrective of indi-

> vidual variations and disproportions, whereby (also in the field of production) in the face of the privileged and the powerful it supports the less favored with the joining of forces, and so it is a guarantee of freedom and balance.[53]

All this, Toniolo adds, is possible under precise ethical-civil conditions — namely, respect for honesty and justice, the sense of personal freedom, the spirit of self-sacrifice and social charity.

This law of the tendency to association also emerges clearly from the history of the economy. It flourishes in a particular way in the Middle Ages, "the age of associations par excellence, also in production":[54]

> The spirit of association, thus transfused into the blood of the medieval populations, but stripped of Christian ideals and virtues in the period of the Renaissance and the Reformation, is passed on to the modern peoples and there multiplies its forms and power, but at the same time causes its degeneration. From the sixteenth to the eighteenth century, association, divorced from any remnant of freedom, becomes an exclusive instrument of the most powerful, with *privileged companies* in industry, in commerce, on the seas of Holland, England, France, for the exercise of monopoly and the suppression of the lower classes. From the nineteenth century to our day, restored to freedom, they penetrate, spread, and loom large everywhere, in mining, in railway transport, in shipping, in banking, in world trade, but at the same time, under the impulse of selfish interests and unbridled competition, they are perverted with colossal frauds, with fictitious speculations, with monopolistic consolidations (trusts), with calculated collapses, with stock market cracks, and with bank failures.[55]

So, it is urgent to "bring association back under the rule of ethics and law."[56] With this corrective, association expresses all its positive potential, without forgetting, however, that in it there are objective limits that cannot be crossed with impunity. They vary depending on the types of industries and their ends. If these conditions and limits are respected,

> association, also in its applications to *productive enterprises*, remains the most expansive coefficient of the same, so that in their internal organization they tend more and more to turn from individual businesses (belonging to a single owner-enterpriser) into collective businesses (belonging to companies).[57]

And if historically the first to be established were associations of only owner-capitalists, and then associations of only workers (cooperative production companies), Toniolo sees in the near future forms of "mixed collective enterprises"

> in which the company will be formed *between owner-capitalists and workers together*, following the medieval example of métayage (sharecropping) and limited partnerships. There are already experiments that tend to consider capitalists and workers as partners in the same factory (participation in capital or profit) and promise to reproduce the physiognomy of a hierarchical social economy. Then association will have involved all the factors of production within an enterprise.[58]

The factors of time and place

> From the sum of these observations, which concern the establishment and management of businesses, it follows that the ways and means of achieving progress in production in the hands of enterprisers, of these pioneers of economic initiatives, consist in an ever more fitting application of the law of proportion (qualitative and quantitative), of the factors of production, and of the businesses' own complex laws of organization (technical, personal, legal); hence a growing effect of utility and a relative decrease of expenses. This as concerns the mechanism of businesses, which, it must be noted, still depends on the ability to put them in relation with three other extrinsic elements: time, place, and society in the degree of its development.[59]

Briefly: Time — that is, the rapidity of production operations, by which the effect of utility is a function of mass (of the means of production) multiplied by velocity (of exercise). Place — a company's utility effect is a function of its appropriate location or headquarters, taking into account the security and promptness of consumption, transport costs, etc. Problems that are intertwined with those of social transformations, in the different conditions of city and countryside, with all the pros and cons of choices that occur a priori but must be constantly modulated with historical, social, and technological change. "What rearrangements will be made in this distribution of industry with electric energy, which can be transmitted over great distances?"[60] A question that today would be translated: What will become of production processes, their management, their placement, with the development of the internet?

The dream of Paris

The didactic tone of the *Trattato* sometimes conceals sentiments. So, to me it seems helpful to provide an excursus in which Toniolo, precisely on this topic of cooperation, drips passion. July 18–20, 1900, in Paris — we are in the heart of the *belle époque* (eleven years earlier Paris had become the showcase of the world with the World's Fair and the Eiffel Tower) — the International Congress of Rural and Workers' Credit Unions was held.[61] Toniolo was to give the closing speech.[62] He had just arrived from Italy, feeling like "the laborer of the eleventh hour."[63] The tone is immediately passionate, indeed provocative: He would speak of cooperation "in crisis" — economic, social, and moral crisis — but with the proviso that he does not mean the word "crisis" in a negative sense. On the contrary:

> We all know that, as in the physiological and ethical life of individuals, so in the social life of institutions there are *crises* whose outcome is not illness or death, but rather health flourishing to the fullness of life.[64]

In this sense he addresses the economic aspect of the crisis of the cooperatives (with the focus on those of Christian inspiration): These, in their triple physiognomy as cooperatives of consumption, production, and credit, had until then carried out an important task, but mainly in reducing negative effects on behalf of the most disadvantaged classes:

a. decrease in consumer costs;
b. attenuation, in the sector of production, of the capillary pull of profit to the detriment of just wages;
c. easing of onerous loan conditions.

These may be all good, but it is time, our author urges, to move forward, with a positive program:

> Without giving up its first aim, which is to lessen the multiple difficulties of life for the lower classes, cooperation aims higher for the future, that is to procure a private capital or fund of their own possession.[65]

Concretely, Toniolo hopes that cooperatives may not limit themselves to spending their savings for the immediate benefit of members but set aside what is necessary to establish actual businesses:

> It is a question, through cooperation, of raising the agricultural or industrial proletariat to the level of capitalist, of supporting small businesses in the face of big ones, of transforming modest users of mobile capital into owners of fixed capital. … This solution aims not so much to add a few pennies to the wages of the rural or city worker as to restrict, within the limits of the possible, wage *earning itself*, setting up in its midst a strong and growing nucleus of small and medium businesses in which the capital would be concentrated in the hands of the worker himself.[66]

Toniolo knows, and he highlights this, that it would be illusory to think of abolishing big business and large land holdings, and he is also realistically aware that cooperatives will certainly not be the ones to completely eliminate wage earning. Yet they can contribute to the growth of small and medium business and of ownership on the part of the independent worker, thus organically reconstituting a new social class. It is in this direction, he notes, that history seems to be going, if one looks at the development of the trade unions in England, of the *Genossenschaften* or *Gewerbsvereine* in Germany, or of the French *syndicats*. For our author, it is a providential historical trend that drives "toward the destruction of the reign of individualism, with the caution that this does not refer to individuality, but rather to the individualism that is its degeneration."[67]

The obligatory course for removing society from the pathological individualistic structure is the transition from cooperation to corporation, understood as a professional order guaranteed by twofold protection: (1) economic, of an independent fund, and (2) legal, of recognition by the state. And this in order to have real survival and bargaining power with respect to organized capitalist pressures and the centralized state itself:[68]

> Catholics, especially among us, have never had systematic prejudices about the function of the state in social progress, but they ask (according to sound philosophical-social criteria) that it promote, aid, and sanction the social organization that comes to fruition by its own virtue, and not impede, divert, and truncate or overwhelm the natural, historical, and normal development of the nation.[69]

The cooperative movement, in its various expressions (Toniolo makes no secret of finding himself closest above all to those along the lines of Friedrich Wilhelm Raiffeisen[70]), and the corresponding corporative design (libertarian, autonomous, grassroots) represent, in the eyes of our author, the two pillars of a new socioeconomic-political order removed from atomistic liberalism and oppressive statism:

> This was truly a wise and original merit of the medieval Christian spirit, of its having been able to generate and interpose between private property and the public property of the state a series of social (or collective) properties, both immovable and movable, which, not belonging to a particular entity, remained assigned to the common social good.

> The modern spirit has destroyed this social property and these social institutions that served as a link and transition between private property and the public property of the state and were for the benefit of all, but of the humble and small by preference.
>
> Just as the *corporation* (professional unions, in any form) is destined to resurrect the *universitates personarum* or social juridical entities of the past, *cooperation* likewise seems to be called to recompose, in modernized form, the *collective property* of tomorrow. In the face of the individualistic atomism of the present, this is the great social task of the cooperation of the future.[71]

A dream, the one expressed in Paris, that expresses the highest point of Toniolo's Christian-democratic maturation, his perspective on the future, with a vision that by this point has left behind the traditionalist Catholic tendency to address the social question mainly with top-down charity and aims to lift the fortunes of the humblest classes starting from their capacity for self-management and self-construction. A discussion that, on the economic level, rhymed with what he was developing during the same period on the ecclesial level, but with an evident political reflection as well, to resolve the acute controversy between the "old" and "young" of the Opera dei Congressi. Looking above all to the young, he lamented the inability of an entire Catholic generation to reconcile itself with the democratic spirit of the times, even if this did need to be corrected and brought back to its Christian soul. It is interesting that just a few days after that talk in Paris, almost continuing his dream in Val de Bois, as a guest of Léon Harmel, he was able to experience up close how practicable that ideal was, and not simply a utopia. He confided this in a heartfelt letter to Cardinal Mariano Rampolla del Tindaro:

> The best works of the clergy, of Catholics, of rich philanthropists, fail if they maintain the character of patronage that descends from above and do not scrupulously respect the dignity, freedom, and initiatives of the workers, of the working masses,

> who even under the intelligent promotion of the upper classes want to reserve for themselves a broad task of self-command and self-rescue. So, it is suitable to remove not only the suspicion of wanting to bring the country back to political forms that offend the current republican regime based on universal suffrage, but also the suspicion of undermining for the future the dignity of workers and the importance of the fourth estate.[72]

Self-command; do it yourself. At least in this phase,Toniolo had come to fully grasp the spirit of the time, freeing himself from any paternalistic claim. He was likewise convinced that this development of the future would not be possible without an ethical consolidation, which he did not see as achievable without a revival of the Christian spirit. The explicit "Catholic" naming of the cooperatives was also intended to serve this reconstructive purpose: not to discriminate in aid based on the faith of the needy — far from it — but to guarantee that moral tone of the cooperative institutions without which they also lose their efficacy.[73]

Chapter XII
Territorial Industry

Between discovery and ownership

One chapter of the *Trattato* is dedicated to territorial (land-based) industries. It is the first level of application of what Toniolo calls the laws of industrial progress (to distinguish them from those of the private economy of production in each business). There are three of these laws: of specification (each industry tends to differentiate itself), of gradual increase, of integration (industries complement one another).

The "original territorial" industries include hunting, fishing, sheep farming, the mineral industry, forestry, and, finally, land cultivation (the latter directly preparatory to rural industry). From the picture of the extensive historical information, we will limit ourselves to highlighting those elements that express significant value orientations.

In the history of the territorial dimension of the economy, Toniolo points out the transition from free primitive forms to those that are consolidated up to the occupation of a territory:

> From the arts of catching or acquiring natural products —that is, the animals living in the territory — by hunting, fishing, sheep farming, the next step is the occupation of the territory itself,

> either in its geological structure, or in the physiological organisms rooted in it, or in its physico-chemical composition; hence the *mineral, forestry,* or *land-cultivation* industries. [This leads to] logical and historical progress, with which humanity deploys its power no longer on the spontaneous product of nature, but on the very system of its productive materials and forces, and so reinforces and completes its sovereign mastery over the globe, thanks to the legal economic fact of *property,* which by common consensus is not such as long as it is limited to the exclusive claim on derived and incidental goods and does not yet extend to the domain of their *generating sources.*[1]

The mineral industry

One fundamental area is the mineral industry. Great attention is dedicated in the *Trattato* to the mines, after a quick look at the quarries (where mineral materials are collected or detached from the ground in the open):

> The laws of development of the mineral industry are best followed in the *mines* — that is, in the *excavation* from the subsoil of common metals (iron, copper, tin, etc.), other precious materials (gold, silver, diamonds), and fossil fuels (coal, oil, etc.).[2]

Throughout the cycle of pagan antiquity, mining work had not yet given rise to a real industry with a class of mine operators, but was rather linked to "speculators (publicans banded in *sodalitates*) under whom, together with a few free workers, slaves, and those condemned *ad metalla* groaned."[3] In the Middle Ages a "first type of mining class" is formed, based on the "right of every prospector to occupy mineral-bearing terrain as long as it should remain viable, and to work it through associations of miners, long respected by feudal lords and municipal cities,"[4] a right recognized and regulated in the general interest and protected in the name of the "freedom of the mine" in the face of claims of surface ownership. Things changed with the first two centuries of modernity, when mines were developed on the new continents, while in Europe the excavations became deeper, down to a thousand meters. Then the mining operations of the worker-owners gave way to the large enterprise of powerful capitalist-enterprisers. The new opportunities, especially with the discovery of America, left themselves open to perversions. Toniolo's assessment is severe:

> Subsoil exploration was aimed exclusively at the search for precious metals, and for a long time not for other materials needed for industry. It was the work not so much of systematic enterprises and operations, but of adventurers driven by the accursed hunger for gold (*auri sacra fames*), who considered the discovery of a mine as a game of chance, a source of sudden fortune or ruin, indeed not of meritorious economic production, and exploited it mostly at the hands of slaves, with cutthroat tactics under the impulse of greedy speculation on the famous "nuggets" or of financial aims, outside of any sense and criterion of lasting social good. It is the story of the feverish greed and cruel passions of the Portuguese, Spanish, Dutch, English in the subsoil of the virgin Americas to unseal the golden and silver treasures with savage hammer blows and inundate Europe, in the meantime deserting the main road of the industries and corrupting the modern mining class in its genesis.[5]

Meanwhile, the mining industry also develops in Europe, and this certainly does not escape the kings and emperors who, taking up Roman and feudal traditions, increase the so-called royalties on precious metals and then on other products. From the eighteenth century, with Dutch, Anglo-Saxon, and French capitalism, and with the big domestic and colonial companies, the mining industry registers a great development, with obvious economic implications: "With respect to the mines, no other age like ours can be called the *age of metals*."[6]

Economic and legal development

From the point of view of the laws of development, the mining industry has a character all its own: It tends to produce a monopoly (in that it is linked to a specific territory) and privilege (as the extraction of the product can certainly be increased, but at a necessarily progressive cost). Like other industries, then, it tends to become increasingly technological. This leads to the formation of gigantic capitalist companies, necessary to cope with the random character typical of this industry, in which "a great deal of capital is depleted in unsuccessful explorations."[7] On the whole this is an exciting development, a source of economic and civil progress. The absence of this industry would have left "the talent unfruitful, that is, the treasure that the provident Father had throughout the immense geological ages hidden in the bowels of the globe, for all the industrious generations of the future. And glory be to these cyclops of civilization of every time."[8]

The analysis then turns to the legal-economic side, specifically to the theme of the ownership of mines, historically divided into three different forms: ownership of the mine as distinct from ownership of the surface; mine ownership coupled with surface ownership; and state ownership. What our author judges to be normal is the first, based on the consideration that

> the rational justification of every particular property lies in the quality of *utility* for human preservation and improvement inherent in the matter, together with a concrete act of will and industriousness whereby the person lastingly connects limited individual pieces to himself, without offense to the previous individual activity of others, indeed to the general benefit.[9]

Here, too, the usual Toniolian comparison comes into play: In ancient and pagan civilization, state pantheism and slavery often disturbed the spontaneous process of private appropriation; the Christian Middle Ages found the right balance, generally establishing the legal-economic principle according to which the mine is

> the object of high sovereignty (rather than ownership) of the state, whereby this makes arrangements for it for public utility, granting its acquisition and regulating its exercise in the interest of society and industry, except, in homage to sovereignty and later for financial reasons, collecting a percentage of the income (royalty).[10]

This was a principle that endured until the modern era, when, for example, Philip II granted, in the sixteenth century, in all of Spanish America, ownership to the discoverer (but the state still demanded 50 percent of the gold!).

There was a gradual reappearance, not without resistance and setbacks, of the individualistic doctrine of Roman law, according to which the ownership of land includes everything found in its bowels. The legislation of the French Revolution reached a compromise in 1791 by granting the surface owner the right over the mine down to 100 feet, but by 1804 the Roman principle was inscribed in the French code. "Thus private individualism sacrificed every social consideration in the regime of mine ownership."[11] An adjustment due to the "genius of Napoleon" (a surprising recognition from the pen of Toniolo) brought back the medieval tradition of state concessions:

> The French law of 1810 and those based on it distinguish … three phases in the *concession* that the state, indeed not the owner of the subsoil but the guardian of social interests, makes of the mine as a thing belonging to no one (*res nullius*): *exploration*, whereby anyone with government permission can search for minerals on private land, and having found them acquires the right, all else being equal (*coeteris paribus*), to be preferred in the concession; *conferral of the mine* by sovereign act upon the one who demonstrates to the authority that he possesses the best guarantees and means for a fruitful operation, which gives him permanent ownership of the mine; the inherent *obligations*, which are the exercise of the mining industry, without which the state can pronounce forfeiture, and the payment of a triple "redevance" (contribution): two small fixed payments, one to the discoverer (if he was not preferred in the concession) and one to the owner of the surface (by way of fairness), and a proportional payment to the government. Quarries of stone, sand, metalliferous earth, and peat bogs, however, cannot be cultivated except by the owner or with his consent.[12]

In the eyes of our author, this appears to be a balanced formula with which the state on the one hand recognizes private property and on the other reserves the right to regulate it on behalf of the general good. He notes that in his time the principle of "mine to the state" is being resurrected, either through the *nationalization of the revenue* (the proprietary state leaves the rental methods to free competition, allocating the revenue for the social good) or *socialization,* by which the state expropriates the mines, transferring their ownership and direct operation to capitalists and workers linked in a national or international trust. Toniolo's judgment is complex. Expropriation seems problematic to him, and the monopoly of a single organization is not beneficial. "In general it must be said that mine ownership and operation by the state can also be legitimate and sometimes useful, but indeed not in an exclusive and permanent form."[13]

As for the internal regulation of the mining industries, Toniolo notes that "the mine by its nature sooner or later becomes the compendium of the most complicated regulatory rules of human activity (advanced technologies, legal problems, social-economic issues like working hours, the exclusion of women for the most part, special guarantees for individuals, etc.). All matters of extreme importance, if one considers that, in his time, in Great Britain alone the class of mine workers (employees and families) comprised an eighth of the whole population.

The forestry industry and environmental balance

Here, too, we find a history of different phases, from natural empirical art to artificial-scientific industry. Considering the importance of wood, one understands how a historical-social law should be delineated whereby the forest in every territory undergoes an initial and centuries-long process of destruction, followed by the belated and recent process of conservation and growth. In fact, if in the first phase of humanity's history, our author argues, claiming territories from the woods was an indispensable requirement of human order, first for safety reasons, which demanded that dangerous beasts be flushed out of the forest cover, and second to widen the margin of land adaptable to agriculture and animal husbandry, the third phase that limits wooded areas "is characteristic of economic periods of the rapid and disproportionate development of other branches of industry that require wood as material, coupled with ignorance and greed, often favored by improvident laws."[14] So it is "a selfish utilitarianism that for the enjoyment or gain of a moment sacrifices the *source itself, productive* of perennial social riches."[15] It is the period of the great modern devastations of the forests. The economic motives of the growth of other industries (one could think of the railways, with the use of railroad ties and carriages made of wooden material) were intertwined with that private ideology "whereby all properties were proclaimed *private* and released from any constraints of social and public interest."[16] This led to

> that vandalistic deforestation by impromptu speculators or improvident owners throughout Western Europe and in all the countries around the Mediterranean, not entirely halted there but rather furiously extended (under different … conditions) to North America and Canada, which in a few decades sufficed to destroy ancient forests that Providence had patiently prepared over immense geological ages and that wise institutions and laws kept almost intact for centuries to lasting social benefit, leaving behind … upheavals and social disasters that for the most part human efforts will never be able to repair again.[17]

Such a vigorous condemnation and such an anticipatory intuition deserve to be remembered, while the cry of the wounded earth is still making itself heard, albeit belatedly, with the urgency of a new ecological conscience, of which the social doctrine of the Church has become a prolific interpreter, especially with Pope Francis (see his documents *Laudato Si'* and *Querida Amazonia*).

Toniolo's discussion ends with the prospect of recovery, pointing to the forest conservation and reforestation procedures guaranteed by forestry law and policy. The latter have the task of

> wisely and vigorously assisting technology with the prohibition (absolute or relative) of the destruction or clear-cutting of

woods, with the obligation of periodic cutting in preserved forests, with the strict regulation of easements or rather of public uses of pasture and wood, and above all with the definition of "woodland property." Which, due to the precious, permanent, and inescapable economic-social functions and interests of the forest, must be (without prejudice to acquired rights) maintained in or restored to the hands of legal moral entities (foundations, corporations), or the political-administrative hands of the municipalities, provinces, especially of the state, as an inalienable heritage of the nation.[18]

Chapter XIII
Rural Industry

Land-based and rural industry

With the same descriptive precision, Toniolo moves on to this area, intimately connected to the first. The two industries — territorial and rural — are, by their nature, linked. The soil can be cultivated to the extent that it is tilled. Land-based industry deals with tillage, starting from the hoe-cultivation phase of simple domestic agriculture:

> The hoe is later joined by the *plow*, inaugurating a second phase that, presupposing the domestication of cattle and more complex tools, and so the addition of animal forces to human forces, allows for extensive and continuous tillage on larger and more resistant plots of land, so that the areas put under cultivation are now measured by the daily unit of work of a yoke of oxen (*iugeri*).[1]

This makes possible the third phase of the art of the plantation. The transition does not always occur in a linear manner. But in general there is a law of intensification, with its relative social implications, in land-based industry. If the era of the hoe is linked to societies based on familial and collective associations, that of the plow, presupposing movable animal wealth, leads to the superimposition of upper classes of landowners on the working and servile ones. The era of the plantation allows the re-awakening of the servile class, "which with its own initiatives prepares the way for the autonomy of the strong class of the farmers."[2]

Appropriation

These social dynamics, linked to the condition of the land and the migration of peoples with their progressive settlement, lead to that phenomenon of appropriation whereby "through the boundless common goods (*res nullius*) and the collective use (by turn) of cultivated lands, it is possible to give *definitive* prevalence *to particular property*."[3] A fact — that of property — with significant economic effects:

> Indeed, prevalent particular property (of moral or physical persons), adding to the needs of common preservation the stimuli of special, private, and individual interests, becomes an impulse not only to continue cultivation on new virgin lands, but also (great progress) to *transition* with an intensive working of the soil *to permanent improvements of already occupied land.* And this is natural. These improvements (irrigation, drainage, transformations of all kinds), *the result of accumulations of work and later of capital* above the soil, involve enormous and protracted sacrifices that often only bear fruit for remote generations and so would not be possible without the motives of familial utility and the stability of patrimonial relationships, including those of inheritance.[4]

According to Toniolo, this origin of property from the free initiatives of work is typical of Christian civilization, "whereby in the medieval era not only the working of unoccupied land, but also the cultivation and planting of someone else's land, often gave rise to independent ownership or at least co-ownership with the ancestral lord."[5] Unfortunately, ownership does not always arise from work. Often its genesis is only in the authority that distributes the land. The economic outcomes are different. While acquisition through work stimulates commitment and favors development, acquisition through authority, "legitimate in itself, but often arbitrary and violent,"[6] with the awarding of extensive lands to a few privileged families alien to economic activities leads to a restriction of engagement, so that "*the landed estate of civil-political origin* ordinarily coincides with the fact of *rugged or almost uncultivated lands*."[7]

Taking root in the soil

Agricultural contracts also have a great impact on progress on the land. Those that guarantee the farmer's right to participate in its growing productivity are certainly advantageous. To be considered as an "error and crime" of the modern era, however, is the fact that the creation of the agricultural proletariat, "by disengaging the worker of the land from any stable co-interest with it and with social existence, destroyed the strong farming class, which was always the partner of the proprietor classes in the transformations of the homeland's soil."[8]

Here Toniolo dwells on the analysis of the various forms (a system of clustered houses or farmsteads, a system of scattered houses) and their agricultural and social outcomes. It can be well understood, he underlines, that "through the residence of owners and farmers the entire rural class takes root in the soil and merges in the common interest of land improvements."[9] Decisive for the development of land-based industry, above all following the stimulus offered by the formation of cities alongside the rural extensions, is its becoming "capitalist":

> Cultivation and improvements, previously determined *by the immediate needs of life*, are now regulated and driven *by the profits of the capital employed*; the *monetary economy,* its calculations, its speculations, its mobility enter to some extent into the art and life of the fields, providing multiple impulses and supports for *innovative scientific progress on the land,* but at the same time *new limitations* and obstacles arise where the capitalists no longer find sufficient compensation for the sums invested in land.[10]

Such problems recall the need for a regulatory body, the state, with its land policy and legal instruments aimed at promoting lasting improvements of the national territory.

Progress on the land

These are — all of those mentioned — factors of land-based industry, which in their relationships delineate the laws of progress on the land. Toniolo focuses on them, starting from the demographic data, in consideration of the fact that there is a tendency toward an increase in cultivation and other forms of progress on the land in proportion to the needs, especially for food, of the growing populations.[11] This should, in principle, push populations toward the most fertile territories. In practice, this is not always the case, since historically that rational law is often overrun and increasingly modified by two orders of variable facts — the settlement of populations and the state of technology[12] — so that the choice of lands to be cultivated is made not so much on the basis of their potential productivity as of their ease of cultivation.

We will pass over the analysis of the other factors that affect the progress or regression of land-based industry, mentioning only the basic thesis, reiterated here, of the merits of the Christian Middle Ages, when, thanks above all to the monasteries, "European soil was built."[13] Quite different is the spectacle of the modern era, which sees

> a general and profound regression in the condition of European land. The age of geographical discovery and of the Reformation was disastrous in this respect. The abandonment of lands for transoceanic adventures; the civil and then religious wars (from the fifteenth to the seventeenth century) in England, France, Germany, which there, together with the plague, reduced the population by half (A. Marshall); the financial exploitation of the countryside for the wasteful new absolutism of the Tudors, the Spanish, the Bourbons; the reconstitution of the fideicommissa of a rapacious courtly aristocracy, accompanied by new servitude and legal spoliation and sometimes (as in Great Britain) by the true destruction of the farming class, caused the spread of the uncultivated landed estate and the untaming of lands previ-

ously redeemed by the age-old sacrifices of generations.[14]

But modernity, too, is ransomed with a return to the land. It falls to the French physiocrats of the *Encyclopedie* to interpret this "irresistible need of all of Europe, which after three centuries of the exhaustion of rustic lands and peoples was getting back to rebuilding the territory of the nations."[15] A renewal that, prepared in the seventeenth century, inaugurates a new era in the mid-eighteenth century. Then there is the resumption of investing to conquer uncultivated lands with cultivation and to improve those under cultivation. Irrigation canals are built. And land legislation defines the "ownership of public and private waters, with a growing tendency today to extend their public character for the general interest (nationalization, see F. S. Nitti)."[16]

Rural industry

Prepared for by land-based industry, the farming or agricultural industry properly so-called arises, "which aims at the generation of plant products from the soil itself."[17]

With a historical process parallel to that of the industry of the soil, agriculture also follows the course of progress that is expressed in the three laws of specification, intensification, and coordination. This is clearly visible on the level of the technical order,[18] in which, for the purposes of specification, a preponderant factor is constituted by "the *physico-chemical zones*, thanks to *science*, which increasingly discovers and varies the physiological plant species and assigns them to the respective qualities of land that must nourish them."[19] Farming is then enhanced, thanks to the means of production, changing from extensive to intensive.

Similar tendencies of development manifest themselves at the level of professional organization, with the progressive configurations of agricultural enterprise, which, from the domestic enterprise stage, tends to develop in the division of labor and skills, resulting in a landscape of small, medium, and large enterprises. Toniolo insists on the fact that each of these configurations of agricultural enterprise has its function, so that "maximum agricultural progress is achieved only with the mutual integration of all the proportions of enterprise."[20]

The same three laws (specification, intensification, coordination) emerge at the level of the economic-legal system. The wisdom of the law, with respect to the needs of each enterprise and of the common good, makes the difference. It is desirable, for example, that the law not penalize small farming properties in which economic interest is blended with love for the domestic roof and the native soil, with the undoubted effect that A. Young expressed by saying that "the magic of property turns sand to gold." So it is a pity, our author notes, that this small property should be undermined by laws shaped by liberal individualism. A typical case: the inheritance regime, which obliges the father at his death to divide all or a large part of the land into equal portions between his children, with the consequence of a segmentation that makes them all poorer, while it would be more reasonable to leave a farm intact, with the requirement that the recipient provide for the other members of the family.[21] An interesting observation, which however cannot escape an objection: Wouldn't this require a degree of integration between family members that rarely occurs, especially nowadays with the general crisis of the family? Yet the fact remains to be reckoned with: A pulverization of property impoverishes everyone. Toniolo presented this very example in a commentary on the Milan Program (1894), in which the guidelines of a Christian-inspired policy were laid down in the face of insistent socialism.[22]

The considerations along the lines of a law favorable to agriculture continue with a whole series of examples. In general, Toniolo advocates integration between large landowners and farmers. One model, in his eyes, is Baron Burghard von Schorlemer-Alst, "who in Rhenish Bavaria multiplied *rural unions* around 1870, living among the country people and striving with them in mutual duties, rights, interests, and was called the 'king of the farmers.'"[23] The people also erected a statue of him.

Agricultural contracts

With a view to this integration of classes, Toniolo examines the various forms of agricultural contracts, showing their advantages and disadvantages. Emphyteusis is fundamental, "a form of economic-legal enterprise in which the farmer takes on the cultivation of land on a long-term or perpetual basis, upon payment of a fixed and unalterable fee to the owner."[24] This was a form of contract that, already existing in the classical world, was perfected in the Christian Middle Ages on the holdings of the Church. When this form is best realized, "it creates a *class of autonomous farmer-owners,* added to the original landlords, true *co-owners* with them."[25] In the form of metayage, instead, "the product in nature is divided in a set portion between the owner and the cultivator, hence the names of half share, third share, quarter share."[26] This solution, too, which is a form of partnership, has its positive effects. Economic advantages for one thing, because it is in the partners' interest to increase production by stimulating intensive cultivation, and social, for another, given that the farm, especially with sharecropping, favors the large family unit (it is in the farmer's interest to have more domestic workers available) and social harmony, in uniting the interests of the owning and working classes. But the condition is an ethical, cultural, and social climate; once this is lost, everything degenerates. When, for example,

> farm families, thinned out by the two-child theory or by emigration (as in France and Italy), are no longer sufficient for the work of the farm, and when respect for honest traditions and customs (a great safeguard of common interests) is replaced by frequent evictions, or trust [replaced] by the suspicion of disloyalty, and worse, class hatred, can one be surprised that metayage should decline, as followed back in the past and today under the influence of the social crisis?[27]

Toniolo does not hesitate to affirm that the assaults of socialism against this figure of the agrarian contract "appear quintessentially anti-scientific and anti-democratic."[28]

The third type of contract is rental, with which "the farmer assumes the operation of the agricultural industry at his own risk and for his own profit, upon payment to the owner of a conventional annual fee for the duration of the contract."[29] The advantage of this contract is in the maximum boost it gives to progressive production, given that it is in the tenant's interest to produce to the maximum, to increase his profit margin. This applies both to small-scale rental limited to a family business and to large-scale rental (capitalist), in which "the tenant (farmer) is a true enterpriser-speculator; he takes on the technical-economic management of the crop, having it carried out by workers at his own risk and for his own profit."[30]

The boost to production (given certain conditions, like the long-term duration of the contract) is maximal. This is the trend of modern industrial agriculture.

The wage earner

But the disadvantages of large-scale rental are also notable, especially on the social level, if one looks at the sad condition of the wage earner:

> The large tenant farmer is by the very nature of the contract a speculative enterpriser, and therefore, not being able to avoid either the heavy fee paid to the landlord or the substantial use of capital necessary for large profits, he is led to whittle labor costs down to the minimum. So, he replaces workers with machines as much as possible and reduces the indispensable few to the condition of temporary wage earners, whom he hires and releases day by day according to need, saving on the wage fund.[31]

The result is the spectacle of an agricultural proletariat in which men, women, and children roam around offering their manual labor, often for subsistence wages: "the last form, crushed and corrupted, of the strong Christian farming population that played such a large part in rural progress from the early Middle Ages onward, this proletariat without God and homeland today transfers the worst socialist ferment to the countryside."[32]

When he was writing these lines, Toniolo had before his eyes the agrarian unrest that was devastating Emilia Romagna in those years. He strove to recommend a policy that, while reaffirming property rights, would show itself open to the needs of the most disadvantaged classes, easy prey for socialism.[33] In the *Trattato* he puts the principles in order, ever more convinced that the social crisis is before all else an intellectual crisis.

Grassroots and legal remedies

What remedy can be found for the problem of the wage earner in capitalist rental or small-scale subletting? Toniolo considers worthy of the Christian economic school the idea of collective rental, in which an association of farmers enters into a contract agreeing to pay rent to the landlord of a vast property, "then dividing the cultivation among themselves on smaller farms, like small tenant farmers."[34] This distinction of cultivation among tenant farmers differentiates this formula from the one preferred by socialists, for whom not only the contract but also the management is in common, which for Toniolo does not seem destined to hold up in the face of the rural economy and "rustic psychology." In any case, this collective contract formula is a true answer to the problem of the dispersed wage earner, because it combines

> large-scale (capitalist) rental with small farm rents, while it excludes a middleman who exploits small farmers and perpetuates sporadic day labor; it generates or restores an autonomous farming class, reconnects it to the soil and uplifts it economically and civilly, presenting all the value of a prudent populating of the estate for the correction of wage earning or similar antisocial forms.[35]

Alongside these grassroots initiatives, wise social legislation is also necessary, like that developed in Great Britain, which Toniolo notes with admiration[36] before continuing the assessment for other European nations. We will limit ourselves to focusing on the conclusion: Keeping in mind the selfish tendency that leads to the prevalence of legal systems that reinforce the more vast and centralized economic organisms (landed estates and capitalist enterprises), there seems instead to be a normal balancing in

> the function of laws that strive to support and spread medium and small ownership and farming with more suitable legal rules and forms of agricultural possession and exercise, to maintain or restore balance not only in the interest of social solidarity, but of labor-intensive farming itself. Legislation thus intervenes to en-

sure the law of defined proportions, which, just as we have seen operate within each business, also applies to the same businesses as a whole.[37]

Chapter XIV
Manufacturing Industry

Advantages and problems

Manufacturing industries (Toniolo mostly prefers to say "manufactural") are to be understood as those that "through physico-chemical processes modify the substance or form of the products prepared by the territorial and agricultural industries."[1] So they are intimately linked, and also follow them in the fundamental laws of specification, increase, and integration, but with characteristics of greater uniformity, rapidity, and scale.

It is a true enthusiasm, as we have already had the opportunity to note, that our author shows technological development applied to industry. He had been captivated by it since his younger years, as emerges from his 1876 letter to his brother Piero after a visit to Alessandro Rossi's wool factory in Schio. Referring to the poem "Work" by Giacomo Zanella, it seemed to him that the reality of modern industry, with its "strict applications of numbers and physical laws," was more fruitful of true poetry than the "artificial and overused combinations of winsome maidens, and brooklets, and satyrs and nymphs."[2]

> Amid this positivism, what always stands out is man, not indeed subjugated by an enervating Arcadian nature, but in all the pow-

> er of his ingenuity triumphant over the same.[3]

Industrial progress seemed to him to be a sort of revelation of God, projecting itself into the future, which he saw as "entirely new and grandiose."[4] Thirty years later he does not recant, even if his presentation becomes more cautious when he switches to the social consequences of a technological economy that gets the upper hand over the human. That of technology — we'll skip past the details — is the first level of his analysis of the laws of development.[5] The second is that of the professional organization of businesses, which, starting from familial industry, became increasingly specified in the emergence of tradesmanship, of handicraft, up to the factory, the typical modern form, characterized by the "agglomeration of many workers in just one building under a single centralized management."[6] Toniolo recognizes the advantages of this development (relatively lower costs, powerful advanced technology, more complete and effective professional organization, ease of sale), but also points out its drawbacks. A critical side is presented that smacks of condemnation:

> *Through industrial concentration,* the factory, breaking up the family with its perpetual idyll of work at home and sacrificing the small autonomous workshops to gather men, women, and children into a single industrial enclosure, absorbs in the few captains of regimented work *the capacity, expertise, and virtue* of *industrious initiatives*, which were previously distributed among many smaller vital nuclei. It is the oligarchy that replaces democracy in productive enterprises. Indeed, within the bosom of these it contributes to degrading *even the individual value* of the workers, in production weighing them down uniformly with the demoralizing influence of the division of labor and of machines. And it generates a new *industrial feudalism,* which most exalts the capitalist enterpriser with his despotic functions and his accumulated profits, just as it abases and levels the multitude of workers with miserable wages. All of this accompanied by hygienic, moral, and social disorders, inseparable from the

> crowding in the factory.[7]

A painful picture. Did it necessarily have to be this way? Toniolo puts the blame on historical conditions, but also on the selfish and greedy "spirit of utilitarianism"

> already brazen among the capitalist gentry of Reformation-era Great Britain, and ultimately triumphant among the industrial and mercantile bourgeoisie of all Europe, which equally availed itself of its ability and fortune, as well as of its errors and deficiencies, to subjugate and exploit the working masses, so that these found themselves cast to the depths of poverty, degeneration, and moral brutalization, storing up hatred for the future revolutionary socialism.[8]

The remedies

And yet, no nostalgia for the past. The present must be addressed with appropriate remedies. First of all, our author is convinced that the establishment of the factory does not necessarily have to sweep away tradesmanship and handicraft. As for the impact on the family, it is mixed:

> The economic unity of today's working family is not always compromised, the sum of wages received by parents and children now scattered in the factories often bringing to the common coffer incomes equal to or higher than those of yesterday.[9]

Economically, therefore, the family gains. The problem arises on the moral side:

> The moral unity of the working family, due to its dispersion in the factories, is profoundly shaken and must be made up for with spiritual energies of higher ethical-religious derivation and with indirect social educational influences, which is still far from happening for the modern wage earner. A serious and urgent duty![10]

Remedies are also to be sought in the way in which the factory is organized, from the point of view of remuneration and relationships. It is necessary to go beyond the fixed daily wage, establishing more direct relationships of *co-interest,* "like the wage per task (by invoice), already widely used in the textile industries, and the participation of workers in the profits."[11] It is then necessary to limit the sovereign power of the capitalist enterpriser: Here Toniolo makes reference to experiences like the participation of workers in the factory board (*conseil d'usine*) to negotiate with the enterpriser over wages, internal regulations, and disputes. Also positive is worker participation in the capital of the factory, through the purchase of shares that make the workers partners of the capitalist-enterpriser.[12] As for problems of hygiene, health (occupational disorders), morality, etc., Toniolo sees the possibility that the organization of work could be improved — also by virtue of legislative interventions — to overcome these drawbacks. One conclusion:

> The drawbacks of the factory and its indefinite expansion in its specific field do not outweigh the economic advantages, which are immense and confirm how it represents a normal order of productive progress and can still be translated into valuable social benefits, such as a more ready and intense means of education of populous working classes. But this is on one condition, which bursts forth from the sad and happy experiences of this regime — namely, that the purely utilitarian operation of the factory be coupled with greater performance of the ethical-social duties that it itself creates and imposes. There is a whole field open: to new initiatives of higher justice and fairness, of wise and disinterested patronage on the part of capitalist enterprisers, who, before benefiting from factory systems, must first work to correct their economic, moral, and hygienic consequences to the detriment of the workers; to new combinations of solidarity among the multitudes of factory workers, to ensure their collective interests, dignity, and elevation; to new legal provisions, proportionate to the more complex relationships of the factory itself. … But in the meantime, from all this arises the solemn confirmation of the truth: that ev-

> ery instance of material progress must be accompanied by an elevation of social responsibility and of the consequent moral duties for all, and so the fulfillment of these broader duties of justice and charity becomes a prerequisite for the utilitarian law to be fruitful. Only on this condition does the triumph of the factory result in progress for civilization.[13]

Is small business finished?

Toniolo maintains — he spoke out on this since one of his first studies in 1874[14] — that the expansion of big business does not necessarily have to lead to the disappearance of the small. The two are destined not to fight each other, but to become integrated (law of integration). He illustrates this principle starting from the very dynamics of the industrial economy. If in fact it is evident that the big business, due to the economic advantages that distinguish it, in an initial stage tends to absorb the small one, it is also true that

> in the long run the static law of integration turns into the dynamic, and *the factory prompts the rebirth and expansion* of handicraft and tradesmanship ... directly, by giving small industries more objects and opportunities for their work, and indirectly, by increasing general well-being and so the demand for their products. In the meantime, it should be noted that small businesses have a triple function: of *adaptation* to the final use ("finissage"), of *restoration and completion* ("adjustage"), of *refinement and ennoblement* ("affinage").[15]

A few examples: With the growth of instrumental equipment the opportunities for repair grow, and "every mechanical factory also provides a quantity of repair work for external craftsmen's workshops."[16] With the prosperity spread by big business, "the demand for products suitable for the small is aroused and increased."[17] Then there is a growth in luxury or cultural goods, which are products of small rather than big businesses. But this proportion and integration is not an automatic and immediate fact. It occurs only "at the end (note well) of the necessary displacement of small businesses from one object or domain to another, of the laborious process of disappearance and resuscitation, and of a renewing transformation, giving rise in the meantime to crises and *conflicts*."[18] A process that requires a general readjustment. It is necessary to elevate the technical education of the new artisan: "to transform, as in the Middle Ages, the artisan into an artist; in this are the main salvation and the hopes of small businesses."[19] It is also important that the artisan be able to find specific help, such as the availability of credit (role of credit unions), also finding support in cooperatives. Toniolo looks ahead: "It can be foretold that in the manufacturing system the commercial function will pass to strong cooperative companies."[20] Finally, the role of the "state (or better, provinces, regions, municipalities) cannot be lacking, with provisions of law and economic policy, especially suited to the congenital weakness and the present suffering of these minute but valuable organisms."[21]

A task of civilization

The data that Toniolo collects show that this scenario is actually achievable; it is not just a hope. He affirms this by relying on the very course correction internal to socialist ideology, but above all by showing that in the relaunching of small business, integrated with big business, a great question of civilization is at stake:

> F. Engels and K. Marx could hope, since 1847, that all the artisans of the small businesses would disappear, leveled by wage earning in the factories, to precipitate the catastrophe of industrial capitalism with the social revolution. But E. Bernstein, among the collectivists themselves, today contradicts them, and on the contrary every sociologist-moralist sees in the reconstitution of small business an obligatory task of civilization. Indeed, the trade on its own or coordinated in manufacturing rests on the responsible initiative of numerous small enterprisers; small business is therefore an exercise in personal and domestic autonomy, a school for free peoples. If all humanity were to be guided by the bell of the great establishment, this would sound the death knell over the grave of individual freedom (F. Hitze in V. Brants). Small

business is indispensable for solving the problem of female work. Back in patriarchal life, in the guild regime, as in the modern system, woman always had a large part in production. But today the factory, where women en masse are scattered together with men and adolescents, shatters and corrupts the working family, and in-home female work itself, in the service of the big warehouses (a degenerate form of manufacturing), accomplishes the individualistic crushing and subjugation of womanly activity. Only the reorganization of the domestic workshop or coordinated in-home work (without excluding woman from well-regulated factories) can keep mothers at the cradle and the hearth, as their husbands' partners, and restore the routed fortunes of those who ply the needle. The unity of the family and the honesty of woman in the solitude of the home depend on it.

Finally, for more than a century, with the big factory, the powerful upper class of industrial enterprisers was formed and the lower class of wage earners spread in large numbers. So, a robust organization of small business is destined to prepare for the *new industrial middle class*, or at least its nucleus ("Kern des Mittelstandes," Pesch), necessary to restore to the other two classes and to society as a whole the center of balance, that middle class which has always been the stronghold of the nations.[22]

Industrial policy from classical times to the Middle Ages

The relationship between work and politics is one of the central nodes of Toniolo's thought, concerned with drawing a line of balance between the opposing tendencies of an absorbing state (or pantheistic, as he loves to say), which limits — to the point of annihilating it — personal, social, and economic freedom, and an absent state, which in the name of freedom actually hands over to the powerful the fate of the have-nots.

Is the faculty, Toniolo wonders, to establish and run an industrial enterprise and to exercise it freely with all the modalities of forms and means compatible with the general interest, on the part of any person (individual, social, public), as a common right, always recognized by *positive laws*? The answer is complex. If this result has been achieved, it has come about thanks to complex historical processes, with a fundamental difference between pagan and Christian culture, and in the latter registering three characteristic historical orders: the guild regime, government concessions, industrial freedom.

In classical antiquity, industry is based on slave labor, and free artisans find themselves regulated by increasingly restrictive rules. Only state industries (arms industry, marble production, shipbuilding, etc.) reach notable stature. Fresh air comes in with the Christian climate, where the right to freedom of work is affirmed, also expressing itself in associative or guild law. This let loose a spontaneous teeming of multiform businesses, which

> remained subject to *conditions and norms of operation*, thanks to their statutes of incorporation. But in the first centuries of the Middle Ages these did not as a rule impose technical prescriptions, but rather moral conditions for the dignity of the artisan class (exclusion of illegitimate children, of men with criminal convictions), or economic prescriptions to ensure product quality (inspections), or finally, in the name of a certain *right to work*, market and consumption constraints to ensure industrial activity and prosperity for artisans.[23]

What is the logic of this freedom, regulated yet never trampled upon? The principles lie entirely in the Christian vision of life:

> In it, industrial work is considered as a child of the moral personality of man, who accepts it as a freely chosen duty and exercises it as a function that God has entrusted to artisans for the moral and material good of each one, of the class, and of the generality, and that therefore attributes a *right to work*, which is for all of them a qualification of equality and brotherhood before the owners and capitalists (Janssen), a right that has its full expression in the faculty of becoming a master — that is, of establishing one's own business. So it is seen how at this time the artisan guilds did not appear as the source of this right, but only

> as legal organs for recognizing it and a condition for its exercise, and how these remained *open*, in the sense that to found a trade it was not necessary to belong to them, or if sometimes it was, everyone was admitted under common conditions.[24]

A climate of well-ordered freedom of economic initiative also influenced civil society: the artisan class, proud of its freedom and equality of work, became "the bulwark of the civic autonomies."[25]

Modern restrictions and liberal reaction

Toniolo reproves the pagan spirit of the Renaissance and the individualism of the Reformation for the fact that, in the artisan class from the fifteenth century on, the sense of Christian freedom and solidarity was replaced by class selfishness, so that the capitalist-speculative merchants with their greater guilds or associations gained predominance in the government of the cities and of the state, excluding small craftsmen and their lesser associations from political activity. The formation of absolute monarchies also contributed to this process, with their interest in "pushing the democratic working class down,"[26] binding the capitalist bourgeoisie to themselves. Thus the system of closed and chartered corporations prevails, with the coercive exclusion of the common right to work and sell on one's own account.[27] The principle is imposed that industrial companies are to be established by state concession. The liberal reaction was to be expected and began in France with the minister R. G. Turgot in 1776. States declined to take any positive action to balance the interests of the national industries. The merits of this trend reversal on the level of industrial growth could be seen, thanks to the accentuation of individual interest as the propellant for economic initiative, regulated by competition:

> In this field it was the triumph of *individualism, idealistic* in French physiocracy ("laissez-faire, laissez-passer") and stingily *utilitarian* among the English (Manchester school), which, fused together in the more recent European liberalism, implied (note well) *the root and branch rejection of any industrial legislation.*[28]

What was the overall outcome? Experience showed that freedom is not enough in itself:

> With unbridled competition the individual rights and interests of the weak were cruelly sacrificed to the strong; with the suppression of guild systems the class struggle between industrial capitalists and workers erupted disastrously; with the abstention of the state from any positive interference in production the unity and industrial power of the nation was sacrificed to a hybrid cosmopolitanism, and the social question grew to giant stature within the very bosom of the most flourishing industries.[29]

Social legislation

Thus opens the grand scenario of the welfare state, which, while recognizing the freedom of economic initiative, intervenes to regulate it with a view to the common good, a necessary intervention from the viewpoint of the protection of workers (prescriptions regarding industrial architecture and mechanics, hygiene, childhood education, duration of work, etc.). State intervention would also be necessary to regulate the labor contract, and our author laments the fact that, in his time, this has not yet been accomplished, thus leaving the confrontation between enterpriser and workers to anarchy and arrogance.[30] The state also intervenes in promotional terms, creating educational initiatives and institutions favorable for access to work. With these and other interventions a real industrial policy is delineated, also through the tools of international trade policy:

> This is, after the long years of anarchic liberalism, a *rebirth* appropriate to the grandiose contemporary production of industrial legislation and policy, which, still revolving around freedom but regulating it in the individual and collective interest, approaches in its final intentions (though not in its prescriptions) the guild statutes of the municipalities of the Middle Ages.[31]

So, the final judgment is fundamentally positive on this regulatory trend, but with concern over deficiencies and abuses. This is a scenario in progress, in need of fundamental principles that for our author can be no other than those of the Christian vision. This is also important for modern industry:

> Thus solemn experiences impose the warning that the supreme spiritual rationale in the life of the peoples is an indispensable condition for the normal progress of production, indeed for the very triumphs of modern industry.[32]

Chapter XV
Distribution: Concepts and Questions

Youthful lessons

Moving from the ponderous volume of the *Trattato*, dedicated to production, to that dedicated to distribution (the fourth of the *Opera Omnia*) gives the immediate sense of a slimmer volume and, in a certain way, of one patched together. In effect, what Toniolo had in mind was not given to him to write. Fortunately, since 1878 he had published, as an aid for students, a small volume on the subject that collected the "lectures" (he prefers to call them "notes") that he gave for four years in Padua.[1] It is a monograph that Cossa admired.[2] Our author notes, in the introduction, that it was the students themselves who insisted on having "at least an outline of that part of the lectures which refers to the distribution of social wealth, and which due to the specific nature of the objective manages to be, in comparison with other areas of the science, more interesting and at the same time more complex."[3] In his maturity, in 1895, those lectures would appear lacking to him. Indeed, he would amend some of their points in dialogue with none other than Cossa, during the review of the tenth edition of *Primi elementi di economia politica* by the economist from Pavia:

> We also confess that we ourselves had adhered to those propositions, but later, led by the hand by the principles of Christian ethics and law, having been induced to modify them, we found ourselves comforted by the very criticism of them that, from the strictly economic viewpoint, has been established by recent utilitarian economists who do not accept our Christian ideas.[4]

So we are within an approach that the author himself considers, at least in some points, still far from the spirit of the Christian economic school that would become his identity card. But, in the meantime, it has the merit of allowing us to meet Toniolo the professor in his most workaday moment, that of dialogue with his students. Compared with his usual style, rather soaring and copious, the *Lectures* are characterized by a particular sobriety and didactic formulation. It must also be noted that, in the volume put together for the *Opera Omnia*, that booklet is republished together with other contributions. But here we are referring precisely to it — without neglecting later developments — finding there the advantage of clarity and synthesis. In the logic inspiring us, we will not follow the details of the notions that Toniolo borrowed from the scientific context of the time and would be found *tout court* in any introduction to economic science. Nonetheless, we will highlight those elements that in some way, although still needing to ripen, anticipate the vision of the mature Toniolo.

Let's start from the incipit that defines the object of the book:

> The distribution of wealth as part of the science of social economics includes the study of the natural economic laws by which in human societies the wealth produced is divided among those who contributed to producing it.[5]

Distribution: Of what? To whom?

The young professor explains first of all that the dynamic to which economic science refers in terms of distribution concerns not so much wealth on the whole, but additional wealth, that which is added in terms of revenue through the productive process. More precisely, what is in question is net revenue — that is, what remains after the amount needed to replenish the wealth advanced to produce it (capital) has been removed from the overall wealth produced (gross revenue).

The net revenue is distributed among all those who cooperated in the production. It is interesting that, in breaking down the recipients, Toniolo should start with the workers, who have invested their human faculties in it and so have the right to a wage, and then move on to nature, through which the relative owners have the right to a return, and finally end with the capitalists, who expect interest on the capital provided, and the enterprisers who look for their profit. Wage, return, interest, profit are the great chapters of the distributive economy.[6]

The legal-economic qualification to participate in company revenue is that of "having contributed to the production, and so of being a co-owner of the resulting product."[7] It should be emphasized that the worker is called "co-owner." In effect, Toniolo underlines, the laws of distribution retrace those of production and are based on the "great institution of property; in other words, they have their guarantee in the supreme principle of justice: that belongs to each one which is the result of his own work."[8]

It is here that the questions come thick and fast, putting the very truth of a just economy at stake: What is to be the logic of distribution? It is easy to say, in the abstract, that what makes the difference is the value of the respective cooperation. A word — that of value — over which economic theory has practically racked its brains. A concept to be applied — but the matters are economically related — both to the value of the products and to that of the services offered to produce them.

And here the quintessential realm of complexity opens up, since the application of the concept of value to the human world brings about a shift from the constancy of physical laws to the dynamism proper to anthropology and psychology. And all this not only with the variety of sentiments and subjective appraisals, but also with the influences of history and culture. The mature Toniolo is already anticipated here, when he will affirm:

> In no other part of the economy is the connection between the

> order of facts and that of ideas so direct and evident. The difference, for example, between the division of wealth in ancient and modern societies corresponds to the substantial opposition between the moral and religious doctrines of paganism and Christianity. And so every recourse of Christian ideas to the pagan spirit hints at resurrecting in other forms the characteristics of the ancient distributive economy.[9]

This is an issue that interferes not only with the economic order, but also with the political and social order, to the point that "the crisis of economic distribution even takes the name of *social crisis* or question."[10] When Toniolo writes this, there are thirteen years left until *Rerum Novarum,* but the young Paduan professor shows that he already has his ideas clear and knows which side to take.

Workers' wages

> A *wage* in the strict sense is that part of the value of the net revenue which is due to the worker as such, for having contributed his work in the production carried out at the risk and for the profit of others.[11]

On this basis, he begins a broad analysis[12] that — first distinguishing the "nominal-monetary value" from the "real value" (the quantity of product that can actually be purchased with money) — grapples above all with the concept of the value of labor: a detailed analysis which, however, we will take at a good clip.

Two big points of view: On the one hand the determination of the wage on the basis of the intrinsic causes of the work itself, and this is the "general normal law" of the wage; on the other, the extrinsic influences on this determination, which have to do with the "labor market," hence the "commercial or current law" of the wage.

Even if, unfortunately, the concrete wage is determined more by the market than by the intrinsic valuation of the work, for Toniolo it is important to focus on the latter, to grasp the ethical and human stakes of the problem, examined not only from the individual or company point of view, but also at the national level. From this viewpoint, the productive power (in both degree and kind) of the workers of a nation being equal, the value of work, and so also the respective right to compensation, is measured "by the sum of the sacrifices (general averages) necessary for workers to acquire that same power and translate it into action."[13] Sacrifices to be measured not only in the moment of work, but also in what prepares for it (studies, training, etc.). Of course, our author admits, it is quite difficult to weigh the value of human sacrifices, which are in themselves internal and immaterial. So, for pragmatic reasons, instead of sacrifices, the satisfaction of human needs is evaluated, from the more fundamental to the more accessory, a perspective that, no less than that of sacrifices, brings out the human character of work. Unlike the other two factors — nature and capital — the labor factor is intrinsic to man: "Indeed, it is man himself considered in the exercise of his personal faculties."[14] With this shift toward consumption or needs as the criterion for determining the wage, the theoretical difficulty of calculating its amount is resolved with an eminently practical rule: "The normal wage is measured by the *usual consumption of the working classes*."[15]

Easy to say, one might immediately object: Even consumption and its respective desires are subject to infinite variations, in which personal, psychological, social, territorial, and civilizational factors have an influence. In other words, quite the puzzle. In concrete terms, to get out of the dead end,

> the wage tends to be commensurate with that sum of wealth which, supplying the workers' usual satisfactions, is sufficient to determine their willingness to provide (with the maximum relative constancy and energy) work in the service of others.[16]

Ultimately, on the practical level, it is the worker who decides what wage he is willing to work for.

But here, too, problems arise. It is easy to evaluate needs and related consumption dictated by necessity — that is, those that determine life, or at least health. These primary needs strangle the worker by forcing him sometimes to accept a subsistence wage. It is understandable why physical consumption (including that of food) should represent the "hard line" of compensation.[17] In principle, however, the calculation of sacrifices and therefore of the value of work must also include those needs that, although not of survival, have a fundamental human impact that also affects work (and so the economy as such cannot disregard it). In particular, among matters of *social consumption,*

> most decisive are those brought to bear by the family, an institution through which the species is perpetuated and with it the *labor factor* itself. The wage is not only equal to the worker's personal consumption but extends to what is needed to support a family. Also in distributive teaching the economic unit is the family, not the individual. Everything that contributes to keeping this family nucleus firm and respected supports the wage; everything that is meant to dissolve it in favor of individual isolation tends to *individuate* (if the word is permissible) compensation as well and to reduce it. Beautiful harmony between the laws of social morality and of utility.[18]

In summary, the normal wage lies between two impassable boundaries:

> [The maximum limit] is determined by the degree of efficacy of the work itself, since the enterpriser is not normally willing to pay, as compensation for the work, more than its useful effect. The lowest (absolute) limit is marked by the consumption essential to sustain physical life.[19]

But up to this point we are in the intrinsic assessment of labor value. What decides, concretely, is the extrinsic situation of the labor market. "The wage varies in direct proportion to the demand and inversely to the supply of labor in the general market of the nation."[20] It is the most realistic aspect, but also the most ambiguous, tough, and sometimes cruel: If there are many workers waiting for employment (labor supply), while the demand for labor from enterprisers is low, competition between workers pushes their wage expectations down. They content themselves with a low wage only because they know that, if they refuse it, someone else willing to accept it will easily be found. Hence, we have war between the poor! Part of the value inherent in their work is thus subtracted from the workers' wages, cynically leveraging their needs.[21] Toniolo analyzes the different cases, with an approach in keeping with the economic science of the time.[22] He points out a series of variables that make the law of the wage, both normal and commercial, highly unstable, linked as it is to a multiplicity of factors ever in movement. Important, for the ends of the possible social remedies, is the observation that this law of supply and demand, applied in the labor market, normally sees the worker in a situation of weakness: "One cannot speak of true *moral* freedom under the servitude of essential needs."[23] Hence the protective and defensive reactions, which range from the concerted action of workers' associations to the extreme form of the strike, which is not a modern reality (there are medieval examples, from the Ciompi Revolt to the Siena strikes of 1371 and 1384, respectively), but in our time it becomes more frequent, with the need that this type of reaction remain within certain limits of social order: "legitimacy of *intentions,* appropriateness of *occasions,* temperance of *means*."[24] The analysis goes into the details, with examples that still have a certain interest. But in the meantime, the professor drew from this a conclusion that he would develop ever more in his economic-social thought: There was an urgent need for legislation to regulate the labor contract in order to protect the freedom and mutual interests of the contracting parties[25] with the introduction of effective institutions for preventing or tempering strikes. He mentions "boards of labor," "elective tribunals," "councils of arbitrators." With the development of his thought within the horizon of the Christian democratic school, he would say much more, and with more intense passion. But here we are still at the *first* Toniolo, more professor than social catalyst.

The interest for the capitalists

Interest is the part of the value of the revenue due to the person who provides the capital — that is, the sum of instruments (buildings, machines, etc.) that makes the work possible, or the money that represents it (monetary capital). How to evaluate the "share" (proportion, rate) of interest? Here Toniolo opens an analysis similar to that made for the wage, distinguishing the intrinsic aspect (normal law) and the extrinsic aspect (commercial law). For the first aspect, the concepts of utility and limitation come into play:

> On a par with the productive efficacy of capital, interest tends to be equal to the general average sum of the sacrifices necessary to form (compose) the capital itself and make it available for production.[26]

The commercial law, instead, depends on extrinsic causes — that is, the capital or lending market — so that interest varies according to supply and demand. Here Toniolo reviews the various criteria that have been applied on this topic.

The first system is linked to the perspective of the Church, which in former times substantially rejected any interest, considered *tout court* as usury, in the name of the gratuitous lending of capital. This was a way of sanctioning the duty of charity as a general social law, important in times in which lending was made "for purposes of consumption and not of production, and in popular hands industry itself was carried out for *subsistence* rather than for profit."[27] With the progress of the economy, the general principle began to be developed, providing for a certain compensation of capital. But in the meantime,

> canonical legislation contributed to maintaining the distinction (also very important in economic terms) between loans for consumption purposes (consumptive) and loans for production purposes (productive). And it also helped to favor the direct participation of the capitalist in production, and with this the formation of the vital and industrious class of capitalist enterprisers, limiting the untimely and immense growth of a class of simple rentiers, rich only due to the almost privileged ownership of capital on a par with the class of landowners, equal to it in terms of leisure, but in terms of moral virtues and civil traditions far inferior.[28]

The second system, entirely based on political discretion, is that which relies on restrictive intervention by the laws, which specify a maximum beyond which interest becomes usury: at bottom, a realistic procedure aimed only at preventing abuse.

The third system is that of freedom in the contracting of interest. Here competition acts as the regulating principle. But it remains a very random adjustment:

> The good effects do not depend only on the multiplicity of loans and their ease of access, but likewise and more so on their destination for *productive* or *unproductive* ends — that is, depending on whether they are aimed at supporting production or instead at encouraging superfluous and wasteful consumption; directed toward solid production in the general interest (e.g., agriculture, the manufacture of common products, etc.) or short-lived industries serving privileged consumers (sumptuary industries); or worse, fuel reckless, random, dishonest speculations (e.g., stock market games).[29]

In the system of competition there are thus pros and cons. For the market to remain within positive proportions, corrective and integrative interventions are necessary, both on the part of laws and through economic institutions

> that may encourage savings and facilitate lending on honest terms to all social classes, especially the lower ones. Such economic institutions (like savings banks, credit unions, the system of unsecured loans connected to mutual aid societies, etc.) are of the highest practical efficacy, and to them must be attributed much of the contemporary mitigation of usury with respect to times gone by.[30]

Return on land

Saying, in the current jargon, that one lives on returns can have different nuances. In some cases, an accent that is not entirely negative (e.g., for a scholar who lives by his previous education), in other cases decidedly pejorative (for someone who leads an idle life because the returns on his assets leave him with no financial troubles). Return always suggests the idea of what is received without the need to earn it with the sweat of one's brow. In the technical terms of economic science, Toniolo defines it as "the part of the value of the net income that is due in certain circumstances to the owners (as such) of the agents of nature for having contributed the latter to production."[31]

This thinking is something similar, in short, to the interest on capital, when not directly intertwined with work, and is not involved in business risks, thus ending up becoming pure return.[32] Discussing this with Fedele Lampertico, Toniolo did not deny the extension of this interpretation to capital, but underlined that the main reference of this notion must remain that of land ownership.[33] Why this clarification? Likely at play was the concern that a negative concept of return should not go so far as to bring land ownership itself into question. Linked to this latter return did not have, in his eyes, the negative meaning of the usurious interest of monetary capital separated from work. Return on land, of course, also risks fueling parasitism, but it can also encourage people to make property available so that it can fulfill its social function. The owner of land who makes this available so that it can produce, generating at the same time a benefit for the worker and the capitalist, has the right to expect his share, with a dynamic that Toniolo analyzes in the various differentiations also used for the previous entries — that is, distinguishing "normal return," established in relation to the usual concepts of utility and limitation, and "current return," concretely defined with the mercantile law of supply and demand. We will leave the details aside. Interesting — at least as a page in the history of customs, far from our current social and cultural climate — is what Toniolo assigns as a moral task, one might say a vocation or mission, to the landowning class, which in his eyes somehow explains and legitimizes its living on returns. In fact, he somewhat idealizes this class. Not absorbed as it is in the care of material interests, Toniolo sees it turning

> to the culture of the *spirit* and so to the sciences, the arts, charity, civil and political functions. This helps to illustrate the history

> of the landowning classes, especially the *clergy* and *landed aristocracies,* and therefore the early and constant cult of knowledge and beauty among the former, the vocation and traditions of political life among the latter, and moreover, in both, that nobility and persistence of moral character which sets the tone for the whole life of a nation. This is the great providential office connected with the institution of *return,* which is then reflected indirectly to the benefit of the whole economic magisterium.[34]

This is a discussion that, to tell the truth, transposed into the circumstances of our time, would be rather idealistic and utopian.

The profit of the enterprisers

An enterpriser is "the person (individual or collective) who, having the productive factors at his disposal, concretely organizes production and carries it out at his own risk and for his own benefit."[35]

One characteristic element of enterprising activity is business risk. In the abstract, the enterpriser is different from the other agents of production (nature, capital, labor), but in practice, to inspire trust and guarantee the fulfillment of obligations toward the other agents, he also has his own assets. In this sense it is necessary to specify that enterprisers, belonging to the social category of capitalists, "under a more restricted point of view make up the special class of capitalist-industrialists and therefore employers of capital, distinct from that of capitalist-lenders of capital."[36] A crucial distinction for Toniolo, when one wishes to establish the comparative importance of the two categories: The one who deserves a higher valuation is the capitalist-enterpriser, the one who risks.

Once again, with respect to the profit due the enterpriser, the analysis of "normal law" and "commercial law" opens up. The reasoning is similar to that carried out for the other factors of production. In the normal course, profit is what is due the enterpriser on the basis of the utility-sacrifice pairing — that is, how significant his competent and generous commitment (sacrifice) is to the success of that particular enterprise and, at the same time, how concretely limited the availability of similar enterprising skills is in a given context. In practice, profit is dictated by the market, with the common law of supply and demand: on the one hand, the demand of consumers to have certain products thanks to the commitment of capable enterprisers; on the other, the willingness of these latter to take on — for the most varied reasons — this expectation, producing what is requested.

What Toniolo expects from enterprisers is significant (which further justifies the profit to which they have a right):

> It is they who in the concrete organization of production make the great applications of science to industry, and who in their autonomous management, with bold initiatives, extend the margin of production to the advantage of all who have productive agents at their disposal, and finally of consumers. It is not enough to have trained workers, abundant capital, the favors of nature, without elements of organization and the enlightened and daring action that sets these disconnected and inert forces in motion for universal benefit. The economic greatness of modern civilization must be attributed above all to the large, powerful, cultured, industrious, and still deserving class of the contemporary enterprisers.[37]

Chapter XVI
The Circulation of Wealth: The Laws of Exchange

Between things and the human

After production and distribution, the circulation of wealth comes into focus with the third part of the *Trattato*. In the *Opera Omnia* it corresponds to the fifth volume. Toniolo did not get the time to edit the publication of this part. After the author's death, Jacopo Mazzei would see to this in 1921, on the basis of the drafts left behind.[1]

One who undertakes the reading of this part comes across, for a good span of pages (the first one hundred sixty), a different tone from that of other Toniolian pages, quite otherwise inspired and driven by the concern to bring out, at every step, the reference to Christian civilization. Here one finds instead a rather dry analysis of use value and exchange value, and of the laws of trade, substantiated with concepts of and references to the human sentiments ("economic psychology"), with an approach not unlike that of similar textbooks of his time (with the exception of diagrams, which were truly not to Toniolo's liking), such as those of Valenti,[2] Supino,[3] Pantaleoni,[4] which he expressly cites.

In reality, beyond the first impression, also in this long analytical segment the "higher" perspective does not fail to peep out, when, for example, at the end of the rigorous conceptualization Toniolo underlines that

> the complete law of use value and exchange value in itself and in its progress is therefore nothing other than *the application of the hedonic law to the private and social appraisal of economic goods* in civilization. And in this two factors are reflected — that is, *man* with his needs and faculties, hence the qualitative physio-psychological elements, and the *external world* with its properties, hence the quantitative material elements.[5]

He emphasizes here that in the genesis, as in the final law of progress, it is the human element that holds the primacy with the exercise of physical, intellectual, and moral faculties. And this is the link for opening up to the transcendent:

> It remains only to be asked if then the first and final reason by which these virtues emerge and become active and are expressed with growing vigor is in turn connected with some fact pertaining to man. Yes, this fact is the conception of the objective ends of life, which are above him.[6]

The conception of the "dignity of individual and social existence" intervenes in these dynamics. "If that concept is uplifted, needs, strenuous activity, enjoyments rise up; if it is brought low and extinguished, everything slows down and stops."[7] Hence the conclusion:

> In this way (decisive observation) the judgment of useful material things, which is converted into value, in itself, in its laws and their progress, is dependent on the esteem of man and his higher ends, to the extent to which it is translated into the awareness and customs of the peoples. The material world, which has the character of a means, is ultimately judged by the human world and its moral ends. This ancient philosophical conception finds confirmation in modern economic psychology.[8]

Use value and exchange value

Considerations like these serve to show us the moral watermark hidden in the meticulous analysis that Toniolo makes, taking up again and exploring several concepts already presented in the treatise on production regarding the use value and exchange value that man attributes to things, and that influences the attitude with which he treats them in the various economic fields. Among these, precisely the great sphere of trade represents "that complex function or operation by which wealth is exchanged between men according to the criterion of equivalence, under the rule of the supreme hedonic law of economics"[9] (we recall that by hedonic law we mean the tendency to obtain the maximum result with the minimum effort).

The discussion begins with a general picture of the phenomenon of trade, which has seen an evident development in history, registering a special impulse with the "enormous accumulation in the American and European markets, especially in the sixteenth century, of *money*, the universal means par excellence of the circulation of all wealth, both goods and capital."[10] A means that then found its multipliers, which, "by replacing money itself in habitual use, virtually increase indefinitely the velocity of it and of trade."[11] These are the commercial credit instruments, including bank notes:

> Indeed, this powerful driving mechanism of circulation, while imparting maximum speed to the flow of movable wealth, manages to dislodge to a growing degree even the most immobilized wealth, and this thanks to the new *representative securities* of co-ownership and guarantee not only of industrial and commercial capital, but also of territorial assets. And so the endless capital invested in land, in mining subsoil, in railways is trafficked on the financial exchanges on a par with merchandise in the form of stocks and bonds, transferable between the most diverse and distant people and nations, finally connecting to the other ebb and flow (for non-productive purposes) of public revenue securities.[12]

The human consortium seems converted, Toniolo observes with Valenti and Messedaglia, "into a single universal society of commerce."[13] He adds that in this lies "our tremendous economic power, but at the same time, in some sense for concomitant reasons, our moral and civil fragility and weakness."[14]

There follows a detailed survey of the laws of exchange, starting from the concept of "equivalence":

> If the *object* of circulation is the commutative exchange of fungible useful things (*do ut des*), distinct from retributive exchange (*do ut facias*), the specific point of view is designated by the criterion of the reciprocal value of the things themselves, as the directive norm of exchange.[15]

So for trade to take place, an estimate of the value of the things to be exchanged is needed, to establish their "exchange value," typical of the social economy, which presupposes the "use value" typical of the individual-private economy. A thing acquires economic value for the person if it is both useful and limited — it is on the one hand desirable for the satisfactions it provides, and on the other achievable only with a certain sacrifice (cost) — to which the person will feel disposed to the extent that it is worth the trouble. With the intent of calculating this relationship, the intersection between the utility curve and the sacrifice curve is outlined: One will be willing to procure something until the sacrifice to acquire it is not greater than its utility. There is a point where the two curves meet, at which utility and sacrifice cancel each other out — at that point the subjective value of that thing becomes zero. But immediately above that zero point,

> there remains a fraction or unit of good relative to which the sacrifice (cost) to produce or obtain it leaves a minimum of net utility — that is, exceeding the sacrifice itself. So the appraisal made of this unit, placed at the border or margin of the decreasing series of higher units, before falling to the zero point of indifference receives the denomination of final or marginal value (or limit value) of the series itself.[16]

This is the well-known marginalist theory, according to which the margin of utility that still justifies a sacrifice is also the basic measure of the economic value of that specific reality. Having established this principle, Toniolo also applies it to exchange value, first analyzing the simple case of private exchange between two people, and then the complex cases in which the calculation of value occurs on a large scale and with many components in play. Exchange value,

> being nothing but an expression, in the vaster domain of the social economy, of use value, follows those subjective criteria of needs and sacrifices that are proper to this, such that no one exchanges a useful thing for a useless one, nor an unlimited and gratuitous thing for a limited and onerous one, and trade is carried out in that measure of exchanged wealth in which each of the contracting parties deems he will obtain a satisfaction that exceeds his sacrifice, and for that very reason, in the social economy exchange value participates in the law of use value, which by virtue of the expansion and contraction of need and of the concomitant subjective, physio-psychological facts leads in the private economy to the *limit value* (marginal, final), with all of the outcomes for the partial and total value.[17]

Society, trade, market

How does the simple exchange of goods between people become the organized exchange that gives life to a special profession, that of the merchant, and to a well-defined institution, that of the market, in its simplest and most complex expressions, up to the global market? Following Valenti, Toniolo applies what has been said about value-based exchange to the complexity of a developed society, in which

> each individual does not produce all the goods he needs, but only those that are more convenient to produce — that is, that offer him a greater utility of production — and these he produces even if they only satisfy the need of others, because he can exchange them for those that satisfy his own need. So that in this

> organic society, specialized in its economic offices, with respect to each individual object or good there is a series of producers distinct from consumers, and therefore soon a series of sellers distinct from buyers of the same good, which give rise to the phenomenon of trade.[18]

Having reached this level of division of labor and social complexity, trade occurs according to the law of supply and demand. In essence, the current or commercial exchange value is decided in the relationship between a series of goods that are supplied and demanded, with the facilitation of a third article, money, which has the characteristic of representing all the other goods, allowing the comparative appraisal of their value. The current value of a good, for the ends of trade, varies in direct proportion to demand and inversely to supply. The latter is a truly elementary principle in economics, understandable on the basis of our everyday experience: The seller who has many things to sell lowers the price, for fear of not selling them; the buyer who is interested in a good that he knows is limited unintentionally pushes the seller to raise the price. Hence the many fluctuations in market prices, until they reach a point of equilibrium.

Once again the "normal" and "commercial" laws of exchange value come into play. Ultimately, they practically coincide. But determining the normal law is important in order to understand the intrinsic logic of value starting from its components — that is, on the one hand, the value of production (the cost incurred and the related compensations demanded by the industrialist), and on the other the value of consumption (ultimately it is the consumers who justify production, to the point that if no one buys a product anymore, not only trade but production itself falls off). The market is thus the place of a sort of "debate" between producer and consumer, "behind the manifold impulse of individual interest and of regulative competition between producers and consumers, which trade broadens and intensifies in all of society."[19]

It should be noted that Toniolo is writing against the backdrop of a production crisis of more than thirty years: "Our powerful production structure throughout the continent does not find a proportionate absorption capacity on the part of consumers, leading to product prices that are exceptionally lower than costs and fair compensation."[20]

The discussion on normal exchange value obviously does not only concern national and continental markets, but also the global market. Let us underline, in the whole of Toniolo's analysis, one key element: The condition for this normal law to be realized is the freedom that allows true competition. And yet, no matter how great the desire to guarantee this, frictions and limitations that block its full expression must be reckoned with. This is a fact linked to the very nature of production, as well as to the different levels of social power of the classes involved. These problems have become topical today in the global market, where the dual face of competition clearly emerges. On the one hand, it forces prices to be kept low, to the advantage of everyone; on the other, this happens to the detriment of the human dimensions of work, especially for the weakest.

I don't deny that, reading these pages by Toniolo with the eyes of today's situation prone to savage competition, I would have expected a different warmth, up to the tenor of his pages and thoughts of strong social commitment. In this part of the *Trattato*, the language seems encrusted with the didactic-academic purpose, in which value judgments are expressed in a rather cold way and almost left to the conclusion of the reader. One could almost get the impression — and it would be a betrayal! — that here he makes his own the Smithian view of the market, against which he has spoken his entire life. Here his passion is bridled by the professorship. Thus, for example, he observes that unilateral competition between producers

> encounters natural barriers in that very specification of industries which is the condition presupposed for the development of trade, because professional groups form corresponding circles distinguished by technical-economic characteristics, so as to make difficult, sometimes impossible, the concurrent transfer of capital and men.[21]

A phenomenon whereby, if an industry is brought to its knees by the lack of consumption of its product, it will hardly be able to switch its instrumental capital over to other more attractive industries. An indisputable fact, against which very little can be done. But can a society turn a blind eye, in this case, to the suffering of the many people left unemployed? Here Toniolo is silent. A problem of resistance to free competition is also seen on the side of the workers:

> Will arms and minds long accustomed to and trained in the highly specialized metallurgical industries suddenly be able to offer themselves effectively to the cotton factories?[22]

This too is a truth: But would it be a good thing for workers to shift about like pawns, from industry to industry, without ever having a minimum guaranteed future?

Competition between consumers also has its impediments (I would say, good thing, too!):

> Do not the habits of an old clientele, the persistence of debts for ongoing purchases, the convenience of closer shopkeepers often lead to buying at prices higher than those of the common competition?[23]

As for the bilateral competition between producers on one side and consumers on the other, this is weakened (and here instead one should say, too bad!) by the fact that the producers are stronger on the organizational level. It would be desirable — and here the social Toniolo once again prevails over the detached economist — that consumers should organize themselves. There was need for this in Toniolo's time, and perhaps even greater need in our time, to make the voice of consumers really count in directing industrial decisions toward what is most productive of the common good and most respectful of common goods (the "voting with the pocketbook" advocated by the school of "civil economics"[24]). Toniolo, for his part, outlines the factual scenario, but also brings forth an alternative:

> By virtue of the organization of companies (industrial and mercantile), producers find themselves constituted in an organic

> whole that moves as a unit in the defense and promotion of its own interests, while consumers almost always live and operate apart, and so are powerless to act in concert and effectively on the market, and thus the balance of exchange, due to disproportionate mutual competition, rises mostly in favor of producers and to the detriment of consumers. Hence the contemporary question of the organization of consumers, two aspects of which are the buyers' league (*des acheteurs*) and the (consumer) cooperatives.[25]

These are scenarios that Toniolo outlines from the point of view of the laws of the market, perhaps indulging the influence — even though he stigmatized it all his life! — of the liberal-competitive vision of the market. I wonder if these posthumous pages with a scholastic flavor — a bit like his *Lezioni sulla distribuzione* of 1878 — would not also have been subjected to a sort of revision and integration if he had had the possibility of a final rereading for the purposes of publication. Fortunately, in the same volume of the *Opera Omnia* there are specific essays that have a more critical and passionate flavor on the side of social urgency.

The special case of monopoly

One last analytical look could not be left out of this chapter of the *Trattato*, and it is that which concerns monopoly. Here competition, on the side of producers and sellers in their mutual relationships, is practically eliminated. In some cases this is an inevitable process, belonging to the very nature of men and things — for example, in the case of natural goods that cannot be produced by man (one could think of pearls and diamonds), or of goods linked to the singular talents of men, like the paintings of a painter. Another case is deliberate monopoly, when goods in themselves producible without the limitations of special characteristics fall to the mercy of just one or a few through unions of producers and merchants (trusts). In these cases the normal law of exchange in a free-market regime cannot be realized. The competing interests of the same active categories of production and trade do not contribute to the formation of the price. The only factor that can act as a counterweight, and so force a "debate" that would regulate the price, is the behavior of consumers. In fact, they have some possibility of escaping the monopolistic imposition of prices, and therefore of controlling them, by taking alternative paths of consumption, driven by unacceptable prices to search for and multiply other similar or replacement products, substituting — to stick with the inevitably dated examples of Toniolo, following Valenti —

> artificial pearls for natural ones, copies or photographs or engravings for original oil canvases, chromolithography for hand-painted artistic miniatures, or turning to other satisfactions of needs that may be different but are less expensive, as for the friend of the arts replacing the purchase of paintings and statues with frequent artistic trips or attendance at theatrical performances: *twofold substitution, either technical or physio-psychological,* which contributes to diverting or attenuating the demand for and price of monopolized goods.[26]

Economic laws and universal order

So even the case of monopoly does not completely escape the law of "normal value," in which the fluctuations tend in any case to find a point of equilibrium. A consideration that pushes Toniolo to see the economic order of circulation within the universal order:

> Thus everything is aimed at the best implementation of the law of *normal value*, which is the central scientific law par excellence, regulating exchange in the whole of society, in perfect analogy with the order of the universe, in which every system of forces and relationships operating within it converges in general, regular, lasting behaviors and processes.[27]

Here, one would say, the contemplative Toniolo emerges. Even economic laws lie within a providential order. How could this be disputed? It is a fact, which, however, must be interpreted with a thousand "distinctions" that are not brought out sufficiently in these Toniolian pages. Thus, for this point of his *Trattato*, the somewhat disappointing impression remains that the contemplation of order is not sufficiently balanced by indignation over disorder — that is, insofar as in the economic order it occurs at the expense of concrete men and women who find themselves, through no fault of their own, in the category of the less fortunate. But we cannot stop at the Toniolo of these pages. What prevails is the complete Toniolo, the economist of passion and prophecy, beyond the formal and composed academic.

Chapter XVII
Commerce and Civilization

From psychology to sociology: The first factors

Here he is again, Toniolo! He doesn't take long to return to the stage, with his typical bearing, with a reflection dedicated to the "coefficients of circulation." If in the analysis of economic psychology (the appraisal of value) his thought scarcely differed from the "vulgate" of his time, now the professor returns to carve out his own niche of more specifically sociological contours, which allows him to frame the phenomenon in a constellation of coefficients that explain the vitality of trade or lack thereof, indeed its normalcy or lack thereof, in the various fields and contexts in which it takes place. It is no longer just the rational-psychological law of exchange value, of its universal nature, but everything that concretely influences this law.

The first factors of influence — true cornerstones of social being and living — are the same that govern all economic action, but they have specific expressions in the dynamics of exchange: man, territory, population.

Man first of all, with his needs and faculties. History shows how the development of trade is linked to the quality and quantity of needs:

If the needs for a complex of historical and local conditions con-

> tract, become habitual and unchanged, trade comes to a halt and remains for centuries at that level of development which suits traditional customs, as in the patriarchal economy and that of the Chinese races.[1]

One wonders, faced with this last example, what would Toniolo have said looking at today's China, which has reached the top levels of the world economy? History truly has its surprises. Irrefutable, however, is the principle that commerce flourishes with the growth of needs, to the point that advertising is entrusted with the task of tapping into them, and indeed of arousing them. A similar argument applies to the human faculties: If they are more or less developed, there will be more or less flourishing trade. As usual, Toniolo verifies this principle by taking as a working hypothesis a precise historical-theological vision, tending to clearly distinguish the cycle of pre-Christian civilization and that of Christian civilization.[2] An approach that offers a stimulating perspective on the relationship between ethical-religious principles and economics:

> Hence two major distinctions in the history of trade, which reflect the analogous distinctions of *pagan civilization*, which together with its trade, after manifold events, became rigid and immobilized in the Orient and disappeared in the Near East, in Greece and Rome, and of the ever-vital *Christian civilization*, which still today carries the banner of culture and trade from the Mediterranean and European peoples to the whole world.[3]

It is impossible not to take note, when reading observations like these, of how much water has flowed under the bridge (a century of theology, sociology, economics, and customs)!

The second factor is territory. The argument appeals to evident reasons: The characteristics of a territory can facilitate or not facilitate trade. For example, regarding marine environs, it is explained how

> that sea entirely enclosed by the three continents of Europe, Asia, and Africa, intertwining and assimilating in its currents the ac-

> tion of all the races and cultures of the world, that *Mediterranean Sea, "mediterranean"* par excellence, we repeat, in the midst of which Italy stretches out and which was called the lake of civilization, was able to gain and maintain primacy and almost monopoly in universal trade for the three ages of ancient, medieval, and part of modern history, not without, in the present time, foreshadowings of new destinies. And already now, beyond the oceans, two other Mediterraneans are being designated, the *Gulf of Mexico* between the Antilles and the American continents and the *Yellow Sea* between China, Japan, and the Sunda archipelago, where in the near future the major mercantile flows of the Atlantic and of Polynesia will perhaps converge through the Panama Canal.[4]

Hard to object. But how many new spaces have emerged — sometimes absorbing physical space — by virtue of that digital economy which Toniolo could not foresee, and which is increasingly our world? In the meantime he glimpsed, in the diverse continental history of trade, the "providential hand" that, while "it shaped the continents, also remotely marked in them the fate of civilization and trade together, born in Asia and then progressively propagated from Europe to the entire globe."[5] As for population, "it is clear that trade develops with the multiplication of populations."[6] The approach completely skips over the Malthusian theory. Toniolo had already criticized this in the aforementioned article of 1886, in which he had laid down the index of the *Trattato*:

> If it is true that the multiplication of the population on the one hand tends to reduce the share of individual apportionment and consumption, on the other hand it itself, with the denser human coexistence and the greater difficulties of life that accompany it, pushes the population to more energetic and skillful work, to more prudent capital savings and so to more copious production, and at the same time, with the improvement of the system of exchange instruments, it makes circulation more rapid and less costly, and the population itself is drawn to greater and more

> widespread emigration, while this whole process is examined and validated by the surer safeguards of science, of civil orders, of moral virtues, in a word of civilization, which as a rule increase and gain momentum amid the more intimate and varied relations of populous societies.[7]

The derived coefficients: The social and political constitution

On the basis of the primary facts — man, territory, population — the "derived coefficients" are developed.

> By this expression we mean those further social facts that, by tightening and multiplying the growing human bonds and relationships among those first elements, give rise to the constitution of society and the state, and also those predominantly spiritual products that, resulting from the accumulation and prolongation of the psychical and ethical energies and virtues of generations under the guidance of a higher cause, appear as continuous historical-social phenomena, such as the culture, the moral education, the civil life of nations, which wealth serves; upon which meanwhile those derived coefficients exert an influence by composing new environments and adding new impulses to commercial activity itself.[8]

As for the influence of the social constitution on trade, Toniolo distinguishes, with Durkheim, Schaube, and Huvelin,

> two *typical forms of the ordering of civil societies:* one simple, which can be defined as the unitary family (others say, unhappily, *segmentary*); the other complex, which can be called organic-hierarchical.[9]

We are at one of the key points of Toniolian sociology in its relationship with the economy and trade. The first ideal type is in turn embodied in two typologies, very different in their overall physiognomy but of similar inspiration: the one constituted by

> autonomous patriarchal societies, in which each family represented by its head makes up a distinct whole, alongside other autonomous and parallel families.[10]

The other takes the form of national political society,

> in which the social unit is absorbed by a supreme civil power, so that the immense number of families brought to the same level serves as a uniform pedestal to rise directly to that political center which represents the whole nation in all its functions (religious, juridical, political), as a great entity of common paternity.[11]

In this ideal type of society, the impact on trade is rather restraining. They are societies in which the "father is priest and kinglet,"[12] and personal freedom, spontaneous association, personal property are absorbed into the collective patriarchal or national unity. In both cases there is an effect of closure to the outside, also in the exchange of goods.

The second social type, the organic-hierarchical, is quite different. If the first is encountered in pagan civilizations, the second distinguishes Christian civilization. It comes about

> when on the roots of those same familial cells intermediate class organs are formed, being coordinated hierarchically at the top to compose the national constitution of the society as distinct from the state.[13]

Here society is formed from below, in terms of freedom and initiative. These societies

> prepare and foster the expansion of commercial relations between that variety of hierarchical organs and circles in the growing domestic market and then in the international, and so this constitu-

> tion of society becomes a positive coefficient of exchange, which progressively drives and expands it. This is the characteristic of European trade, which ultimately became global.[14]

Corresponding to the social constitution, one decisive coefficient is the political constitution. Depending on whether it is defined in more centralized and absolutist or more decentralized and liberal terms, the effects on trade are negative or positive:

> In monarchical and centralized political regimes, trade soon undergoes general regulationism, which levels, compresses, and crystallizes it in the name of the collective national interest; this is what marks economic legislation and policy in China at various times, in America under the dynasties of the Incas and the Montezumas, and back in Egypt, later reproduced by Diocletian in the Roman Empire, which copied that Oriental political pantheism. Instead, in democratic or in any case more or less decentralized political regimes, without escaping intermittent influences of pantheistic regulationism, for example in the Greek archipelago and Sparta, individual initiatives or those of autonomous classes still tend to assert themselves and prevail, causing the spontaneous genesis of a customary law, emerging from the very bosom of the mercantile classes.[15]

The role of culture

It is not hard to understand the impetus that commerce receives from the growth of culture in all its aspects. And this not only in reference to the greater awareness of the economic dynamisms that shift trade from empirical exercise to rational-scientific, but also in relation to culture in terms of geography, technology, finance. It is this cultural progress that enabled the transition from the long era of a natural economy to a commercial economy. The former,

> in which the consumer uses and exchanges, by preference in nature, what he himself produces, lasted until the municipal re-

> surgence in the Italic and Flemish cities, but did not disappear in Europe until after the sixteenth century. The latter starts in the modern era and continues up to our own day, subdivided into two successive periods according to the use of the means or instruments with which exchange is made, metallic money or endorsable credit securities; hence for Europe in general an economy of monetary exchange from 1500 to 1750, and then of fiduciary exchange, now predominant since the middle of the nineteenth century.[16]

Equally significant progress in trade occurred with the geographical discoveries, which allowed trade to become universal. Also important was the transformation from the class-based civil economy, represented by the merchants' guilds, to a national state economy, up to today's international economy. All made possible by the development of communication tools.

Ethics and the education of peoples

But the development of knowledge is not enough for the normal path of commerce. Also necessary is the safeguard afforded by moral and legal education, without which "economic utilitarianism, more than ever in these relationships, tends to deviate and ultimately destroy itself."[17] More than ever in commerce it is important that utility be wedded with the honest and the just:

> The concept of the useful, particularly in trade, is so permeated with that of the honest and the just that although it does indeed admit of a methodical distinction in science, it does not in the practice of life. In a transaction, is it the economic concept of the *equivalence* between two exchanged values or rather the ethical and legal principle of "to each his own" that prevails over the other? Or is it not, perhaps, the external material (economic) form of the moral norm, of lawfulness and of commutative justice?[18]

This is an illuminating consideration that makes the economic mechanism of trade, according to a valuation of the equivalence of goods, an expression of commutative justice. The Toniolo of the "ethical element as an intrinsic factor of economic laws" returns. And by the natural development of thought he joins the Toniolo of the "Christian economic school" in highlighting that, ultimately, the ethics that must be the point of reference is certainly the natural and universal, but reiterated and deepened by Christian revelation. A page that deserves to be reread in its entirety:

> Nothing more than commerce (this is a common historical observation) is inclined to fuel boundless individual greed with the unjust exploitation of social needs, which attracted the suspicions of philosophers and the curses of the common people in every age; hence the lesson that commerce abandoned to utilitarian instincts (without moral and juridical restraint) prepares its own suicide in the rapacious selfishness of personal and class interests, as among the mercantile capitalism of Carthage, the publicans of Rome, and the monopolizers of the modern trusts. Hence also the warning that this mercantile education, in order to become a true moderating coefficient of trade, must be both economic and ethical-juridical, thanks to that sense of social solidarity — that is, of coordination between individual and social interests, which is destined to compose the psychological environment entirely characteristic of commercial soundness.
>
> But then one understands how, amid such vehemence of mercantile selfishness, natural morality should appear more powerless than ever to maintain the solidarity that is thereby continually disturbed, and how this moderating authority should be found primarily in religion, the source of ethical and juridical dictates guaranteed by supernatural sanctions. And this is not only because in the sacred books of the great Eastern religions one encounters certain precepts of justice and fairness applied to trade, but is due to much more general and protracted influences. Indeed, depending on whether the cults, varying and succeeding one another throughout history, are informed by religions of the domestic type (familial) and at the most national (racial), or are

> inspired by the concept of universality, they become an obstacle or an impulse to trade, educating the peoples in economic habits of internal life or vice versa of external expansion. In fact, due to these influences of the religious coefficient on trade, two immense cycles in history are definitively designated: of populations closed to mercantile vocations, whose center of economic activity falls within, and of populations open to the relationships and impulses of trade, whose center progressively gravitates outward, extending to the horizons of the globe. As its final tendency, the former was the case with the pagan peoples; the latter became and is characteristic only of the Christian nations, and trade followed the respective vicissitudes.[19]

Commerce between war and peace

For centuries trade found itself compressed and sacrificed by the "absorbing *political-military* function of the governments themselves."[20]

> The dual spirit, either *conqueror* with arms or vice versa *ruler* with legal sanctions in the life of states, becomes an alternately negative or positive coefficient that profoundly determines the emergence and development of commercial relationships.[21]

Trade, in other words, needs peace: "Regular and advancing commerce presupposes peaceful relations protected by law at home and abroad."[22] Also in this aspect, Toniolo observes, the positive influence of Christianity is visible:

> It was necessary that *peace* be promised to *all men of good will*, that is, governed everywhere by the same divine morality, and that analogously the law, the child of this, should become the responsibility not of the citizen alone, but of all humanity inside and outside of the individual states, so that trade, by its universal nature, should seek protection and help not in the *ius civile* (of citizens) but as was said in the *ius gentium* (of all humanity), thus developing, thanks to popular customs, an autonomous

> body of commercial laws in favor of trade; a slow and hindered work, deferring its development. But in the meantime it remains established that the juridical-political concepts and orientations of the state form a decisive coefficient for the fate of commerce.[23]

Toniolo laments, in this regard, that Christianity's influence on trade has not been well appreciated by economists and jurists. Apart from the question of individual theories of the Church and of canon law — the reference is clearly to the issues of usury — in which prejudices were imposed that should have fallen by now after the studies of Ashley and Brants, in order to lay down a good foundation for judgment it is necessary to look at the merits that Catholicism acquired "in preparing that social order of civilization in the midst of which commerce was to arise and then be perpetuated."[24] And on these general merits the *Trattato* offers another significant page here:

> With the doctrine of the dignity of every man, called to sublime supernatural destinies and to corresponding functions down here, on the basis of freedom and responsibility, it educated all without distinction in that energy of individual initiatives in common competition which is the life of commerce.
>
> When, repeating the divine word of the first origins, which "invested man with sovereignty over the world" and commanded all human generations to "grow, multiply, and fill the earth," removing the obstacles to this common domination and expansion posed by the inequalities of social conditions, religion, race, proclaiming "that there is no longer Gentile or Jew, barbarian or Scythian, slave or free," it opened the globe to the bold and tenacious explorations of the future, prepared ever new markets for the growing and migrating populations, and among them all it cast the net of universal trade.
>
> With the doctrine of dutiful and sanctified work and of temperate and parsimonious customs it established the two balanced fundamental cycles of production and consumption between which the function of commerce would interpose itself,

> to which it then assured indefinite prosperity, subjecting it to the law of strict commutative justice, enlivened by diffusive charity.
>
> And when the right proceeded remotely not indeed from inexorable public needs, nor from concessions of princes, nor from the power of conquests, as a privilege of the few in contrast with the subjugation of the many, but from a divine moral law that reigns over all men and so brings it forth proximately from the original quality of man and not of citizen, thus associating it with individuals, with classes, with society, with countrymen, with foreigners, with all states, themselves equated in their independent juridical personality, it predisposed with its long arm that indefinite breadth of national and international relations, protected by laws, which indispensably fuels trade and for which it became a minister of peace and progress among all peoples.[25]

The chapter could conclude with this inspiring (if somewhat idealistic) definition of trade as a "minister of peace and progress."

But Toniolo doesn't stop there. It is necessary to at least mention his intense last remarks, in which he draws on the support of economists like Marshall, sociologists like Kidd, historians like Janssen, Taine, Macaulay, writers on international law like Olivi (against Bluntschli),[26] noting — it seems important to me to underline this — that his claim in favor of Christianity is not intended to deny "that other previous forms of civilization under pagan influences" also intuited and "to some extent translated into action some of these concepts and institutions."[27] But, he adds, there is no comparison between the two scenarios. In Christianity

> commerce, not compressed or artificial, is progressively intertwined and consolidated with the developments of a general economy, typical of cultured and progressive peoples, and taking its lead from free individual energies, supported by multiform flexible and powerful associations, it subsequently expands to connect families, classes, nations, humanity, pervading the entire social organism. Here, amid the resurgent aggressions of mercantile selfishness, the utilitarianism prosecuted by the public

conscience definitively yields to the moral imperatives of commutative justice and of the general good, which regulate trade and its monetary instruments, and indeed of the psychological fact of trust, nourished by growing guarantees of honor, and commerce becomes a support for more daring impulses of circulation on credit. Here, not indeed through state regulationism but through the spontaneity of popular customs and habits inspiring written laws, detaching itself from civil jurisprudence, an autonomous commercial law is constituted, which sets free the accelerated course of mercantile transactions and then reverberates in civil law itself.

There is nothing in the setting of pagan civilization that can match the characteristic attitudes of commerce in the civilization that has come down to us. And if in it there were moments of a profound decline of trade, or if today we are pressed by anxious worries about its future, the main reason lies in the partial deviations by the peoples from this Christian civilization, from whose bosom alone commerce derives the virtue of perennial vitality.[28]

Chapter XVIII
Historical-Geographical Development of Commerce

The historical landscape

After having focused, in the exchange of wealth, on the "hedonic law" (minimum effort for maximum result), starting from the first facts and the coefficients, the *Trattato* opens two chapters, as concise as they are erudite, on the development of commerce in the historical-geographical landscape. "The rational genesis, which for methodological expediency portrays the first or general laws of trade solely on the basis of the abstract utilitarian motives of *homo oeconomicus,* must now be followed by the positive search for those secondary laws that reveal themselves through the subsequent social events in history."[1]

At the origins

Taking his lead from archaeology,[2] Toniolo observes that many clues lead one to think of trade as an original propensity of the human being, certainly under the utilitarian impulse, but also "under the warmth of *sympathy* — that is, of moral sentiments between men,"[3] fruit of the ethical-religious law that God has impressed upon reason. The other side of the coin does not escape our author — that is, the human *antipathies* expressed in wars, pillaging, and conquests:

> But it is to be observed that *rapacious violence* against the property of others *is not an intrinsic origin* or *generating cause* of trade, which normally consists of consensual and peaceful relationships in society; rather, it is the negation of it at the root.[4]

Examining the development of trade, the first look naturally goes to the family, which

> implements a system of internal economy (direct or private) in which all members produce in order to consume; this nonetheless prepares the way for the external economy (indirect or social), and this thanks to *the division and exchange of services in the household,* in which economists recognize the seed of the *exchange of goods in society,* which tomorrow will mark the transition to the social economy.[5]

This is followed by a focus on patriarchal families, in which exchange is limited within the perimeter of the family itself, with the phenomenon of hospitable exchange on behalf of the stranger. The case is different with the locality, in which the phenomenon of exchange takes place in the form of an interfamilial market. Added to these first two circles of exchange is that of the tribe, the seed of the political society or state. In summary,

> trade is aimed at and takes place primarily within the framework of institutions (the family, local associations, the state) of a substantially ethical-civil character, in which economic benefits are superseded by the higher ends and needs of preservation and procreation, honest custom, legal defense, and therefore by the similar sentiments of domestic affection, social solidarity, civil heroism, or the different concepts of personal, collective, political law, and which in order to protect all those final human goods can sometimes foster utilitarian motives and exchange,

> sometimes limit and sacrifice them.[6]

In all of this, peeping out once again is religion:

> Where the monotheism of a personal God looms large over all human beings, faith in the common *divine paternity* also entails that of equal *human fraternity*, and then custom, law, politics, arising from that supreme source, are inspired by concepts of *universality,* so that the patriarchal family first and later the *gens,* the tribe, the state tend to open up in varying degrees to relationships of general trade. Where, on the other hand, religion becomes fragmented and shrunken with polytheism in the cult of ancestors, heroes, national myths, in turn the authority and efficacy of ethical norms, juridical faculties, and political action are restricted to those participating in the domestic, aristocratic, political group, and then the family, the territorial associations, the tribe, the states tend to close in on themselves, and so to cut off outside trade. Indeed, a similar thing happens under the different religious influences of the *faculty of exchange* within the state. If darkness falls on the concept of a God as *the first source of the moral and juridical law,* whence *positive* human laws descend, gradually the *immediate author and arbiter* of those positive norms (*ius civile*) is seen in the state, since in the presumed fullness of its powers the one who represents it is also ascribed the faculty of *creating and revoking every right* (independently of that supreme source), and *of conferring and taking it away from others at his whim*. And then in the *ius civile* or domestic law there is an inclination to recognize private rights themselves (based on human nature) only in those who participate in public government with the title of *citizens*, and similarly the right of commerce also remains a privilege of some classes within the state itself. And if on the contrary religion instills the conviction that private personal rights have their immediate and inalienable source in the one who shaped human nature, the *ius commercii* also tends to be associated with the totality of the members of

> the state itself.[7]

Development over time

First on the stage appear the peoples in the state of nature (*Naturvölker*), in which trade long remains linked to collective exchange or barter. There follow the "semi-civilized peoples," among which — surprisingly, with respect to our current perspective — Toniolo places Egypt, India, China: "populations that, despite having grown to certain even elevated degrees of spiritual life and therefore of civilization, were not able to continue in this, either because their civilization became corrupted and disappeared or because it stopped at half height."[8] The tendency of these civilizations is the transition from aristocratic social groups to "*powerful and complex states* with century-spanning monarchies, in whose unlimited centralizing sovereignty came the *pantheistic* blending of religious authority and political powers, withstanding until the fatal hour of protracted dissolution or inert fossilization."[9] In this configuration, trade finds itself in the grip of a "vigilant regulationism of caste, administrative bureaucracy, or central government."[10] It is certainly to be recognized that this unity obviously also produces great advantages and results on the economic level:

> But as those ethical-religious ideals gradually degenerate into the sensualism of the Egyptians, into the Buddhist nirvana, into the skeptical-utilitarian rationalism of Confucius, with the analogous perversion of the powerful social and political orders that they generate in a selfish traditionalism of class, of race, of vaunted culture, assimilated with the state, trade tends to *halt inside* in rigid immobility and *to close itself to outside relationships* in a growing aversion toward the foreigner (xenophobia). It is historically certain that the populations and governments of those very ancient states long welcomed foreigners within themselves to trade, and that they had historical moments of external expansion, not only religious, demographic, political-military, but also to some extent mercantile (China itself toward India and Malaysia), while *xenophobia* prevailed in later times. But on the

> other hand the *final exhaustion of civilization* is evident, which is not total inanition but atrophy and anemia, of which those races and their institutions still today present a miserable spectacle, having indeed survived but powerless to progress, until they are overwhelmed, like Japan, by the living wave of Western Christian civilization. These are the definitive events and fates of trade in what are called the semi-civilized peoples.[11]

A diagnosis, that of the backward economy of Oriental civilizations, that today stimulates at least a discussion, in the face of the surprising development of the economy of those civilizations in recent decades. Toniolo's thesis, with the example of Japan, would suggest that the capacity for development that they have demonstrated in recent times, as an innovation in their age-old history, would be explained by their openness to Western culture, historically shaped by Christianity. There's enough there for a debate.[12]

It is then the turn of the peoples of "normal civilization"; a connotation that Toniolo reserves for that civilization characterized by "perenniality and universality of progress," which marks true civilization. The obligatory reference is to Christian civilization. Normally, as we know, Toniolo presents this in total opposition to pagan civilization. In this case what prevails instead — and it is a modulation of no small importance, also in terms of a broader theological rereading of the history of humanity[13] — is a perspective that we would call evolutionary, with a period of preparation among the populations of the Near East and then of Greece and Rome, and a

> period of implementation in the new Christian civilization, subsequently spread to all peoples. Two periods connected to each other, because that first culture, although defunct, passed on to the second a few sound proximate traditions, which it, with its original virtues, was able to re-fertilize and perpetuate until today.[14]

In the field of trade, the first move of this progressive path must be situated in the Near East, in which the Jewish people from Chaldea stand out. A people in which the light of revelation ensures an ethical inspiration that is on the whole favorable to universal trade.[15] On the other peoples of the classical Orient (Chaldeans, Babylonians, Phoenicians), Toniolo's judgment is ultimately severe:

> At the end of the fatal historical course of dazzling prosperity for these races (mostly Semitic and Cushite), turned to inexorable decadence due to utilitarianism and corruption (through which Babylon, Sodom, Gomorrah, Carthage itself remained in abomination), *there is a glimpse of the rise to definitive preponderance of the Aryan races* in the Near East.[16]

He then recalls, among the Persians, the epics of Cyrus, Darius, etc., to move on to Greece and Rome, arriving at Christian civilization:

> For this reason, the scepter of trade did not leave the hands of the *Japhetic* (Aryan) race, representative of indefinite progress. The populations of the Near East, finally assimilated by the genius of the spent and dying *Persian Aryans*, nonetheless passed on to the upstart, raw, warlike *Pelasgian Aryans,* who in the meantime with millennary marches had transmigrated from the Near East itself via the Caspian to the European continent and the Mediterranean lake; they passed on, we repeat, admonitory examples that lasting and fruitful trade has its roots in spontaneous energies, in the awareness of social solidarity, in state provisions of public order. These Oriental traditions, re-fertilized by the ideal expansive genius of the Hellenes and by that of the *imperium* of the Latins, prepared the way for the universality of commercial relationships themselves in Christian civilization.[17]

Greek law was the first "to trace out the concept of juridical-economic relations based on universal reason."[18] From this is born an expansion of commercial culture. Roman law gave a similar welcome, but with a deep-seated resistance toward a truly universal conception based on the transcendent reference to the one God. Even when there was openness to the concession of the right to trade, this was always understood as a right of *freemen of the empire,* not of men as such:

> Indeed, there always endured in the emperors, as in the broader sentiment, the original prejudice that *public law* (*ius suffragii, ius honorum*) was indeed not only the guarantee of private law (*ius connubii, ius commercii,* which included every economic faculty), but the *source of private law,* so that in the later imperial age it ended up perverting and compromising all the personal and patrimonial rights of citizens, by virtue of the predominance (with Diocletian) of an Oriental pantheism of the state, which deifies the all-powerful whim of the prince even in private laws: Whatever pleases the prince has the force of law.[19]

The effects on trade were disastrous:

> Commercial exchange, therefore, in the period of the broadest and most intense circulation, is centered on the worst form of exploitative capitalism, later slows down amid bureaucratic shackles, and finally tends inexorably to exhaust itself. Because the commerce of the long imperial age was always *passive,* that is, consisting of an immense importation of all kinds of foodstuffs, manufactured goods, sumptuary and precious objects, which from the countries around the Mediterranean, from Africa, from the Orient, from all continents, descended upon Italy, and especially Rome, *without a return of proportionate exports.* So the corpulent and voracious city, consumer of the products of the whole world, found itself gradually despoiled through paying out the coin it had usurped in the conquests, accumulated in the thrifty days, and in the long run found itself forced to interrupt universal trade. With monetary capital and movable wealth largely gone, the few proprietors of the soil in whose hands landed wealth was concentrated returned to the enjoyment for themselves and for their numerous dependents and slaves of the products of the earth and of the domestic industries on their enormous holdings. After the division of the empire,

> first the western part and later (despite Constantine's transfer of the capital to Byzantium in AD 330, for political and commercial ends) also the eastern part inexorably retreated to the *economy of nature.*[20]

The Christian cycle

On the basis of the evangelical conception of the world and of life, a progressive and radical movement of conversion of culture and society begins, which also has a positive effect on commerce. There are various signs of confirmation of this broad process. The conditions for a new commercial impetus are gradually being prepared. But there was no lack of internal obstacles. The time of flowering was the age of the municipality.

> The weakness of the Carolingian successors, opening the way in Europe for the fragmentation of political sovereignty and with it for the spread of the isolated and organized violence of feudalism (between the ninth and eleventh centuries), left more than ever on the shoulders of the Church the urgent and definitive *resumption of social reconstitution*. It brought this about *by restraining the strong and supporting the weak*, for this purpose *relying on the people* with three historical means, which definitively redounded to great profit for trade.[21]

The three means to which Toniolo refers here are the Truce of God, with which the Church called for peace, that is, the temporary and finally lasting suspension of private wars; pilgrimages, which were an important factor of openness and knowledge that also facilitated commercial relations; and finally the Crusades, with which the Church, while reiterating among the sacrifices of the undertaking *the duty and solidarity* of the "peace of God" among all Christian nations,

> poured out kings, emperors, feudal lords, and populations in masses, almost an immense "armed pilgrimage" from the entire European West to the Mediterranean beaches of the Asian Orient, to defend in the name of religion the new "society or repub-

> lic of Christian peoples" against the enemies of the Cross and civilization, the Muslims.[22]

It would be completely anachronistic to react to these last words with our sensibility shaped by Vatican II. Toniolo's words are in tune with the theology of Vatican I and with the Leonine cultural climate. Besides, the point of view is not that of a moral evaluation of the Crusades, but rather of their effects on trade:

> The unexpected and immense result, among the greatest events in history, was the *resumption of trade between several continents of the world*, in a round of mercantile relations that expanded well beyond the borders of the ancient Roman Empire to the Indies and China. The Crusades thus mark the completion of the evolution of trade, which from familial, aristocratic, local, now becomes *intercontinental* again, and from now on it will never lose this vocation and character (whatever its circumstances).[23]

This is not just a matter of favorable events. These were also accompanied by theological and canonical development, translated into a series of general legal norms more suited to Christian society also in relation to trade. In particular, canon law contributed to the development of commercial exchange in three ways: with the concept of positive law, with the general notions of the economic order, and with the doctrine of the just price. On the first level, by placing positive law in a subordinate relationship to divine law, a liberating conception of human beings developed, whereby "trade itself was forever legitimized as *a right of nature* in the name of the moral equality of men, which the state must sanction for the general good."[24] Another result of this was a correct conception of peace, understood as "the tranquility of order" — that is, "the security of all under the common observance of the ethical and juridical law together."[25] As for the economy, the entire natural order of wealth was placed under the protection of the useful and the just, and not only the useful, giving work spiritual value as well and disciplining the consumption of wealth with adequate distribution, looking not only to the individual but also to the social good. In this context, for the ends of trade, one significant debate was that on the just price, the elements of which were developed starting from the equivalence between goods, and so in terms of commutative justice, within the framework of a broader justice,

> up to this point the strict rule of *justice in trade,* of what is called *commutative justice*, between equal and equal. Except that this, in the concept of those theologians and canonists, needed in turn to be subordinated to *distributive justice*, concerning the relationships between upper and lower classes, not violating the proportional interests of each and above all not exploiting the weaker multitudes with prices, as well as respecting *legal or general justice,* not damaging the entire society and the state with monopolies or hoarding.[26]

These are a few highlights with respect to the detailed Toniolian pages. His final thesis can be found in the following statement: "Trade did not reach its essential theoretical conception and practical efficacy except in Christian civilization."[27]

Space and providence

One could not speak of the variables of trade if one did not take into account not only time and history, but also space and its geographical determinations:

> God (W. Roscher wrote) prepares the territories for the peoples with his own hand and then leads them there. This truth concerns not only economic sociology or production or consumption, as is admitted by most, but also the *economics of trade.* Because geographical space is not just the continuity of mathematical points on the surface of our earth, but results from a system of immense accumulations of matter, forces, and cosmic influences variously intertwined with each other and situated with respect to place, which the Creator, through indefinite geological eras, prepared, deposited, and arranged on the earth's

> crust, so that all of humanity might find, through its own activity, the conditions of its own existence and well-being throughout the ages of civilization.[28]

All of this with a clear influence on trade. With an abundance of data, Toniolo extends his gaze to universal geography, moving from China to Russia, from Egypt to India, from Brazil to England:

> And so, after recalling man's everlasting attraction to the natural products that the beneficent hand of God has spread over the globe, such that it has been written that in history salt itself played a greater role than gold in establishing regular trade relationships between distant regions (Brunhes), it must be concluded that such geographical-economic investigations fall within the scientific study of causes that is necessary to illustrate the development of trade. Still today the intuition of free competition and the calculations of colonial imperialism converge on this: to discover and occupy in advance the points on the globe marked out by nature around which the patterns of future trade will revolve. And what a disaster to get it wrong![29]

Applying the organic concept in some way to the physical world, too, Toniolo sees in the distinct territorial units an "organic constitution" of the entire surface of the globe.[30] The consequences develop one after the other: "Those distinct telluric and economic-productive units form the basis and outer shell of as many distinct autonomous markets, within which certain typical differences of trade are accentuated by virtue of the predominance in each of its own specific groups of goods."[31] The directions of the respective flows of trade are also delineated in space, based in part on location variables and mutual distance.

To this material element must be added the anthropic and demographic element. There are privileged regions, like the Near East, whose heart is Mesopotamia. According to a view largely taken from the biblical story, or in any case in keeping with it, here

> the first Noahide populations (after the flood) originated and soon multiplied, then divided into the first fundamental lineages, and finally dispersed with a thousand branches and ethnic derivations throughout the world. And from Mesopotamia these very ancient offspring brought with them everywhere the manifold traces (physical, mental, linguistic) and the primitive memories of this Near East, which was witness to divine revelation, the cradle of the historical positive religions, the seat of the greatest empires, the hearth of the most splendid Oriental civilizations.[32]

Also geographically, this region was destined to become a land of transition. "The true *vagina generis humani,* the Near East was thus able to disseminate humanity across all the continents through the millennary events of successive transmigrations in search and conquest of those natural telluric units … destined to become territories of industrious settlement and the autonomous market of distinct peoples and states, between which trade relations would then continue."[33]

We won't follow Toniolo's presentation in its further analyses of the dynamics that presided over this diffusion of humanity, also in terms of the circulation of wealth. There were different demands, from the fundamental needs to the enhancement of personal health or safety to religious passions and racial oppositions in terms of conquest, not without internal psychological coefficients (dreams, hopes, wishes, sense of man's sovereignty over the earth). And all of this within the different guidelines of relocation drawn by natural conditions over land or sea routes, with modes of relocation that depend on the possibilities offered by the use of animals or other means of transport that are progressively developed, until the realization of the "lasting and industrious settlement of populations in their own territory, stably connecting man to the soil with public utility, material interests, and affections,"[34] giving rise to the homeland, nationalities, states. Hence rural and urban markets, national and international markets. The analysis proceeds in detail with the contemplation of a grandiose and manifold phenomenon that builds the long history of *incivilimento* and civilization. One fundamental thesis that Toniolo develops and with which he concludes his discussion: There have been many civilizations in history that have had long periods of blossoming, only to then regress to the point of "complete reversion to the economy of nature."[35] The truly new fact is the commercial cycle of Christian civilization,

> which is distinguished by the resumption of a *cycle of trade* that is no longer moribund, but *indefinitely progressive* in space and time. And this by virtue of the predominance that *spiritual factors* gradually acquired also in trade and commerce — that is, free personal initiatives, the widespread habit of work, contractual honesty and justice, individual and collective responsibility, the awareness of the common good — above the *purely natural and extrinsic* coefficients.[36]

Reading, a century later, this thesis, the backbone of Toniolo's thought, according to which the great world of Christian civilization — practically coinciding with European-American civilization — cannot help but bring up questions, especially if one considers the condition of crisis in which Christianity finds itself precisely in Europe, glaringly ever more distant from its Christian roots, in a world in which the prevailing religion seems to be precisely the materialistic one of economic-technological progress. Toniolo might respond to such a consideration by recalling the element of human subjectivity, called to a responsible dialogue with Providence, with all the risks of freedom, which can also produce long regressive cycles in Christian civilization, which the historical path will somehow bring back to positive phases of conversion and resurrection.[37] But here we are in the perspective of faith and prophecy, and no longer in that of the factual and predictive principles of social economics.

Chapter XIX
From Monetary Economy to Credit Economy

Money

The treatise on circulation concludes with the theme of money. The text is clearly incomplete. It is missing a conclusion. It is missing a summary. The editors of the *Opera Omnia* have filled the gap by adding a series of contributions by Toniolo on credit.

Presenting, as usual, a broad historical account, Toniolo explains how money is brought in to solve the practical problems of a trade economy based on the exchange or barter of goods for goods. The difficulty of measuring the comparative value of the different goods to be exchanged prompts the desire for a good that can be used not only for its value in itself, but also as a good representative of other goods, and therefore suitable for measuring their value:

> Such is metallic money, especially precious metals (gold, silver), which obviates the difficulties of any exchange between goods in nature, dividing the exchange into two successive operations between distinct contracting persons and making money serve as

> the common instrument of the same two operations. One who is hindered or blocked in his need and intention to give up a horse to his neighbor in order to get some sheep first exchanges the horse for a sum of money, and later gives up a part of these coins to get some sheep, in any circle of people and places where the money is recognized and accepted as an intermediary of exchange. Thus the creation of this instrument of circulation became of general interest, and barter exchange was turned into monetary exchange.[1]

Having illustrated the genesis of money, Toniolo explains, in the classic textbook manner, its function, which

> in its complete cycle is threefold: to quantitatively measure the value of all goods in the same way as a common unit of appraisal (of the value itself); to concretely represent the value of specific goods with a corresponding sum of a generic good exchangeable par excellence, and therefore to be passed physically from person to person; to lend itself to the preservation, accumulation, and lasting purpose of all wealth.[2]

It was not easy, in the history of human development, to discover what good could perform this function. It had to be a good equipped with its own economic worth, containing great value in a small volume for convenience of transportation, in its physical properties homogeneous, unalterable, divisible, suitable for minting, and finally for natural and historical reasons endowed with a certain rarity. After different experiences in various cultures, the general inclination went to metals, and in particular to precious ones like gold and silver.

Monetary economy

A decisive moment in the history of economic exchange was the accumulation of money, which thus becomes a powerful wealth of production, a capital:

> This is an innovatory fact, by which the accumulated gold and silver, in addition to acting as a means of purchasing final goods, rises to the function of a means of forming instrumental productive goods, represented potentially by a particular metallurgical mass destined for this purpose, which in this case takes on the title and importance no longer of money but of "monetary capital," and this in turn would become an opportunity and stimulus for particular and varied forms of exchange, which would intensify and extend circulation.[3]

Thus a dynamic is born in which money is not only a neutral translation of the value of the goods exchanged, but itself has a value that, as for all goods, varies based on utility and rarity. Therefore "the variations in the dual value of merchandise and money are reflected in price, so that, taking money as the term of comparison (estimative module), the variations in the price of each individual good appear in an inverse ratio to the value of the money itself."[4] If the value (and so the purchasing capacity) of money increases, the price of a good that can be purchased with it decreases. Conversely, if the value of money decreases, the price of goods rises. An elementary reasoning, within the reach of every good homemaker. A similar dynamism applies when money as a metallic stock is replaced with "fiduciary symbols," "which, being grafted onto the metallic stock and making up for its incidental deficiencies, help to raise the top and virtually expand the volume of the monetary pyramid, adding ease and balance."[5]

The *Trattato* closes with these basic notions, enriched with a historical survey that we will skip. Fortunately, various writings by Toniolo tell us something more, and we will draw from them to explore the problem of credit, which is now at the heart of the economy, but also at the center of our author's interests.

Agricultural banks and credit unions

In fact, the very first title of Toniolo's scientific bibliography from 1871 concerns the banking world. The approach is social: In developing, as a function of agriculture, his interest in popular credit,[6] drawing above all from the teachings of Luzzatti, Toniolo insists on the necessity that the agricultural world be guaranteed, no less than the manufacturing industries, the possibility of access to credit, in order to increase those possibilities of capital that are instrumental to the development of agriculture in a modern and competitive sense. A few years later, in 1879, he would revisit credit unions[7] with a proposal to integrate ordinary banking functions with a charitable function to be structured in a way suited to the logic of banking, but in terms still useful for reviving the fortunes of the poorest, to keep, for example, a poor farmer unable to easily resort to a "Mount of Piety" from ending up in the hands of a usurer.[8] The desired aid instrument was a system of "vouchers" with which the bank advances the costs of a product to the farmer, with the commitment that he repay the sum in "small, long-term" installments, without interest but with a percentage compensation (5-6%) in terms of savings — that is, buying a bank share:

> Once he has become *a shareholder,* he may possibly make further applications to the bank, but under the ordinary conditions of the statutes and on a par with all other members. Thus the loan made for needs of personal consumption, which is usually a steep slope leading to servitude and ruin, through intelligent charity becomes an opportunity for the exercise of foresight and a means of regeneration. It is the charity that lifts the fallen and enables him to proceed further on his own.[9]

In short, we are in the logic of aid that tends not only to help, but to promote: a generative support.

The problem of credit

So with an interest developed since his first forays as an economist, Toniolo was convinced that the credit economy, which historically follows the monetary economy, was in itself a form of progress. But under precise conditions. He would have the opportunity to return to the topic in 1884 in relation to a book on credit by Fedele Lampertico.[10] His quintessential treatment of this phenomenon would however take place, as we mentioned before,[11] at the Second Congress of the Catholic Union for Social Studies, held in Padua August 26–28, 1896.[12] According to his assessment,

> the question of credit represents the apex of *modern economics*, in its doctrines as in its applications. And indeed all classical economists, distinguishing three successive eras of historical development — the *natural*, the *monetary*, and the *credit economy* — recognize in the latter the highest system of economic relations, which, based on trust in the facilitation of capital, imparts to all the wealth of the peoples vigor, refinement, and marvelous expansion, and enumerating its indefinite *benefits* all discourse of the almost magical, abounding power of credit.[13]

He recalls that, on the contrary, others see the credit economy — identified as capitalism — as a vicious system:

> Thus the question of credit, amid the clash of opposing currents, amid the still enduring triumphal echo of an optimistic liberal economics and the gloomy predictions of a pessimistic sociological economics, aggravated by the vehement protests of the doctrinaire socialists who intone the avenging hymn of destruction, grows to giant stature before the intellects of thinkers and the awareness of the peoples, and the solution to the *problem of credit* indeed constitutes the great expectation of the future.[14]

From antiquity to the Middle Ages

According to the dichotomous scheme dear to him, starting from the classical-pagan economy, Toniolo sees Babylon, Carthage, Greece, Rome "crushed under the weight of usurious capitalism."[15] Christianity produces a radical turning point by condemning all usury — that is, "every intrinsic fruit of capital on loan."[16] A position that, in the modern age, will seem excessive to many, but in reality concealed a profound truth, as many of Toniolo's time recognized, and not only among the socialists from Proudhon to Rodbertus to Karl Marx. The *Wucherfrage,* the question of usury, by this time registered a spirited literature. And there was reason for it. With the breaking of that medieval dam of the firm condemnation of usury,

> the *capitalism* that from Reformation-era Germany establishes itself as in an incubation center in Holland, passes into England under William of Orange and the Puritans, and triumphs in France in the early stages of the revolution, in our day pervades all of Europe and America with sordid usury at the bottom, with the centralization of banking legalized at the top, with the dishonest speculations of anonymous companies, with the bloating of public debt, with the colossal games and cracks of the financial exchanges, with unbridled and violent competition, with the gigantic monopolies of the American corners and trusts, with the overpowering monopolies of the contemporary barons of finance.[17]

The facts are matched by the theories, all the way to the open defense of usury as a fundamental canon of classical economics. Hence "the social crisis, of which credit with its abuses is perhaps the greatest economic factor."[18]

In 1745, with *Vix Pervenit,* Benedict XIV had reiterated the traditional doctrine, condemning any profit for reasons intrinsically linked to the lending of capital. But he had left open the prospect of compensation for the capitalist for extrinsic reasons. In this space of possibility, the topic is also debated among Catholics, with a range of positions from rigorism to possibilism.[19] It is time, Toniolo hopes, for the "Paduan" congress of Catholic scholars to make some kind of synthesis. To this end he offers a few criteria for discussion.

First of all, he explains the logic of the Church's doctrine on lending, clarifying that it was not a slavish repetition of the Aristotelian thesis of the sterility of money, but rather was articulated in a constellation of attitudes, both negative and positive. Negatively, together with the ban on the usurious loan, mercantile speculation was curbed and monopoly combated, especially of the money supply. Positively, some interest on loans accompanied by extrinsic titles was admitted, promoting the direct alliance of capital with industry (limited partnerships, land taxes), and all of these social relations or institutions concerning credit (like public lending or the "Mounts of Piety") were assured the character of service to public social utility:

> There arose as if by magic an economic order in which the ruler was *human person*, with his work the true author of wealth; *capital* was made his minister and subject, and by blunting among the jealous possessors of money the keen incitements to sudden wealth snatched up by fortune and extortion, the law of justice among individuals and of social charity among all was made to prevail.[20]

The "rapacious usury" of modernity

The scenario changes with the modern era. The colors are somber:

> Today it is absolutely the opposite. After four centuries of *cultured* rebellion against those principles of economic and civil wisdom we find established in our midst and towering over us a *credit economy* in which: (a) the usurious loan is the hinge of all economic relationships; (b) through it capital dominates and subjugates the hardworking and enterprising *person;* (c) speculation and monopoly threaten and engulf universal interests in favor of a powerful few. Thus one understands in all its greatness the task incumbent on Catholics when … Leo XIII, in the encyclical *Rerum Novarum*, urged them to direct their industrious care to the "*rapacious usury*" that reproduces itself in new and monstrous forms, and thus one interprets with fullness of truth the instinctive sentiment of the populations that, amid so many disillusionments and collapses of the banks and financial markets, today turn their silent and trusting gaze to the Catholics.
>
> In fact, teacher and faithful ask that a *capitalist economy* epitomized by the lending of capital to the enterpriser be replaced with a *human economy* par excellence, so that capital may

> become a follower and ally of the industrious *person.*[21]

It is a text that we have cited several times, given its encapsulatory and strategic importance in Toniolo's thought. On the basis of these premises he develops his theses on credit, explaining its concept and function, outlining its legal discipline, and, finally, considering its concomitant conditions of efficacy. An organic discussion that fits in well as a supplement to the *Trattato*, which remained unfinished.

Concept and function of credit

Starting from the meaning of the word credit — that is, trust — a *credit transaction* means "that act whereby, on the basis of trust in the honesty and solvency of others, capital is transferred to others in such a way as to give up its ownership, reserving for oneself only the right to get the equivalent back."[22] Consequently, by *credit economy* is meant "that series of social practices by which the great majority of economic relationships rely on lending, and in which especially the transfer of capital in service of the industries is done by means of loans."[23]

What is the place of credit in the economy? For Toniolo it can only have a "secondary and complementary" function, in the sense that:

a. "the normal mode of the economic structure is the direct and permanent union of *capital* with *work*, either in the same person or in several people through the association of the *capitalist* with *the worker,* both contributing to the purposes of production and sharing the profits and risks."[24] When this occurs it is to the benefit of both the producers, united in the endeavor, and the consumers, given the absence of fixed charges like interest paid to a lender. The social advantages are also evident, with the coming together of capitalists and workers, but with a legitimate preference for the worker, meaning by the term "worker" not only the manual worker, but also the industrial enterpriser.

   It is clear that this worker of a higher order, who with his mind and personal performance orders and directs production, translating it into action (through factories, agricultural companies, commercial operations), has the greatest merit in it. This being said, the capitalist lender, who on the contrary contributes nothing but an instrumental means (e.g., machines, fertilizers, raw materials, or their corresponding value) feels the need to give primacy to — that is, to rely on the inventive and directing action of the true enterpriser. … This is the case with the capitalist who entrusts (*commendat*) his capital to an *industrialist* in that eminently Christian form of the *limited partnership* in which the one makes the capital bear fruit with his intelligent personal industriousness, and the other, by contributing this same capital, brings to industry the guarantees of his responsible oversight and of real value. What solidity and expansion a social order thus presents, which thanks precisely to the absence of usurious lending, excluding the privileged and idle holders of wealth, unites all classes in the legitimate and fruitful daring of productive enterprise![25]

b. "Conversely, the transfer of capital to industries through the loan is for that very reason an exceptional relationship."[26] The short-term loan is necessary for large-scale "speculative" commerce (not carried out to order, but with the product being offered without a definite sales forecast) subject to unpredictable market fluctuations; the long-term loan serves to start or carry out forms of production in which the necessary capital is slight in comparison with the manpower and profits that can be obtained with it. It is natural and legitimate

> to seek in all of these cases a temporary support that does not involve association between the two elements and transfers the ownership of the capital entirely to the working industrialist, excepting the repayment of the equivalent. This is done precisely through the loan of fun-

> gible things, and generally of monetary capital, which, being able to be converted into the many technical forms of capital, represents all of them.[27]

Credit in the strict sense (loan or mortgage), being nothing but an instrument of production (a horse, a vehicle, etc.), is economically justified within the limits and with the consequences of the nature of the loan. For the purpose of this valuation it is necessary to keep in mind

- that capital, of any kind and in any technical form, is productive only potentially — that is, it has "the possibility of becoming productive, but only actually becomes so through work";[28]
- that monetary capital on loan completely separates "the *capitalist* from the *working industrialist,* that is, from the productive use *that others make* of his capital and therefore from the events and risks of production, so that whatever the final outcome, even to the ruin of the business, the capitalist always pits himself against the industrial enterpriser to fully recover the capital lent."[29]

A consequence stems from this, which explains the traditional doctrine of the Church:

> The lender, who does not participate and does not want to participate in the productive use of his capital, neither immediately by adding his own activity to that of the enterpriser, nor mediately by running the risk of the possible loss of his assets in the industry, the lender, we repeat, *by intrinsic virtue of the loan contract* (*ratione mutui*) has no right to earnings beyond the simple repayment of the capital value.[30]

If he can request compensation, this is due to him not on account of a right linked to the loan as such, but by way of indemnity, in consideration of extrinsic circumstances that bring him harm through having transferred his money to others: circumstances that result in blocked activity, in the loss of profit, and in the danger of incomplete repayment. This indemnity, normally called interest (as distinct from usury), "can never be higher than the *profit* that the *enterpriser* (capitalist worker) can normally make, but must remain below its average."[31]

Even with this caution, however, the fact remains that "the support of capital through lending, that is, the habitual use of *credit,* always represents an imperfect and dangerous system, economically, juridically, socially."[32] A forceful judgment, almost a withering verdict that falls not only on much of the economy of Toniolo's time, but even more so on the economy of our time, which has seen great crises due to the development of reckless finance linked only to financial market games. Such a type of credit, when from exceptional it becomes habitual,

> generates a class of idle *rentiers* that enriches itself, outside of any personal industriousness, with the preestablished and fixed interest of the loan, subjects to itself through the servitude of debt the industrialists who are truly deserving for their enlightened enterprise and for beneficial daring in production, and stands aloof from the economic progress of the nation.[33]

Degenerate capitalism

At this point Toniolo's pen becomes a sharp blade. Juxtaposed with the Christian ideal of the primacy of work, the modern primacy of capital is an authentic disaster. This vigorous *j'accuse* must be read in its entirety:

> In this Christian structure the ideal was always that all capitalists, made partners of the (working) enterpriser and under his primacy, would cooperate lastingly and directly in the stability and progress of the social economy. In the modern structure the center of gravity is the opposite; all industrialists find themselves made more or less dependent on the capitalists through the system of lending, and almost the entirety of national production is erected and supported on accidental and transitory relation-

> ships, that is, on the unsteady and onerous foundation of debt.
>
> Nor is that enough, but the ease of lending — that is, the facility of rapidly and continuously drawing on the capital of others — which has passed into the general habits and been increased by the *transferability* of the credit securities that represent it, provides constant and boundless nourishment for the intemperate expansion of *industrial* production and so of *mercantile* speculation, and finally for unbridled competition between producers and speculators, and therefore succeeds in multiplying *commercial crises* in the strict sense and at the same time *banking crises*. Indeed, the credit securities representing the loan of monetary capital, multiplied and distributed universally, in turn become the object of *speculation* on the natural or artificial fluctuations of their value and cause *financial market crises*. Finally, this dizzying cycle, based on this *general and constant system of the accidental, provisional, short-term loan* on the part of the capitalists, enables those who control *monetary capital* to set themselves up as moderators, arbiters, despots of the entire circulation of wealth, and they then find themselves drawn to monopolize (with those colossal agreements that the progressive era grants for their exclusive profit) the *money supply* and the *representative securities* that are instead destined by their nature for the final benefit of *universal exchange*, and with this they rise to dominate the whole social economy.
>
> This is the pinnacle of the contemporary *capitalist* system. But it is nothing other than the ultimate result of the theoretical and practical justification of the usurious loan. How much wisdom in the derided and opposed precepts of the Church regarding the gratuitousness of lending![34]

It is time to put an end to this chapter, although Toniolo's 1896 talk in Padua continues with interesting pages regarding what could be called the "economic policy" of credit. We will return to it. Suffice it to say here that at that conference this lucid and courageous page met with resistance from two important priests: Romolo Murri, who led the young Christian democrats and unfortunately over time would come into conflict with the Church, and Giorgio Gusmini, who would become bishop of Foligno and then archbishop of Bologna and cardinal. To both of them, Toniolo's rigor in putting restraints on the capitalist model seemed too tied to the past and hardly open to the conditions of the current economy. What would they have said rereading this page of Toniolo in light of the global financial crisis of 2007–08, which revealed the fragility of a global financial system made up of an unlikely swelling of credit securities not corresponding to the real economy and always teetering on the brink of a crisis with devastating effects? We have had the opportunity to mention the outcome of that interesting dispute.[35] This page by Toniolo has the spirit of prophecy.[36]

Chapter XX
Socialism Between Protest and Ideology

A predictable reaction

"The poor know little of the motives which stimulate the higher ranks to action — pride, honor, and ambition. In general it is only hunger which can spur and goad them on to labor." "It seems to be a law of nature, that the poor should be to a certain degree improvident, that there may always be some to fulfill the most servile, the most sordid, and the most ignoble offices in the community." "Considering the numbers to be maintained, they work too little, they spend too much, and what they spend is seldom laid out to the best advantage." Such statements are simply horrifying, but an Anglican physician and vicar, J. Townsend, made them without scruple in 1786, during the English Industrial Revolution.[1] Toniolo finds himself condemning this degree of barbarism in the company of the socialist Achille Loria.[2] To prevent his readers from getting the idea that Townsend was a singularly "heartless" man, he noted that Voltaire himself — yes, precisely the champion of the age of the Enlightenment, devoted to the program of "crushing" the Church (*écraser l'infâme*) — had made a similar pronouncement: "The laborer, the worker, must be reduced to what is necessary in order that he may work; such is the nature of man."[3]

Faced with such a landscape of inhumanity elevated to ideology, Toniolo is not surprised that, as a predictable and in some way justified reaction, socialism should erupt. But if this was now a fact visible to the naked eye, in order to deal with it adequately it was necessary to proceed with a thorough analysis of its causes, scientifically developing what Leo XIII had taught in *Quod Apostolici Muneris* (1878), the encyclical against socialism, and in *Rerum Novarum* (1891), the encyclical on the social question. Toniolo dedicates himself to it with analytical precision in a series of essays included in the volume of the *Opera Omnia* entitled *Capitalismo e socialismo*.

The genesis of socialism

Toniolo obviously knows Karl Marx's *Das Kapital*,[4] and he had certainly not overlooked the *Communist Manifesto* of 1848 signed by Engels and Marx, with the famous appeal, "Workers of the world, unite," an appeal that our author adopts to some extent, with a Christian reconfiguration: "Proletarians of the whole world, unite in Christ under the banner of the Church!"[5] Yet the "father" of Marxism is not his privileged interlocutor. In his time it was not at all obvious that that voluminous work on capital and that agile and incendiary "manifesto" would have so much success, giving us a twentieth century broadly marked by Marxian ideology, with experiments that for decades divided the world into two spheres pitted against each other until the collapse of the Berlin Wall and the defeat of real socialism, with the subsequent eruption of a new era with the liberalist global market. Another reason for not taking Marx as his privileged interlocutor was the fact that, by the term "socialism," Toniolo meant much more than the political-economic theory aimed at collectivism. For him socialism is a vision of society whose connotations emerge repeatedly in history, since ancient times, and in the contemporary era are expressed with many variations by a series of thinkers and agitators who, even with lively disagreements between them, are characterized by an underlying convergence. It is this convergence that particularly interests Toniolo, the "common thread" that is raveled out in the socialist phenomenon in all its vastness and complexity.

To understand Toniolo in this further critical kernel, we must always keep in mind his basic thesis on the opposing historical cycles, pagan and Christian. The latter — and this is already the first point of open contrast with Marxian historical materialism — highlights the primacy of ideas, and so interprets social and economic processes in relation to the ideal values that govern them. The first idea that makes the difference is that of God. The closer a religion comes to the truth, our author argues, the more positive the influence it exerts on the socioeconomic system. Since the Christian religion is that which, by virtue of revelation, has the most authentic connotations, the consequence follows of itself: proximity or distance with respect to the "ideal type" of Christian civilization also determines the physiology and pathology of social and economic processes.

How does all this apply to socialism? Toniolo explains that the pagan cycle of civilization has always found itself, albeit with very different expressions, reckoning with the pantheistic tendency, which implies the confusion between religion and politics, to the point of making the state itself — however conceived and structured — the place of the genesis and consolidation of ethics. The state, in other words, in paganism and its variants, tends to perceive itself and to be perceived as God, with the presumption of manipulating the social structure as it pleases, not respecting its intrinsic rules established by the Creator. In reality this same tendency to make oneself out to be God is also latent in individuals, when they act as a rule unto themselves, exempting themselves from an objective norm. This gives rise to a social dynamism always lurching from the tendency toward individualism (each individual by himself and for himself, without ethical responsibility and recoiling from organic relationships with his peers) to the tendency toward a massifying socialization, controlled by the sovereign of the moment, always inclined to claim a divine character. It is a short step from the individualism that shatters relationships by "atomizing" people to the power that governs them in an arbitrary manner. "Egalitarian individualism inevitably leads back to state pantheism."[6]

The Christian watershed

Christianity, anchoring religion to revealed truth, distinguishes (but does not separate) the religious and political spheres ("Give to Caesar what is

Caesar's, to God what is God's," Mt 22:21). What Toniolo calls the social order of civilization is born, in which everyone is guaranteed, in hierarchical order, his own place; everyone is recognized as having his dignity; all is bound with the thread of solidarity and placed under the aegis of the moral norm. To this latter everyone, including the sovereign, must submit. The Christian Middle Ages is the era in which this "normal social order" was expressed in bold relief. And not, Toniolo warns, because all was smooth sailing from every point of view. The points of fragility, resistance, inconsistency, are countless:

> In political relations, in social and economic relations, neither the absolutism of princes, nor the oppression of the weak by the upper classes, nor the rebellions of the multitudes were unknown. The tyrants arising again from time to time in our municipalities — the Ezzelini, the Duke of Athens, the Visconti, John Lackland, Philip the Fair, not a few Germanic emperors — attest to this. The slave trade always stained social relations by means of our own republics, so proud and jealous of the dignity and freedom of the citizen. Nor is there any lack of usurious exploitation of the poor, nor, alongside the scourge of the political parties, was it rare to see the outbreak of social revolutions like those of the Albigensians at the beginning of the thirteenth century, the "Jacquerie" or uprising of the French peasants led by Guillaume Cale (1358), the Ciompi revolt in Florence (1378), up to Wycliffe together with W. Tyler (1381), continued by the Lollards (1401) in England, up to Jan Hus in Bohemia, condemned by the Council of Constance (1415).[7]

But the very recognition, in the culture and in the laws, of the normal profile of the social order and of the Church as its protector and promoter meant that for centuries that order was able to endure. The cornerstones remained firm:

> God is the first cause and ultimate end of man, and so human-social existence and life, in its natural earthly order, is also con-

> nected down here to the supernatural and eternal order; all human relationships (personal freedom, marriage, family, work, property) from which society results are subject to the ethical-religious law supported by legislation; through it society, a moral entity, is the basis of the state, and this merely completes it with its external juridical-civil means, and this human social order, which finds positive and complete implementation in the Christianity represented by the Catholic Church, is destined to promote an *indefinitely perfectible civilization* marked by progressive *spiritual elevation,* by *unifying* power, by *universal expansion.*[8]

The modern involution

Toniolo identifies the point of fracture, which by logical development leads to the socialist crisis, in the Renaissance and particularly in humanism, a process of liberation of the human from God, dressed up as a return to classicism. Toniolo knows well that there was also a humanism of Christian inspiration.[9] But this was not the one that asserted itself. Interest in classical culture fomented a return to the pagan vision of life: It is "the transition from the *Middle Ages* to the *modern age*, from the Christian social order ripened by the Church to the human social order generated by pure reason."[10] Neoclassicism, exalting the Roman Empire with its cosmopolitical uniformity and imperial omnipotence (Caesarism), "predisposed the popular consciousness and the minds of the doctrinaire to princely absolutism."[11] On the social side, the echo of classical philosophy tends to disdain economic activity and the

> type of the landed estate in the imperial era, which with the sweat of thousands of slaves ensures corrupt wealth for the leisure of the owners amid the decay of Rome, the spectacle of the monopolizers of money and of their boundless power over the plebs and the magistracies, predispose and encourage the new society, amid the growing economic difficulties, to disavow the honorable industriousness of its ancestors and to rely on the fruits of the past, and from this comes the impulse for the con-

> centration of land ownership and the sterile accumulation of monetary capital, living on lending, usury, and speculation, amid the degradation of the farming class and the demoralization of the artisans.[12]

In the social structure, then, the intermediate organisms collapse: a true disaster! The useful is severed from ethics; social relationships crumble to the detriment of the weakest:

> So the intemperate cult of ancient doctrines and classical institutions, resuscitated at the time of the Renaissance, had to obfuscate the abstract concept of an *ethical law* governing social relations and replace it with simple *utility*, and at the same time, in the struggle over the useful between the strong and the weak, it had to undermine and finally disperse this *nucleus of intermediate forces* to leave society divided into two opposing camps: *politically*, on one side the multitude that obeys and on the other the boundless arbitrariness of the few and of the one who alone reigns; *socially*, the more numerous class, burdened only with duties and sacrifices, and a small and privileged class entitled only to rights and enjoyments; *economically*, the dispossessed on one side, the plutocracy on the other; and, in the conflict of these constrained forces, alternating episodes of *anarchy* at the bottom and growing *absolutism* at the top. The whole history of antiquity vividly represented this artificial structure and this fatal cycle. Restoring ancient wisdom to honor without correcting it with the doctrines and historical experiences of Christianity was tantamount to preparing profound social upheavals and multiplying the seeds of future socialism.[13]

To the disgrace of early modernity, the new geographical discoveries in Africa and America even lead to the revival of slavery, amid fruitless opposition from the popes.[14]

Taking his inspiration from the thought of W. Hohoff,[15] Toniolo continues his analysis of the drift of modernity, focusing on the three great successive revolutions: the religious-social revolution of Germany in the sixteenth century, the English Revolution of the seventeenth century, and the French Revolution of eighteenth century.[16] To grasp Toniolo's overall vision, this consideration should suffice: "It is often said that we are the children of the French Revolution: This view is still too shortsighted, and we must openly recognize that we are the belated grandchildren whose forefathers were the Italian *humanists* and the Germanic *reformers*."[17]

From the working class to the proletariat

On the properly economic side, the progressive trend of these three revolutions and the final outcome can be summarized in the following way. In the fourteenth and fifteenth centuries, as a mature fruit of the Christian configuration,

> the working class acquired an economic strength and a civil importance that it has never regained. This power was contained, in the countryside, in the strong lineage of farmers (leaseholders, sharecroppers, long-term cultivators, small landowners) sown throughout Europe; in the city, in the populous and rich class of artisans, coordinated (without offense to their autonomy) by powerful mercantile firms that handled trade at national and international markets and fairs.[18]

Toniolo knows well, as we have seen, that social unrest was not lacking even in that period, but he relates it precisely to this state of power then enjoyed by the working class, which, organized as it was, could also defend itself and dictate its conditions:

> But once the ethical ideals so favorable for the hardworking classes have declined, the fate of the latter is downgraded to the point of completely tipping the scales. The robust association between worker-owners and capitalists is split to make way for the *wage earner*, pushed down further into the *proletariat*, which in turn gives way to *pauperism*. Three descending degrees that correspond to the progressive elevation of the possessors of the

> productive instruments, that is, land and capital.[19]

The first to be born — with the growth of the big business that absorbs the small, with the disruption of the balance in the management of arable land between ownership and participation in it with various forms of stable work relationships — is the agricultural wage earner. "The crowds expelled from the ancestral fields and flowing into the cities form the first and numerous recruits as wage earners in the manufacturing industries."[20] The condition of the wage earner gradually stabilizes as, with technological progress, direct labor is replaced with the machine, as happened early in Great Britain in the second half of the eighteenth century. There is registered

> that fever which from then on takes hold of the industrialists (and which our Romagnosi labeled with the sad name of *industrialism*), by which the profits of the capitalist enterprisers seemed to benefit to the extent that the worker's position was more precarious and necessitous.[21]

Now wage earners and capitalists confront each other from two opposing camps. But it's not over:

> To touch bottom requires descending yet another level … passing on to *pauperism,* which expresses the misery of multitudes of workers capable of working but rejected from the normal industrial occupations.[22]

With the decrease in wages, profits grow, and with them the enormous accumulation of capital, aided by the arrival of American precious metals, and even earlier (starting from the fourteenth century) by the spread of usurious lending. Speculation on goods, on the money supply, and on credit securities develops. The big national and international commercial companies "not only ruin small businesses with monopoly, but in the form of *bearer share companies* they let the general public participate in the fever of speculation."[23] The public debt of the states provides abundant material for this "fever." Financial market speculation is propagated, regarding credit securities representing a value.

Socialism between theory and action

On the basis of these facts there takes shape the vigorous and informative overview of theoretical and practical socialism to which Toniolo dedicated a course at the University of Pisa, and then a publication in 1902.[24] Socialism is approached "indeed not as an aspect of economics alone, but of the sociology or doctrine of *incivilimento*."[25]

It is a socialism that has its first theoretical and practical expressions already in ancient society. In the journey from the Middle Ages to the modern age the focus is on the social shocks and the utopias according to Moro or Campanella. But the analytical center of gravity falls in the contemporary period, in the nineteenth century, when socialism accelerates and universalizes its development "through *three processes of scientific elaboration:* one *philosophical,* the other *positive,* followed by a third of *universal coordination*."[26] With his typical tendency toward synthesis (with the risk of schematizations that are not always persuasive, but always stimulating), here Toniolo recognizes two souls, one individualistic, the other statist, attributable to two points of view embodied respectively by Kant and Hegel.

We will skip the detailed assessment — besides, it is a well-known story[27] — to highlight some of the more specific accents of the Toniolian vision. Interesting also for today's situation is one of his intuitions of the future: In the comparison between the two souls of socialism, collectivist and anarchist, the "final prevalence of individualist socialism" is likely.[28] This may seem an airy-fairy prediction if we recall the imposition, for decades, of real socialism with a Marxist imprint, and so of the collectivist soul. But today it is clear that that era, which seemed rock solid, has passed. What leaps into our view is the triumph of individualist ideology, what Baget Bozzo in the 1970s characterized as "radical culture,"[29] embodied in various expressions, from the untamed liberalism of the economy to the shattering of the family and sexual identity, to the dissolution of cultural, social, and national physiognomies in global standardization, down to the autonomism of each individual opinion that presumes to impose itself as truth in the fluid world of social media, often without any guarantee of scientific documentation and evaluation, and generally with a reflection of public pretense, as if everyone could configure as his own "acquired right" what he subjectively considers as such. I don't know if all this is exactly what Toniolo had in mind, but it seems to me at least very close to the syndrome that he defined as "anarchist or individualist socialism." What contributes to it, more than any other factor, is

> the spirit of modern culture, which, from the free inquiry of the first Protestant reformers in the fifteenth century to the systematic skepticism of the entire nineteenth century, substantially and progressively denies any religious, moral, or doctrinal authority. In vain did the idealistic *dogmatism* of Hegel, or the *positivist* fact-based philosophy of A. Comte and the *empirical metaphysics* of the neo-Kantians, which would like to find and impose something *relatively fixed* in human knowledge, presume to react to it, even in our century. Criticism, dissolving everything in the name of individual free reason, introduces and perpetuates *intellectual anarchy,* which, through *moral anarchy,* finally ensures the triumph of *anarchist socialism* also in historical-doctrinal affairs.[30]

In light of this intuition, it was natural for him to rule that Marxism should at this point be considered a theory in crisis (history would prove him wrong for a period of time, from 1917 — the outbreak of the Russian Revolution — to 1989 — the fall of the Berlin Wall — but right in the long term, which extends to us and now seems to have on its side — but for how long? — the future. Marxism, in his eyes, was already losing, paradoxically defeated by its own internal evolution, as E. Bernstein in particular led him to think with his "critical socialism":[31]

> The fundamental economic laws of Karl Marx, under the pressure of scientific analysis by the disciples themselves, were shaken and invalidated, so that it can be said that there is no longer any of them (even among the most solemn, like the iron law of

> wages, the theory of value, that of profit or "Mehrwert," of capitalist production) that has not undergone the influence of dissolving criticism.[32]

There fell the illusion (the thunderous thud, however, would only occur after three quarters of a century!) of a fated law of history that, through the growing impoverishment of the proletariat, would have led to the revolution, and so to the reversal of the relations between proletarians and capitalists, with private means of production abolished and placed in the hands of the state, with a view to the future classless society. With Bernstein, "the program of *socialist revolution* of K. Marx had been turned into a program of *social reform*."[33]

So was there no more reason to fear the revolution? Time to let down one's guard? Not a chance! This repackaging of socialism appeared to Toniolo no less dangerous and, if anything, more treacherous, as it would facilitate the spread of the socialist utopia among the masses. Socialism, even as an error, had to be taken seriously, and deserved an adequate response from the Catholic side, in science and practice.

> No one, therefore, has the right to disdain an error even in the most transcendental ideas, since history teaches us that, sooner or later, its fruit will be tears of blood for the peoples. In this case, the socialism looming over modern civilization today in all its forms is the belated but sure revenge, matured over four centuries, for the rejection, in the neo-pagan Renaissance and the rationalistic Reformation, of the supreme religious and scientific ideas that in the Middle Ages had historically generated Christian civilization.[34]

Chapter XXI
Christian Democracy: A Social Vision in Political Perspective

The prescriptive alternative

> We ask nothing of doctrinal socialism, which under the guise of emancipation is preparing a more cruel and universal servitude, and we also reject the name of Catholic socialism that is sometimes attributed to us or thrown in our face, because socialism is the intrinsic negation of Christianity, and its program is the antithesis of ours. Socialism is *atheistic*, and we are religious; it overthrows particular property, which we want to revive and spread; it is destructive, and we want to rebuild the hierarchical order and through it legitimate freedom, proportional equality, and solidarity in the final aims of civil life.[1]

With these solemn declarations, the Catholic Union for Social Studies chaired by Toniolo approved in Milan, on January 2-3, 1894, the "program of Catholics in the face of socialism." In the background was the violence of the Sicilian Fasci (Workers Leagues) of the previous summer, subdued with the intervention of the army.[2] The text is clearly of Toniolian coinage. The contrast with socialism was stark. But it likewise distanced itself from individualistic liberalism:

> We are not seeking to prop up some fragments of this social structure that is wavering and collapsing on every side, and that is being leveled in atomistic disintegration under thankless servitude to the plutocracy.[3]

This passage on liberal ideology and the type of society and economy it delineated could not be clearer. The stated alternative, far from being limited to general principles, took to the field with a concrete program. It was not simply the saying of a "no": An agenda was developed, starting from the reproposal of the "law of Christian duty," which on the economic side "is translated into the law of work, from which no one is absolved except to replace it with other higher and more universally profitable forms of activity."[4] When in its first article the Italian Constitution states that the republic is "founded on work," this expression echoes, in some way, the "Milan Program."[5] On this basis it moved on to consider property, underlining on the one hand its legitimacy, and on the other its intrinsic social function, with precise consequences above all in agriculture, like the program for the diffusion of small ownership and for the participation of workers, on different levels, in the rights and benefits of owners. In the industrial sphere it was asked that the capitalist lender be connected more directly to the enterpriser, in such a way as to induce the former to shoulder the risks of the latter, contributing with him to the health of the company and so to the well-being of the workers, not limiting himself to profiting from the pure lending of capital. In commerce it called for a fight against the monopoly on credit, with the reproduction in updated forms of the legal repression of usury, subjecting the financial exchanges to strict legislation. Finally, the state was asked to intervene with laws to protect workers, but — to avoid any statist or paternalist temptation — it was specified that this was to be understood as "exceptional and transitory," expressing the hope that the stable function of this protection be carried out by the workers themselves through the reconstitution of "professional unions or corporations," in principle open to workers, owners, and capitalists, but which in the case of refusal by the latter could legitimately be configured as "exclusively workers' professional unions." In short, a program of social and economic renewal starting from the bottom and looking in preference to the most disadvantaged classes. The tone ended up being menacing:

> That if in order to reach this ideal, which bears with it the guarantees of the most splendid period in history, of what were called the *ages of the people*, it were, against our wishes, necessary to side with the *people* alone, we would not hesitate for an instant between the weak and suffering on the one side and the strong and thriving on the other.

Thus is born the program of "Christian democracy" (the movement, not the party). A program that looks at society in its various aspects and levels, including, ultimately, the political (at the time off-limits for Italian Catholics due to the "Roman question" and the injunction of the *non expedit* that kept them out of parliament), which in any case included precise guidelines of what today we would call economic policy.

Christian democracy

In 1900 Toniolo publishes an essay entitled *La democrazia cristiana*,[6] collecting in it several articles developed for the *Rivista internazionale di scienze sociali e discipline ausiliarie*.[7] The recent years had been "hot" due to the intensification of socialist uprisings, repressed in Milan in 1898 with the cannon fire of General Bava Beccaris. A leading priest, Davide Albertario, director of the *Osservatore Cattolico*, had been arrested as a subversive (he would serve a year in prison), and Toniolo had testified at his trial to explain to the judges that Christian democracy had nothing to do with socialism; it was, indeed, the alternative.[8] This makes clear the historical-strategic importance of this book, with its scientific stylings and prophetic tone. It was a question of finding a flagship name, an identity, an ideal point of convergence for the social commitment of Catholics. The name was precisely "Christian democracy," based on the following preliminary definition of democracy:

> Democracy in its essential concept can be defined as: that civil order in which all social, legal, and economic forces, in the fullness of their hierarchical development, contribute proportionally to the common good, issuing in the final result to the prevalent advantage of the lower classes.[9]

The addition of the "Christian" connotation served to clarify that this "normal" definition of democracy has not been historically realized and is not historically realizable, at least in full, except within the horizon of a Christian society and to the extent that a society approaches the model of Christian civilization.

The aspects inherent in this definition deserve a more analytical examination than is possible here.[10] The concept was calibrated down to the milligram, so that it could be accepted by all Catholics of different sensibilities. This was anything but an easy operation, given that the word *democracy* was full of ambiguity between its different historical interpretations. To many Catholics it seemed suspicious due to the echo of democracy linked to the French Revolution or the socialist threat. Toniolo had to do some chisel work.[11]

I will limit myself to highlighting two aspects that have a direct connection with economics. First, it is a vision in which democracy is expressed as a "civil order" — that is, linked to society itself in its fundamental elements prior to the political structure, as an order conceived in terms of an organic and hierarchical cooperation of forces directed to the common good. Among these forces are obviously the economic, which immediately bring to mind the organization of the working classes (guilds, professional unions). The other element, decisive also for economic ends, is that contained in the last line of the definition: the prevalent advantage of the lower classes. Toniolo translates this into a very effective formula: "He who can do more owes more; he who can do less receives more."[12] A concept that the professor does not scruple to illustrate with the ideal triad of the French Revolution — liberty, equality, fraternity[13] — but detaching it from its individualistic substrate and relating it not so much, or not only, to individual people, while still recognizing their dignity and autonomy, but to people in relationship, that is, seen in their respective aggregative units, natural and voluntary, from the family to associations, institutions, social classes.

This whole organic convergence and cooperation has as its end the common good, but within it, as a special and qualifying end, the advantage of the "lower classes." Indeed, Toniolo emphasizes, the "special protection and concern for the lower multitudes" is the very substance of democracy well understood.[14] A vision entirely inspired by Christianity, as Toniolo is quick to illustrate with a series of biblical extracts from the Old and New Testaments. In particular, he points to the words and example of Jesus, insisting on the fact that his "promises of relief and reward lavished on the most numerous and downcast" do not only concern the future life, but also the present (so nothing that could make religion the Marxian opium of the poor).

The normal dynamic of this protection and concern for the weaker classes is "the ministry of the upper classes, of the rulers, of the wise, of the strong, of the wealthy, charged with representing his own supreme royal and paternal authority and with continuing the work of his justice and charity in the redemption, also down here, of the humble and oppressed."[15] This input given by Christ develops in the age of the Church. The examples multiply. A lyrical page emerges, with almost mystical accents:

> Oh! Truly from that day in which Jesus was seen bending his knees before twelve fishermen, and despite their reluctance washing their feet, prescribing that from then on they should also do the same; from that solemn day the world witnessed the new and moving spectacle of the entire social hierarchy, which by degrees, amid the resistance of a prideful nature, bends down to serve the ignorant, poor, suffering multitudes. This is Christian democracy! … In short, it is the whole Christian hierarchy, which without descending from the height of its rank or detracting from its dignity recognizes its own duty, its own greatness, and its own glory in genuflecting, following the example of Jesus, before the poor, the humble, the derelict, to serve them and lift

> them up from their abjection, so that the people, both in conception and in historical fact, have become the supreme emblem of the concerted industriousness of all the upper classes and of the public rulers. This is how Christian democracy understood and realized the *sovereignty of the people*![16]

Too ideal a picture? Toniolo does not hide the fact that this "building with an admirable aesthetic outline" is always found, in practice, "in some part disrupted, corroded and ruined."[17] Nonetheless, with the Gospel a way had been opened, and the democratic movement had become a "historical law of civilization," so that it is possible to conclude that the Church is "the creator of true democracy!"[18]

As can be seen, the exclamation marks come thronging. In Toniolo's language on democracy there is lyricism and passion. The Christian apology and love for the poor are two sides of the same coin.

With all of this we are still at the level of social democracy. Political democracy is another thing. Toniolo does not rule it out (the topic was then being debated among Catholics[19]), but sees it as a rational and historical consequence:

> Once the people have been freed, honored, elevated, educated, it is natural that sooner or later they should also gain importance politically and find their place in the government, to the point of hastening in certain cases, if desired, a type of republican government. But this political democracy in such a case is a consequence of the social, juridical, and economic democracy, and not indeed vice versa.[20]

If this consequential order is not respected, democracy is perverted. So it is necessary to distinguish between true and false democracy.[21] Outside of the Christian perspective, the pre-Christian democracies and the rationalistic ones of post-Christian and anti-Christian modernity are tainted at the root; they lose the sense of the social order, of the common good, of the hierarchical organism of the classes, of the commitment of the upper classes to make themselves "ministers" of the lower ones, of the right of the latter to become the gravitational center for the interest of the whole society, and this not only in being helped (passive dynamic), but also by growing proportionally in exercising rights of participation (active dynamic). The social question, by this time become explosive, condemns the failure of democracy:

> And in fact contemporary democracy is generally blended and embodied in a specific type of parliamentary government on the basis of universal suffrage, and in it, amid the atomistic legal dissolution of every organism of class, only one stands out and imposes itself, the economic-bourgeois one (of mobile capital), which in fact makes the others serve its own interests and prejudices. So all these pseudo-democracies (which sometimes turn into demagogueries or ochlocracies), whatever their name and appearance, are the denial of true Christian democracy.[22]

The professor warns those Catholics are therefore deluding themselves who esteem the liberal structure as if it were the last bastion of a social order respectful of freedom. The law is one thing, the fact another. Formal democracy is one thing, substantial democracy another. Although in law the contemporary structure "is egalitarian par excellence," in fact, "it is as oppressive as ever."[23]

The Catholic heirs of socialism

On the strength of this conceptual and prescriptive identification, but also by reading some signs of sociology's coming to its senses, straddling the nineteenth and twentieth centuries, in the rediscovery of the spiritual and religious element Toniolo manifests what I would call a true prophetic fever in the anticipation and preparation of the future of Christian democracy. In reality, between the lines of his warm and encouraging accents there also emerge the struggles of an Italian Catholic world that, precisely in those years, was experiencing a tension that would lead to the rupture, in the Opera dei Congressi, between "young" (Christian democrats, led by Romolo Murri) and "old" ("*paganuzziani*," linked to the president, Paganuzzi). His attitude is that of a mediator who tries to hold together and mend an increasingly difficult unity. His enthusiastic accents on the future must also be read in this logic: Rather than predictive, they are strategic. It is the logic of a commander who promises victory to elicit effort and enthusiasm. For example, in a passage like the following:

> Today the mysterious and powerful regenerative forces of a profound social rebirth can be felt trembling all around, and everyone points, beyond the storm that rumbles formidably over the tag end of the century, to a new world that is developing and emerging. Now then: beyond the metaphor, this "... infernal hurricane that never rests" (*Inferno* V, 31), but bit by bit rages all the more, is socialism, which engulfs in its chaotic vortex all the antisocial and antireligious forces, growing denser from the Reformation to our day. But whether socialism should burst forth ruinously, thanks to a sudden catastrophe, as Karl Marx predicted and Bakunin hoped for in his destructive hatred, or whether it should pervade unnoticed the fibers of this senile society so as to gradually transmute its intimate structure, as Bernstein and the critical socialists advocate today, it is certain that it will not endure, and at that solemn hour, *the heirs of socialism will be the Catholics.*[24]

The reform of the social pyramid

In understanding Christian democracy from the economic perspective, a simple but decisive concept stands out: "that economic reform depends mostly on a problem of social justice, equity, and charity."[25] Thus is asserted "the essentially human-moral character of the entire economy of wealth, initially considered as a material mechanism, behind which man disappeared, forgotten and oppressed."[26]

Toniolo sees framed within this vision a twofold movement of reform: at the base (the condition of workers) and at the apex (state duties). But all this would not be enough if, between base and apex, the social body were not reconstituted with an organic redefinition of the relationships between the classes, once the "lower class" should be reconstituted:

> Until now Catholics (it is worth noting this aspect of their historical action) by preference worked to achieve a twofold aim, which in the economic reorganization of society represents its *base* and its *apex*. For one thing, they set out to improve the too slender and uncertain incomes of the lower classes and to favor their more prudent use; this was achieved with the extensive and fruitful messaging of mutual aid associations, cooperative societies for consumers, for rural and industrial credit, for workers' housing, for collective purchasing, and associations of every kind, and other institutions of a *quasi-private character*. For another, they displayed great and successful zeal in advocating *state legislation* for the protection and relief of the lower classes, and this with those laws on hygiene in factories, on the duration of work, on limits and prohibitions on the occupations of women and adolescents, on associations for the prevention of injuries or for workers' pensions, or with those others for the preservation of small properties or against usury among the people etc., all of which have the quality of measures of public order. … But on closer inspection this intense work applied to the *foundations* or to the *apex* of the social pyramid is only up to a certain point compatible with the maintenance of the contemporary *individualistic* structure of a disintegrated and faltering society. So beneficial endeavor must be integrated with a more broadly *social* office, aimed at *reconstituting the relationships between the various social classes,* in order to turn the contemporary proletariat (the characteristic morbid product of our century) *into an organic class, and reproduce the future solidarity among all.* Thus the base will be firmly joined to the apex, through the central body of the edifice, and this will acquire solidity.[27]

It is therefore necessary to undertake a comprehensive social reform. Understood properly, rather than a reform or small adjustments this is a matter of genuine transformation, in a rediscovered harmony with the DNA of democracy and society.

Chapter XXII
Economic and Ethical-Civil Reforms

The reform of the labor contract

One of the vicious points of the economy at the time is the labor contract that had emerged from the First Industrial Revolution in England: an illegitimate, immoral, antisocial contract, with which enterprisers had taken advantage of the proletariat they themselves had created,

> then justifying such cruel behavior with the supposed Ricardian law of the *supply* and *demand* of labor, and with the *Malthusian* theory, which makes the multitudes themselves responsible for the excess of impoverished and unemployed workers because they are unable to renounce marriage and procreation.[1]

A dramatic situation that between 1830 and 1870 swamped all of Europe and America. On the strength of *Rerum Novarum,* Toniolo sets as the first criterion that "the part of the wage that meets the necessary ends of the existence of the honest and upright worker cannot be reduced by any contractual act."[2] The state must keep watch that this minimum not be disregarded. Furthermore, economic reason itself shows that "the improvement of the worker's wage translates into an increase in profit for the enterpriser,"[3] so that "the example of the voluntary increase in wages is reproduced in Europe amid common satisfaction,"[4] at the same time as the movement of the "spontaneous and fruitful reduction of working hours in factories."[5]

A similar example is set by the system of workers' participation in profits[6] and the consolidation of peaceful relations between industrialists and workers through conciliation boards and arbitration tribunals. But it is a journey still in its earliest stage, and from which many groups of workers remain excluded. The charitable patronage of industrialists is not enough. Some duties of patronage are strictly of justice, and "it is not legitimate to grant in liberality what is due in justice without upsetting and irritating the natural sense of the workers."[7] Authentic charitable patronage finds nourishment and inspiration in the Christian vision.[8] Examples like those of Baron Schorlemer-Alst in the Rhenish countryside or that of Léon Harmel in Val de Bois in northeast France lead Toniolo to conclude that

> this patronage, no longer *utilitarian* (rational-liberal) nor completely *patriarchal* (of authoritarian beneficence), but quintessentially Christian, promises to profoundly transform the labor contract and all the relationships between capital and labor in the workplace.[9]

A duty that the ruling classes cannot shirk:

> The legislative intervention of governments would be in vain without this spontaneous organic and psychological elaboration of the ruling classes. And this again for the sake of rigorous restorative justice.[10]

Unfortunately, the reality is different:

> *Chronic forms of contracts* survive throughout Europe, especially in the field of rural industries, in Ireland, in Hungary, in our Ita-

> ly: in Sicily, in the Neapolitan region, in the Roman countryside, in the prosperous Po valley, which under the guise of ancient and degenerate customs of leaseholding, sharecropping, and rent, or of the supposed economic needs of a temporary wage earner without ties to the land, to the domestic roof, to family, betray the arrogance of the wealthy and the greed of speculative enterprisers, reveal the abiding and flagrant disregard for the duties and functions of landed property, and end up casting all of the burdens, risks, and oppressions onto the rural common people, forsaken and impoverished. They are usurious contractual forms that Catholic morality has scourged in all times and against which medieval canon law thundered condemnation, and that are the ever-flowing spring of a proletariat that empties the countryside, swells the cities and the periodic transatlantic migrations, solidifying in the meantime age-old hatreds exploited by socialism.[11]

Moving from the rural world to that of the manufacturing industry, the problems are similar. At first glance it would seem right for the enterpriser to agree with each individual worker on his wages. But this formal justice is undermined at the root by the difference in influence that ensures nothing for the worker, and this makes the presumed justice entirely unjust:

> What is certain is that today, in the organization of the big modern industries, the capitalist enterpriser has the only weight on the scale where wages are measured and debated, as an enormous centralized power in the face of thousands of disconnected workers, each of whom, in a solitary discussion of compensation, almost an imperceptible atom, finds himself overwhelmed and induced to accept any agreement with no relation to his merit. And in such a case, bringing all of the factory's workers together to collectively negotiate their interests with the enterpriser, far from being arrogance, appears to be an association necessary for restoring balance and ensuring effective (and not just nominal)

> freedom in the consensual establishment of the agreement.
>
> Nor can there be any doubt that the internal regulation of a factory (both in its voluntary modalities and in the application of the laws in force), just as it concerns the *ius imperii* or at least the *ius gestionis* of the owner-enterpriser, so likewise, with measures of personal health and safety, with working hours, with the division of the sexes in the rooms, with nighttime or holiday rests, with methods of remuneration, etc., it comes into contact in a thousand ways with the integrity, with the moral duties, with the tenor of domestic life, with the personal freedom of the workers. And in such case, calling the workers to agree on this internal regulation with the employer, for the common interest and for its reciprocal observance, seems recommended by eminent reasons of fairness and by personal respect for all participants in industry.
>
> Finally, ensuring with mutual contractual agreements *a more direct and lasting bond* between the two sides within that industry, which becomes the common training ground for the resourcefulness and sacrifices of capitalist and workers, both *excluding* the sudden ("at will") breaking of the contract on either part and regulating *a priori* the forms of mutual dissolution, and *directly involving* the two sides in the *earnings of the company* — that is, allowing workers as well to participate to some extent in both the risks and the profits of the industry — does that not designate a more correct and elevated form of contract, responding to the concept that industry is a technical-economic system in which by his nature the *worker is a partner* (albeit subordinate) rather than an instrument or tool of the capitalist?[12]

All of this, Toniolo observes, should happen by natural inclination of beneficial patronage, but under normal conditions there may be other models that have greater plausibility and efficacy. So it is necessary to keep one's feet on the ground and not close one's eyes to a dialectic that has been developing over time:

> The proletariat divided from the wealthy and ruling classes is a product that is too long-lived; the suspicions and aversions against capitalism are too deeply rooted; the mechanical arrangements so expensive and predominant in the modern factory cause too great a separation today between the enterpriser who manages the work and the workers who execute it to give promise that the fusion of the thoughts and volitions of all under an intelligent and provident *patronage* will always be intimate and sincere. In this case it seems preferable that the enterpriser, often already in partnership with other capitalists, and the mass of workers, themselves gathered together in association, should compose two *distinct entities* at every factory, each maintaining its autonomy while keeping in constant relations with each other thanks to a *mixed council* of delegates, for the definition and observance of the work agreements and everything that concerns the common interests of the industry.[13]

Cooperation as "Christian brotherhood"

But there aren't just the big businesses. As exhausted by competition as they may be, medium and small businesses also survive. Moreover, the strain of the relationship with the managerial classes

> drove the proletariat itself to seek, apart from any transaction with capitalism, its own independence, that is, concentrating capital and labor in its own hands and thus elevating itself to an autonomous position with respect to the big companies. Economic-popular associations, under the name of *cooperation,* converge directly on this further transformation of the proletariat in our century.[14]

In this tendency there is something that, in Toniolo's view, contains "happy promises for the future."[15] He refers to the fact that cooperatives (for consumption, credit, collective instrumental purchasing, production), far from limiting themselves to achieving less onerous economic living conditions,

> in recent times aim to acquire a profit with their operations, and

> thereby to set aside capital for the future, and this, either belonging to the participants themselves, whose association would thus rise to the level of capitalist, or (note well) belonging to the class as such, in the form of an indivisible (collective) asset that would be reserved for the perpetual benefit of all present and future members of the class itself.[16]

While sharing this perspective, which excites him, Toniolo recalls the most representative names among Catholics (from Ketteler to Raiffeisen, from Cerutti to Durand) who took on initiatives in competition with those promoted by Lassalle, Shulze-Delitzsch, Luzzatti, Wollenborg. "It is a whole new world that is perhaps being developed under this name of cooperation,"[17] a new world that is in profound harmony with the Christian vision of capital, because it tends "to bring capital back to one of its most noble and legitimate functions, which the Church has always assigned to it — that is, to be an instrument indeed not for keeping the working class down, but for emancipating it."[18]

A new class of independent worker-capitalists is thus formed, and in this way there is a reproduction in modern form of "those collective or common goods, those juridical patrimonial entities that are the natural defense of those new social strata and have always been considered as a guarantee of the popular economy."[19] By this means the workers grow, do it themselves, and alongside the patronage for their benefit on the part of the upper classes they develop a "*Christian brotherhood* that lifts up the proletarian and teaches him to *do it himself,* equalizing him fraternally in independence."[20]

The professional unions or associations

But where to aim, ultimately? Toniolo has his ideas clear:

> In this almost universal proletariat, which in the near future will find a twofold organization in association with capitalists in big businesses and then in the widespread autonomy of medium and small businesses, but which in the meantime remains disjointed, fluctuating and threatening among the rural and in-

dustrial multitudes, there has penetrated, grown, and flared up in recent years a *class consciousness*. Well then, this frightening psychological and social fact, which has been compared to the ignition and flashing of sparks in a mass of incendiary powder, is the third fulcrum on which Catholics count on setting up the lever of the redemption of the proletarian multitudes, quite otherwise than for the social catastrophe invoked by Marxian socialism, but rather for the *reconstitution* of those multitudes into *an ordered class, thanks to the associations.*[21]

Toniolo sees growing signs of this, despite ambiguities that seem to usher in the fear of the menacing class struggle of Marxian stamp. In particular, the English trade unions seem to him to be a significant instance of this type of association, which ideally should be thought of as a collaboration between the working class and the enterprising class, but in concrete terms can only be hoped for as working-class (after all, capitalists don't think twice about uniting in groups of their own):

This threefold series of measures on behalf of the multitudes — the reforms of the labor contract in big companies, the recomposition of medium and small *autonomous popular businesses*, and the *associative representations of the working class* — forms the most urgent economic program of the future, and it is to be seen how this takes on a *truly social character,* aimed at reconstituting the connective tissue of the economic organism.[22]

What springs from this is a glimpse of the future, a flash that has the savor of utopia and the form of prophecy, and that in reality is a program entrusted to the common responsibility and in particular to the efforts of believers:

The age of the capitalist will be followed by the age of the worker. But this transformation, which today appears absurd, will not be a reality tomorrow except by virtue and almost by a miracle of Catholicism.[23]

The primacy of civil society

Over all of this, like a light appearing on the horizon, Toniolo sees the emergence of a new spiritual imperative that surpasses purely material perspectives and offers the very issues of the economy and work a framework of higher values, linked to "the being of man, to his spiritual nature, to his necessary ends that are therefore by their nature prior and superior to any coercive relationship."[24]

A natural consequence is the distinction of society from the state, indeed, the primacy of society over the state. To his eyes there is

> the clearer reappearance in intellects and consciences of a distinction (not separation) of *society* with its substantial ethical-civil ends from the *state* with its strictly juridical-political offices, which is extrinsically added to and coordinated with it.[25]

Among the historical causes of this recovery, Toniolo sees also the fateful words of liberty, equality, fraternity, words that, although used ideologically by the revolution, meanwhile "sounded like a protest of spontaneous private and social life against artificial political orders."[26] The very laisser-faire, laisser-passer of an individualistic liberalism made its contribution, albeit equivocal, to the rediscovery of private and social life. The global expansion of the economy beyond state borders also contributes, and, paradoxically, so does the "rising of the socialist tide"[27] itself with its systematic criticism of the state. Most of all, the religious factor influences it with the awakening of the Catholic Faith, showing that the social question is essentially moral, and

> the first genesis of the social crisis is concealed in the vicious ethical-civil institutions of society, which the state itself contributed to arbitrarily tampering with, whereas it has no right to unsettle that which has immediate origins in ethical-religious law, generator of *universal human society*, which ultimately *political society* must serve, and not vice versa. This affirmation of the virtual and logical anteriority and superiority of ethical-social goals with respect to the political, and so of the hierarchical co-

> ordination of the *state* with *society,* which holds the pinnacle, was the great doctrinal novelty and the inestimable real merit of the Church since its origins.[28]

A long historical page flows here beneath Toniolo's pen in justification of this statement, to reach the prescriptive conclusion:

> Faced with the modern state, arbiter and tinkerer of the social order, *to vindicate the autonomy of the fundamental social-civil institutions,* whose moral essence, untouchable by any political action, remains under the immediate custody of the eternal ethical law, of religion and of the Church, and so to demand from the public powers that they cease undermining and perverting them, limiting themselves to guaranteeing them juridically and to coordinating them for the common good. And three ethical-juridical demands chiefly impose themselves today: for personal and private freedom, for the reconstitution and function of the social classes, for the moral unity and historical vocation of the nation.[29]

Freedom in personal and private life

Faced with the tendencies of state centralization or of true statism that are realized in both the liberal and socialist visions, Catholics

> demand: the freedom of faith, of moral-religious conscience and of the Church; the freedom and inviolability of Christian marriage and the family; the freedom of voluntary and private associations in all honest forms; the freedom of educating and instructing children and the people; the freedom of charity, of its pious foundations, of their religious spirit, and of their management.[30]

Of course, this freedom has its intrinsic limits within the boundaries of the true and the good. The freedom of error and evil is not conceivable,[31] even in the awareness that "error and evil themselves must be *tolerated* within certain limits when in certain factual circumstances this is (hypothetically) required by the least damage or the greatest common good."[32] It is on this basis that the principle of freedom in social life is demanded. But Catholics also support it on the strength of "sound sociology":

> In fact, they consider *personal freedoms as a necessary seed of civil resurrection*. Every social rebirth logically and historically begins from the vital cells of private autonomy. In fact, individuals and families are the primary elements on which society is built and nourished. Is it possible to imagine the greatness of nations and states without the greatness of individuals, that is, without a high personal awareness of one's moral ends, of one's responsibility, and the duty to achieve these thanks to one's own meritorious energy of thoughts and works, and in other words without *civil freedom*, which is the condition, school, and safeguard of all this? What hope of resurgence for a people in the midst of which the *personality* has lost the concept of its own dignity, where the moral character is perverted, where the family is no longer a sanctuary, where the house is no longer a nest, a refuge, a castle, where the spirit of association is weak and where, with daring private initiatives extinguished, the individual is reduced to a cog in the powerful state machine or to an unconscious atom of the future collectivism?[33]

Catholics demand freedom as "the substance and leaven of future democracy."[34] A right assured not just for the privileged, as happened in the democracies of Greece and Rome:

> Even in the most open democracy, the participation of all citizens in wealth and political power will never be translated into action except within the proportions and limits of the capacity of individuals, nor will everyone in it become proprietors and statesmen. But there is a minimum of moral goods enclosed in the citadel of freedom and making up its content, like respect for personal dignity, paternal authority, the faculty of raising children, the exercise of work and of charity; legal and de facto

> goods that can be shared by all, wherever a man is found in the state or even in the world, and this is why in a healthy democracy freedom is blended with civil equality.[35]

A personal and civil freedom that must be better guaranteed for the multitudes with the protection of the law:

> Hence freedom equally for man and woman (corresponding to the nature and offices of each), but more protected for the latter due to the frailty of the sex; for adults and children, but supported more for those who suffer the weakness of age; for rich and poor, but upheld the more for those who experience economic inferiority, so that, by proportioning the defense of the law to need, freedom may remain equally intact for all. The rationalist democracy in its twilight equalizes us all in a nominal legal freedom that in fact only benefits the strong and pushes down the weak. The dawning Christian democracy promises a potential and proportionate legal freedom, the value of which will be measured by both the power of the great and the security of the small.[36]

The reconstitution of the classes

With this heading we come to one of the themes dearest to Toniolo, but also one of the most difficult to grasp in its true sense. The very word *class* is now rather obsolete. In Marxism it was linked above all to the dialectical perspective of the class struggle. For its part, fascist statism favored the concept of corporation, also used by Toniolo, as a function of an economic system — corporatism — integrated with the authoritarian state: and this was as far as could be from Toniolo's thought.

The theme of the class or corporation (or even professional union) in the thinking of our author is to be understood entirely within the horizon of freedom; indeed, it is grafted onto the concept of personal freedom and autonomy, removing the latter from individualistic atomism (society as an amorphous juxtaposition of isolated individuals), to highlight the natural process by virtue of which, person by person, society is constituted into an organism of social groups with their identity within a harmonious whole:

> Catholics (in full harmony with scientific doctrines) in the genesis of classes recognize: a natural process of expansion of personal energy, which for one thing is reproduced and broadened in families, and for another, in certain family groups that are respectively more alike (by location, by economic status, by traditions of office), amplifies and perpetuates the original or acquired varieties of talents, virtues, vocations, education, habits of the individuals themselves, instilling and finally transmitting in each of these groups the awareness of a special *moral duty* to be fulfilled with a variety of offices and unity of ends for the common good of society.[37]

This elaborated and harmonious vision of society, flourishing in the Middle Ages, found itself constrained in the modern age by individualistic liberalism or by the threat of collectivist state pantheism:

> But in the face of these age-old devastations and of such public aversions and prejudices, Catholics rise up to invoke: that *class consciousness* be reawakened in the populations, that is, the concept and sense of the existence of the Christian function, duties, and virtues proper to the various social classes; that the state respect, facilitate, and promote their natural reconstruction, and recognize and guarantee their legal personality, with all personal and patrimonial rights; and that the state itself grant associations due autonomy for the management, defense, and development of the moral, civil, and material interests of the respective classes.[38]

A vision that applies to the whole of society and to all of its components, but in particular places itself at the service of the weakest class:

> The Girondins, inaugurating [a] false liberal democracy, persuaded themselves that the abolition of class privileges on the night of August 11, 1789, had equalized the social hierarchy for-

> ever. But our age, almost in protest, witnessed the unprecedented rising up of the capitalist bourgeois classes in opposition to the landed noble classes, in the subjugation of the working artisan classes, and it heard the proclamation of the class struggle as a condition and fated law of progress.[39]

In hoping for the organization of society into the respective classes, Catholics do not mean to support situations of privilege for some of them to the detriment of others. All must collaborate proportionally for the common good. Classes understood in this way are not closed castes, but completely open circles of aggregation. One can move from one class to another, horizontally or vertically. And in any case those who are weaker will find support in class organization that they certainly could not have if they were to remain isolated, as happens in the modern proletariat:

> But the only hope of the individual, almost an atom lost in the amorphous mass of the people, lies in the accumulated experiences and vocations of his confreres, in the assiduous mutuality of affections, aspirations, material and moral services among his associates, so as to find adequate compensation for his personal deficiency and stimulus to release his personal energy, to remove himself from downward pressure and become the architect of his own fate in the future. In this is potentially the secret of the good democracy: not in pushing down the exalted, but in lifting up the humble, that is, in multiplying the social supports and protections on behalf of the latter, so that they may raise themselves up in status with the fulcrum of personal merit. But the lower classes cannot draw upon this bundle of collective energies and this powerful virtue of elevation coming from below except on the basis of vast and historic associations.[40]

This was a crucial point of the Christian democratic program, which our author proposed, at least in progressive form, to the whole Catholic world, in part as an alternative to the spread of chambers of labor inspired by the socialists and instrumental to a new socioeconomic structure.[41] Making, in 1902, a survey of the vast development of the international trade union movement in Europe and the United States, and underlining the development of class consciousness in the working world,[42] Toniolo observed:

> And just as once before, in the Middle Ages, the industrial and mercantile bourgeoisie came to separate itself from the landed nobility and to win its own autonomy alongside it, so now in this maturity of the twentieth century, from this bourgeoisie erected on movable wealth (and which has become quintessentially capitalist in the modern sense), which long kept the proletariat as its appendage and dependent, this latter laboriously struggles to constitute itself distinctly, with its own functions and rights, in the complex of social life.[43]

It is therefore the genesis of a "fourth estate."[44] Everything contributes to this spontaneous movement of the social base, even if sometimes in problematic ways (as in the early stages, marked by secret associations akin to Freemasonry in England and by the developments of socialism in its various forms). It is a movement that, as one would say in the biblical language that we rediscovered with Vatican II, is a "sign of the times." Toniolo sees this as a providential path, a harbinger of a rosier future, as its physiognomy gradually comes more into line with the demands of the Christian-Catholic vision of society, based on the concept of organic cooperation aimed at the common good:

> This function of the social classes and their corporate order will perhaps remain the most original and sure characteristic trait to distinguish the equally fallacious liberal and socialist democracies from the old and new Christian democracy.[45]

But for this it is necessary to define its identity well: as a radical overcoming of leveling individualism,

> the corporation, as in the past so also today, is understood as an autonomous and permanent association between all those

> engaged in similar economic offices, with the aim of representing, protecting, and favoring the multiple interests (material and moral) of their own *class* coordinated with respect to those of the other hierarchical classes of society.[46]

As such Toniolo reiterates that, in principle, mixed corporations should prevail — that is, those made up of workers and enterprisers. But the upheaval of modernity has led to a conflict between the two classes that is difficult to resolve. Catholics take note of this: "Capitalists and workers now make up two profoundly distinct classes that will perhaps never assimilate again."[47] This is not a matter of a utopian project, Toniolo explains by pointing to the example of England, "where the people organized in the trade unions have acquired material well-being, an autonomous existence, a degree of culture such as to carry out for fifty years (and more so since 1871) a notable function in the legislation and political life of the nation."[48] Ultimately, to understand in terms closer to our lexicon what our author means when he talks about corporations — without diminishing his complex sociological-organic plan, which did not rule out, in principle, hoped for mixed associations of enterprisers and workers — we should translate the word *corporations* with *unions*.[49]

Special attention is to be paid to the spirit of the corporations. To this end Toniolo did not hesitate to say that, for Catholics, these had to be proposed to the working world without excluding or marginalizing the religious dimension: "If man is religious by nature, why would the *institutions* sprung from and serving him not be so?"[50] In the contrast between the socialist and Catholic approaches, openly declared in their antithetical perspectives on religious issues, for Toniolo the very future of society was at stake.

Nation as mission

The concept of nation also arises in the organic vision of society. Toniolo means by nationality "the complex of those specific qualities that mark a special group of the universal human family":[51] corporeal qualities (physical temperament, typical stature, skin color, etc.) and mental qualities (spiritual temperament, inclinations of the spirit expressed in forms of thinking, feeling, operating), but above all spiritual characteristics, which prevail in giving the distinctive imprint to the nations:

> Hence a *nation* is definitively the result of a more intimate union of souls, connected to each other by a special affinity of ideas, affections, and habits of work, with regard to a common civil purpose especially assigned to them by Providence in the course of civilization.[52]

All of this shaped in the national history. In particular, "*religion* (a supernatural and historical fact at the same time) is the factor that, more than any other, generates the being and unity of each nation."[53] Under Toniolo's pen the examples flow, with a special look at Italy, marked by the mission of the pontificate:

> Catholics invoke the recomposition of the *moral unity* of every nation, and in particular of Italy, thanks to the new refulgence of the concept of its own respective mission in history. Without a great idea that may unify the thought of all and that, converted into sentiments of duty, may give a vigorous and constant impulse to industriousness and common sacrifices, there is not a nation, but a mass of people.[54]

In Toniolo's eyes, the German people stand out with "the proud promise of F. Hegel, that after the ancient predominance of Semitic Oriental civilization, after the triumphs of the Greco-Latin culture of which the Italic was a continuation, the hour of the hegemony of the Germanic race was launched."[55] At the same time, with colonial policy the English assert themselves "with the awareness of being the *new Romans*, called to dominate the whole world with civilization,"[56] while the Anglo-Saxons of America "are exhilarated at having the primacy in the next century, as representatives and pioneers of progress in all forms."[57] To Italy falls

> *the vocation of coordinating in unity*, that is, of reconnecting to itself, through the multiplicity of its ethnic elements, through its

> ready contacts with three continents, through the assimilation of many influences of ancient and modern cultures in its history that goes back several thousand years, through the flexibility and balance of its talents, of reconnecting, we repeat, merging, and harmoniously representing the genius, thoughts, aspirations, traditions of all peoples, and thus of serving as a means and intermediary to draw them near to the hearth of Christian civilization in Rome.[58]

While he was writing these things, echoing the Guelphic accents of Vincenzo Gioberti's *Primato*, he certainly could not imagine that this ideal of the nation would soon be undermined and perverted by the nationalist *virus*, and that the fascist regime would feed on it for aberrant conclusions similar to those of Hitlerian Nazism. The Toniolian perspective is completely different, democratically conceived and guaranteed by the Catholic spirit of the nation:

> Everything among us must become Italian again, once more Catholic. This character must be restored in our intellect, our sentiments, our private and social institutions: the family with the simplicity of its traditional customs; the social classes with their dignified mutual intimacy; city life with its urbane and lively exuberance; charity with its eager and fruitful religious inspiration; the economic systems with their social physiognomy, from the artisanal associations to the civic savings banks; the rapport between clergy and people, made brothers in the majesty and love of religion; the greatness of papacy and homeland; we must lead our literature, our arts, scientific genius, and popular education to that source and nourish them there, enlivening everything with memories, traditions, ideals that are Catholic and national at the same time. For this purpose it is appropriate to draw most extensively on the study, the examples, and the teachings of the Italian Middle Ages, the unique and great historical period that, through our democratic societies of the thirteenth to the fifteenth centuries, and together with the primacy

> of the pontificate in the world, presented the frank and splendid physiognomy of Italian civilization, forever shaping the national type, thanks to the harmonious assimilation of the most varied elements *unified and dominated by the Catholic papal idea.*[59]

A nation with a universal scope

The national mission — not to be forgotten — in Toniolo's vision is conceived without any prejudice to the universal unity of the peoples. On the contrary, it contributes to it, in the perspective of a universal order of civilization. In this too, Christian culture has made the difference with respect to pagan culture:

> *Nationality is a condition of social order.* Of the three objects of human love down here — family, homeland, humanity — it has indeed been written that pagan culture recognized and valued only the second, for the sake of the country immolating the family and opposing every people that was not included in it. Quite otherwise in the Christian conception, nationality, for one thing, with the shared participation in ideas, desires, and meritorious works for the good of all, coordinates into unity the special good of each class, just as this latter harmonizes the private good of each family, and for another, by attributing to each people its own special task in the work of human progress, it is an intermediary for the realization of the universal order of civilization.[60]

An ideal, demanding vision, the dawn of which Toniolo saw in the resumption of ecclesial life in the Leonine era and, in this climate, also in the role that the pontiff himself assigned to, among others, the Franciscans, linked in their origins to the moment most representative of the Christian Middle Ages.[61] For this reason, he allowed himself to entertain a hope:

> May God therefore raise up, in his saving mercy, a new St. Francis. And indeed, neither the Church nor our Italy can forget (and today less than ever) that an apostolate of faith, penance, and

> love was that of the little poor man of Assisi, but that Christian and Italic democracy emerged from there, having repercussions throughout the world, with an entire renewal of civilization.[62]

The political perspective

Starting from the person, in his concentric expansion into families, associations, corporations, territorial bodies, nations, Toniolo assigns a far from marginal role to politics, understood as a special task of the state. There is no normal society or thriving economy without adequate politics.

Toniolo returns repeatedly to this theme, framed in the broader context of the discussion on civilization, but in particular in the last chapters of his *Indirizzi e concetti sociali all'esordire del sec. XX*. He shows how the doctrine of the Church, especially in the systematic exposition of Leo XIII, has much to say on this point. The fundamental principle is that

> the sole reason for the political power (of this authority that comes from God) and so the definitive title of a government's legitimacy (always with the exception of justice) and therefore also the measure of its perfection, lies in the common good.[63]

It is not a question of any particular form of government structure or political regime. The Church is neutral toward the monarchical or republican constitution. What matters is that the "fundamental political constitution" be adapted to the "social constitution of the nation."[64] Hence not only respect for private civil liberties, but also for "*broad local autonomies,* which for the sake of the common good the state must guarantee and integrate, not harm and suppress."[65] Hence also "the *participation* to varying degrees *in the powers of the state on the part of all social classes* (constituted in turn, as we have seen, in autonomous form), in order to represent and proportionally assert the good of all."[66] Hence also, finally, "the formation, above these autonomous local and social bodies, of *political units* that are no longer mechanical, but *eminently organic*, to strengthen the general interests of the nation in more natural solidarity."[67]

The perspective of a politics organized with great respect for local autonomies, starting from the municipality, is the one that best corresponds to social life in general and, for Italy, to its history. (Luigi Sturzo would faithfully echo this principle in the platform of the Italian People's Party.[68]):

> Not that the resurgence of local freedoms is alone a happy prediction of the future, but with the fall of the rationalistic dogma of popular sovereignty (that the state has the powers necessary for its office by divine order of Providence, and not by approval of the multitudes), the future will nonetheless be marked, as the clues increasingly indicate, by participation in the government of public affairs by all classes of the population, organically constituted.
>
> Against the persistent liberal prejudice that after the proclamation of universal suffrage the monopoly of narrow factions is erected on the whirlwind of floating atoms, and against the socialist threats to bring the multitudes to the helm of the state, this will be a reform particularly due to Catholics.[69]

It is necessary to work toward state figures "resulting from the coordination of various concentric circles of autonomous municipal, provincial, and regional life, in a vast federal *national political unity,* no longer mechanical, but *organic.*"[70]

This state mechanism is entirely directed to the common good of the nation, but must in turn "be coordinated with the universal and perennial ends of civilization."[71] Grafted in here is the politics of humanity, the universal perspective, also conceived in an organic way:

> And indeed the historical political mission of every state finds its reason for being in its correspondence with the common goals of humanity, in which the universal good is perpetuated and then flows back to the good of the individual nations.[72]

But where to find the point of convergence of this universal unity? With the ardor of a believer who does not take his lead from the news but interprets the profound tendencies of history, Toniolo has no doubts: The moral authority capable of this sort of miracle of universal convergence can be no other than the Catholic Church, and in particular the pontificate, which encapsulates and authoritatively expresses its mission, not only spiritual but in some way, through indirect influence, also social.[73] Here begins a long page in which theological, historical, and sociological motivations follow one another to justify this thesis that, in light of the facts as we see them in our time, seems the most anachronistic imaginable, in the context of our multicultural and multireligious world. For Toniolo, on the contrary, it was evidence to which history itself, sooner or later, would yield. At the end of his life, amid the rubble of the First World War, making to Pope Benedict XV the proposal of *a Catholic institute of international law* at the service of world peace, he was still dreaming that the pope, assuming its initiative and direction, could in some way carry out that unifying and pacifying task which the historical trend would instead entrust[74] — with results that in truth were rarely brilliant — first to the League of Nations and then to the United Nations. Checkmate against the prophecy? Yet if one reflects on the role that the popes have progressively taken on in recent history,[75] on the level of moral influence, with their statements of condemnation and inspiration with respect to the great directions of world politics, one can legitimately get the impression that, if not in the form Toniolo hoped for ("the coming century holds the promise of a reproduction of the times of Innocent III, when a supreme moral and supernatural force presided in the name of religion and civilization over the social and political relations of the world"[76]), at least in the form of a presence as authoritative as it is gentle and humble, the Church offers itself as a point of reference for a worldwide audience and carries out something of what Toniolo foretold. His dream and his appeal, however, remained down to earth when, for this ideal, he appealed to the condition, never adequately realized, of an ecclesial testimony worthy of the Gospel, and so of holiness, concluding his impassioned argument with this "vision":

> But we believers feel in the depths of our souls and urgently proclaim it here as a legitimate conclusion that the one who will definitively save the present society will not be a diplomat, a scholar, a hero, but rather a *saint*, indeed a society of saints.[77]

Chapter XXIII
The Role of the State in the Economy

Interventionist state?

The function of the state was a thorny issue for the Catholics of Toniolo's time.[1] To their eyes the state projected the shadow of centralism and absolutism, even when it conducted the policy of laisser-faire, laisser-passer. It was all the more frightening in the version of collectivist socialism that was configured as true statism. The position adopted by the Toniolian-inspired Christian democrats was that of a moderate interventionism which on the one hand expressed the entirely subsidiary character of state intervention, and on the other was required, under precise conditions, for the benefit of the weaker classes.[2]

An intervention that should certainly be limited, if not ruled out, in the area of education. The concern refers to the state's tendency toward the ideological standardization of society. Subsidiarity was therefore not excluded in providing state school opportunities for the benefit of all, but this was meant to be well delimited by the "right to education" that has as its first subject the family. What Toniolo said in this regard at the "world days" of Milan in 1907 was loud and clear:

> We desire that the state not monopolize the brains of our children; that private instruction also be recognized in its early initiatives, with the kindergartens and elementary schools; that absolute freedom be granted to give the characteristic imprint of our religion to instruction, as others are able to give the characteristic imprint of their doctrines.[3]

But there are areas in which the state has a duty to intervene. Toniolo summarizes them:

> The state has not only the task of maintaining the legal order and promoting general progress, but also a function of balancing and harmonizing between the various classes; this function must unfold according to the criterion of an *equality proportional* to the needs of the various classes, so that the protection of rights and the promotion of well-being may be more lively on behalf of the classes less fit to provide for themselves, and thus become *special* protection and assistance of the weaker and more suffering multitudes. But the action of the state, which always remains supplementary and integrative of individual (private) initiative or of that of the individual classes (social-corporate), must, in exceptional circumstances of social crisis, be exercised with even extraordinary breadth and intensity. And this particularly today, due to the gravity of the *public threat* stemming from the conflict between capitalism and the proletariat; also due to the deleterious action of the state itself, which is responsible for a full restitution of the rights it has violated and offended, and for an effort to repair all of that damage which in the past and even now (either with despotic and antisocial legislative measures, or with the culpable absence of any law, or in general with rash and nefarious political operation) the modern state has done to the civil order in general and to the humblest classes in particular; and finally due to the lack or insufficiency of intermediate bodies between individuals and the state, such as, for example, the corporate organization of the classes and the complete auton-

> omy of the municipalities, for which many disciplinary social measures would by their nature remain more usefully reserved.[4]

So on this basis there is no doubt: The state must also intervene with specific legislation:

> It is urgent that the arduous and complex relations between the multitudes of workers and the capitalist enterprisers of the big industries and of modern agricultural cultivation, relations that today unfold almost outside of the law, at the mercy of conflicting forces, between alternating lockouts and strikes, between convulsive interruptions and mutual harassment, should be brought back under normal legal discipline that may harmonize individual and social interests in the name of justice.[5]

Workers' social legislation

> By the name of *workers' social legislation*, today is meant a series of *special* laws and public provisions for the more direct relief of the multitudes, not substituted for those *general laws* (civil codes and statutory laws) in whose common observance civil equality consists, but rather added to them, in order to bring back and maintain the harmonious unity between the various classes of the social body. And it, in correspondence with the threefold function of the state as guardian, coordinator, and promoter of the common good, tends to be expressed with a threefold concrete purpose.[6]

The salient points of the debate on this topic between the 1800s and 1900s can be deduced from an international conference held in Zurich in 1897 on the initiative of the International Association for the Legal Protection of Workers,[7] in which Toniolo had been unable to take part personally, but in which some Catholic representatives from various European nations had participated, in direct confrontation with the socialists. From Italy and at Toniolo's prompting the lawyer G. M. Serralunga had taken part. On the basis of an account drawn up by the latter, who signed the article with him, Toniolo writes an extensive report on that great "social experiment," going into the details of the discussion and its outcomes.[8] The discussions had focused on the Sunday rest, the work of adolescents, and the employment of women in the industries.

The priest J. Beck had been a passionate and thoroughly prepared speaker on the Sunday rest for the Catholic side.[9] Speaking to an audience largely made up of socialists, he had deftly quoted Marx and Kautsky in their highlighting that it is capitalism and not socialism that undermines the family, even keeping parents and children apart on Sunday.[10] The discussion was resolved in favor of the Catholic position.

Not so for the other items on the agenda. As for the protection of children and adolescents, Catholics and socialists converged in wanting work under a certain age to be prohibited, making education compulsory. But at what age should the limit be set? Should it be the same for all types of industry? The position of the Catholics was complex. In the end the socialist stance of the age limit of sixteen had won.[11] A similar outcome on the issue of working hours: The socialist proposal to limit working time to eight hours a day had prevailed, whereas the Catholics, "while agreeing on a maximum limit to be defined within a certain range, also by international law, advocated a wider margin of variation and application."[12] But the socialist Vandervelde himself had given a tempered interpretation of this resolution, noting that the eight-hour limit was not to be understood as uniformity without exceptions.[13] An all-out confrontation had taken place on the subject of work for women, which had the problem of the family behind it. Catholics were particularly concerned "about the generalized abuse of the capitalist production system by which women, welcomed, indeed wanted by and drawn to the big factories, are torn away en masse from the domestic hearth."[14] The Belgian Catholic parliamentarian Carton de Wiart had formulated his proposal in these terms: "The congress vows that the work of women in factories and mines *should be gradually abolished*."[15] The debate was heated. The socialist from Stuttgart Klara Zetkin had spoken out in favor of women working in factories in the name of their emancipation. The female response from the Catholic side had fallen to Baroness Vogelsang, who had illustrated the ideal of the familial role of women and so the appropriateness of limiting their employment in factories by privileging and developing domestic work.[16] The two major speeches on the topic had been given for the one side by the Catholic Decurtins and for the other by the socialist Bebel.[17] A short sword duel, with the final victory of the socialist position, at least according to the numbers, given that Toniolo concludes, "The cause of the *family* seemed lost this time, by the number of votes, but the audience judged that by virtue of reason it was won gloriously."[18]

The discussion on workers' legislation would continue, and increasingly with the participation of states and with a growing awareness of the need for international legislation.[19] An emblematic moment came in Zurich in 1897. On the one hand, Catholics and socialists found themselves united in criticizing the capitalist system, both promoting social legislation; on the other, albeit with substantially correct and respectful manners (the socialist Liebkneckht compared the meeting to a "Truce of God"[20]), the different and irreconcilable points of view of Catholics and socialists emerged clearly. The two "armies" could not be confused, but in the meantime they had identified the common enemy and workers clearly found, not only in the socialists but also in the Catholics, a point of support. Toniolo translated the lesson from this for Catholics: It was urgent to roll up one's sleeves, going to the people, working and enlightening. The people will return to the Church

> on the day when with *action* and equally with the *light of truth* Catholics will have shown this to them, not indeed as a stepmother, but as a mother, minister of justice and charity, initiator of every demand of the people, loving guardian of the weak and oppressed.[21]

Zurich was once again a moment in which European Catholics showed themselves united, beyond matters of detail, on the general outlook. Toniolo writes:

> The Catholics, finally, acquired another merit at this conference: that of having demonstrated a full understanding of the

> profound transformation that is taking place in contemporary society, and of having similarly traced the main lines of the reorganization and mission of the working class in the future restoration of Christian society: to gather the scattered and now disconnected members of the working class in every civilized nation, ensuring their preservation and integrity with protective international laws; to prepare along with such protective legislation the reconstitution of industrial associations, which may better foster the application of those laws in the act whereby it attributes organic vitality and their own social function to those classes; to further bring these safeguards to bear on the rebirth of the first cell of every civil organism, that is, on the recomposition, solidity, and vigor of the working family; in this way to restore to the proletariat that moral dignity which Christianity has connected with work, family life, and class spirit; and finally to educate the proletariat, that is, the great mass of the people, so newly redeemed from the corrupting dissolution of individualism, in the awareness of their mission in Christian society as a factor of social preservation against the snares of socialism.[22]

Protection of the just labor contract

It is not enough, Toniolo wrote in 1906, that the law on the *labor contract,* concerning the wage earner, ensure with freedom of negotiation and agreement the mutual obligations, their observance, and the modalities of exceptional breaches of the bond, but it is necessary that this should imprint upon the labor contract itself (*locatio operarum*) a *collective character.*[23]

So, there is a need to avoid as much as possible that workers negotiate their pay in an isolated way: They would always be the losers! It is instead necessary that they feel assisted by the associative force, and this also in the case of in-home work, "to put a stop to the exhausting meagerness of sweating wages and uplift the lot of female work in the family."[24]

By giving legal force to the association of workers, Toniolo explained in 1902 in *Provvedimenti sociali popolari*, the state fulfills the function of *guardian* toward them, aimed at

> ensuring the integrity of rights and so of freedom (personal, of workers). Lacordaire's saying applies here, that "between the strong and the weak, it is freedom that oppresses and law that liberates."[25]

Lengthy examples of this state protection follow — we will skip these, in part because, at least on the European landscape, this is a condition already in place — derived above all from English and German legislation. The state is also recognized as having a "coordinating" function, with measures taken on behalf of workers under agricultural or industrial contracts. As for the former, Toniolo insists on the need for the relationship between workers and owners of the land to move ever further away from the condition of "temporary wage earner," to express itself in forms of "partnerships" of different types (leaseholding, metayage, sharecropping, rental) in which the personality of the worker is respected and the working of the land itself is favored, as would hardly be possible on landed estates where swarms of workers arrive only at haphazard, in a completely precarious way.[26]

> We must by preference set the wage earner as much as possible on the path toward the higher relationships of leaseholding, sharecropping, and small ownership, in keeping with the legitimate aspirations of the common rural people themselves, who demand not so much a less meager wage as a more stable and dignified economic position.[27]

Our author expresses his admiration for the practice of "collective rentals" in which farmers previously bound to the yoke of the Lombard or Sicilian sub-landlord felt supported and freed by the work of priests like Sturzo in Sicily and Portaluppi in Lombardy.[28] It is indispensable that such protections be guaranteed by the intervention of the state within the framework of international labor legislation,[29] which seems important to Toniolo in part for a reason that today, in the global market, we feel is particularly urgent, namely the need to

> exert pressure on every government so that, by each adopting its own disciplinary labor laws, the working classes may be protected wherever they are; nor should it happen that the nation that refuses to put a stop to the abuses of capitalism to the detriment of workers should by the sacrifice of these engage in unfair competition with the peoples that are more attentive in ensuring, through a higher sense of morality and justice, the protection and relief of the working classes.[30]

Recognition of professional unions

As we have seen, the social program of Christian democracy attributed the utmost importance to professional unions. It called for their establishment and development at home, but also abroad among emigrants.[31] It was requested that all this be expressed legally, through "the conferral of legal personality on the professional unions themselves, so that they may access the courts and acquire their own assets; hence the constitution of *collective property* belonging to the class."[32] This type of recognition "must be granted to any group of workers, under the sole condition of registering its statutes, so that it may be seen that these do not offend the public order."[33] Therefore, upon the corporate orders of workers and capitalist-owners in agriculture, in industry, in commerce, the state is called on to confer

> *legal personality*, that is, the ability to represent their interests in court and to own assets; a *jurisdiction*, that is, the faculty to rule in certain special cases of the profession; a *legislative disciplinary power*, to determine (subordinate to the general laws) and apply certain regulations for the best good of production and of the respective class.[34]

Can one go so far as to make associations compulsory? Would that be a threat to freedom? For Toniolo it is instead an increase in freedom. Nothing that has to do with the use that the fascist regime would make of corporatism, rendering it instrumental to the totalitarian regime:[35]

> So the *obligatory nature* of law implies only that the individual, in *economic life* itself, is in no case free to remain isolated, with the risk of harm to himself and others, but must enjoy the protection and help of his class and participate in the deliberation and observance of the measures adopted by it and for it. And what a precious right and what an increase in freedom (in exchange for a few mutual observances and services) for a group of owners, industrialists, workers, to give themselves in the bosom of fellowship *a law of their own* and *ensure that it be respected,* according to the needs of profession or place, rather than to live in an *anarchy* that is the triumph of the domineering, or to suffer the rigid and incompetent regulations of the distant government! The like holds true for all of private and public life. The individual, for example, today remains fully free to set up or transfer his domicile anywhere, inside or outside the nation, but no one among modern peoples is allowed, in order to live outside of the law, not to belong to any municipality or any state.[36]

Toniolo does not dodge an objection: but aren't abuses by associations to be feared? Answer: Of course, but there are no fewer abuses in the current

> decadent regime of freedom, or rather of anarchy, under which the coalitions, the strikes, the boycotts, the mutinies on the part of workers, the oppression of the poor, the mass expulsions from the factories, the new feudalism of the stock exchange, the conspiracy of the speculators, of the industrial and mercantile unions, the colossal monopolies of the trusts on the part of the capitalists, sadly fill the history of the nineteenth century, during which, together with liberalism, socialism was able to extend its conquests to the whole world.[37]

So one cannot, given the possibility of abuse, condemn an institution that is good in itself, but only conclude "that the state must intervene with its laws to protect freedom and justice, also in the face of the future associations."[38] On the other hand, in the constitution of professional unions[39] everything comes from below, responding to the natural aggregative needs that develop not only around purely material interests, but also around moral and spiritual needs. Hence also the role of religion in them, albeit with respect for the personal conditions of faith and religious practice of each member, but in any case in such terms that in each professional union the workers may feel as if they are in a "vast family that facilitates all the legitimate satisfactions of a proper and dignified life."[40]

Support for small property

The insistence on fostering small property is a recurring motif in Toniolo's thought, an insistence that has a clear summary in the following passage:

> In the zones of large-scale, intensive cultivation, the introduction of *collective rental* should be facilitated, on behalf of small farmers and laborers associated in solidarity with each other, with the various combinations already successfully undertaken in Italy; in the regions (to be designated by law) of the landed estate left uncultivated or under extensive cultivation, the exceptional provision of obliging the owners to divide their holdings into *modest parcels*, to be given in leasehold to small farmers, should be applied more decisively.... With the intent of ensuring permanent social interests in conjunction with the land, the collective properties of the forests and mountain meadows should be kept in the hands of public bodies, and all general deforestation in forests in private hands should be absolutely prohibited, the law reducing this to regular periodic cutting. On the land assets of the state, the provinces, and the municipalities, *civic uses* should be respected, that is, customary rights of wood gathering and grazing in favor of the village communities, and on private properties subject to similar easements of collective use that encumber lands susceptible to intensive cultivation, legal authority should distinguish the rights of the owners from those of the users, allowing the former to free themselves from the general

> burden on their lands by granting a portion of these to the municipality, which will turn it into coppice woodland and stable meadows for the collective use of wood gathering and grazing, on behalf of the small farmers and laborers of the population, almost a dowry of small property and sustenance of the have-nots. Finally, on the extra-European continents that are the destination of our migratory throngs, the state should see to ensuring for them with diplomatic agreements the conditions for a sound, productive, and definitive colonization of the foreign lands that are almost an extension of the soil of the homeland.[41]

A reform thus globally conceived opens itself up to political implications, since these large organic and vital bodies, equipped with social-civil faculties,

> could also become *political*, turning into *electoral colleges* for sending to parliament three distinct sets of deputies or representatives: of landowners, or of immovable wealth; of industrialists and merchants, or of movable wealth; and of workers, thus realizing the desired political representation by class.[42]

The regulation of credit

One of the strategic points of economic policy is to intervene on credit — essentially on the banks and stock markets in their respective operations — with precise criteria. According to the aforementioned report at the 1896 conference on credit, the fundamental criterion remains the principle that capital must not overwhelm labor, but be at its service. This also applies to monetary capital.

Hence the consequent guidelines on the duties of the state:

a. "legal prescriptions according to which the ordinary interest on private loans is kept in relation to the state of the market";[43]
b. criminal sanctions for any clear extortion;
c. introduction of land taxes favorable for small properties, in such a way that the capitalist, while acquiring — by virtue of

his loan to the owner of the land — the right to land income transferable to third parties, may not demand the repayment of the capital, "still preserving for the landowner the right to release himself from the tax burden by returning the capital itself according to certain procedures;"[44]

d. "with respect to direct credit for large properties, the gradual replacement of private lending, which is usually difficult and onerous, with the habit of long-term lending through land credit institutions, fostering as much as possible the development of these as preeminent centers for the flow of funds toward land and their distribution to owners under milder and more favorable conditions;"[45]

e. "similarly, also in commercial credit operations, favoring lending through the intervention of banking institutions rather than through private loans, moreover establishing the institutions themselves indeed not in the form of a for-profit company, but rather of an *entity with legal personality and with its own assets,* which therefore, freed from any regard to particular interests, may serve solely the general interest, as an institution of public utility;"[46]

f. alongside these credit institutions with legal personality, the spread of simple credit companies at which deposits may be subject to minimal interest (of pure indemnity for the bank), and when the deposit is protracted may take on the character of "a *joint* venture between the investors (depositors) and the clientele as a whole (producers), funded and represented by the bank, such that the collection of interest on deposits and the return of the capital deposited itself may be subject to the condition and measure of the realization of profits and the preservation of the bank's capital;"[47]

g. "that preference be given to the interests of the middle and lower classes, fostering both small savings and small loans, thus correcting the greatest vice of the modern age, whereby credit tends by preference to provide capital indefinitely to those who are already rich, while by its nature capital is

> destined for a function of equalizing social differences, providing this powerful means to those who are defenseless and equipped only with personal aptitudes, hence the appropriateness of the multiplication of credit unions."[48]

All of these policies must be accompanied by measures aimed at "restricting that *illegitimate expansion* of credit which has given rise to the universal custom of basing the entire economy of nations on *lending* and so on the monopoly of monetary capital, instead pushing capital to seek return in direct, normal, lasting association with work."[49]

Hence the urgency of a series of restrictions:

- to bring the bill of exchange back to its characteristics of a "commercial security" linked to a real transaction;[50]
- to reduce to exceptions, well controlled by law, joint stock companies with limited liability, "which with the variations in the value of the shares often fuel dangerous and unfair speculations,"[51] while collective companies with unlimited liability and those with mixed liability (limited partnerships) must be considered normal;[52]
- public credit is to be considered legitimate as the purchase and sale of a perpetual return without the obligation of repayment of the capital by the state, but an end must be brought to "the increase in these public liabilities and other forms of state debt that remove from productive employment much of the capital destined for industries and provide enormous and incessant material for random and often dishonest speculation;"[53]
- to tax company stocks as well as income producing securities;
- to increase, with respect to taxes on movable wealth, taxes on bond payments, since they constitute "an income that does not involve personal services;"[54]
- that commercial shares, like government bonds, if registered, be subjected to lower transfer taxes;
- "to prohibit with strict laws all financial market operations

that have the character of gambling or give rise to it";[55]

- finally, "to favor partnerships in commerce and industry in all forms, that is, those in which the partners are personally responsible with the fullness of their honor and their substance, and to promote the establishment, among merchants or industrialists, of class corporations or associations that, by restraining dishonest competition by mutual agreement, may emancipate them from the excessive need for credit, remove them from servitude to the large banks, and conversely induce capitalists to ally themselves directly with producers, becoming permanent partners of the companies."[56]

It is a long series of corrective interventions entrusted to the law, and so to the state. Here one would expect that Toniolo would also like the idea of a single state bank of issuance. And instead the idea finds him opposed, in contrast with the prevailing direction in Europe, and this because of his underlying concern over a slide from liberal individualism to state omnipotence.[57] One of his great-grandsons, Gianni Toniolo, an economic historian, would present interesting contextual considerations on this position.[58]

Ultimately, the way out of the problems of credit was to be found, according to our author, in the multiplication of credit institutions as closely linked as possible to the people and places they serve, and for Catholics, of institutions linked to the ecclesial world, which would allow the social control necessary to keep credit from deviating from the ethical guidelines that must regulate it. He dealt with this in detail in a report given at the XIVth Italian Catholic Congress.[59] The accent is on the morality of credit transactions, as well as on the motives of distributive justice and general utility, "so that the dispensing of credit may not follow the motives of personal profit, but may be based mainly on public well-being, as a social function."[60]

There could be debate over Toniolo's concrete approach in relation to the evolution of the credit economy of our time. Nonetheless, observing what we have experienced even recently, for example in the global financial crisis of 2007–08, it is hard not to conclude that his concern regarding the growing pathologies of this aspect of the contemporary economy was well-founded.

The tax system and progressive taxation

Another significant theme — that of progressive taxation — was on stage at the previously mentioned conference of the Catholic Union for Social Studies in 1896. Here a report proposed by Anastasio Rossi, future archbishop of Udine and afterward prelate of Pompeii, was to be put on standby so as not to cause divisions among Catholics. Toniolo spoke out in support of the cause defended by the speaker.[61] It was a brilliant speech in terms of tactical ability, diplomatic style, and bold attitude, aimed at getting approval for the most demanding solution. He knew well that

> from the times of the municipalities, later absorbed into the principalities, to those of the *ancien régime* that precipitated the French Revolution, up to the present day, in which generally a crushing and overloaded financial system suffocates economic life and harshens class struggles, the question of taxes and their distribution was always a primary and decisive part of social upheavals.[62]

But not taking a position, timidly circumventing the problem, he argued, would not be a good witness and would mean losing a golden opportunity to show the strength of the Catholic approach to the social question. That if, on this issue, the socialists also thought the same way, it should not be frightening:

> We must also once and for all reclaim our right and indeed our priority in every cause where the true and the just are at stake. The usurpers are our adversaries, and we are doing nothing but bringing every noble cause that affects civilization back to its pure and sublime source.[63]

The financial policy of a state is no small thing, he added, adopting the thought of another, given that "legislating on finance can bring about a greater revolution than that of 1793."[64] He then dedicates himself to demonstrating that progressive taxation, as compared with the proportional, responds to true justice.[65] In this he endorses the previous remarks by Angelo Mauri, recalling

> that the preferred doctrine of financial science today for the distribution of tax burdens is that of the *ability to contribute,* which is in fact the result of two components: the *wealth possessed* by each taxpayer (real element) set in relation to the subjective ends (personal element) that the wealth serves. And therefore one who possesses so much wealth that with an initial part of it he has provided for the essential ends of private existence can contribute more extensively to the state with a second part that still remains and serves only his secondary ends. I would like to add that this financial doctrine coincides with the economic doctrine of the *decreasing final utility* of wealth. Of three equal units of wealth owned by the same person, the value of the first unit, which serves essential needs of life, is high, but the value of the second, which serves accessory needs, is lower, and the value of the third, intended for saving and perhaps squandering, is even lower. So, if the revenue authority, in order to provide equal treatment, wants to withdraw the same share of value by way of tax for each unit of wealth owned, it must hit the second unit more than the first and the third unit more than the second. Let this criterion be applied to three distinct contributors of wealth differently graduated and the fairness of the progressive criterion is evident. In this sense the true proportional tax is the progressive.[66]

He concluded with a warm invitation to Catholics that in this matter, too, they should show themselves champions of justice in favor of those who are weaker.

Free trade or protectionism?

Also on the subject of trade policy, Toniolo does not forsake his balanced position, always based on recourse to principles. And these say first of all that the exchange of wealth is a value. This must also be applied to universal trade. At the same time, it is necessary to hold firm the principle that wealth is instrumental to the human person in his relational existence, and so must take into account the hierarchy of his social relationships (family, nation, international society). His synthesis in a correspondence with Luigi Caissotti di Chiusano is enlightening. Considering that economics studies "individual human activity, which unfolds to achieve and use wealth in the bosom and with the participation of society," there is established "the right and certainly the appropriateness of exchanging wealth wherever this is most useful to its full use and enjoyment, both domestically and abroad,"[67] but precisely for this reason this must be done to the degree that trade not harm social ends. The activity of trade

> first, therefore, must be coordinated for the economic ends of national society, which forms its own organic unity and is closer to individual private existence, and further for the ends of universal society. This latter may seek general free trade as the ultimate tendency; the former, as its immediate provision, the constitution and preservation of the organism of the national market, and thus, within certain limits, protectionism.[68]

Toniolo specifies that all of this must also be regulated by distinguishing the qualities of the products and the social circumstances (normal or abnormal times). He recalls, for his time, the crisis of overproduction:

> Today, for example, there is an evident excess of production overconsumption, which determines competition to the death between nations, which in turn has repercussions on the phenomena of wages and unemployment. And likewise today there weighs heavily in the balance the competition between ancient lands and those saturated with capital, such as those of Europe and the new and virgin ones of America.[69]

He then reminds his correspondent that, since freedom of trade is ultimately aimed at more abundant consumption, the interests of production cannot be neglected: "The low price of foodstuffs would be of little use if many workers were unemployed and had no means to buy them."[70] Ultimately, free trade, yes, but not as an absolute that does not allow exceptions. A healthy economy is made up of many aspects and many dynamics. It is the task of politics to operate with discernment.

The discussion then becomes problematic, from our contemporary point of view, when the theme of relations between nations slides onto the terrain of colonial and imperial geopolitics. In Toniolo's time imperialism was in vogue, particularly in the England of the Chamberlains, the Balfours, etc. In a letter dated 1903, again to L. Caissotti di Chiusano, our author summarizes his point of view.[71] Beyond the political and cultural aspects, which lead some European nations to expand into other continents, integrating some peoples "into the circuit of Christian civilization"[72] (a perspective so distant from that of today!), Toniolo dwells on the economic aspect of the phenomenon:

> Imperialism has its economic aspect, and how! That of customs duties is subordinate to it. All of the grave agitation of free trade in our times, even more than in the year 1846, would impose or suggest universal freedom of commerce. But this is opposed in part by the aforementioned tendencies of groupings of races, one against the other, and also by a profound and common difficulty: the permanent and universal crisis (as from 1870–82) of production and consumption. On the whole, modern civil states have a structure — that is, a technical-capitalist system of industries so powerful that they are able to produce much more than what civil society, at the normal rate of trade, is capable of buying and consuming. … Hence the tendency of every state to close itself off with a protectionist customs barrier, to exclude foreign sellers and ensure domestic consumption for its own industries. And at the same time it must of necessity acquire foreign markets throughout the world as an outlet for national production, and in this twofold way restore for the nation itself the balance between production and consumption.[73]

This dynamism explains the English tendency to increasingly widen the circle of its colonies, facilitating their commercial relations with the motherland and closing "this ethnic-economic circle to the competition of other international ethnic circles that stand before it."[74] In this regard, he wondered: "Shouldn't there be a federation of Latin States? In this, what providential plan is hidden for Christian civilization?"[75] But with quite different sentiments, ten years later, faced with Germany's declaration of war on Russia (August 1, 1914) and immediately afterward on France, he would wonder:

> What will the king of hosts, who is also the king of peace, conclude from this immense conflagration of the military forces of more or less Christian but still practically pagan states, which in the name of selfish nationalism, each of them greedy to impose a violent, racially exclusive imperialism on the other autonomous lineages of Europe and the world, trample on and reject the universal society founded on the equality and brotherhood of all human beings, children of the common divine paternity?[76]

Conclusion

Perspectives and Provocations

An economist ahead of his time?

> With the dizzying speed of our times, in which years count as centuries, events have come headlong that, for good or for ill, in the domain of ideas as in the experiences of social life increasingly testify to the truth of and need for Christian scientific principles.[1]

Words written in 1896. Speaking of the acceleration of time, they seem to have been written today, in the full-blown era of the internet. Could this, our own, be the hour of Toniolo? Two Catholic economists separated by more than half a century — Francesco Vito and Stefano Zamagni — agree in considering the Pisan professor an unlucky school founder. The thinking he set in motion was not received and developed as much as it should have been. It may be true that his redundant style, his open and insistent perspective of faith (in his time, as today, a challenge to political correctness), and a series of accidental causes contributed to this. But doesn't history have its resources and, in Giambattista Vico's parlance, its recourses?

Zamagni today describes Toniolo as an "economist ahead of his time." In what was he ahead of his time? Francesco Vito observed, with a hint of disappointment, that our author did not leave behind any principle that could be called a law of economics.[2] Is that so? It seems to me that this last evaluation can be upheld only if one looks at the more technical aspects of economic dynamics, what the Pisan professor called the "operational order," to distinguish it from the "constitutive order."[3] But wasn't Toniolo's interest — I would say his fascination — precisely the fundamentals? He spent a lifetime vindicating them, maintaining that the economic edifice (and not only it) is at risk of collapsing when it lacks solid foundations. This applies to economic practice as well as to science. It is here that one must seek out his originality and legacy.

By way of a hermeneutic hypothesis — aware that I am writing not as an economist, but with the unconcealed hope of *provoking* economists (and politicians!) — I will try to outline some characterizing aspects of his thought, proposing them in terms of *principles* (so as not to confuse them with the technical *laws* of economics).

Our time, in all areas of practice and knowledge, and therefore also in economic matters, struggles to find agreement precisely on principles. It rejects them as a relic of *metaphysical* times that can no longer be proposed, with the sad consequence, also in economic science, of "a Babelic confusion of languages."[4] While languages are confused and theories wasted, we are grappling with formidable questions (*dum Romae consulitur Saguntum expugnatur* — "while Rome deliberates, Saguntum is stormed!"[5]), not least that of the world economy, which experiences its cyclical crises, and in any case lives in a state of imbalance if one looks at the issues of poverty, inequality, social hardship. "Today," Thomas Piketty has written, "we have no reason to believe in the automatically balanced nature of growth. Today it is more urgent than ever to put the question of inequalities back at the center of economic analysis and return to posing the questions left without adequate answer in the nineteenth century."[6] How can a problem of these dimensions be addressed without criteria? Returning to the fundamentals is not a waste of time, but a gain of future. In reality, even economists who espouse a post-metaphysical perspective ultimately adopt as axioms or methodical postulates principles they at least consider reasonable. Empirical research itself needs them so as not to be reduced to a meaningless game. Chase metaphysics out the door and it will come back, perhaps in false guise, through the window.

Leaves that fall, trunk that remains

In offering this attempt at a summary I will limit myself to what I consider essential for the ends of economic discussion. I know well that Toniolo is a man of his time, and so there is no lack of dated aspects in his thinking, in some cases to be frankly considered obsolete. Everything invites us to rediscover him; nothing obliges us to make him into a myth. In his mental world, typical of a man of culture, faith, and multiple social relationships, there are many lights, but also shadows linked to the inevitable ecclesial and historical-cultural influences.[7] One who rereads his thought from the point of view of the theological background, placing it under the scrutiny of the Second Vatican Council, will find on the one hand aspects in which he appears to be a forerunner (for example on the theme of ecclesial commitment in history, with an intense need for lay coresponsibility and an authentic lay spirituality[8]), and on the other hand aspects in which he is affected — like many of his contemporaries, starting with the popes of his time — by a "pyramidal" conception of the Church, in need of diving back into the "familial" spirit of the Christian origins; theological dimensions also influence his social thought. I could go on: I think of his view of the social order, based on classes in terms of a hierarchical conception that, although animated (may it not seem contradictory) by a great democratic aspiration and based on the centrality of the poor and the corresponding duty of service of the upper classes, nonetheless exposes itself, in one case or another, to the risk of paternalism, perhaps underestimating — but not without glimmers of an opposite character — how much the poor, helped and supported, can and must do for their own redemption (hence a social action not only *for* the poor, but also *with* the poor). Something, in reality, not at all excluded from Toniolian thought, which on the contrary pushes in this direction. Yet he was held back not only by the dominant worldview, but above all by the nightmare of socialism. Going to another point, his conception of woman, although open and appreciative (a view certainly favored by his happy marriage to Maria Schiratti), still reflected the prevalent tendency at the time toward a distinctly domestic interpretation of the female role,[9] a perspective quite far from today's sensibility, even when unacceptable extremisms are to be, and should be, avoided. The same can be said of the way in which he conceived, in the process of "*incivilimento*," the civilizing task of colonialism, which at the time was a common attitude in Europe. On this front he shows himself, albeit with some well-placed critical hints, still far from being aware of the limitations and errors of that system, which today are visible much more clearly after the end of Eurocentrism in an increasingly multipolar and multicultural world.

All things, these, that also on the level of the economic perspective (what doesn't have to do, at least indirectly, with the economy?) have their weight.

The "Toniolian optimum" or the "integral good health" of the economy

So let us take Toniolo with his limitations, without making any allowances. What remains? Many things. As regards the foundation of economic discourse, there remain some principles that I will call principles of correlation applied to economic action as a whole (but the consequences on the individual sectors of the economy can be readily deduced and developed).

By correlation I mean the link between a reality A and a reality B, in which A is the economy understood as the practice and science of material wealth in its more "technical" aspects (business, production, costs and revenues, distribution and trade, money, finance, market, etc.),[10] B represents, at various levels, the social order (it will be remembered that Toniolo defines economics as the science of the *social order* of wealth).

With this attempt at a synthesis I hope to recover, at least in part, a chapter that our author was not given to elaborate, but that he had in some manner planned in that document, which we analyzed,[11] of 1886, adopted by the second section of the Opera dei Congressi,[12] in which the themes and structure of the future *Trattato* were essentially anticipated. In it, after having distinguished the introduction, and then the fourfold thematic articulation of the "economic social order" (a. production; b.

exchange of goods or circulation of wealth; c. exchange of services or distribution of wealth; d. consumption or use of wealth), our author also added a fifth articulation indicated as a "comprehensive law of the economic order and of the consequent material well-being of society."[13] What did he mean by "comprehensive law"? I don't know if what I am proposing in this conclusion is an answer to this question. It nonetheless seems to me at least a hermeneutic attempt well founded in the whole Toniolian magisterium.

I start from the consideration that current assessments of the economy usually speak of its "state of health," and the "good health" of an economy (a company, an economic sector, the economy in general) is seen as a condition in which the numbers add up and profits are made. So, it is usual to check on "good health" by reading the balance sheets, analyzing the fiscal, economic, financial position. For countries, everything is analyzed starting from the gross domestic product (GDP). At most, in all of this there is introduced — and it is already a specific step forward in economic thought — some element referring to satisfaction, overall interest, well-being, and happiness, as elements that concern the human world implicated in economic processes, remembering that the fundamental principle that characterizes economic reasoning — the "hedonic" one, or the maximum benefit with the minimum cost — is a rational and therefore profoundly anthropological principle. But the human-hedonic element is only one aspect: the more subjective one, which recalls and presupposes an objective aspect of the human. Experience says that in people's psychology the subjective aspect (happiness, satisfaction, sense of well-being) does not always fully correspond to the objective one, given that in the evaluation of objective aspects there is always room for error. In other words, the motives that lead to happiness, at least in the immediate future, do not always coincide with authentic anthropological needs and sometimes cause damage and sadness that manifest themselves only over time (one could think of the satisfaction that can be felt by one who uses intoxicants, or of the shady gratification of one who profits from drugs, or of the horrifying cynicism of a hardened criminal in committing a murder or making a deal). So the aspects of "objective human health" cannot be underestimated in judging the balance sheets of an economy that, as it is made by the human person, must also be made *for* him. If also in the evaluation of physical health it can sometimes happen that one feels good, only to discover later that this feeling did not correspond to good health, this is no less true in the psychological-economic order.

I understand that such a consideration stands in tension with the relativistic climate of the current culture, devoid of certainties even in what is fundamentally human, but it is an unavoidable challenge. It is impossible not to appeal to the objective-human, even if trying to determine it with humility and in dialogue with various cultural approaches. The Christian vision — and with it the Toniolian — of the economy starts from the rational certainty, confirmed by revelation, of the existence of an objective ontological order that supports the human as a stable axis despite the variety of historical situations and models.[14]

Toniolo outlines an economy that, in principle, is intimately correlated with this ordered condition of the human being, his identity, his relationships. When he speaks of an economy that works well, he means an economy in which not only the company's accounts add up, but so do the accounts of the human, of society, of civilization. Only then is an economy in a truly healthy state (Toniolo often distinguishes between the physiology and pathology of the socioeconomic order[15]). In this regard, I would propose the expression of "integral good health," with the question: What are the principles or criteria, or "laws" — however one prefers to call them — that must function if an economy is to be in a state of "integral good health"?

Among the best-known concepts of economic thought is that of the "optimum" proposed by Pareto.[16] I wonder if there is a Toniolian "optimum"? Having to look to an ideal, to a basic criterion, how does Toniolo imagine the optimal condition of the economy?

I believe that first of all he would explain that his "optimum" is not a mechanical formula, but a specifically human dynamism, and so its pursuit will always take place as a tension, a journey "toward," a goal to aim for, perhaps not underestimating the popular wisdom of the proverb "the best is the enemy of the good." In history, with the presumption of the best, utopias devoid of concreteness have been designed, resulting in revolutions in which the blood shed certainly did not produce the results dreamed of or hoped for. The Toniolian optimum — that is, the ideal of an "integral good health" of the economy — is not a mathematical equation to be balanced at any cost, but a conceptual tension to be allowed to mature in minds and in history. Toniolo would put all of this in the following terms, which he characterizes as the "law of civilization":

> The higher the vision of the internal ends of humanity (*Weltanschauung*), the better the predisposition to invent the external means that serve as a ladder.[17]

Wanting to dissect this "law of civilization" on the basis of what we have learned in the systematic analysis of Toniolo's texts, I believe that his optimum can be summarized in the following three principles, which, after a lexical explanation (with apologies for a few Greekisms or Latinisms, preferred only because they are useful for summarizing), I will try to explain in terms of theses and related commentary. The Toniolian theses should not be understood as explicitly formulated by him, but as extractable from his thought (theses, I would say, of Toniolian inspiration).

1. Principle of humanistic correlation: economy ⟷ holo-oiko-personalistic view of the human

Terms:

- *humanistic/personalistic:* to indicate the reference to the human person as the center, subject, and end of the economy. Man and woman understood in the full sense expressed by the concept of person dear to philosophical personalism of Christian inspiration, but no less rationally founded;
- *holo:* from the Greek root *holos* (whole), to indicate the complete expression of the human person in the entirety of his dimensions (rational, volitional, affective, corporeal, relational);
- *oiko:* from the Greek root *oikos* (house, family) — whence

the words *economy* and *ecology* — to indicate a "familial" vision of the human being, according to which society is not a simple aggregate of monads (single "individualities"), but a weaving of social and fraternal relationships both within the human world and, in some way, in the relationship with the cosmos itself (in the manner of Francis of Assisi: "brother sun," "sister moon," etc.), a weaving based, more or less consciously, on the transcendent foundation of the creaturely and filial relationship with God.

Toniolian thesis: An economy that is efficient on the technical level is in integral good health to the extent that the human person, grasped not only in the multiple dimensions of his individual being but also in his complex relationship with other human beings, with the material-animal environment, with the transcendent (God, for believers; for everyone at least the mystery in which existence is shrouded), is placed at the center of appraisals and decisions, being respected and promoted as the point of gravity for the factors cooperating in economic processes (work, nature, capital).

Commentary.

a. The debate that runs through the economic science of our time does not fail to register, in the jumble of highly diversified trends and positions, a (growing?) line of thought that distances itself from a "separated" view of the economy. This is a rediscovery — coming back in some way to Toniolo — of the essentially integrated character of economic action and social action. It is now openly confessed, with the amazement of Andersen's famous fairy tale, that "the emperor is naked"[18] — that is, that the presumed *homo oeconomicus* on which pompous theories dressed up with mathematical language have been built is in reality a *fictio*, a pure mental model. *Homo oeconomicus*, to put it bluntly, does not exist! Man exists in the complexity of his dimensions, which can certainly be distinguished for the purposes of study, but cannot be separated. Science that does not take everything into account (the holistic approach) turns out to be false in its assumptions and a harbinger of disaster in its consequences.

b. In the light of two centuries of development of the economy and economic science, between the extremes of the broadest market freedom on the one hand and the most stringent statist regulation on the other, the Smithian framework appears increasingly inadequate, in the classical or neoclassical version (as of Léon Walras[19] and his admirers — in Italy, Pantaleoni, Barone, Pareto — up to the neo-Walrasians[20]). A system will not hold up if it is plastered together on the abstract methodical assumption that "*only individual agents exist*, their decisions are not influenced by any type of interdependence or externality, and their social relations are not mediated by any institution other than the competitive market."[21]
c. In the context of the current debate — rich in positions and nuances (such as, for example, on the subject of welfare economics and market failure[22]) — I believe that interest could be aroused, at least as a provocation, by this law of humanistic correlation of Toniolo, who based his entire economic teaching on the holistic approach, in the vein — which he frequented, not without a critical spirit — of the German historical school, also opening himself up to some mitigated positions of the classical school itself, finding, for example, allies like Marshall,[23] who had more luck than he but still did not significantly influence the long-term course of economics, with the possible exception of the "heretic" John Maynard Keynes, with his insistence on corrective state intervention in the market through monetary policy.
d. Accepting this first line of correlation means aiming for an integral economy, reintegrating the human being into its laws in terms that, contrary to the concept of the individualistic, selfish, and separate *homo oeconomicus,* can be defined

— in harmony with the substantial if not the lexical configuration of Toniolo — as *homo holo-oiko-nomicus*: It is this integral man who is the subject, the engine, and the end of economic action.[24]

e. If the center of gravity of economic activity remains *homo* understood according to this *holo-oiko-personalist* anthropology, this will have notable positive consequences. Two examples: that of respect for the environment, as an integral dimension of a good economy, and that of a curtailing of the capitalist-financial aspect of the economy, at least through rigorous control of it so that it may not domineer over the human aspect of the economy, keeping this latter anchored to actual productivity with a view to wealth to be adequately distributed to each human being. The wealth of the *holo-oiko-nomic* man grows, not if money increases, but if the things that money represents and helps to acquire grow for the benefit of the human person and his integral development, which, in the parlance of Paul VI, is not such if it is not the development of the "whole" man (and woman) and of "all" men (and women).[25] Finance must yield to productivity and not replace it.[26] It is necessary to interrupt the vicious circle of a financial wealth that takes resources away from real wealth, and of a real impoverishment that drives investment in ephemeral financial wealth.[27] The economy — micro and macro — must return from paper to things, and from things to the home. Wanting to give in to naivety, I would like it if, to recall all of this, there could sooner or later be a single world currency — is it really impossible to dream of it? — that would be called the *oikos*: no more dollar, euro, yen etc., but *oikos,* with which to buy and spend, to remember in every transaction the humanistic, holo-oiko-personalistic sense of economic activity.

f. A chapter that Toniolo could not foresee, and is therefore a challenge entirely our own, is that which sees us engaged in managing the digital age, in which the human *oikos* increasingly coincides with the internet, artificial intelligence, and online relationships that have an enormous impact on individual and collective existence. There is talk of "post-human" and "trans-human." There is talk of *homo algorithmus.*[28] The decisive question is whetehr we are leaving humanism behind, or deepening it?

Optimism and pessimism can face each other here in a no-holds-barred match, depending on whether one sees more of the lights or of the shadows. In the digital world, will the human still be at the helm? Or will it allow itself to be overrun by its own production? There are those who see above all the beauty of a technological progress that will bring greater freedom, creativity, and ingenuity, with an organization of working relationships capable of putting the human person at the center.[29] And there are those who see the digital world obscured by the shadow of a global dictatorship that will control everything and everyone and definitively crush human subjectivity.[30]

Can this scenario, premature in Toniolo's time, be addressed with a consistent application of Toniolian principles? I think so. Indeed, I believe that precisely for this new world the Toniolian principle is more relevant than ever. Holo-oiko-personalism, as the foundation, soul, and structuring principle of economic rationality, can guarantee precisely the primacy of the human pole in the human person-machine relationship. The challenge (a particular task of culture, of philosophy, of the proclamation of faith) is to recover and strengthen a renewed humanistic awareness by opening it to the integrally human, in which the economic factor develops in full convergence with ethics, culture, environment, politics, and religion.

g. Without this conversion of the economy to holo-oiko-personalist anthropology, even without wanting to be catastrophic, it is hard not to take into account an enormous risk. If humanity in fact stays put or even retreats, in its typ-

> ically human prerogatives, while the machine progresses at exponential speed, how can one not fear, at moment *x*, the suicidal self-surrender of humanity to its machines? Evoking the biblical scenario of the first destruction of humanity in the time of Noah, there is to be feared a universal deluge not of water but of machines, with the progressive reduction, to the point of thinning down close to zero, of self-awareness, of responsibility, of the transcendent openness that characterizes the human world. One could then only hope for a new Noah's ark [moment], for a resumption anew (Toniolo would say a palingenesis) of humanity's journey: an ark that is always possible (the believer hopes for this for reasons of faith; the nonbeliever by vital instinct). But it could only be built by the residual capacity of resilience of the human (in any case supported, in the eye of the believer, by the grace of God), by its capacity not to be definitively overrun, reacting to the instrument and learning to dominate it. A true rebirth of humanity would be needed.

Ultimately, humans and robots are destined to interact ever more. Woe, however, if the robot should get the upper hand.[31] But here the discussion and the challenge inevitably move from the side of reality to that of responsibility, which Toniolo enunciates in the third principle of correlation that we will encounter shortly and that arises at the level of moral conscience, the ultimate reserve of humanity.

2. Principle of solidaristic correlation: economy ⟷ organic, hierarcho-diaconic, imo-centric vision of society

Terms:

- *organic:* expresses the vision of society as a moral organism;
- *hierarchical:* emphasizes the diversity of social functions, detracting nothing from the equality of dignity of the human person, but respecting the directive functions and responsi-

bilities at the different functional levels of the social order (in this sense, as Toniolo expressed it, superior or hierarchical functions);

- *diaconic:* from the Greek term *diakonia* (service), indicates the role of service that each element of society is called to express at its level of social position and possibility;
- *imo-centric:* from the Latin term *imus* (low or deep[32]), indicates the strong attention to the least (the most poor, fragile, discarded) to be placed at the center of interest, both as recipients of care (welfare state and welfare society) and as protagonists of their own redemption (class organization for self-defense and self-management).

Toniolian thesis: An economy that is efficient on the technical level is in integral good health to the extent that it develops within a socio-institutional framework characterized by the right proportion and correct relationship between human groups linked by healthy bonds (therefore distinguished well from immoral and criminal ones), necessary or voluntary, so that society may be respected as it is, as a structured whole (a moral organism), with its internal functions and responsibilities, and primacy be ascribed to the civil society as opposed to the political (state), the latter operating by way of subsidiarity and solidarity with a view to the common good, to this end lifting the weakest members from the bottom of the economic-social ladder to the center of attention and promotion (imo-centrism).

Commentary.

a. To determine this principle one can make use of some of the voices in the economic debate. In particular, a certain affinity with Toniolo's thought emerges in those positions collected under the name of institutionalism,[33] united by the criticism of the free market and by the insistence on corrective and regulatory intervention carried out by the institutions, well protected however from totalitarian policies (Marxian socialist planning or that of the fascist corporate state). In this institutionalist approach the economy is removed from its mercantile solitude dominated by the fetish of perfect competition, and is seen in its inevitable intertwining with social dynamics and, within them, with specifically political-institutional dynamics.[34] There is resemblance to Toniolian thought in that of Thorstein Veblen,[35] father of institutionalism, or the holistic economics of Allan G. Gruchy, for whom economics must be a science of culture, developing in symbiosis with sociology, anthropology, politics, historiography.[36] On the level of psychological analysis, a similar direction is taken in the thought of Tibor Scitovsky, who on the basis of Wundt's research underlines the need for an economy that takes more into account creative goods and relational goods (relationships of family, friendship, affection, etc.), from which more satisfaction, indeed more happiness, can come than from the necessary elementary goods (food, health, home, comfort, etc.).[37] This approach is also followed by the school of civic economics that is being consolidated today, and that I believe finds, in many aspects, a forerunner in Toniolo (I found many points of similarity with Toniolo's synthesis in Kate Raworth's *The Doughnut Economics: Seven Ways to Think Like a 21st-Century Economist*).[38]

b. These affinities, however, do not extend to the overall specificity of Toniolo's vision. Equidistant from liberal individualism and socialist massification, equally opposed to absolute market freedom and excessive state intervention, it develops by looking at the process of genesis of social classes. The point of origin is the family based on the stable and generative relationship (marriage) of the man-woman couple and the children who come from it. Here is the fundamental cell, the first nucleus of social relationships that expand, almost in concentric circles, as a progressive or simultaneous weaving of relationships between families and then between groups of families (tribe, *gens*), from which emanates the social organism, called so because in the moral organism of society, people and families take their place in relation to different histories, needs, capacities, and functions (hence the various groupings of culture, economy, religion, territory, nation, etc.). So the social organism is born and develops as a natural process, configuring itself not only as a sum of individuals, but as a network of relationships. Little by little, as the relational pool grows, and with it also functional specialization, social classes are structured, understood as relatively stable and cohesive human groups. The genesis of classes thus has its roots in the very nature of the human person.

c. In that it is organic (a network of social bodies or classes), generated by the human person with his relationships, society draws its value from the person himself. It is the person who gives value to society, and not vice versa. Furthermore, by virtue of this genesis from below, society has a primary character with respect to the state, which is born as a function linked to social complexity, and so due to its intrinsic requirement,[39] in need as society is of being served by an institution that may ensure the common good and some special goods that people and their groups are unable, with their own efforts, to produce. The consequences of this principle on economic policy are evident. Excessive intervention by the state where the subjectivity of civil society could manage on its own, in addition to a public indebtedness that makes the entire system more fragile and precarious, slackens the creative energies of society, takes away resources that the state should instead ensure for weaker elements, and sometimes, with the phenomena of corruption and clientelism, masks a creeping totalitarianism of policy. The slogan "less state, more society,"[40] which was circulated a few years ago in the vein of liberalist recovery, need not be understood as a surrender to the untamed market. Achille Ardigò, precisely in Toniolo's footsteps, in an unsuspecting era, had presented the urgency of "starting again from civil society."[41] Today it is hard not to recognize that "since the end of the twentieth century the welfare state has entered into crisis, due to the aging of the population, the increased costs of services, and the rise of new forms of poverty. This imposes a rethinking of the model toward greater involvement of civil society, moving from the welfare state to the welfare society."[42]

d. Social groups, which are formed according to a logic linked to different abilities and opportunities, as well as to different histories and circumstances, tend to place themselves, according to Toniolo, not only in a diversified horizontal position (territorial, organizational, etc.), but also in a diversified vertical position: hence the expression "hierarchy" of classes. A word that today may sound doubtful and hardly appealing, especially if understood in tension with the equality of dignity of all human beings. For our author, who has no doubts about the latter, the emphasis on social hierarchy expresses the objective fact of an organic specialization of society, perfectly balanced by the ethical-diaconic imperative — that is, of service and responsibility. In short, those who are higher up have greater responsibility and must serve more. Toniolo's thought is clear: "Every form of superiority, be it of talent, wealth, or virtue, entails special duties on behalf of the less favored."[43] The hierarchy is thus not ontological (with respect to human dignity) but functional, to the advantage of the social organism, which develops and expresses itself in a healthy manner when the individual classes, far from closing themselves off in the protected enclosures of impenetrable castes and privileges defended tooth and nail, open themselves up to the dynamism of the growth and freedom of people, who can therefore present themselves, thanks to their talents and effort and with the support of private and public solidarity, for entrance into social and economic classes different from those of origin. To deny a hierarchy understood in this way is, for one thing, to deny the evidence of functional diversity, and, for another, to conceal and foster crypto-leadership phenomena fueled by populism and perhaps resulting in dictatorships.

e. The service of both civil society and the state is a function of the common good. It can be called such to the extent that the operational energies of the state and society converge to the special advantage of the classes that, due to their conditions of need, find themselves at the bottom of the social ladder. The class hierarchy, from this point of view, is resolved, for Toniolo, in an "inverted pyramid" (imo-centrism). In the eyes of our author, this very inversion is Christianity's great contribution to civilization.

f. The manner, then, of conceiving this service to the least, toward the bottom, cannot be limited to a paternalistic type of action (charity), but must rather be promotional in character, as an intervention that supports and stimulates the subjectivity of the lower classes: This is the democratic perspective (which, in the Toniolian sense, although social in the first place, does not exclude the political, but rather prepares for and establishes it). However, the organization of classes — also legally recognized by the state — implies that the primary service to the common good is entrusted precisely to the intermediate bodies of society. So institutional intervention, also in the economy, does not concern only or even mainly the state, but directly concerns precisely the social institutions, in which the various classes also operate. The nightmare of the Toniolian vision is the disintegration of the classes, which makes society a shapeless mass — or at least unstable and liquid (to use the words of Zygmunt Bauman) — of isolated, atomized individuals, therefore easy prey for power. In an organic society the economic and financial intervention of the state is itself licit and useful (I believe that Toniolo would accept, albeit moderately, Keynes's view), but it must be balanced by a society rich in strong and stable intermediate bodies, which bring individuals together in common interests, enabling them not to find themselves alone before the *Moloch* of power, be it state, financial, media, etc.

g. In moving away from this organic balance, society is inevitably exposed to conflict, to the domineering of the upper classes, to the reaction of the oppressed, and to class struggle. Thus both social peace and the good health of the economy are at stake. So it is not enough to rely on the logic of the market, bringing drops (trickle-down) of well-being upon the lower classes, deluding oneself moreover that this will be done automatically by the "invisible hand" of Smithian memory. There is an urgent need for an economic and political culture that puts at the center the issues of poverty, inequality, and "waste" (as Pope Francis used to say).

3. Principle of ethical correlation: economy ↔ ethico-transcendent Christotypical vision

Terms:

- *ethical:* indicates here not only the moral aspect in the strict sense (the moral norm understood by conscience), but also the *ethos* understood as the sharing of values, approaches, attitudes, culture, customs, that gives to a group and to society as a whole, depending on its local, regional, national, etc., groupings a fundamentally unitary configuration, still in freedom and with social dynamics that can foresee diversity and even conflict, but within a fundamental framework of a few unifying values, without which a society is a pure aggregate and not a true society;
- *transcendent:* this is the perspective that removes human consciousness from self-centeredness, opening it to the other, to being in all its expressions, and, ultimately, to God;
- *civilization:* with this term we refer on the one hand to what Toniolo meant by it, that is, "the participation of human society, to the highest degree possible, in the essentially moral

good, coordinated with that supreme otherworldly good in which is perfection and happiness, as well as with the subordinate goods that prepare for and validate it,"[44] while on the other hand we think of a structural-functional concept of society in which the whole of society is clearly distinguished from the state that is a function of it. This second sense of the term was also dear to our author, who asserted that Christian civilization had brought out this distinction. Applied to the economy, therefore, the Toniolian concept of "civil" refers to both senses;

- *Christotypical:* the reference is to Christ, with what distinguishes him according to Christian faith in his divine-human mystery, revealing at once God and man. We do not use the term "Christological" — specific to theology and so to faith — but "Christotypical," to evoke those aspects of the Christian message and of Christological dogma itself that have a reflection on human experience, and therefore can be grasped as a point of reference (in the Weberian sense of the "ideal-type"), to indicate a specific way in which society and culture situate themselves, to varying degrees, within or close to the Christian vision, also in appraisals and attitudes regarding the economy.

Toniolian thesis: an economy that is efficient on the technical level is in "integral good health" to the extent that the individual and collective behaviors of economic actors are guided by precise ethical norms, shared in that they respond to the very nature of the human person and of society, and therefore recognized as normative not on the basis of a subjective, arbitrary, and precarious perception, but by virtue of the objective dependence of worldly being on God, recognized by right reason as the God of creation and grasped ever more clearly as the God revealed in Christ, in his Gospel, and in the Church that proclaims him (in this sense Christotypical ethics).

Commentary.

a. This third thesis, fundamental in Toniolo's thought, is undoubtedly the most provocative. In the loss of religious and moral certainties in which a large part of humanity finds itself,[45] even in the regions of ancient Christian tradition, this view, which for our author is characteristic of the ethical-Christian school of economics, is one of those options that would immediately close off dialogue with nonbelieving or in any case non-Christian interlocutors. And yet looking at these matters more closely in the light of economic rationality, and so even leaving aside the specific imperatives of faith, this thesis shows a logic that is at least respectable and less strange than it may appear at first glance.

Modern culture marked its greatest point of distance from medieval culture when it expunged from scientific knowledge not only supernatural revelation but the very dimension of values and ethics (due to a presumed neutrality or absence of value judgment). What the Middle Ages distinguished but did not separate — that is, ethics, faith, and science — have appeared incompatible in modernity. The result, when things went well, was Gould's theory of nonoverlapping magisteria,[46] which codifies the parallelism between religion and science. When Toniolo chose to go against the tide with his thesis of the ethical element as an intrinsic factor of economic laws (1873), the debate on method in economics (*Methodenstreit*), already in the air for some time, was about to be formalized by Carl Menger (1883). The Austrian author, in dialectic with Gustav Schmoller, maintained that "the so-called ethical orientation of political economy is a vague postulate devoid of any profound meaning with respect to both theoretical and practical problems, a confusion of thought."[47] Almost half a century later, in 1932, Lionel Robbins would reiterate the neutrality of economic science, practically reducing it, in its specific aspect, to the formal economic logic of the hedonic principle that inevitably arises in every circumstance in which an end must be achieved with a scarcity of means available.[48] The ethical in economics buried forever?

Never say never! In reality that alleged expungement of ethics was already in itself an ethical choice, but one of questionable ethics. In fact, it ended by making material utility coincide with ethics itself. Today, not only the social doctrine of the Church, but a Nobel laureate like Amartya Sen,[49] and with him a good group of scholars,[50] present the rediscovery of ethics in economics as an indispensable perspective, if a convincing answer is to be given as to why a global economic structure that seemed to have found the path to perfection in the free market regulated by the "invisible hand" instead finds itself having to deal with the disasters — human and environmental — of an economy devoid of soul. If anything, the problem will be to determine what kind of ethics (even the ethicists of economics, united by the ethical postulate, end up divided as soon as ethics is expressed in concrete terms). In any case it is a positive fact that there is a revival — in economics as an inseparably theoretical-practical science — of interest in ends and in the legitimacy of ways for achieving them. "The conviction is now widespread that a pure economic theory, meaning one scientistically indifferent to values, which completely disregards ethical points of view in the establishment of norms, is not up to the scientific understanding of economic action."[51]

This is the outlook of the school of civic economics or of the economics of communion. Then, opening the perspective to the global horizon, isn't an ethical recovery applied to economic policy what is outlined in the seventeen global goals of sustainable development (2030 agenda) proposed by the United Nations as millennium objectives?[52]

b. Up to this point Toniolo's thesis is perhaps once again having, at least to some extent and for a good number of economists, an easy game. I suppose that the greatest resistance is to be expected in relation to the second part of the thesis, where the blessed economist (not by chance "blessed"!) explains that the ethics to which he appeals has Catholicism as its point of reference, not only in its ethics, but in its very dogmatics and its consequent ecclesial vision.

To understand Toniolo on this point a premise is needed. That the believer finds in faith the point of reference for his choices in the theoretical and practical field is a foregone conclusion: Tt is a question of consistency. He certainly does not expect the nonbeliever or one who believes differently to do economics on the basis of his religious beliefs. Two aspects, however, can be brought to the table for comparison: one of a historical-positive character, which is the question of how much a religious horizon (dogmatic and ethical) affects the dynamics of the economy, influencing the motivations of economic rationality and setting precise guidelines and boundaries for economic action; the other of a philosophical-theological character, but also with economic repercussions, referring to the extent to which some dimensions of a certain religious vision of life, in this case the Christian vision, can be accepted as plausible or reasonable even independently of faith, thus influencing the motivational considerations underlying the economic process.

c. As for the first aspect, Toniolo, thanks in part to his research on the medieval economy, showed how the historical influence of religion is an irrefutable fact.[53] Moreover, others like Weber and Sombart, although with theses different than his on the origin of the spirit of capitalism, reiterated the same concept. Walter Benjamin and Pavel Florensky would later characterize capitalism itself as "religion."[54] Today Vera Zamagni, questioning why Europe has had such an influence on world economic development, finds herself pointing to its Christian soul,[55] while Elisabetta Basile and a group of institutionalist economists, examining the case of China and India, highlight the role played in the recent economic development of these countries by philosophical, religious, and traditional ideas.[56] A discussion therefore, that of Toniolo, that is anything but shelved. The theology-economics relationship has been marginalized with a sort of cultural removal, but it is inside of things, and it cannot be addressed correctly except by bringing it to light. "We would need," L. Bruni wrote, "a serious theological analysis of capitalism to understand it and perhaps try to change it."[57]

So on the second point — that is, on the extent to which the relationship between economic science and Christianity can become a significant theme apart from the profession of faith by economists — it can be remembered that some aspects of Christian dogma and ethics can also be translated in terms of rational values, although not reduced to them. Toniolo highlighted this in his ardent Eucharistic talks.[58] From the theological point of view, there is a specific reason to admit this, and it is the fact that revelation, while it surpasses reason by virtue of its supernatural character, is not in conflict with it; on the contrary it finds in it a connection on the basis of the underlying unity of God's plan. From the historical-cultural point of view, the data demonstrate this in many aspects. This is why, in the thesis that I am illustrating here, as a summary exposition of Toniolian thought, I have used the adjective "Christotypical" rather than "Christian" (which Toniolo certainly would have preferred, indeed specifying, to avoid any misunderstanding, "Christian-Catholic"). In the dialogue necessary in a multireligious and multicultural society, the adjective *Christotypical* offers a comprehensive connotation that includes, for one who professes it, the Christian vision in its full meaning, but at the same time allows an encounter with cultures of other origins, on the basis of the objective influence that the Christian Faith also exerts in relation to economic dynamisms.

d. A few examples: Let's take the Christological dogma of the hypostatic union — that is, the union, without confusion, of the human and divine natures in the person of Christ. This view helps to distinguish, without separating them, God and the world. Is this concept really a matter of indifference for the ends of economic action? Is it a matter of indifference, for example, from the point of view of the attitude toward men, things, nature, to divinize them (as in pantheism) or to consider them as pure matter (as in materialism), or even to consider them negatively, as happened in some well-known philosophies and ideologies (Manichaeism, Catharism, etc.)? Also sentiments, values, motivations for economic action — those that then influence economic laws — cannot help but be affected by these convictions. And again, if the Christotypical vision of existence is also an eschatological vision, aimed at the construction of a future and the pursuit of a goal (*eschaton*) that is both earthly and transcendent, is all of this a matter of indifference from the point of view of economic engagement? Marxism reproached religion for being the opium of the people: an unfounded and ungenerous reproach toward Christianity, at least when it is lived consistently. Maritain returned the accusation to the sender, interpreting Marxism itself as a Christian heresy,[59] for having borrowed the eschatological principle from biblical-Christian culture, secularizing it and reducing it to a project for the construction of an earthly society marked by justice. How influential is the lowering of eschatological tension in today's culture, also due to the crisis of thought and the weakening of the meaning of life, in discouraging engagement to build a different world, out of responsibility for future generations and for the fate of the environment? One who has before his eyes only the present, and perhaps only "his" present, will easily assume, in economics, an attitude different from that of one who instead experiences the present in terms of sharing and the future as a great intergenerational responsibility. A final example: To accept

> or reject the values of the Sermon on the Mount, the great manifesto of the kingdom of God in the words of Jesus (poverty of spirit, meekness, forgiveness, justice, etc.),[60] is this a matter of indifference for an economy worthy of man and friendly toward peace?

Toniolo maintains this with vigor: Christological or at least Christotypical ethics is made to influence the integral good health of economic processes. That this awareness, on the Catholic side, must develop in dialogue with other religious and non-religious visions of life, in which many seeds of truth are present, is what, after Toniolo, we have learned from the great lesson of Vatican II. Toniolo gave all he could in the ways possible to him. But his certainty that the Christian vision of life, bringing to fulfillment the vision of man and objective universal ethics, is a great secret source of inspiration also for the renewal of the economy, is a legacy that we have no reason to renounce and that can still be presented, with the strength of a certainty that is not only of faith but also rational and historical, as long as it is expressed in the meekness of consistent and sincere dialogue.

"Watchman, how much longer the night?"

This question that we find in the Book of Isaiah (see 21:11), the cry of a people experiencing a tragedy and calling for liberation, can well close these conclusions and provocations, but it could also act as a horizon of inspiration for this entire book, explaining its subtitle: the lesson and prophecy of Giuseppe Toniolo.

Our world hangs in the unstable equilibrium between incredible potential and searing defeats, between a technological miracle and a profound human crisis, between a growth in wealth and a growth (at least relative) in inequality. It took a pandemic like that of COVID-19 to teach us (perhaps!) that if the pyramid of selfishness is not overturned in favor of the least fortunate, their painful fate will cause the entire social edifice to collapse. If not for strictly ethical reasons (that would be enough!), at least for a minimum of economic realism it is necessary to reverse course, to use a title by J. E. Stiglitz, Nobel laureate in economics.[61]

Even economics needs prophets! In the afterword to a book by Federico Caffè, *L'economia senza profeti*, Riccardo Bellofiore said of him, "An economist who never wanted to become a prophet, and yet who knew how to be a master."[62] I think we can say both things about Toniolo: He was a master and also a prophet.

If today the Church asks for a pact for the renewal of the world economy (see *The Economy of Francesco*, the movement of young economists, entrepreneurs, and change makers wanted by Pope Francis aiming to this goal), the rereading of Toniolo can constitute at least an opportunity. In the era of the post-human, which exalts us with its algorithms and disturbs us with its challenges, Toniolo's economic-humanistic thought, although dated, remains generative, at least provocative. He belongs, as L. Bruni classifies him, to the "defeated economists of the twentieth century."[63] But it may happen that the defeated of the last century will show themselves victorious in the next. He outlined the "integral good health" of the economy, which, also in light of the current turbulence of world capitalism, I believe can and should be considered, at another level, an ideal of the "optimum" no less interesting than the Paretian optimum. Toniolo was a watchman of the human in economics, an unheeded prophet of our possibilities and our misfortunes. A little more than a century after his death, perhaps the time has come to drop the veil that has progressively hidden him and establish a dialogue with his thoughts as a scientist and believer. "Watchman, how much longer the night?"

Notes

Introduction

1. "*Criteri scientifici etico-economici intorno al credito dal punto di vista cristiano*" [hereafter *Criteri scientifici*], in *Atti del II Congresso cattolico italiano degli studiosi di scienze sociali* (Padua, August 26–28, 1896), in *Trattato di economia sociale e scritti economici* [hereafter TES], I–V, preface by F. Vito (Vatican City, 1949–1952). The quote is in TES V, 491.

2. *L'economista di Dio.* Giuseppe Toniolo, preface by F. Miano (Rome: AVE, 2012) [hereafter *Economista di Dio*]. It essentially reproposes, supplemented with an anthology, the previous *Giuseppe Toniolo. Una biografia* (Cinisello Balsamo: Edizioni Paoline, 1988).

3. Giuseppe Toniolo. *Una Chiesa nella storia* (Milan: Vita e Pensiero, 2012) [hereafter *Chiesa nella storia*]. It is essentially the re-edition of the previous book with the same title, published by Edizioni Paoline in 1987 with a preface by Giacomo Martina.

4. Fundamental for a biographical approach is F. Vistalli, *Giuseppe Toniolo* (Rome: Comitato Giuseppe Toniolo, 1954). Interesting due to the author's direct experience is E. da Persico, Vita di Giuseppe Toniolo, new edition edited by G. Campanini, D. Castenetto (Rome: AVE, 2012; 1st edition 1927). Among the more recent biographies, in addition to that of the present author cited in note 2, see E. Preziosi, Giuseppe Toniolo. *Alle origini dell'impegno sociale e politico dei cattolici* (Milan: Edizioni Paoline, 2012); M. Andreazza, Giuseppe Toniolo. *Un laico cristiano, un docente, un testimone* (Pisa: ETS, 1988). Popular presentations: M. Zabotti, Giuseppe Toniolo. *Nella storia il futuro* (Rome: AVE, 2018); S. Falzone. *Toniolo senza baffi. Una biografia del maestro dei cattolici italiani* (Rome: Ecra, 2018).

5. It is known that the university circles of Toniolo's time, simply because he was

openly Catholic, were not favorable to him. Significant, therefore, is his being mentioned — along with G. Ricca-Salerno, M. Pantaleoni, A. Loria, etc. — in L. Cossa, *Introduzione allo studio dell'economia politica* (Milan: Hoepli, 1892). The author mentions some of his writings, recognizing in Toniolo "the theoretical precision of the instructor, with good historical and philosophical research, and with conscientious teaching aimed at high moral ideals" (524). For the decades following Toniolo's death, mention should be made of C. Bresciani-Turroni, *Corso di economia politica, I, Teoria generale dei fatti economici* (Milan: Giuffré, 1960; 1st edition 1949). In a brief but detailed chapter dedicated to the evolution of economic thought, he also dedicates a paragraph to "the Catholic school" of economics, "whose most illustrious representative in Italy was Toniolo" (ibid., 59). Over time his memory, even among Catholics, has inexplicably faded. I hope that the *Dizionario di economia civile* (Rome: Città Nuova, 2009), edited by S. Zamagni and L. Bruni, in an upcoming edition may dedicate at least one entry to Toniolo. (This hope has been satisfied, as I myself could write the entry for the second edition, 2024.)

6. I will limit myself to pointing out a few names, leaving the titles (in any case not an exhaustive list) to the final bibliography: P. Pecorari, A. Spicciani, R. Molesti, A. Cova, F. Manzalini, A. Acerbi, etc.

7. One could think of the fact that the period of Catholic political presence that could have enhanced it the most — Sturzian popularism — was soon buried by fascism. With the collapse of the regime, the Degasperian rebirth of "Christian democracy" certainly remained linked to Toniolo's thought, but it now developed above all on the political side, which Toniolo had only been able to hint at, due in part to the limitations posed by the Roman question. His economic thought was partly taken up by scholars of the Catholic University (F. Vito, A. Fanfani, etc.), but Toniolo had no real followers, as acknowledged by Amintore Fanfani in the introduction to G. Toniolo, *L'odierno problema sociologico. Studio storico-critico* [hereafter OPS] (Vatican City: Comitato Opera Omnia, 1947): "But although many Italian economists, politicians, and sociologists have passed through his school and many others in a generic sense have been called his disciples, the truth is that Toniolo did not leave real students and followers" (ibid., xii). Considerations on this lack of "follow-up" for Toniolo can be found in R. Molesti, *Il pensiero economico e sociale di Giuseppe Toniolo* (Pisa: Ipemedizioni, 2017), 79–82. Furthermore, one should not forget that, in the climate of post-fascist Italy, culture and society in Italy, despite the political role of Catholics, were affected by the strong Marxist ideological presence that also passed like a steamroller over the memory of Toniolo. For the debate on his work in both Catholic and Marxist contexts, cf. F. Tamassia, "*La rappresentanza politica organica in Toniolo come momento del corporativismo cattolico*," in M. L. Fornaciari Davoli, G. Russo (eds.), *Attualità del pensiero di Giuseppe Toniolo* [hereafter *Attualità del pensiero*] (Milan: FrancoAngeli, 1982), 71–152. R. Faucci shines a spotlight on him in *L'economia politica in Italia. Dal Cinquecento ai nostri giorni* (Turin: UTET, 2000), 206–8. Precisely on the basis of the Degasperian success of Catholics in postwar politics, also traced back to Toniolo's groundwork, the author concludes, "In this respect, the controversial Toniolo has left a much more lasting trace on Italian society than many economists more cele-

brated than he" (ibid., 208).

8. The *Opera Omnia* are now to be found almost exclusively in libraries. Romano Molesti's initiative to put some of Toniolo's texts back into editorial play is well deserved.

9. Piero Barucci wrote in 1981, "I am sure that today's theoretical economist would not spare even one page of Toniolo, and I am sure that, if his work should end up in the hands of one of those young lions of economics who feed only on refined algorithms and sophisticated simulations, the judgment would be more or less this: a woolgatherer, to be placed midway between sociological and political studies": Various authors, *Contributi alla conoscenza del pensiero di Giuseppe Toniolo* [hereafter *Contributi alla conoscenza*] (Pisa, 1984), 22; proceedings of the conference "Economy and Society in the Crisis of the Modern State: The Thought of Giuseppe Toniolo," organized by the University and Chamber of Commerce of Pisa (December 18–19, 1981).

10. It was an agenda-setting decision, as Toniolo himself emphasizes, recalling the dedication of the volume to his teacher Fedele Lampertico. In a letter to Professor Sebastiano Rumor dated August 22, 1914, Toniolo wrote, referring to Lampertico, as a tribute to this thinker by whom he himself had been inspired in his conception of the relationship between economics and sociology, "Indeed, after his ever regrettable death I allowed myself to dedicate to his memory an introductory volume to political economy, much of which is a compendium of sociology, in which the broad outlines of the social order of civilization are presented, since this is preliminary to the science of wealth." The letter, published with the title "*Pensiero filosofico-scientifico di Fedele Lampertico*," in S. Rumor (ed.), *Scritti in omaggio a Fedele Lampertico* (Vicenza: Tipografia San Giuseppe, 1924), 75–84, is found in Toniolo's *Opera Omnia* in the volume *Dei remoti fattori della potenza economica di Firenze nel Medio Evo e scritti storici* [hereafter RF] (Vatican City, 1952), 516–23. The quote is from page 516.

11. M. Bianchini, outlining the economic styles, in reference to the "institutionalist" economics rediscovered today in reaction to the individualism of the classical economy, traces back to Aristotle, and precisely to the perspective of the house (*oikos*, whence *oikonomia*) as opposed to chrematistics (from *krémata*, wealth), the "first kind of economic reflection written in an institutionalist vein": *La parola e la merce. Una guida al pensiero economico* (Reggio Emilia: Diabasis, 2005), 211.

12. I received a basic education in political economy and economic policy some fifty or so years ago in the political science degree program of the University of Rome La Sapienza. I have kept myself informed on further developments in the science of economics above all in relation to my ethical-theological interests, with particular reference to the social doctrine of the Church. Evidently too little to presume myself an economist!

13. An in-depth work on some of Toniolo's economic categories, with a meticulous bibliography, is F. Manzalini, *Elementi di economia politica in Giuseppe Toniolo* (Siena: Cantagalli, 2009). In the bibliography one will find the names of economists or historians of economics who have dealt with them, from Vito and Fanfani to Barucci, Spicciani, Molesti, Bodega, Cova, Carera, Zalin, Stefano and Vera Zamagni, Bruni, Becchetti, Bazzichi, etc. For the most part they either focus on some aspect or provide an overall view. A

systematic examination is still awaited. The present work came about precisely with the aim of filling this gap.

14. For example, "*servigio*" for *servizio*, "*imo*" for *basso* or *fondo*, "*stromento*" for *strumento*, "*dee*" for *deve*, "*perocché*" instead of *perché*, "*uopo*" for *bisogno*, "*ruina*" for *rovina*, "*incivilimento*" for *cammino verso la civiltà*, etc. For the term "*medioevo*" we will leave, in the quotations, the way in which Toniolo expresses himself, which for the most part is "*medio evo*."

15. We document the essentials of this in the bibliography, but we will largely make account of it along the way, whenever the topic suggests doing so.

16. Cf. D. Bodega, A. Carera (eds.), *Economia e società per il bene comune. La lezione di Giuseppe Toniolo (1918–2018)* [hereafter *Economia e società*] (Milan: Vita e Pensiero, 2020). The conference was held on November 24, 2018, in Milan, at the Catholic University of the Sacred Heart. In addition to my introductory report, a first session was dedicated to "Economics, Ethics, and the Common Good" (D. Bodega, S. Zamagni, F. Manzalini, L. Becchetti, L. Bruni), a second to "Substantial Democracy in Action: Social Thought and Action" (M. Truffelli, L. Ornaghi, V. Negri Zamagni, A. Carera, R. Molesti), a third to "Good Politics: Society, Democracy, and Peace" (A. Giovagnoli, N. Antonetti, U. Villani, M. Magatti).

17. This is the initiative that Pope Francis launched with a message dated May 1, 2018, addressed to young economists, enterprisers, and change makers, to invite them to make a "pact" for the renewal of the economy in a more fraternal and supportive sense.

18. Cf. Pontifical Council for Justice and Peace, *Compendium of the Social Doctrine of the Church* (Vatican City: Libreria Editrice Vaticana, 2004).

19. One could think of *Caritas in Veritate* (2009) of Benedict XVI, and *Evangelii Gaudium* (2013), *Laudato Si'* (2015), and *Fratelli Tutti* (2020) of Pope Francis.

Chapter I: The Motives of Economic Activity

1. Cf. G. Toniolo, "*Cenni commemorativi: Angelo Messedaglia,*" in *Rivista internazionale di scienze sociali e discipline ausiliarie* [hereafter RISS], 1901, vol. XXV, 683–85; now in RF, 480–84. Toniolo, who took his courses and replaced him for a while at the University of Padua, praises above all his encyclopedic and unified presentation of economics.

2. The correspondence between the two is interesting: cf. P. Pecorari, *Carteggio Giuseppe Toniolo-Luigi Luzzatti (1869–1918)* (Vatican City: Biblioteca Apostolica Vaticana, 2017).

3. *Dell'elemento etico quale fattore intrinseco delle leggi economiche. Prelezione al corso di economia politica nell'Università di Padova, 5 dicembre 1873* [hereafter *Elemento etico*] (Padua: Edizioni Sacchetto, 1874); now in TES II, 266–92. Quote on page 267.

4. *Elemento etico*, in TES II, 266.

5. He cites Hermann, Wagner, Schmoller, Schönberg, H. Contzen, Scheel, and Schäffle.

6. Antonio Genovesi (1712–69), founder of the newly rediscovered school of "civic

economics," had the first chair of political economy in Italy, in Naples. The work that made him famous is *Delle lezioni di commercio ossia d'economia civile* (Naples, 1765).

7. Pietro Verri (1728–97), friend and colleague of Cesare Beccaria (who had also laid down the *Lezioni di economia* alongside the more famous *Dei delitti e delle pene*), wrote *Meditazioni sull'economia politica* (Livorno, 1771).

8. Lodovico Ricci (1724–99), known for his insights into the "principle of population." Among his works: *Riforma degli istituti pii della città di Modena* (Modena, 1787).

9. Gian Rinaldo Carli (1720–95), a man of various interests, including literature. Among his works: *Dell'origine e del commercio delle monete e dell'istituzione delle zecche d'Italia* (1751).

10. Melchiorre Gioja (1767–1829), a former priest with a tumultuous life intertwined with politics. He published essays in Milan between 1815 and 1816 on the production, distribution, and consumption of wealth.

11. Marco Minghetti (1818–86), a statesman who held several ministries and was twice prime minister, cited by Toniolo above all for his work *Dell'economia pubblica e delle sue attinenze colla morale e col diritto* (Florence, 1859).

12. *Elemento etico*, in TES II, 291.

13. Ibid., 292.

14. Ibid., 268.

15. Cf. TES II, 90.

16. Cf. L. Cossa, *Introduzione allo studio dell'economia politica* (Milan: Hoepli, 1892; (revised 3rd edition of the *Guida allo studio dell'economia politica*). This author, a professor in Pavia, makes extensive use of Greek etymology in the chapter dedicated to the denominations and definitions of political economy, cf. 68–9. Toniolo dedicated repeated reviews to the various editions of this work, as well as to similar publications by Cossa, which can be found in TES II on 297, 304, 311, 313, 317, 353, 358, 363, 421, 424, 430, 449. Such an interest on the part of Toniolo, with many points of agreement but also some politely declared differences, leads me to consider this author as particularly significant if one wishes to make a comparison between Toniolo's approach and that of the economic science of his day.

17. Cf., for example, this distinction in his volume on circulation: TES V, 113.

18. *Trattato*, in TES I, 15. Toniolo's definition is not original, given that it is considered by other authors, but Toniolo develops it with a special emphasis stemming from his neo-scholastic training, for example on the hierarchical, finalistic, theological sense of the social order: cf. F. Manzalini, "*Il credito e la circolazione della ricchezza*," in A. Carera (ed.), *Giuseppe Toniolo. L'uomo come fine. Con saggi sulla storia dell'Istituto Giuseppe Toniolo di Studi Superiori* [hereafter *L'uomo come fine*] (Milan: Vita e Pensiero, 2014), 154 (proceedings of the conference held at the Catholic University of the Sacred Heart on March 21–23, 2012). On the relationship of this concept of social order in Toniolo with G. D. Romagnosi and L. Taparelli d'Azeglio, see A. Acerbi, "*Giuseppe Toniolo, tra filosofia neoscolastica e scienza economica,*" in *Contributi alla conoscenza*, 59–85, especially 68–73.

19. *Dei fatti fisici e dei fatti sociali nei riguardi del metodo induttivo*, published in

Archivio giuridico, vol. X (Pisa, 1872), 178–212; republished in TES II, 219–65. In the first note he expresses his gratitude to his professors Angelo Messedaglia and Luigi Luzzatti, whose thought he takes as inspiration. Indeed, he says of the latter that he offered him "the outline of this work": TES II, 220.

20. Cf. F. Ferrara, "*Il germanismo economico in Italia*," in *Nuova Antologia*, vol. 26 (Florence, 1874), 1010.

21. Toniolo cites the second edition of M. Minghetti, *Della economia pubblica e delle sue attinenze colla morale e col diritto* (Florence: Le Monnier, 1868), 83–6.

22. Cf. J. S. Mill, *Essays on Some Unsettled Questions of Political Economy,* 1844. Toniolo emphasizes that Mill proposes to add to the definition of the "laws of wealth" the clarification "insofar as they depend on the human spirit."

23. He taught this in Pisa from 1879 until his death. Copies of the "notes" for that course were found in materials produced by students, and then in 1902 came the first printed edition (subsequent editions: 1907, 1912). Not published in the *Opera Omnia*, the 1912 edition of *Lezioni di statistica* was republished in 1998: G. Toniolo, S. Burgalassi (ed.), *Lezioni di statistica* (Milan: Vita e Pensiero, 1998).

24. *Elemento etico,* in TES II, 268.

25. Ibid.

26. Ibid., 268–69.

27. Ibid., 269.

28. In effect, Smith's thought is far from unambiguous, to the point that it has been called "Smithian schizophrenia": cf. E. Screpanti, S. Zamagni, *Profilo di storia del pensiero economico* [hereafter *Profilo di storia*], *I, Dalle origini a Keynes* (Rome: Carocci, 2004; 6th reprint 2017), 114. The authors observe that Smith's approach is less egocentric than a current interpretation might lead one to believe, especially if one compares the approach of *The Wealth of Nations* (1776) with that of his other work, The *Theory of Moral Sentiments* (1759). But already an economist of Toniolo's time and one whom he esteemed, Cossa, distancing himself from the "German historical school" that our author, albeit critically, alluded to, pointed out that it is not possible to make against Smith, "to their fullest extent, the accusations of individualism, materialism, absolutism, and even less that of excessive idealism, that are hurled against him by the economic school now dominant in Germany": cf. L. Cossa, *Introduzione allo studio dell'economia politica* (Milan: Hoepli, 1892), 319. Today there is a reassessment of Smith: cf. P. L. Porta, "*Il problema del metodo*," in *L'uomo come fine,* 42–3. Regardless of this biographical-hermeneutical question, Toniolo was interested in distancing himself from a view that, in its de facto reception, was traced back — rightly or wrongly — to Smith. Furthermore, our author conceded that Smith had been able to reconcile "rational principles with positive ones, nor did he divorce economics from morality," while still contesting his type of morality "founded on sentiment" (and so not on an objective recognition of the moral norm): cf. *Trattato*, TES I, 149.

29. *Elemento etico*, in TES II, 270.

30. Ibid.

31. Ibid., 268.

32. Ibid., 270.

33. Ibid., 270–71.

34. Ibid., 271. Reflections on the relevance of this vision in the light of current research in behavioral economics in L. Becchetti, "*L'attualità di Toniolo nell'economia civile*," in *Economia e società,* 59–69, especially 60–3. In particular, the author recalls C. Engel, "Dictator Games: A Meta Study," in *Experimental Economics*, 2011, 14 (4), 583–610.

35. *Elemento etico,* in TES II, 273.

36. Ibid., 277.

37. Ibid., 278.

38. Ibid.

39. Ibid., 281.

40. *Homo sum, humani nihil a me alienum puto*. Ibid., 283–84.

41. M. Minghetti, in *Della economia pubblica e delle sue attinenze colla morale e col diritto,* uses the expression "circumscribe." In the second edition reprinted in 1881, on page 82, he states: "The fundamental principles of morality and law *circumscribe* economics within its rational limits, and for this purpose provide it with certain postulates, without which it could not well understand all its laws, nor solve all its problems" [italics added]. On page 295 he states, "Economics is distinct from but connected and subordinated to law and morality."

42. *Elemento etico*, in TES II, 289.

43. Ibid., 292.

44. Review in *Archivio giuridico*, 1888, vol. XXXIX, 551–54, of L. Cossa, *Introduzione allo studio dell'economia politica*, *I*, *Economia sociale* (Milan: Hoepli, 1888); now in TES II, 424–29, especially 428.

45. It was the third edition of the book by Cossa (Milan: Hoepli, 1891); Toniolo's review in RISS, 1893, vol. I, 128–33; republished in TES II, 430–36.

46. TES II, 432–33.

47. Cf. V. Pareto, *Manuale di economia politica con una introduzione alla scienza sociale* (Milan: Società editrice libraria, 1906), 15, par. 24.

48. Pareto himself begins the second chapter of his *Manuale* by stating, "The foundation of political economy and of every social science in general is evidently psychology," 31, par. 1.

49. I refer, on this whole topic, to *Chiesa nella storia,* 179–200.

50. "*Donde il progresso della scienza economica*," in RISS, 1897, vol. XIII, 191–214; now in TES II, 464–94. Toniolo here provides an account of the positive echoes in the Catholic world of the conference of the Catholic Union for Social Studies held in Padua in 1896. Quotation on 478.

51. Ibid., 483. The text cited by Toniolo is V. Cathrein, *Die Moralphilosophie* (Freiburg: Herder, 1893), pt. 1, 232–36. On this structurally neo-scholastic configuration of his economic thought, cf. F. Manzalini, "*Toniolo e la scienza economica del suo tempo*," in *Economia e società,* 48–54. On his neo-scholastic formation, cf. P. Pecorari, *Giuseppe*

Toniolo e il socialismo. Saggio sulla cultura cattolica tra '800 e '900 (Bologna: Pàtron, 1981), 49–70. On the topic of ethics-economics in Toniolo, cf. F. Manzalini, *Elementi di economia politica in Giuseppe Toniolo* (Siena: Cantagalli, 2009), 167–200.

Chapter II: Economics as a Science

1. An adjunct professor since 1879, he became a full professor in 1882.

2. "*Lo sviluppo del cattolicesimo sociale dopo l'Enciclica Rerum novarum (15 maggio 1891)*," in RISS, 1902, vol. XXIX, 3–11; now in *Democrazia cristiana. Concetti e indirizzi* [hereafter *DC* I and II], preface by A. De Gasperi (Vatican City, 1949), *I*, 306–17. Quote on page 313.

3. Cf. *Dei remoti fattori della potenza economica di Firenze nel medio evo* (Milan: Hoepli, 1882); now in RF, 1–287. Toniolo, referring to the period from the remote beginnings to 1250, identifies the factors of Florence's economic power in "natural telluric" influences (geography, climate, etc.), in ethnic tendencies (starting from the Etruscan ethnicity and culture), and in historical-civil events and moral virtues (with particular reference to Christian-ecclesiastical influences). His intent is "to reiterate, with the example of a city in which, more than in any other, in our medieval resurgence all the manifestations of culture shone in wonderful harmony, that the factors of economic life coincide with the very causes that generate and govern the culture," RF, 8. In Florence, in particular, "the economic revival coincided with all the other higher manifestations of culture and was under their sway," RF, 237. For Toniolo, the economic superiority of the Florentines ultimately confirms "the dependence of the material order of wealth on the immaterial order of thought and morality," RF, 241. A harmonious vision that responded to the balance expressed by medieval scholasticism: cf. "*Scolastica ed umanesimo nelle dottrine economiche al tempo del rinascimento in Toscana*," lecture given for the academic year 1886–87, in RF, 291–371.

4. With the *Storia dell'economia sociale in Toscana*, Toniolo won a competition (in two successive phases between 1884 and 1887) organized on the initiative of L. Cossa by the Royal Lombard Institute of Sciences and Letters. He then began its publication but was unable at the complete it (probably due to the commitments he was taking on in the Catholic movement at the time). He made various partial publications of it. The edition of the *Opera Omnia, Storia dell'economia sociale in Toscana nel Medio Evo* [hereafter SEST] *vol. I, La vita civile-politica, vol. II, La vita economica* (Vatican City, 1948), reproduces the part of the work preserved in the printed sheets and in the proofs. In the introduction Toniolo declares his intention "to illustrate in what way and to what extent the movement of economic doctrines has contributed to the general intellectual and moral progress regarding the higher ends of existence, in which the essence of civilization consists" (SEST I, 35). In general, his judgment is that "from the extrinsic influences of nature to the hidden ones of the bloodlines, up to the most sublime actions that operate on the spirit, everything converges to form a microcosm of Tuscany destined, in general, to provide the highest and purest manifestations of Italian civilization," SEST I, 51.

5. Cf. "*Cenni commemorativi: Guglielmo Roscher*," in RISS, 1894, 522–25; now in RF, 454–57. Toniolo notes that this school, especially with Hildebrand and Knies, had fallen into an excess of historical relativism, of which however the master Roscher was not guilty. Cf. for a survey of the "old" and "young" historical school (Schmoller), I. Cervelli, "*Lo storicismo economico tedesco dell'Ottocento nei suoi rapporti con la storiografia*," in *Contributi alla conoscenza,* 117–37.

6. Cf. A. Spicciani, "*Giuseppe Toniolo, un economista storico*," in *Contributi alla conoscenza,* 155–202.

7. Thus ends his pamphlet *The Civil War in France* (London, 1871).

8. Cf. *Economista di Dio,* 73–7.

9. A summary of the general state of the country in this period is in G. Mori, "*Economia e società in Italia fra '800 e '900*," in *Contributi alla conoscenza*, 41–58.

10. Ibid., 45.

11. "A different Italy had arisen. Less antiquated, less unpleasant, and less static than the previous one, it has been said. But the tensions and fractures of territory, class, politics, and culture attributable to the upheavals that had generated it, to a vitalistic and nationalistic reorientation of a large part of the intellectual world, and to the persistent weakness of the country's international position in a world increasingly dominated by incurable and threatening rivalries, were not overcome, or even reduced, despite the sagacious, lively, and insistent attempt at mediation conducted by Giovanni Giolitti. The entry into the First World War — for which an Indian historian used the expression 'European civil war' — vertically split the country, the great majority of which was against it, and even divided the ruling classes into opposing camps" (ibid., 53). On the general situation of Italian economic development, cf. Gianni Toniolo, *Storia economica dell'Italia liberale (1850–1918)* (Bologna: il Mulino, 1988).

12. Cf. "*L'eredità di Leone XIII*," in RISS, 1903, vol. XXXII, 517–49; now in *Scritti spirituali, religiosi, familiari e vari, I-II* [hereafter SS], preface by F. Costa (Vatican City, 1952), *II*, 22–61.

13. It was published in *Il popolo italiano,* republished in *Democrazia cristiana,* DC I, 260–63.

14. Cf. *Economista di Dio,* 81–4 and 95–100.

15. Cf. N. Raponi, "*Toniolo e la preistoria dell'Università Cattolica*," in *Vita e Pensiero*, May-August 1985, 248–82; "*Toniolo e il progetto di università cattolica*," in P. Pecorari (ed.), *Giuseppe Toniolo tra economia e società* (Udine: Del Bianco editore, 1990), 257–302.

16. Letter to Msgr. Giovanni Bressan, the pope's secretary, dated November 19, 1907, in LL III, 132.

17. Cf. A. Spicciani, "*Giuseppe Toniolo, un economista storico*," in *Contributi alla conoscenza,* 186.

18. Cf. F. Vistalli, *Giuseppe Toniolo,* op. cit., 293–94. See also a letter from Toniolo to S. Medolago Albani of May 30, 1888, in LL I, 110–11.

19. In the decree on the heroic nature of Toniolo's virtues (Paul VI), it is said that "the Servant of God was one of those very learned people whom Leo XIII consulted to

draft the aforementioned encyclical," cf. *Economista di Dio,* 330. This is confirmed by the statement of a witness in his cause for beatification, in *Sacra Congregatio pro Causis Sanctorum, Pisana beatificationis et canonizationis servi Dei Iosephi Toniolo Viri Laici. Positio super virtutibus,* Rome, 1970. It is from the deposition of Fr. Clienze Bortolotti: "And to those who, in a conversation, wanted to congratulate him for having taken part in the compilation of *Rerum Novarum,* Toniolo took care to state that the great pontiff had indeed also wanted his judgment on the matter, like that of others, but that the encyclical was entirely due to the pontiff and to some of his closest and most direct collaborators" (ibid., 397).

20. Not signing the articles published by the *Opera dei Congressi* has to do with a precaution that Toniolo took during those years — also taken by friends of his in the *Opera* — of not making himself conspicuous, given his role as a professor at a state-run university, within the context of the official activities of organized Catholics, which for the Italian state, due to the dispute with the pope, was considered as bordering on the subversive. Cf. F. Vistalli, *Giuseppe Toniolo,* op. cit., 287–28. In his "Rules of Life" he writes, "Then to help the *Catholic movement* in those forms and to that degree which in my position will be possible and useful, according to the advice of my confessor," SS I, 19.

21. "*Una sapiente proposta,*" signed X, in *Movimento cattolico*, I (1880), 220–25, republished in *Iniziative culturali e di azione cattolica* [hereafter IC], preface by G. Dalla Torre (Vatican City, 1951), 309–16. In this epistolary contribution, addressing a "very dear friend" (perhaps the secretary of the *Opera*, the lawyer Casoni), he began by apologizing for not being able to do more — "not being able to provide (as I would like) direct and active work." He noted that he had long been asked to at least offer suggestions in the economic-social field. Responding to this invitation, as a first point he suggested giving maximum attention to the principles ("the fundamental principles of the *doctrine of utility* currently need to be revised, corrected, harmonized with *moral-Christian* doctrine and with the supreme truths of philosophy," IC, 309–10). For this reason he recommended that a translation be made of C. Périn's book *De la richesse dans les sociétés chrétiennes.* As for practical issues, a book that would highlight the mission and duties of the "upper or ruling classes" (landed aristocracy, clergy, industrial and commercial classes) seemed urgent to him, with a view to a renewal, under the banner of Catholicism, of the social order, violated to the detriment of the working-class world.

22. "*Dell'odierno indirizzo delle scienze sociali-economiche e dei corrispondenti doveri degli studiosi cattolici,*" *Movimento cattolico, VII* (1886), 236–52; now in TES II, 392–93.

23. Published in Bergamo, Tip. S. Alessandro, 1886; now in TES II, 367–91 [hereafter *Linee e quesiti*].

24. TES II, 379.

25. Cf. F. Vistalli, *Giuseppe Toniolo,* 259–69.

26. *Linee e quesiti,* in TES II, 368.

27. Ibid., 369.

28. Ibid., 373.

29. Ibid., 374.

30. Cf. ibid., 374–375.

31. Cf. *Economista di Dio,* 84.

32. On Talamo, cf. F. del Pizzo, *Salvatore Talamo e la rinascita moderna della dottrina sociale della Chiesa* (Soveria Mannelli: Rubbettino, 2018).

33. "*Ragioni e intendimenti degli studi e dell'azione sociale fra i cattolici d'Italia,*" in *Movimento cattolico, IX* (1888), 337–64, which in turn anticipates *Proposta di un ordine di studi e di azione sociale in Italia,* published in Bergamo, 1889, later incorporated in *Ragioni, costituzione, opera, programma scientifico dell'Unione cattolica degli studi sociali in Italia promotrice del congresso,* published without signature in the proceedings of the first Italian Catholic congress of social science scholars held in Genoa in 1892 (Padua, 1893), *vol. I,* 5–48. Both writings were essentially merged into *L'Unione cattolica per gli studi sociali in Italia. Intendimenti, costituzione, operato e programma scientifico* [hereafter *Programma scientifico*] (Padua: Tipografia del Seminario, 1903); now in IC, 75–133. Especially for the prescriptive part, cf. ibid., 87–133.

34. *Programma scientifico*, in IC, 130–31.

35. *Programma della Rivista internazionale di scienze sociali e discipline ausiliarie* [hereafter *Programma RISS*], in RISS, 1893, vol. I, III–XI; now in IC, 134–42. Quotation on 135–36.

36. *Programma RISS,* in IC, 140. For a general look at the development of the sociological interests of the RISS, I refer to my study "*Gli intellettuali cattolici e le origini della 'sociologia cristiana'. La Rivista internazionale di scienze sociali e discipline ausiliarie,*" in G. Camadini (ed.), *La 'Rerum novarum' e il movimento cattolico italiano* (Brescia: Morcelliana, 1995), 88–151.

37. *Trattato*, TES I, 90.

38. Ibid., 15.

39. Ibid., 59.

40. Ibid.

41. Ibid., 53.

42. Ibid., 54.

43. Ibid.

44. Cf. L. Cossa, *Introduzione allo studio dell'economia politica,* (Milan: Hoepli, 1892; revised 3rd edition of the *Guida allo studio dell'economia politica*), 55.

45. Cf. ibid., 12. Referring to Romagnosi, by political economy the author means "the doctrine of the social order of wealth, studied in its *essence,* in its *causes,* in its *rational laws*, and in its relationships with *public prosperity*." He then asserts its character as a science, but, unlike Toniolo, refers the definition to the part that concerns theory (pure economics), while for the practical part he prefers to speak of art. In the definition he does not include, as Toniolo instead does, the qualification of moral science, meaning by morality the scope of those imperatives that must rather be included in art. Toniolo for his part underlines the moral character of this science, referring not only to ethical imperatives, but to the spiritual being of man, rational and free. G. Valenti also refers to the same "Romagnosian" conception of the "social order of wealth," *Principi di scienza*

economica (Florence: Barbera editore, 1916; 1st edition, 1906), while the distinction between science and art is supported by several authors who were contemporaries of Toniolo (cf., for example, A. Graziani, *Istituzioni di economia politica* [Turin: Fratelli Bocca, 1904], 9–10). Meanwhile, the conception of "pure" economics is consolidated starting from the postulate of *homo oeconomicus* and the hedonic principle, cf. M. Pantaleoni, *Principii di economia pura* (Florence, 1889), which bases all economic science on the hedonic principle. The approach of V. Pareto is similar. If one looks at an author like C. Supino in *Principi di economia politica* (Naples: Luigi Pierro editore, 1904), the approach immediately enters in *medias res* with the "law of the least means" seen as "the starting point and foundation" of political economy, without even raising the problem of scientificity. Instead, V. Pareto would enter into the problem with elbows swinging, explaining in the "general principles" of the *Manuale di economia politica con una introduzione alla scienza sociale* (Milan: Società editrice libraria, 1906), that the scientific claim of economics refers to the typical approach of the experimental sciences, therefore dealing with the laws of economics that can be translated into mathematical language, and leaving to philosophy, religion, etc., the other statements of a metaphysical or moral nature, indeed respectable but of a different scope: "To know a tree completely, we can start from the roots and move up to the branches, or start from the branches and go down to the roots. The first way was widely used by ancient science; the second is exclusively used by modern experimental science, and experience has shown that it is unique in leading to knowledge of the truth" (ibid., 22, par. 33).

46. Light is shed on Pareto's position toward Toniolo and his *Trattato* in a letter from the Lausanne economist to Maffeo Pantaleoni dated November 3, 1907, published in G. De Rosa (ed.), *Vilfredo Pareto. Lettere a Maffeo Pantaleoni (1890–1923), vol. III (1907–23)* (Rome: Edizioni Storia e Letteratura, 1962): "I had the Introduction by Toniolo sent to me, to get a gold mine of metaphysical drivel. . . . And you put me with Toniolo? Oil and water. We are poles apart" (ibid., 75, letter no. 567). For his part, Pantaleoni, writing to Pareto on March 11, 1909, called Toniolo a "murderer" of economic science (ibid., 378, letter no. 15). Cf. F. Manzalini, "*Giuseppe Toniolo e la scienza economica del suo tempo*," in *Economia e società*, 43.

47. *Trattato*, TES I, 81–2.

48. It is well known that the second chapter of his *Manuale* is an "introduction to social science" starting from psychology: "The foundation of political economy and of every social science in general is evidently psychology. Perhaps a day will come when we will be able to deduce the laws of social science from the principles of psychology," *Manuale di economia politica* (Milan, 1906), 35, par. 1.

49. On Toniolo the sociologist, cf. S. Burgalassi, *Alle origini della sociologia. G. Toniolo e la scuola pisana (1878–1915)* (Pisa: ETS, 1984).: "We can readily conclude that Toniolo's is a sociology sui generis in terms of the formalities in which it is expressed, but it is a sociology that starts from the data and leads back to the data, even if the data are illuminated, *antea* and *postea,* by a series of presuppositions of an extra-empirical nature" (214).

50. *Trattato*, TES I, 79–80.

51. Cf., for example, *Trattato*, TES I, 3, which cites the "respected names of Pantaleoni, Pareto, Graziani, Supino, Valenti," and Pareto would appear at least ten times in his writing.

52. He cites him, together with Pantaleoni, in the context of the theory of value, promising however in his general course (the *Trattato* was born as progressively refined academic lecture notes) "to reduce the theory to a certain greater simplicity," since — in reference to the authors mentioned — "their defects are in their subtleties," *Trattato*, TES I, 347.

53. "So they are much in error who accuse the author who studies economic activity — or *homo oeconomicus* — of neglecting, or worse, despising moral, religious, etc., activity — that is, *homo ethicus, homo religiosus,* etc.; one might as well say that the geometer neglects and despises the chemical properties of bodies, the physical, etc. Those who blame political economy for not taking morality into account are also wrong; one might as well accuse a theory of the game of chess of not taking the culinary art into account," cf. V. Pareto, *Manuale di economia politica,* 15, par. 24 (a critical edition of the *Manuale* was made in 2006, but here I quote from the original edition that I have at hand).

54. "Science is essentially analytical; practice, essentially synthetic. Political economy does not have to take morality into account, but one who advocates a practical measure must take into account not only the economic results, but also the moral, religious, political, etc." (ibid., 16, par. 26).

55. For a focus on this topic, in the general sense of the science-faith relationship in Toniolo, cf. *Chiesa nella storia,* 173–200.

56. *Il supremo quesito della sociologia e i doveri della scienza nell'ora presente* (Rome: Un. Typ. Coop. Ed., 1903; the result of articles published in the RISS: 1903, vol. XXXII, 169–96, vol. XXXIII, 18–47; 1904, vol. XXXV, 161–77, 321–45, and 481–509), a study reworked and republished in 1905 in Florence; now in *L'odierno problema sociologico. Studio storico-critico*, preface by A. Fanfani (Vatican City: Comitato Opera Omnia di G. Toniolo, 1947) [hereafter *Problema sociologico*, in OPS].

57. Introduction to OPS, XVI.

58. *Problema sociologico,* in OPS, 350.

59. *Trattato*, TES I, 96.

60. Ibid., 128.

61. Ibid., 152–53.

62. Ibid., 95.

63. Milan: Hoepli, 1891. This is the revised third edition of the previous *Guida allo studio dell'economia politica*. Review in RISS, 1893, vol. I, 128–33; now in TES II, 430–36.

64. Review of Cossa, Introduction, in TES II, 431.

Chapter III: Economics in History

1. Cf. A. Fanfani, "*Il contributo di Giuseppe Toniolo agli studi di storia economica*," in

Various authors, *La figura e l'opera di Giuseppe Toniolo* (Milan, 1968); M. P. Alberzoni, "Giuseppe Toniolo medievista," in *L'uomo come fine*, 83–110.

2. "His aim, also as a historian, was only one: to determine the 'normal' laws of economic development," A. Spicciani, in *Giuseppe Toniolo tra economia e storia* (Naples: Giunta, 1990), 99.

3. Cf. C. Violante, "*Il significato dell'opera storiografica di Giuseppe Toniolo nell'età di Leone XIII*," in G. Rossini (ed.), *Aspetti della cultura cattolica nell'età di Leone XIII* (Rome: Cinque Lune, 1961), 714–19 (proceedings of the conference held in Bologna on December 27–29, 1960).

4. Cf. *Chiesa nella storia*, 113–38.

5. Cf. "*Della storia come disciplina ausiliare delle scienze sociali*," introduction to the volume by A. Main, A. Toti, *Studi storico-sociali intorno a S. Gregorio Magno* (Siena: Tip. S. Bernardino, 1891); now in RF, 391–428. A discussion that aims to demonstrate the importance of history, but conceived of broadly as social history, in comparison with the reductionist tendency interested above all in political history, at the service of sociological synthesis and Christian apologetics itself. Cf. P. Pecorari, "*Giuseppe Toniolo e la storia come disciplina ausiliare delle scienze sociali*," in *L'uomo come fine*, 21–33.

6. Cf. Trattato, TES I, 157.

7. L. Neal, R. Cameron, *Storia economica del mondo. Dalla preistoria ad oggi* (Bologna, il Mulino, 2016; translation of the 5th English edition, 2016), 35–52.

8. A. Fanfani, *Storia economica*, part one, *Antichità Medioevo Età moderna* (Turin: UTET, 1961; 1st ed. 1938), 5–32.

9. Cf. *Trattato*, TES I, 165.

10. Cf. ibid., 176.

11. Ibid., 178.

12. Cf. ibid., 180.

13. Ibid., 181.

14. Ibid.

15. Ibid., 183.

16. Ibid., 184.

17. Ibid., 186.

18. Ibid., 188.

19. Ibid., 192.

20. Ibid., 193.

21. Ibid.

22. Ibid., 194.

23. The concept of pantheism applied to the state as a specific pathology is fundamental in Toniolo's thought. In a talk from 1913 he explains it like this: "Just as religious pantheism equates God the creator with the created universe, and more particularly the divine supernatural with human nature, both in the great pseudo-monotheistic historical religions of the Asian Orient and in the polytheistic cults of Greece and Rome, so also, with inseparable logical and positive correlation, throughout paganism one finds the

state tending, in different but inexorable ways, to seize and assimilate religious authority as well in its juridical-coercive power, and then to absorb, in the unity of its political organism and in its omnipotent action, the whole of man and every derivation and manifestation of social life," *Problemi ed ammaestramenti sociali dell'età costantiniana*, published in installments in the RISS and then with a comprehensive extract (Rome, 1913); now in CS, 3–102. Quotation on 10–11. On this topic in general Toniolo refers to A. M. Weiss, *Soziale Frage und soziale Ordnung* (Freiburg im Breisgau, 1904); for historical applications in antiquity, cf. R. Pöhlmann, *Geschichte des antiken Kommunismus und Sozialismus* (Munich, 1893–1901).

24. Cf. *Trattato*, TES I, 194–96.

25. Ibid., 196.

26. Ibid., 202.

27. Cf. the summary he presents in the first volume of his *Storia dell'economia sociale* in *Toscana nel Medio Evo*: SEST I, 280–360: "The Tuscan republics, and in particular the Florentine, in essence reproduce the free political orders of Europe in the Middle Ages, which, due to being linked in various ways and degrees to many different lineages and historical conditions, are today mainly attributed to the genius of Christianity through the work of the Church" (324). A thesis for which Toniolo refers to C. Périn and G. Romain.

28. *Problema sociologico*, in OPS, 277.

29. Cf. *Chiesa nella storia*, 107–12.

30. *Trattato*, TES I, 205.

31. Ibid., 206.

32. Ibid., 207.

33. Ibid., 207–08.

34. Ibid., 208.

35. Ibid., 209–10.

36. Ibid., 210–11.

37. Ibid., 213.

38. Ibid., 214.

39. Ibid.

40. Ibid., 216.

41. Ibid., 220.

Chapter IV: Between Science and Revolution

1. *Trattato*, TES I, 221.

2. Ibid., 222.

3. Cf. ibid., 228–29.

4. Ibid., 230.

5. Ibid., 231.

6. *Trattato della moneta* (1750) and *Dialoghi sul commercio dei grani* (1770).

7. *Lezioni di economia civile* (1765).

8. *Elementi di economia* (1768).

9. *Meditazioni sull'economia politica* (1771).

10. *Dell'economia nazionale* (1774).

11. Cf. *Trattato*, TES I, 235.

12. Ibid., 236.

13. Ibid., 238–39.

14. Ibid., 241.

15. Ibid., 242.

16. Ibid., 244.

17. Ibid., 245.

18. Ibid.

19. Ibid., 245–46.

20. Cf. F. List, *Das nationale System der politischen Ökonomie* (1841); W. Roscher, *System der Volkswirthschaft* (1854–194); B. Hildebrand, *Die Nationalökonomie der Gegenwart und Zukunft* (1848); K. Knies, *Die politische oekonomie vom standpunkte der geschichtlichen methode* (1853). For a summary view cf. I. Cervelli, "*Lo storicismo economico tedesco dell'Ottocento nei suoi rapporti con la storiografia*," in *Contributi alla conoscenza*, 117–44.

21. Cf. A. Schäffle, *Das gesellschaftliche System der menschlichen Wirtschaft* (1861); G. von Schmoller, *Grundriss der allgemeinen Volkswirthschaftslehre* (1900–04); A. Wagner, *Lehr- und Handbuch der politischen Ökonomie* (1876).

22. *Trattato*, TES I, 255.

23. Cf. G. Toniolo, *Capitalismo e socialismo* [hereafter CS], introduction by S. Majerotto (Vatican City: Comitato Opera Omnia di G. Toniolo, 1947).

24. Cf. P. Pecorari, *Giuseppe Toniolo e il socialismo*, (Bologna: Pàtron Editore, 1981), 175–246.

25. *Il socialismo nella storia della civiltà. Linee direttive* (Florence: Libreria Editrice Fiorentina, 1903; the result of several articles published in the RISS); now in CS, 267–446. Citation in CS, 411. Regarding the "laws" enunciated by the Marxian theorist, Toniolo observes, "It can be said that there is no longer any of them (even among the most solemn, like the iron law of wages, the theory of value, that of profit or 'Mehrwert,' of capitalist production) that has not undergone the influence of dissolving criticism, instilling a kind of eclecticism" (ibid.). Indeed, he sees emerging signs of a decline in collectivist doctrinairism of the Marxian type, to the advantage of individualistic socialism.

26. H. Sidgwick, *The Principles of Political Economy* (1883).

27. A. Marshall, *Principles of Economics* (1890).

28. *Trattato*, TES I, 258.

29. Cf., for example, L. Cossa, *Introduzione allo studio dell'economia politica*, 524.

Chapter V: The Christian Economy

1. I refer, on this issue, to *Chiesa nella storia,* 173–200.

2. *Trattato*, TES I, 267.

3. Ibid., 274.

4. Ibid., 274–75.

5. Ibid., 375–76. Typo alert: speaking of the German protagonists, the text reads "Monfang" for "Moufang" (Franz Christoph Ignaz).

6. Cf. A. De Gasperi, *I tempi e gli uomini che prepararono la Rerum novarum* (Milan: Vita e Pensiero, 1945). A comparison between Ketteler and Toniolo in P. Pecorari (ed.), *Ketteler e Toniolo. Tipologie sociali del movimento cattolico in Europa* (Rome: Città Nuova, 1977).

7. Toniolo highlights — also to emphasize his conception of economics in the broader framework of society and ethics — that the whole of Leo XIII's magisterium must be considered in terms of *pars destruens,* in the condemnation of socialism (*Quod Apostolici Muneris,* 1878), and of *pars construens,* in the relaunching of Christian thought through the revival of scholastic philosophy (*Aeterni Patris,* 1879), of the Christian concept of the state (*Diuturnum,* 1881), of the remedies to the workers' question in *Rerum Novarum* (1891).

8. Toniolo mentions the historical studies on the first Christian centuries by P. Allard and the social history of the Church by U. Benigni, the rediscovery, with U. Chevalier, of the institutions of the medieval age "in which was recognized the youth of the Catholic Christian order" (TES I, 278), studies on the crisis of modernity from the Reformation to the French Revolution (J. Janssen, H. Denifle, and H. Grisar), up to studies on the recent Catholic revival (G. Goyau). Sociological studies took advantage of this historical rediscovery, in monographic or summary form (F. Hettinger, J. Mausbach, V. Cathrein, M. O. Weiss, H. Pesch, etc.).

9. *Trattato,* TES I, 279.

10. Ibid., 280.

11. Ibid.

12. Ibid.

13. Ibid., 280–81.

14. Introduction to the *Trattato*, TES I, XII.

15. This is, for example, the case with some propositions on the wage-population relationship, in which Toniolo accepts as an established fact that wages depend on the supply of labor relative also to the reproductive fluctuation of the working population, "due to three fundamental facts: births, marriages, and deaths, and so to the demographic composition of the same and all the circumstances influencing it, in which respect the law of wages is closely linked to the biological laws of society" (*Sulla distribuzione della ricchezza. Lezioni* [hereafter *Lezioni distribuzione*], Verona-Padua: Ed. Drucker e Tedeschi, 1878), 103–213; now in TES IV, 123–24. A similar view would draw his reproach in 1895, in reviewing *Primi elementi di economia politica* (10th edition) by L. Cossa,

finding in the text "traditional Malthusian phrases that are equivocal as compared with the Christian concepts on the duty of procreation and on the beneficial efficacy that it normally exerts on the status of workers" (TES II, 451). In making this observation, Toniolo also makes a self-criticism: "We also confess that we ourselves had adhered to those propositions in a booklet on the *apportionment of wealth*, but later, led by the hand by the principles of Christian ethics and law, having been induced to modify them, we found ourselves comforted by the very criticism that, from the strictly economic viewpoint, has been established by recent utilitarian economists who do not accept our Christian ideas" (Ibid.). In this regard, in his anonymous text of 1886 *Alcune linee e quesiti di un programma di economia sociale cristiana* (Ibid., 367–91), there is a passage in which he reviews his initial beliefs of a Malthusian flavor, highlighting that population growth does not automatically entail a problem of well-being: "If it is true that the multiplication of the population on the one hand tends to reduce the individual share of distribution and consumption, on the other hand it itself, with the denser human coexistence and the greater difficulties of life that accompany it, pushes the population to more energetic and intelligent work, to more prudent capital savings and so to more copious production, and at the same time, with the improvement of the system of exchange instruments, it makes circulation faster and less expensive, and the population itself is drawn to greater and more widespread emigration, at the same time that this whole process is validated and examined by the surer safeguards of science, of civil orders, of moral virtues, in a word, of civilization, which as a rule become more numerous and robust amid the more intimate and varied relations of populous societies. So, due to the increased wealth that is brought into balance with population growth, material well-being remains unchanged and will perhaps be found to be elevated" (Ibid., 378–79).

16. Introduction to the *Trattato*, TES I, ix–x.

17. Ibid., xix.

18. Ibid., xxxi–xxxii.

Chapter VI: The Logic of Economics

1. *Trattato*, TES I, 288.

2. Ibid.

3. Ibid., 290.

4. Remember that, for example, even a superior intellect like Plato went astray by imagining a social order that a philosopher-legislator could refashion at will, "to the point of equating males and females in all civil functions and justifying slavery as its basis" (Trattato, TES I, 292).

5. *Trattato*, TES I, 294.

6. Ibid., 296.

7. Ibid., 297.

8. Ibid., 307.

9. For the current debate on the dominant role that Europe has played in the world

economy, cf. V. Zamagni, *Perché l'Europa ha cambiato il mondo. Una storia economica* (Bologna: il Mulino, 2015); P. T. Hoffman, *Why Did Europe Conquer the World?* (Princeton: Princeton University Press, 2015). On the economic development of some large Eastern countries, cf. A. Sen, *L'altra India. La tradizione razionalista e scettica della cultura indiana* (Milan: Mondadori, 2006); B. D. Metcalf, T. R. Metcalf, *Storia dell'India moderna* (Milan: Mondadori, 2007); K. Pomeranz, *La grande divergenza. La Cina, l'Europa e la nascita dell'economia mondiale moderna* (Bologna: il Mulino, 2004); E. Basile et al., *Istituzioni e sviluppo economico nel capitalismo contemporaneo. Il caso di Cina e India* (Milan: FrancoAngeli, 2021). This is enough to demonstrate that Toniolo's line of inquiry has not been erased from the scientific agenda, and if anything is coming back into prominence.

10. Trattato, TES I, 306.
11. Ibid., 308.
12. Ibid., 309–10.
13. Ibid., 310.
14. Ibid., 311.
15. Cf. ibid., 312.
16. Ibid., 313.
17. Ibid., 316.
18. Ibid., 317-319.
19. Ibid., 321.
20. Ibid., 322.
21. Ibid., 323.
22. Ibid., 328–29.
23. Ibid., 335.
24. Ibid., 336.
25. Toniolo mentions here, among the historical authors, Whately, J. S. Mill, Cairnes, Garnier, Neumann, Cossa, Lampertico, Ricca-Salerno, and among his living peers, Wagner, Schmoller, Sidgwick, Graziani, Supino, Menger with the psychological-exact school of which Pantaleoni and Pareto are "worthy perpetuators and improvers" (cf. ibid., 338).
26. Ibid., 340.
27. Ibid., 341.
28. Ibid., 342.
29. Ibid., 345.
30. Ibid., 347.
31. Ibid., 348.
32. Ibid., 349.
33. Ibid., 354.
34. Ibid., 356.
35. Ibid., 371.
36. Ibid., 372.
37. Ibid., 375–76.
38. Ibid., 376.

39. Ibid., 377.

40. Ibid., 378.

41. Ibid. It is interesting that, in his review of Cardinal A. Capecelatro's book *Le virtù cristiane* (Rome: Desclée, 1898), Toniolo should underline how, in the scholastic perspective, this law of the maximum useful effect with the minimum expenditure of forces was connected to the virtue of prudence, "which teaches in every human act the proportion of means to end," "*Le virtù cristiane e la sociologia. A proposito di un libro recente del card. Capecelatro*," in RISS, 1898, vol. XVIII, 395–409; now in SS I, 92–109. Quote on page 98.

Chapter VII: Foundations of Social Economics

1. *Trattato*, TES I, 382.

2. Ibid., 383.

3. Cf. ibid., 384.

4. Ibid., 387.

5. Ibid.

6. Ibid., 388.

7. Here Toniolo puts his references for such a statement in parentheses: Schmoller, Roscher, Baudrillart.

8. *Trattato*, TES I, 391.

9. Ibid.

10. Ibid., 393.

11. Ibid., 395.

12. Ibid., 397.

13. Ibid., 398.

14. A discussion that does not lose its relevance, if one only thinks about the protest movement unleashed throughout the world in the spring of 2020 by the killing of the African-American George Floyd in the United States by the police, a protest conducted under the slogan "Black Lives Matter."

15. *Trattato*, TES I, 400.

16. Ibid., 401–2.

17. Toniolo presents the example of the tropical climate, where nature is generous and luxuriant, reducing the concerns for physical work to a minimum and stimulating the higher concerns of the spirit, as demonstrated by the most splendid forms of civilization like those of Egypt and India. But with this largesse of nature the character tends toward inertia and laziness, to the point of falling into immobility and barbarism. Not so in Europe, where need forces one to sharpen one's ingenuity, so that "the tropical zone seems destined to initiate civilization, the temperate zone to perpetuate it" (*Trattato*, TES I, 404).

18. Ibid.

19. Ibid., 406–7.

20. Ibid., 410.

21. Ibid., 411–12.

22. Ibid., 416.

23. Ibid. In 1904, commemorating Frédéric Le Play (in *Studium,* Florence, IV (1909), 5, 266–74; now in RF 500–13), Toniolo declared himself in agreement with him on the vision of woman and the family: "What Le Play writes about respect for woman, and in particular about the dignity of the mother in the family (although calling the equality of the two sexes an aberration), is the best that could be written up to now about the troublesome question of feminism. He was the first, with his comparative observations, to voice the positive judgment that if man makes the laws in assemblies and from thrones, woman makes the customs in the family and in society, and by this means she is an indispensable author of social prosperity. Thus with his proposals he anticipated that solution of feminism which the most sensible reformers are approaching in recent days, calling not for an equalization of the sexes in the entire field of social and political life, but rather for broader and more effective legal faculties and resources for woman, so that she may better exercise those *special functions* that nature entrusted to her and not to men: the functions of wife, mother, homemaker, child-rearer, minister and dispenser of ideals of the truth, of strengthening virtues, and of social charity. That even if woman lays claim to other faculties and rights to be exercised together with man, she requests these only according to the forms, ways, and limits that may become a preparation, a means, and a complement to the special functions of her sex" (RF, 506).

24. The bibliography and plurality of positions are endless. On the issue in general, cf. S. and V. Zamagni, *Famiglia e lavoro. Opposizione o armonia?* (Cinisello Balsamo: San Paolo, 2012).

25. We will return to the topic in the twenty-third chapter, for the treatment of the question at the 1897 conference in Zurich organized by the International Association for the Legal Protection of Workers.

26. *Trattato*, TES I, 418–19.

27. Ibid., 422–23.

28. Ibid., 424.

29. Ibid.

30. Ibid., 426–27. Here Toniolo also adds, among the erosive causes, "the theories of an old and new Malthusianism, which hinders marriage and diminishes its fruitfulness; those of the emancipation of women and free love (Bebel and/or socialists)." In order not to misunderstand the reference to the emancipation of woman as an attitude contrary to the "social" emancipation of woman, it must be said that Toniolo was quite meritorious on the latter — for example, by helping to organize the Catholic Women's Union within the People's Union of which he was president (cf. *Economista di Dio,* 129). Here he refers to emancipation of socialist stamp, with unacceptable ethical principles.

31. Among Toniolo's first considerations on the position of T. R. Malthus in his *Essay on the Principle of Population* (1798), cf. the letter to his fiancée, Maria Schiratti, dated May 26, 1778 (LL I, 53–6): "I think that in most cases there is a balance between life and the means of living, and that marriage is one of the conditions for maintaining it" (55).

32. *Trattato*, TES I, 429.
33. Ibid., 433.
34. Ibid., 438–39.
35. Ibid., 439.
36. It would be interesting to discuss Toniolo's considerations, based largely on statistical data, but also with an eye ever attentive to the influence of Christianity in history. According to Toniolo, Christianity has also played a significant role in the push for biological "vitality," encouraging the multiplication of the species (the biblical "be fruitful and multiply"). It would take a whole chapter to subject this to a critical interdisciplinary approach, verifying to what extent Toniolo's vision holds up in comparison with what has happened in the world, in its different regions and cultures, from the last century up to these first decades of the third millennium.
37. *Trattato*, TES I, 460.
38. Ibid.
39. Ibid., 462.
40. Ibid., 465.
41. Ibid., 466.
42. Ibid.
43. Ibid., 470–71.
44. Ibid., 481.
45. Ibid., 485. Confirmation of this missionary view of emigration is found in Toniolo's correspondence (*Lettere* [hereafter LL], collected by G. Anichini, ordered and annotated by N. Vian, Vatican City, 1952–53). In the letter of November 1, 1912 (LL III, 322–42) to Fr. Massimo Rinaldi in memory of Bishop Scalabrini of Piacenza, meritorious for his service to migrants, Toniolo also sees in the spread of Italians throughout the world "the mission of bringing everywhere with the cross examples of an activity educative of the peoples; they will perhaps be that leaven which the hand of God secretly places in the bosom of every race, of every nation, of every social condition, so that it may ferment and hasten the expansion in the near future of a universal civilization, which will be centered, assimilated, and made fertile again around perennially Latin and papal Rome!" (p. 323).
46. *Trattato*, TES I, 483.

Chapter VIII: Economics and the Social Order

1. *Trattato*, TES II, 1.
2. Ibid., 215.
3. Ibid., 3.
4. Ibid., 4.
5. Ibid., 7.
6. Ibid., 10.
7. Ibid.

8. Ibid., 18.

9. Cf. Pope Francis, encyclical *Laudato Si'*, par. 108.

10. *Trattato*, TES II, 33.

11. Ibid., 35.

12. Cf. J. Elster, *The Cement of Society: A Study of Social Order* (New York: Cambridge University Press, 1989).

13. *Trattato*, TES II, 39.

14. Ibid.

15. Ibid., 40.

16. Ibid.

17. Ibid., 41.

18. Ibid., 41–2.

19. Ibid., 42.

20. Ibid., 43.

21. Ibid., 45.

22. Ibid.

23. Ibid., 46.

24. Ibid.

25. On this I refer to *Chiesa nella storia*, 99–138.

26. *Trattato*, TES II, 48.

27. Ibid., 50.

28. Ibid.

29. Ibid., 53–4.

30. Ibid., 54.

31. Ibid., 59.

32. Ibid., 61.

33. Ibid., 65.

34. Ibid.

35. Ibid., 68.

36. Ibid., 71.

37. Cf. Ibid., 70–2.

38. Ibid., 72–3. Toniolo refers to Périn, de Decker, Lampertico.

39. Ibid., 73.

40. Ibid., 75.

41. Ibid., 77.

42. Ibid., 79–90.

43. Ibid., 90.

44. Ibid., 90–6.

45. Ibid., 97.

46. Ibid., 98. Cf. Toniolo's report at the Social Week of Naples (March 31–April 5, 1910), published, with notes and additions, in RISS, 1910, vol. LII; now in *Democrazia cristiana. Istituti e forme, I–II*, preface by A. Ardigò (Vatican City, 1951) [hereafter DC

III for the first volume, DC IV for the second]. The report we refer to is in DC IV, 6–32. "The family risks becoming the object in which all the hostile forces of the contemporary era meet, to bring about the final collapse of the Christian social order" (8), and "it is about to become (one can say this with all scientific rigor) the heart of the contemporary *social question*" (22).

47. Cf. *Trattato*, TES II, 100–11.

48. Ibid., 106.

49. Ibid., 108.

50. Ibid.

51. Ibid., 109.

52. Ibid., 111.

53. Ibid.

54. I refer to *Economista di Dio,* 149–53. His daughter Teresa's fiancé, Giovanni Corna Pellegrini, dies in the war.

55. "The Voice of the Pope; Peace, Peace, Peace," published in *Vita e Pensiero, I* (1915), 65–71, together with an open letter to Cardinal Lualdi, archbishop of Palermo, published in the single issue *Decennalia;* now in DC IV, 297–315. Quote in DC IV, 305.

Chapter IX: Hierarchy as *Diakonia*

1. *Trattato*, TES II, 112.

2. Here it would be interesting to make a comparison with Pareto, who puts the concept of social heterogeneity at the foundation of his theory of the "circulation of the elites or aristocracies": "The assertion that men are objectively equal is so absurd that it does not even deserve to be refuted. Instead, the subjective concept of the equality of men is a fact of great moment, which works powerfully to determine the changes that society undergoes" (*Manuale,* 126, par. 102).

3. Cf., on the specific topic of the responsibility of intellectuals, J. Benda, *Il tradimento dei chierici. Il ruolo dell'intellettuale nella società contemporanea* (Turin: Einaudi, 2012; French original, 1927). The topic of the "elites" is certainly as important as it is delicate, taking on a certain color depending on the context of value in which it is set. It has given rise, in history, to authentic aberrations (suffice it to think of the role that Nazism attributed to the Aryan and German races). But it cannot be avoided without finding it again in other guises. Today there is a rediscovery of this sociological subject area. Cf. F. De Mucci, *I molti e i pochi. La società "sotto-sopra" dei diseguali* (Soveria Mannelli: Rubbettino, 2015).

4. T. Piketty, *Il capitale nel XXI secolo* (Florence-Milan: Giunti-Bompiani, 2019), 40.

5. *Trattato*, TES II, 112.

6. Ibid., 114.

7. Ibid., 115.

8. Ibid., 117.

9. Ibid., 120.

10. Ibid., 124–25.
11. Ibid., 126–27.
12. Ibid., 127.
13. Ibid., 128.
14. Ibid., 128–29.
15. Ibid., 138.
16. Ibid., 139.
17. Ibid.
18. Ibid., 141.
19. Ibid., 142.
20. Cf. ibid., 150.
21. Ibid.
22. Ibid., 156.
23. Ibid., 158.
24. Ibid., 159.
25. Ibid., 167.
26. Ibid., 169.
27. Ibid., 171.
28. Ibid., 173. The word *sindacato*, in Italian, has undergone a significant transformation over time. In medieval cities, during the communal and seigneurial eras, it indicated a legal and financial control over the operations and management of public affairs by the city mayor (*podestà*), who was entrusted with their administration for a limited period.
29. Ibid., 179.
30. Ibid.
31. Ibid., 180.
32. Ibid., 181.
33. Cf. ibid., 182–200.
34. Ibid., 181.
35. Ibid., 185.
36. Toniolo here generically cites Salvatore Talamo, the director of the RISS, who on this topic had published *Il concetto della schiavitù. Da Aristotele ai dottori scolastici* (Rome: Tipografia dell'Unione Cooperativa, 1908). On this essay cf. F. Del Pizzo, *Salvatore Talamo e la rinascita moderna della dottrina sociale della Chiesa,* 201–54.
37. *Trattato*, TES II, 200.
38. Ibid., 201.
39. Ibid., 204.
40. Starting from his conception of original human nature polluted by social evolution, in his *Discours sur l'origine et les fondements de l'inégalité parmi les hommes*, Rousseau wrote in a biting and ironic way: "The first man who, after enclosing a piece of ground, took it into his head to say, *This is mine,* and found people simple enough to believe him, was the true founder of civil society," J. J. Rousseau, *A Discourse upon the*

Origin and Foundation of the Inequality Among Mankind (London: R. and J. Dodsley, 1761), 97.

41. Cf. P.-J. Proudhon, *Che cosa è la proprietà?*, 1840.

42. *Trattato*, TES II, 205.

43. Ibid., 206.

44. Toniolo expands on the historical development of property, showing how it also evolves as a function of the development of personality. In antiquity, collective property predominated — from the Latin public field to the concentric circles around the Germanic village: the ring of private family farms, the ring of collective ownership assigned for cultivation by lot, with individual families holding temporary possession for a few years, and then a final ring of unplowed collective property, whether natural meadow, forest, or pond, which all are free to enjoy. Subsequently, the doubly absorptive collective property is increasingly transferred to single individuals and legal moral entities. "This historical law confirms the principles of ethical-juridical philosophy, recognizing the *legitimacy of particular property,* either individual or social or public, always coexisting, so the question is only one of relative preponderance. While the Middle Ages in general was the era of collective and individual domination at the same time, balancing social stability with private freedom, the contemporary era, with overwhelmingly individualized ownership and the suppression of collective entities (especially the juridical), brought instability in all social relations, breaking a proportion that today tends toward reconstitution" (*Trattato*, TES II, 211).

45. *Trattato*, TES II, 212.

Chapter X: Principles in Action

1. The first edition published by Libreria Editrice Fiorentina, in 1909, was republished without changes by the same publisher in 1921 and 1944.

2. *Trattato*, TES III, 3.

3. Ibid., 3–4.

4. Ibid., 4.

5. Ibid., 5.

6. Ibid.

7. Ibid., 8.

8. Ibid., 11.

9. Ibid., 13.

10. Ibid., 15.

11. Ibid., 16.

12. Ibid., 17.

13. Ibid.

14. Ibid., 23.

15. Cf. ibid.

16. Ibid., 24.

17. Ibid.

18. Ibid., 26.

19. Ibid., 27. In reality, the concept of "work" and "worker" registers a certain oscillation in Toniolo's writings. Here restricted to the scope of material work, in other pages it is also used in a wider sense, "in the broad sense of any personal activity, whether of hand or thought or moral energy" ("*L'economia capitalistica moderna. A proposito di un libro di Claudio Jannet e di altri studi analoghi*," in RISS, April 1893–94; now in CS, 199–265, quote on page 208). Cf. also the letter of March 17, 1878, to his fiancée in LL I, 33–35: "You must know that the word 'wage' has a special and restricted expression in science: that of compensation due to the worker who works in material production on behalf and at the risk of another. In this sense you see that the phrase corresponds to the concept, since it is a matter of the remuneration of the working classes in the true sense of the word, and not indeed of these workers of thought as … we are lawyers, doctors, professors, educators, priests, statesmen, etc. All of us, all (except the idlers and thieves, as one economist has already said) are included in the great concept of work, and we can call ourselves workers: while, I add, this word 'work' already summarizes the great task assigned to every man by Providence, which put us down here *ut operemur*. But between the workers of the arm and those of the mind there is a great distance, as between direction and execution."

20. *Trattato*, TES III, 30.

21. Ibid., 33.

22. Ibid., 34.

23. Ibid., 35.

24. Ibid.

25. Ibid.

26. Ibid., 36.

27. Ibid., 39.

28. Ibid., 40.

29. Ibid., 41.

30. Cf. ibid., 45.

31. Ibid., 53.

32. Ibid., 55.

33. Cf. ibid., 55.

34. Cf. C. Supino, *Principi di economia politica* (Naples: Luigi Pierro editore, 1904), 36; A. Graziani, *Istituzioni di economia politica* (Turin: Fratelli Bocca, 1904), 194–95. The latter author presents a certain debate on the topic, but opts, like Toniolo, for the definition presented above, based on a few studies in this regard by Cossa and Ricca-Salerno.

35. *Trattato*, TES III, 58.

36. Ibid., 59.

37. Ibid., 63.

38. Ibid., 64.

39. Ibid., 65.

40. Ibid., 66.

41. Ibid., 67.

42. Ibid., 69.

43. Ibid., 73. Cf. L. Becchetti, "*L'attualità di Toniolo nell'economia civile*," in *Economia e società,* 64–6.

44. *Trattato*, TES III, 74.

45. Ibid., 81.

46. Ibid., 85.

47. In reality, Toniolo dedicates only generic and occasional attention to it. Two things probably influenced this: (1) his Thomist formation, in an era in which, with *Aeterni Patris,* Thomism had regained strength; and (2) his apologetic approach, which led him to favor the merits of Christian civilization *tout court* (insisting on Saint Francis could have made one think, as often happens when this great figure is celebrated, of an exceptional case). On the other hand, the rediscovery of the Franciscan school within economic theory and practice is a recent fact. Cf. P. Evangelisti, "*Francescana (Scuola francescana di economia)*," in L. Bruni, S. Zamagni (eds.), *Dizionario di economia civile* [hereafter DEC] (Rome: Città Nuova, 2009), 424–39; G. Toeschini, *Ricchezza francescana. Dalla povertà volontaria alla società di mercato* (Bologna: il Mulino, 2004); O. Bazzichi, *Dall'economia civile francescana all'economia capitalistica moderna. Una via all'umano e al civile dell'economia,* preface by S. Zamagni (Rome: Armando editore, 2015).

48. *Trattato*, TES III, 91.

49. It was the second Congress of the Union, held August 26–28, 1896.

50. Cf. chapter 19.

51. *Criteri scientifici,* in *Trattato*, TES V, 485–523. Quote on page 491.

52. Cf. ibid., 523. On this debate, cf. *Chiesa nella storia,* 219–20; P. Pecorari, *Giuseppe Toniolo e il socialismo,* 163.

53. *Trattato*, TES III, 95.

54. Ibid., 96.

55. Ibid., 102.

56. Ibid., 104.

57. Ibid., 107.

58. Ibid., 116–17.

59. Ibid., 118.

60. Ibid., 121.

61. Ibid.

62. Review of L. Luzzatti, "*Le odierne controversie economiche e le loro attinenze con la protezione e col socialismo*" (Rome: Loescher, 1894), in RISS, 1895, vol. VII, 499–509; now in TES II, 439–48.

63. Ibid., TES II, 446–47.

64. One such passage is in the article "*I veri riformatori sociali*," in *Movimento cattolico, VII* (1886), 165–73; now in SS I, 169–84, in which Toniolo summarizes the work as social reformer of the little poor man of Assisi: "When wealth, accumulated prematurely

in the mercantile cities, in contrast with the general poverty of the common rural people, with the passion for enjoyments of the senses threatened for one thing to exhaust the virtue of work and materialize the incipient culture of the spirit, and for another to harshen the conflict between the wealthy classes and the needy multitudes, he, clad as a beggar, travels through Umbria, Tuscany, Lombardy, crosses into France and Spain, and to the people astonished at his passages he preaches the praises of his bride, poverty, which imposes detachment from earthly goods on the rich, resigned contentment on the disinherited, and the sublime harmonies of charity, which in its immense arms embraces not only human but senseless creatures. The crowds throng after him and the rich sell their substance to distribute it to the poor, and these represent the kingdom of an unexpected universal brotherhood, which, without offending rights and social hierarchy, begins in the commonality of sacrifice and is completed with the communion of charity. … And at the end of his life he leaves behind him numerous religious families to perpetuate in the world the example and apostolate of a new Christian democracy" (173–74).

65. Review of Luzzatti, op. cit., in TES II, 448.

Chapter XI: Laws of Productivity

1. Cf. *Trattato*, TES III, 122–31.
2. Ibid., 131.
3. Ibid.
4. Ibid., 133.
5. Ibid., 135.
6. Ibid.
7. Ibid., 136.
8. Ibid., 136–37.
9. Ibid., 137.
10. Ibid., 137–39.
11. Ibid., 146.
12. Ibid., 146–64.
13. Ibid., 151–52.
14. Ibid., 159.
15. Ibid., 163.
16. Ibid., 163–64.
17. Ibid., 164.
18. Ibid., 165.
19. Ibid.
20. Ibid.
21. "*Il commercio internazionale dei grani. Criteri direttivi a proposito delle odierne questioni sul dazio dei cereali in Italia*," in RISS, vol. V (1894), 177–92, republished in TES V, 465–84. Among the authors he explicitly cites as influences: V. Brants, *La circulation des hommes et des choses* (Louvain: Peeters, 1892).

22. Ibid., TES V, 472.
23. Ibid., 482.
24. *Trattato*, TES III, 166.
25. Ibid., 168.
26. Ibid., 171.
27. Ibid., 175.
28. Ibid., 182.
29. Cf. P. Bianchi, *4.0. La nuova rivoluzione industriale* (Bologna: il Mulino, 2018), 91.
30. *Trattato*, TES III, 185.
31. Ibid., 187.
32. Cf. ibid.
33. Ibid., 188.
34. Ibid., 189.
35. Ibid., 190.
36. Ibid., 191.
37. Ibid., 192.
38. Ibid., 193.
39. Ibid., 194.
40. Ibid.
41. Ibid., 195.
42. Cf. L. Bruni, S. Zamagni, *Economia civile. Efficienza, equità e pubblica felicità* (Bologna: il Mulino, 2004); L. Bruni, *Il prezzo della gratuità* (Rome: Città Nuova, 2006).
43. *Trattato*, TES III, 195.
44. Ibid., 196.
45. Ibid., 202. Among the examples that Toniolo gives here (brawny men for the toughest jobs, women for delicate operations), there is also the example — which now seems outdated to us — of "children for the least painstaking aspects." Nonetheless, it must be said that, although on this point he has not yet reached our sensibility, which in principle rejects child labor, he is moving in this direction. One of his youthful scientific inquiries takes stock of this topic: "*Sul lavoro delle donne e dei fanciulli nelle industrie manifatturiere di Venezia e sopra alcuni criteri di legislazione industriale in Italia. Conclusioni del rapporto della Commissione presso il Comitato di studi economici di questa città*," in *Giornale degli economisti, vol. IV*, 1876–77, 109–27; republished in DC III, 201–23. A. Ardigò, in a lucid introduction (cf. DC I, xiii), emphasizes that this "first" Toniolo, in order to support workers' wages, does not look so much to the intervention of the law as to the technological development of backward companies, given that these, precisely because of their backwardness, dominated by the competition, are inclined to reduce wages. The "second" Toniolo will be increasingly convinced of the importance of social legislation on behalf of workers.
46. Ibid., TES III, 205.
47. Ibid.

48. Ibid., 206.
49. Ibid., 208.
50. Ibid.
51. Ibid., 213.
52. Ibid., 214.
53. Ibid., 216.
54. Ibid., 217.
55. Ibid., 218–19.
56. Ibid., 219.
57. Ibid., 221.
58. Ibid., 222.
59. Ibid., 222–23.
60. Ibid., 228.
61. Cf. "*Il Congresso internazionale delle casse rurali ed operaie a Parigi*," in RISS, 1900, vol. XXIV, 202–16.
62. "*L'avvenire della cooperazione cristiana*," in RISS, 1900, vol. XXIV, 369–81; now in DC III, 510–24.
63. Ibid., 510.
64. Ibid.
65. Ibid., 511.
66. Ibid., 512–13.
67. Ibid., 514.
68. Cf. Ibid., 515.
69. Ibid., 517.
70. Cf. ibid., 518. See also G. Toniolo, "*Per la storia del movimento cooperativo. Criteri e documenti*," in RISS, 1895, vol. IX, 3–27; now in DC III, 477–509. Taking a panoramic look at the cooperative movement, Toniolo insists on the appropriateness that it should openly declare its Christian inspiration and courageously express the final intent of ethical and social reconstruction. "For Catholics, all cooperative organizations are nothing but stones for building up, step by step, the Christian social order. Their final intent is that of making the credit institutions themselves into so many *living cells* which, connected with a mutual exchange of healthy moral and religious energies, converge to ignite the Catholic spirit in all the social orders" (489). On the economic boost that the "confessional turn" brought, at least for then, to the efficiency of the rural credit unions (the story would become more tortuous, registering a penalization especially in the fascist era), cf. A. Leonardi, "*Casse rurali*," in DEC, 166–80.
71. "*L'avvenire della cooperazione cristiana*," in DC III, 520.
72. To Cardinal Mariano Rampolla del Tindaro, August 1, 1900, LL II, 201.
73. "*L'avvenire della cooperazione cristiana*," in DC III, 510–24. The Parisian talk on cooperatives concludes with an appeal to their Christian character: "From now on each cooperative society of consumption and production, each syndicate of collective purchasing and selling, each cooperative bank or rural credit union, in the very act in

which it associates people with the bonds of economic interests, must become an incidental means of strengthening the bonds of charity and Christian faith" (521–22). There is no problem with the service offered also to non-Christians, given that this openness of charity is in the very spirit of Christian charity, as demonstrated by the missionaries who in some Muslim countries "open and run schools for infidels, without even teaching them the catechism" (522). This openness of charity also applies to "the infidels in our unhappy populations that have practically fallen back into paganism" (523), but this must not make us submit to the "secularization" that presumes to make us hide, personally and institutionally, "the banner of religion and civilization."

Chapter XII: Land-based Industry

1. *Trattato*, TES III, 250.
2. Ibid., 254.
3. Ibid., 255.
4. Ibid., 257.
5. Ibid., 259.
6. Ibid., 262.
7. Ibid., 267.
8. Ibid., 269.
9. Ibid., 270.
10. Ibid., 273–74.
11. Ibid., 277.
12. Ibid., 279–80.
13. Ibid., 282.
14. Ibid., 287.
15. Ibid., 288.
16. Ibid., 291.
17. Ibid., 292–93.
18. Ibid., 295.

Chapter XIII: Rural Industry

1. *Trattato,* TES III, 305.
2. Ibid., 308.
3. Ibid., 310.
4. Ibid., 311.
5. Ibid., 312.
6. Ibid., 313.
7. Ibid.
8. Ibid., 316.
9. Ibid., 319.
10. Ibid., 320.

11. Ibid., 325.

12. Cf. ibid., 327.

13. Ibid., 334.

14. Ibid., 335.

15. Ibid., 336.

16. Ibid., 342.

17. Ibid., 343.

18. Cf. ibid., 350–65.

19. Ibid., 355.

20. Ibid., 372.

21. Cf. ibid., 379–82.

22. "*Programma dei cattolici di fronte al socialismo*" (January 2–3, 1894), in RISS, 1894, vol. IV, 168–75, republished in DC I, 1–14. The point we are referring to is on pages 7–8. The program, generally known as the "Milan Program" because it was approved in this city by the Catholic Union for Social Studies on January 2–3, 1894, was signed not only by Toniolo, but also by S. Medolago Albani, L. Bottini, C Sardi, L. Olivi.

23. *Trattato,* TES III, 387.

24. Ibid., 390–91.

25. Ibid., 393.

26. Ibid., 396.

27. Ibid., 401.

28. Ibid.

29. Ibid., 402.

30. Ibid., 406.

31. Ibid., 408–9.

32. Ibid., 409.

33. See, for example, the interview he gave to *Corriere d'Italia*, May 26, 1908, no. 70, reprinted in DC III, 434–37 ("*I cattolici e le agitazioni agrarie. Intervista di Arturo Giometti col prof. Giuseppe Toniolo*").

34. *Trattato*, TES III, 412. To this experiment Toniolo links the names of three priests: Luigi Sturzo in Sicily, Ambrogio Portaluppi in Lombardy, Emilio Cottafavi in Emilia.

35. Ibid., 413.

36. Ibid., 417–22; cf. also "*Riforme agricolo-sociali*," in RISS, 1908, vol. XLVII, 206–19; now in DC III, 400–17, especially 405–9.

37. Ibid., 434.

Chapter XIV: Manufacturing Industry

1. *Trattato,* TES III, 438.

2. Letter of October 20, 1876, in LL I, 8.

3. Ibid.

4. Ibid., 9.

5. Cf. *Trattato*, TES III, 440–47.
6. Ibid., 461.
7. Ibid., 474.
8. Ibid., 475.
9. Ibid., 477.
10. Ibid.
11. Ibid., 478–79.
12. Cf. ibid., 479.
13. Ibid., 484–85.
14. Cf. "*Il quesito delle piccole imprese industriali nell'odierno momento storico. Saggio sulla economia delle piccole industrie*," in *Rassegna di agricoltura industria e commercio*, Padua, II (1874); republished in TES IV, 3–41. An extensively documented study, in which Toniolo reports the results of historical-statistical research by G. Schmoller, *Zur Geschichte der deutschen Kleingewerbe im 19 Jahrhundert* (Halle, 1870); W. Roscher, *Étude sur l'industrie en grand et en petit*, French translation of a study published in Leipzig, 1861. In *Le piccole industrie in Italia* he cites a study by P. Torrigiani, in *Rassegna di agricoltura, industria e commercio*, Padua, vol. III, no. 2, June 1874. Other Italian authors: E. Morpurgo, M. Treves, L. Luzzatti. On the basis of historical-statistical data, Toniolo believes that the discussion on small businesses in the organic framework of economic theory has entered a phase of integration (H. von Mangoldt, A. E. F. Schäffle, A. Emminghaus).
15. *Trattato,* TES III, 488-89.
16. Ibid., 489.
17. Ibid.
18. Ibid., 493.
19. Ibid., 495.
20. Ibid., 497.
21. Ibid., 498.
22. Ibid., 500–1.
23. Ibid., 507.
24. Ibid., 509.
25. Ibid.
26. Ibid., 511.
27. Cf. ibid.
28. Ibid., 516–17.
29. Ibid., 517.
30. Ibid., 523.
31. Ibid., 527.
32. Ibid., 529.

Chapter XV: Distribution: Concepts and Questions

1. *Sulla distribuzione della ricchezza. Lezioni* [hereafter *Lezioni distribuzione*] (Verona-Padua: Ed. Drucker e Tedeschi, 1878); republished in TES IV, 103–213.

2. Cf. L. Cossa, *Introduzione allo studio dell'economia politica* (completely revised 3rd edition of *Guida allo studio dell'economia politica*) (Milan: Hoepli, 1892), 524.

3. *Lezioni distribuzione,* in TES IV, 103.

4. Review of L. Cossa, *Primi elementi di economia politica* (10th edition), in TES II, 449–52. Quote on page 451.

5. *Lezioni distribuzione,* in TES IV, 105.

6. Ibid., 109.

7. Ibid., 110.

8. Ibid., 111.

9. Ibid., 113.

10. Ibid., 114.

11. Ibid., 115.

12. At the same time as the publication of the "lectures," he published an extensive article on the topic "*Il salario. Saggio di una esposizione sistematica delle sue leggi*" [hereafter *Salario*], in *Giornale degli economisti*, 1878, vol. VII, 261–80 and 343–64; vol. VIII, 267–89; republished in TES IV, 214–91. We will take both the "lectures" and this article into account here.

13. *Lezioni distribuzione,* in TES IV, 117.

14. *Salario,* in TES IV, 235.

15. *Lezioni distribuzione,* in TES IV, 118.

16. Ibid.

17. Ibid., 121.

18. Ibid., 120; cf. *Salario,* in TES IV, 271–74. Toniolo insists on the importance of the family not only in the name of ethical principles, but also for the ends of work themselves. Underlining the different role of man and woman in general, Toniolo hopes for work in the family for woman, but also with an openness to factory work with precise guarantees: "It seems that one must recognize that, to a certain extent and under given conditions and guarantees, the admission of women into factories can remain unaffected by these [problematic] economic and moral consequences."

19. *Lezioni distribuzione,* in TES IV, 121–22.

20. Ibid., 122.

21. Here Toniolo cites — without a polemical attitude; indeed, it would seem, in agreement with him on this point — the Marxian theory of "extra value": "A *surplus of value*, K. Marx says (*Das Kapital,* Hamburg, 1872, 2nd edition), of which the worker is actually defrauded to the benefit of the enterpriser; this profit *margin* is the unclean origin of the *capital* of the entire *capitalist* economy of modern times," *Salario,* in TES IV, 231, note 1.

22. He refers here to G. Ricca-Salerno, "*Del salario e delle sue leggi*," in *Giornale degli*

economisti, 1878.

23. *Lezioni distribuzione,* in TES IV, 133.

24. Cf. Ibid., 138.

25. On the different forms of remuneration for work, see an article from 1875 in which Toniolo advocates going beyond the uniform wage, simply "by time," with a view to more varied formulas, adapted to the variety of situations: from wages by task to the fixed wage supplemented with participation in the company's profits, up to the wage supplemented with the worker's participation (through the purchase of shares) in the ownership of the company itself. He sees pros and cons for each formula, in reference to the efficacy of the work, to the harmony between workers and enterprisers, to the dignity of work (the "capital-human person": in TES IV, 56), distancing himself from the leveling communist egalitarianism (the reference is to *Das Kapital* by K. Marx: in TES IV, 51–2). Cf. "*Delle varie forme di rimunerazione del lavoro in rapporto colla partecipazione degli operai ai profitti degli imprenditori*," in *Giornale degli economisti*, 1875, vol. I, 282–301; now in TES IV, 42–64.

26. *Lezioni distribuzione,* in TES IV, 142.

27. Ibid., 152.

28. Ibid., 153.

29. Ibid., 155.

30. Ibid., 156.

31. Ibid., 158.

32. With regard to Toniolo's thoughts on this theme, extending the concept of return also to monetary capital, L. Bruni writes: "Interest on money, or usury, is the consequence of a power that becomes extraction of return, without a justification of value based on human labor. … In this, then, Toniolo shares Loria's analysis on return, which identifies an authentic tradition of the Italian school (from Genovesi to Sylos Labini to Federico Caffè), which saw return as the main disease — the *parasitic syndrome* — of the Italian economy (and in general the Catholic, different here from those of Protestant countries)," "*Toniolo e lo 'spirito del capitalism,'*" in *Economia e società,* 76.

33. In an 1877 text Toniolo presented a subtle discussion of a position expressed by F. Lampertico in *La proprietà* (Milan, 1876), according to which return, understood as "that portion of the total product which, after the expenses and profits of production have been covered, *remains free and constitutes the surplus*, must indeed be seen not as a special attribute of natural agents, but still as resulting from the work of man and of capital, nor indeed as particular to some industries only, but common to all." Toniolo accepts this "broad" vision of return, but proposes a series of distinctions, to conclude that, in a proper and specific sense, they are related to land ownership: G. Toniolo, "*Sulla teorica della rendita. Lettera al senatore F. Lampertico a proposito del suo libro 'La proprietà,'*" in *Giornale degli economisti*, vol. IV, 345–61 and 465–81, republished in TES IV, 65–102.

34. *Lezioni distribuzione,* in TES IV, 170.

35. Ibid., 173.

37. Ibid., 179.

Chapter XVI: Circulation of Wealth: The Laws of Exchange

1. Florence: Libreria Editrice Fiorentina, 1921. It would be reprinted in 1929.
2. G. Valenti, *Principi di Scienza economica* (Florence: Barbera ed., 1906).
3. C. Supino, *Principi di economia politica* (Naples: Pierro, 1904).
4. M. Pantaleoni, *Principi di economia pura* (Florence: Barbera ed., 1894).
5. *Trattato,* TES V, 157.
6. Ibid., 158.
7. Ibid., 158.
8. Ibid., 159.
9. Ibid., 3.
10. Ibid., 12.
11. Ibid., 13.
12. Ibid., 13–14.
13. Ibid., 14.
14. Ibid., 15.
15. Ibid.
16. Ibid., 57.
17. Ibid., 65.
18. Ibid., 68.
19. Ibid., 118.
20. Ibid., 136.
21. Ibid., 140.
22. Ibid.
23. Ibid., 141.
24. Cf. L. Becchetti, *L'economia tra il venerdì e il sabato. Le buone pratiche del cittadino consum-attore,* (Milan: Avvenire/Vita e Pensiero, 2020), 133–46.
25. *Trattato,* TES V, 141–12.
26. Ibid., 150–51.
27. Ibid., 155.

Chapter XVII: Commerce and Civilization

1. *Trattato,* TES V, 162.
2. Cf. *Chiesa nella storia,* 95–138.
3. *Trattato,* TES V, 167.
4. Ibid., 173.
5. Ibid., 174.
6. Ibid.
7. *Linee e quesiti,* in TES II, 378.
8. *Trattato,* TES V, 177.
9. Ibid., 180.
10. Ibid., 180–81.

11. Ibid., 181.
12. Ibid., 183.
13. Ibid., 181.
14. Ibid., 184.
15. Ibid., 186–87.
16. Ibid., 193–94.
17. Ibid., 196.
18. Ibid.
22. Ibid., 201.
23. Ibid., 202.
24. Ibid., 204.
25. Ibid., 204–5.
26. Cf. Ibid., 206.
27. Ibid.
28. Ibid., 206–7.

Chapter XVIII: Historical-Geographical Development of Commerce

1. *Trattato*, TES V, 216. Toniolo refers here to various authors in the sociological, historical, legal, and economic fields, referring in particular to Cognetti de Martiis, Pantaleoni, and Pareto, "critically summarized" by A. Graziani (*Istituzioni di economia politica,* 1904).

2. "From the Paleolithic age in Europe, in the caves of the troglodytes in the Dordogne, in central France, necklaces of shells from the Atlantic along with pieces of rock crystal from the Alps were found, undoubtedly brought there through trade, and from the Bronze Age common weapons and tools marked with Minoan letters in Sardinia and Sicily, transported there by the Cretans (Pigeonneau, Mosso, Mayer in Graziani), while in Asia the legendary memories of rich exchange even over great distances and dating back to several thousand years before the common era have recently been confirmed by the Orientalists, and at least rudimentary forms of them were finally discovered in Africa, America, Polynesia, by explorers and sociologists (Babelon)," *Trattato,* TES V, 217–18.

3. *Trattato,* TES V, 218.
4. Ibid., 219.
5. Ibid., 220.
6. Ibid., 226.
7. Ibid., 226–27.
8. Ibid., 233.
9. Ibid., 234.
10. Ibid., 235.
11. Ibid., 240–41.
12. On the case of China and India, cf. E. Basile et al., *Istituzioni e sviluppo economi-*

co nel capitalismo contemporaneo. Il caso di Cina e India, 115–72; L. Aiguo, *China and the Global Economy Since 1840* (London: Macmillan Press, 2000); J. Drèze, A. K. Sen, *An Uncertain Glory: India and Its Contradictions* (Princeton: Princeton University Press, 2013).

13. In its interpretation of the relationship between Christianity and other religions, Christian reflection has always had a twofold tendency, starting from references equally present in biblical texts, in a more "oppositional-conflictual" or more "harmonizing-dialogical" sense, depending on whether otherness was put under the sign of negativity, even ending up demonized (pagans seen as worshiping not the true God, but demons), or was seen, in its positive "seeds" of philosophical and religious truths (*semina Verbi, logoi spermatikoi*), as a propaedeutic to the Gospel (*praeparatio evangelica*). It is a dialectic that runs through the entire history of Christianity, and that of today also registers significant expressions of it. As is known, Vatican II, with the dialogical option that characterizes it, adopted the latter perspective (see above all the decree *Nostra Aetate* on the Church's relationship with non-Christian religions). The theology of Toniolo's time is more marked by the former perspective, and he is affected by it, but not without interesting nuances of openness. On this analysis, I refer to *Chiesa nella storia,* 271–74.

14. *Trattato,* TES V, 242.

15. Cf. ibid., 243.

16. Ibid., 251.

17. Ibid., 256–57.

18. Ibid., 259.

19. Ibid., 269.

20. Ibid., 270–71.

21. Ibid., 278–79.

22. Ibid., 282.

23. Ibid., 282–83.

24. Ibid., 287.

25. Ibid., 290.

26. Ibid., 297.

27. Ibid., 300.

28. Ibid., 303.

29. Ibid., 308–9.

30. Ibid., 310.

31. Ibid., 311.

32. Ibid., 316–17.

33. Ibid., 318.

34. Ibid., 328.

35. Ibid., 356.

36. Ibid., 357.

37. I refer to *Chiesa nella storia,* 95–138.

Chapter XIX: From Monetary Economy to Credit Economy

1. *Trattato,* TES V, 362–63.

2. Ibid., 364.

3. Ibid., 369.

4. Ibid., 378.

5. Ibid., 376.

6. "*Sull'importanza delle banche agricole,*" essay read to the Paduan Academy of Sciences, Letters, and Arts on June 25, 1871, published in *Rivista periodica dei lavori della R. Accademia di scienze, lettere ed arti*, vol. XX, 81–113; now in TES V, 409–36.

7. "*Il credito di beneficenza presso le banche mutue popolari,*" letter to Prof. Luigi Luzzatti, published in *Archivio giuridico*, Bologna 1879, vol. XXIII, 477–90; now in TES V, 437–54.

8. Ibid., in TES V, 443.

9. Ibid., 446.

10. Review of F. Lampertico, *Il credito,* in *Archivio giuridico*, 1884, vol. XXXIII, 230–35; now in TES V, 455–64.

11. Cf. chapter X.

12. *Criteri scientifici,* in TES V, 485–523.

13. Ibid., 485.

14. Ibid., 486.

15. Ibid.

16. Ibid.

17. Ibid., 487.

18. Ibid., 488.

19. Cf. a focus on the issue in P. Pecorari, *L'economia virtuosa. Orientamenti culturali dei cattolici italiani dall'Unità alla seconda Repubblica* (Rome: Studium, 1999), 35–62.

20. *Criteri scientifici,* in TES V, 491.

21. Ibid.

22. Ibid., 492–93.

23. Ibid., 493.

24. Ibid.

25. Ibid., 494–95.

26. Ibid., 495.

27. Ibid., 497.

28. Ibid.

29. Ibid., 498.

30. Ibid.

31. Ibid., 500.

32. Ibid.

33. Ibid., 500–1.

34. Ibid., 501–2.

35. Cf. chapter X.

36. This is how L. Becchetti considers it in "*L'attualità del Toniolo nell'economia civile*," in *Economia e società,* 64.

Chapter XX: Socialism Between Protest and Ideology

1. *Dissertation on the Poor Laws* (London: C. Dilly, 1786), 13, 34, 85.

2. Taken here from A. Loria, *Analisi della proprietà capitalistica,* (Turin: Fratelli Bocca, 1889), vol. II, 259, cited in *Capitalismo e socialismo* [hereafter CS], preface by S. Majerotto (Vatican City, 1947), 109.

3. *Siècle de Louis XIV*, "*Le manoeuvre, l'ouvrier, doit être réduit au nécessaire pour travailler: telle est la nature de l'homme. Il faut que ce gran nombre d'hommes soit pauvre, mais il ne faut pas qu'il soit misérable.*" Toniolo cites this maxim in *La genesi storica dell'odierna crisi sociale economica* [hereafter *Genesi storica*], in RISS, 1893, vol. I, 39–68 and 223–53; now in CS, 103–98. Quote on page 168, note 5.

4. He cites it in the fourth German edition, *Das Kapital* (Hamburg, 1890).

5. *La democrazia cristiana,* (Rome: Società cattolica italiana di cultura, 1900); now in DC I, 15–172. Quote on page 145.

6. "*Problemi ed ammaestramenti sociali dell'età costantiniana*" [hereafter *Problemi ed ammaestramenti*], in RISS, 1913, vol. LXII, 23–43, vol. LXIII, 3–20 and 330–54; now in CS, 1–102. Quote on page 17.

7. *Genesi storica,* in CS, 117.

8. *Problemi ed ammaestramenti,* in CS, 74–5.

9. Cf. *Genesi storica,* in CS, 111–12.

10. Ibid., 113.

11. Ibid., 114.

12. Ibid., 115.

13. Ibid., 120.

14. Ibid., 145.

15. W. Hohoff, *Die Revolution seit dem sechzehnten Jahrhundert* (Freiburg im Breisgau. 1887). For an exploration, cf. P. Pecorari, *Giuseppe Toniolo e il socialismo,* 180 ff.; *Chiesa nella storia,* 124–38.

16. *Genesi storica,* in CS, 124.

17. Ibid., 191.

18. Ibid., 153.

19. Ibid., 155.

20. Ibid., 162.

21. Ibid., 164.

22. Ibid., 169.

23. Ibid., 172.

24. *Il socialismo nella storia della civiltà. Criteri direttivi* [hereafter *Socialismo*]

(Florence: Libreria Editrice Fiorentina, 1902), published in various articles of the RISS between 1899 and 1902; now in CS, 269–446.

25. Ibid., in CS, 270.

26. Ibid., 353.

27. Cf. the thorough analysis of P. Pecorari, *Giuseppe Toniolo e il socialismo,* 175–246.

28. *Socialismo*, in CS, 414.

29. Cf. G. Baget Bozzo, *La Chiesa e la cultura radicale* (Brescia: Queriniana, 1978).

30. *Socialismo,* in CS, 418–49.

31. E. Bernstein, *Die Voraussetzungen des Sozialismus und die Aufgaben der Sozialdemokratie* (Stuttgart, 1889).

32. *Socialism,* in CS, 411.

33. Ibid., 434.

34. Ibid., 446.

Chapter XXI: Christian Democracy: A Social Vision in Political Perspective

1. "*Programma dei cattolici di fronte al socialismo*" [hereafter *Programma dei cattolici*], approved at the assembly of the Union for Social Studies; now in DC I, 12.

2. Toniolo himself indicated the circumstance that had driven the Union to intervene, introducing with a historical account the conference of the Union in Padua in August 1896: "Nor was the opportunity lacking in which the Union should once again assert itself with greater publicity and vigor, and it was when the painful uprisings of Sicily, embittering the spirits of those country people and touching all honest hearts, gained entrance for socialism to spread through the island, presenting itself, thanks to the collectivist doctrines, as the only shield of defense for those miserable people, and promising social redemption with enticing programs. It then seemed appropriate that the association of Catholic scholars should also lay out a *program of social principles and reforms,* to testify that hearts informed by the justice and charity of Christ did not remain indifferent," *Discorso di apertura del II Congresso cattolico italiano degli studiosi di scienze sociali* (Padua, 1896), in DC I, 244.

3. *Programma dei cattolici,* in DC I, 12.

4. Ibid., 6–7.

5. The exact expression "republic founded on work" is found in Toniolo's writings, and precisely in *Salario,* in TES IV, 265, regarding the institution of the arts and crafts guilds of the Middle Ages, "the most robust and vital organization of work that history records. Everything here was aimed at instilling and growing in the consciousness of the multitudes the sense of the moral dignity and of the great civil mission of the working class, in those republics *founded on work* (and largely manual work), the exercise of which was a condition for participation in the protection and rights of the public order. And all of this contributed in the greatest degree to keeping morale high and expansive, and with it the recompense." Cf. also *Remoti fattori,* in RF, 216.

6. The volume [hereafter *Democrazia cristiana*] was published in the *Piccola biblioteca della cultura sociale* edited by Romolo Murri (Rome: Società cattolica italiana di cultura, 1900); now in DC I, 15–174.

7. *Il concetto cristiano della democrazia,* in RISS, 1897, vol. XIV, 325–69; *L'odierno movimento cattolico popolare ed il proletariato,* in RISS, 1898, vol. XVI, 165–83 (corresponds to the second chapter of the book *La genesi dell'odierno proletariato e la democrazia cristiana*); *Le responsabilità sociali dell'odierno movimento cattolico popolare,* in RISS, 1898, vol. XVIII, 3–18.

8. The summary of the deposition, in DC I, 258–59, taken from book by Fr. Davide Albertario, *Un anno in carcere* (Milan: Bertarelli, 1900), 181–82.

9. *Democrazia cristiana,* in DC I, 26.

10. I refer to what I wrote on this subject in *Chiesa nella storia,* 209–26.

11. Leo XIII would also speak of "Christian democracy" in the encyclical *Graves de Communi* (1901), but limited its meaning to action on behalf of the people. The Toniolian perspective was broader and more comprehensive, ultimately implying a program of social order and reform of a potentially political nature. The tensions in the Catholic movement between traditionalists and Christian democrats continued to make this word problematic, and perhaps even more so in the years of Pius X's pontificate and the Modernist crisis. Toniolo continued to use it, but with all of the "polishing" possible. In an article written for the RISS ("*Dopo 25 anni dalla Rerum novarum,*" 1916, vol. LXX, 3–6; now in DC II, 351–55), he significantly notes, regarding "Christian democracy," "The title can disappear; the substance cannot" (DC II, 354). On these difficult years for "Christian democracy" I refer to *Economista di Dio,* 125–49. The immediate reaction of our author — a very welcoming reaction, but with careful distinctions aimed at defending the substance of his vision — in *Provvedimenti sociali popolari* [hereafter *Provvedimenti sociali*] (Rome, 1902, collecting various articles from the RISS; now in DC III, 1–198).

12. *Democrazia cristiana,* in DC I, 29.

13. Ibid., 29–30.

14. Ibid., 31.

15. Ibid., 37.

16. Ibid., 48–9.

17. Ibid., 49.

18. Ibid., 50.

19. The first official document of the Church welcoming democracy in a political sense would come with the radio message of Pius XII of December 24, 1945. Cf. M. Ciampi, *La 'democrazia organizzata' di Toniolo e il partito dei cattolici* (Rome: Studium, 2020).

20. *Democrazia cristiana,* in DC I, 52 (note). Toniolo further clarifies: "But in its accidental or contingent manifestations democracy can, as regards the political constitution, incline toward forms of popular government, calling the lower class to participate to some extent in public administration or even entrusting to the citizens as a whole the election of the council members and magistrates, or finally by making the head of state

himself popularly elected and at the same time temporary" (DC I, 56–7). Further on, our author advances some hypotheses for the restructuring of the representative bodies of democracy, hypothesizing, in addition to the two traditional chambers of the "lords" and the bourgeoisie (representing respectively landed and movable wealth), another chamber that would express the "directive" element of the spiritual life of the nation (clergy, university, liberal professions, initiators of civil progress) and a chamber of universal representation of the people: "That is, the multitudes, today through universal suffrage the arbiters at the ballot boxes on account of their numbers; tomorrow, rather than clamoring in the squares to sell their votes to treacherous representatives, or conspiring in the resistance leagues against the other classes and the social order, they should enter the parliaments in a distinct body to represent themselves, which means not so much the rights of wealth or intellectual superiority, but rather the inalienable rights of the human person, and the essential interests of the great number" (ibid., 64). At the end he wonders, "Who would call this system artificial?" (ibid.). In reality — let's say it frankly, but with the benefit of hindsight — this expresses genuine appeal, but it is hard not to see how artificial this design is, dreamed up in an armchair, hardly corresponding to historical trends.

21. *Democrazia cristiana,* in DC I, 73.

22. Ibid., 74–7. The concept of "ochlocracy" (from ὄχλος, mass), which indicates a politics at the mercy of the masses, is interesting. In the aforementioned radio message of Pius XII on democracy, the pontiff would distinguish the "people" and the "masses," stating that the latter are "the capital enemy" of true democracy.

23. *Democrazia cristiana*, in DC I, 81.

24. Cf. *Indirizzi e concetti sociali all'esordire del sec. XX* [hereafter *Indirizzi e concetti*], in DC II, 3–282. The volume, which was also translated into Spanish by Armando Castroviejo (Valencia: Ortega, 1907), was published in a first edition by Mariotti in Pisa in 1900 and then by Buffetti in Parma in 1901. It reproduces five conferences that Toniolo gave in Rome at the Circle of the Immaculate Conception.

25. *Indirizzi e concetti*, in DC II, 46.

26. Ibid., 47.

27. Ibid., 53.

Chapter XXII: Economic and Ethical-Civil Reforms

1. *Provvedimenti sociali* in DC III, 1–201. Quote on page 83. The reader is reminded that the acronyms DC III and DC IV correspond, in the present system of acronyms, to volumes I and II of the *Opera Omnia* entitled *Democrazia cristiana. Istituti e forme.*

2. Ibid., in DC III, 94.

3. Ibid., 100.

4. Ibid.

5. Ibid.

6. Ibid., 101.

7. Ibid., 105.

8. Ibid., 106.

9. Ibid., 108–9.

10. Ibid., 114.

11. *Indirizzi e concetti,* in DC II, 54–5.

12. Ibid., 57–8.

13. Ibid., 60.

14. Ibid., 62.

15. Ibid., 62–3. For an exploration, cf. G. Zalin, "*Sistema di fabbrica, cooperazione e solidarismo in Giuseppe Toniolo,*" in P. Pecorari (ed.), *Giuseppe Toniolo tra economia e società* (Udine: Del Bianco, 1990), 53–90; G. Catelli, "*La cooperazione come precipitato economico del sociale,*" in *Attualità del pensiero,* 65–70; R. Molesti, "*Lavoro e partecipazione nel pensiero di Giuseppe Toniolo,*" in *Economia e società,* 107–14.

16. *Indirizzi e concetti,* in DC II, 63.

17. Ibid., 64.

18. Ibid., 64–5.

19. Ibid.

20. Ibid., 66.

21. Ibid., 66–7.

22. Ibid., 74.

23. Ibid., 94.

24. Ibid., 96.

25. Ibid.

26. Ibid., 98.

27. Ibid.

28. Ibid., 99.

29. Ibid., 109.

30. Ibid., 114–15.

31. Ibid., 119.

32. Ibid., 120. Toniolo here recalls traditional Catholic doctrine: error — theoretical and practical — as such has no rights; at most it can be tolerated. Hence the duty of the state to make the Catholic religion its own as the only true religion, limiting itself to tolerating the others. Vatican II would bring a significant development (in a certain sense a "surpassing") of this doctrine in the declaration *Dignitatis Humanae* on religious freedom, basing this not on the truth in itself but on the dignity of the human person, in his right to the free pursuit of the truth, even with the risk of incurring error. This new perspective allows for the acceptance of diversity, including religious diversity, while overcoming the indifferentism toward the truth that was the concern underlying the previous doctrinal formulation.

33. *Indirizzi e concetti,* in DC II, 122–23.

34. Ibid., 126.

35. Ibid., 127.

36. Ibid., 128–29.

37. Ibid., 132–33.

38. Ibid., 135.

39. Ibid., 137.

40. Ibid., 138.

41. Illuminating in this regard is the long letter that he wrote to the president of the Opera dei Congressi, Giovanni Battista Paganuzzi, on January 11, 1896. The latter had, in fact, asked him what Catholics could do for the working world, as an alternative to the chambers or boards of labor of the socialists. Toniolo presents three possibilities: the first is the "people's secretariat" of the type conceived by the Swiss Gaspard Decurtins (essentially a form of patronage with broad functions of assistance), but he sees its limitation in the fact that it is a top-down initiative that does not actively involve the popular classes; the second possibility is the professional union of the type conceived by the German baron Schorlemer-Alst, a mixed union of bosses and workers, with the advantage of class unity but with the limitation of not having "enough popular consensus"; the last type — ultimately the one he prefers, as it is historically the most achievable — is the English (trade union) or French (syndicat) type, certainly with the limitation of unilaterality (workers only), but with the advantage of being achievable, constituting the basis for the reorganization of society in organic terms precisely through the enhancement of professional unions, cf. LL II, 6–14.

42. Cf. *Provvedimenti sociali,* in DC III, 120–38.

43. Ibid., 140.

44. Ibid., 141.

45. *Indirizzi*, in DC II, 139.

46. *Provvedimenti*, in DC III, 143.

47. Ibid., 144.

48. Ibid., in 148.

49. This is the thesis supported by A. Cova, "*Lavoro e capitale nel pensiero di Giuseppe Toniolo,*" in *L'uomo come fine,* 111–38, especially 134–36.

50. *Provvedimenti*, in DC III, 151.

51. *Indirizzi*, in DC II, 140.

52. Ibid., 141.

53. Ibid., 142.

54. Ibid., 145.

55. Ibid., 146.

56. Ibid.

57. Ibid.

58. Ibid., 148.

59. Ibid., 159.

60. Ibid., 163.

61. Cf. ibid., 168. Toniolo reads in this strategic and prescriptive sense the appeal for a new commitment that the pope had made to the Franciscans. In 1882, on the occa-

sion of the seventh centenary of the birth of Francis, Leo XIII dedicated the encyclical *Auspicato Concessum* to the event, encouraging in particular the Franciscan Third Order. In 1897, with the apostolic constitution *Felicitate Quadam,* he had unified with the name of *Ordo Fratrum Minorum* the four families of Observants, Reformed, Discalced (or Alcantarines), and Recollects. Cf. L. Iriarte, *Storia del Francescanesimo* (Rome: Dehoniane, 1994), 448–49.

62. *Indirizzi e concetti*, in DC II, 170.

63. Ibid., 177.

64. Ibid., 178.

65. Ibid.

66. Ibid.

67. Ibid., 178–79.

68. I emphasized, on this point, the Toniolo-Sturzo continuity in "*La 'democrazia' di Luigi Sturzo*," in *Impegno e dialogo: incontri culturali 1985–1986*, Biblioteca diocesana S. Paolino-Seminario di Nola, 117–37.

69. *Indirizzi e concetti*, in DC II, 182. A long note is dedicated to hypotheses for correcting today's parliamentary orders, both in the electoral body and in the representative body. Toniolo imagines that, once the legal entities (corporations) representing the various classes have been established, they will be able to bring to the highest level of national representation people from within the corporation itself. "The corporation of landowners, within a certain territorial district, would elect its representatives *from its own bosom,* that is, from among the members of the same association, and likewise the corporation of industrialists and merchants on their own account, no less than that of the workers or common people. Those *eligible* would thus be, for each corporate association, people already known and esteemed through the experience of all its members, due to continuous contacts in the ordinary discussions of the social interests of the class; the *elections*, among men who find themselves in homogeneous social conditions and are acquainted with the needs, sentiments, and aspirations of the class, would not be disturbed and misled by heterogeneous influences, surprises, and easy corruptions; and the *elected members* of each class would come to represent in the political assembly (where they could vote in three distinct sections) not just individual ideas but the real moral, economic, civil interests of the various permanent bodies of society with their respective traditions and vocations. With greater reason, even before applying to the political representation of the state the same electoral regime based on *classes* would apply to the autonomous representations of the municipality, the province, the region, and the *continuity* between the local organs and the central organ of the public authorities would thus be better respected and guaranteed" (183–84, note).

70. Ibid., 187.

71. Ibid., 190.

72. Ibid., 193.

73. For an analysis of this perspective, also from the point of view of the dominant theology of his time as well as of his spirituality, I refer to *Chiesa nella storia,* 139–71.

74. Cf. his letter to Benedict XV of June 1917 and his memo to the Secretariat of State of the following October, in *Iniziative culturali e di azione cattolica* [hereafter IC], preface by G. Dalla Torre (Vatican City, 1949), 202–26. Cf. also U. Villani, "*Il progetto di un Istituto cattolico di diritto internazionale*," in *Economia e società*, 131–42.

75. Toniolo had before his eyes some of these papal interventions of his time: "Lately we contemplated the Church raising itself to a wider sphere of efficacy with the papal arbitration for the Carolinas, with the offered mediation on behalf of Spain, with the mission for the Italian prisoners in Abyssinia, with the pontifical proposals for disarmament and universal peace, promising to become more and more the natural center of international legal relations in the service of broader social interests. And in the meantime the idea dawns among the peoples and diplomatic cabinets that the pontificate has a legitimate function of its own, to integrate and coordinate in a permanent manner the political action of individual states, and there reappear on the horizon the gratifying outlines of a future republic of the Christian peoples, which under the inspiration and the impulse of the Church in Rome may become the guardian and promoter of universal Christian civilization," *Indirizzi e concetti,* in DC II, 200–1.

76. Ibid., 201.

77. Ibid., 282.

Chapter XXIII: The Role of the State in the Economy

1. A distinction was made, on the one hand, between the school of Angers (Bishop C. E. Freppel), closed to state intervention, and that of Liège (Bishop V. J. Doutreloux), open to reasonable intervention by the public authorities "in harmony with the Christian tradition and with the social legislation of modern states," cf. "*Mons. Victor Joseph Doutreloux, vescovo di Liegi. Una parola di commemorazione e una pagina di storia*," in RISS, 1901, vol. XXVII, 484–92; now in SS II, 3–17. Quote on page 5.

2. At the Social Week of Florence in 1909, Toniolo was challenged by Fr. Agostino Gemelli, who would have liked to attribute greater autonomy of action to the state, while the Pisan professor insisted on its limits: The state "intervenes only where spontaneous personal or collective forces are not sufficient to completely achieve general progress," and relies on the local, municipal, and provincial public bodies, as well as on organizations of owners and workers. Cf. the summary of this discussion in DC III, 236.

3. "*Parole all'apertura delle Giornate sociali di Milano (1907)*," in DC II, 306.

4. *Provvedimenti sociali*, in DC III, 178–79.

5. "*Passato e futuro dell'Azione economica fra i cattolici d'Italia*" [hereafter *Passato e futuro*], in *Azione sociale*, Bergamo, a. I, Dec. 1906, 1–10; now in DC II, 285–300. Quote on page 290.

6. *Provvedimenti sociali,* in DC III, 180–81.

7. *Association internationale pour la protection légale des travailleurs*. Toniolo would become president of the Italian section in 1900. At the beginning he had doubts about this association, due to its neutral character with respect to religious principles. Then he

was convinced that it was appropriate to participate, encouraged above all by the testimony of Gaspard Decurtins. Cf. *Economista di Dio,* 131.

8. The conference had taken place August 23–28, 1897. Around 500 people of different nations, faiths, and parties had taken part. The leaders of European socialism — from Bebel to Liebknecht, from Vollmar to Vandervelde, from Adler to Grillenberger, etc. — were present in numbers. But some, like the Italians Turati, Ferri, Costa, and others, after giving their support, refused to participate so as not to find themselves in contact with "men in cassocks." Among the Catholics, in addition to Decurtins, were the Spaniard Rodriguez de Cepeda, the Belgian Carton de Wiart, Vienna seminary professor Msgr. Scheicher, the theologian Hille of Berlin, etc. Italy was represented by the lawyer G. M. Serralunga. The article was entitled "*Un grande sperimento sociale. Storia, giudizi, ammaestramenti*" [hereafter *Sperimento sociale*], in RISS, 1897, vol. XV, 202–19 and 481–89; now in DC III, 255–323.

9. Cf. *Sperimento sociale,* in DC III, 285.

10. One of Kautsky's statements in particular is taken up: "Those who not only attempt to dissolve but actually dissolve and destroy the family are for now the capitalists, who with prolonged work tear mothers away from children and do not grant parents the happiness of enjoying their children even on Sundays" (K. Kautsky, *Das Erfurter Programm in seinem grundsätzlichen Teil* [Stuttgart, 1892], 28: To me it seems rather that it corresponds in part to page 41). Also cited, generically, is K. Marx, *Das Kapital,* 1867, vol. I.

11. Toniolo summarizes the position of the Catholics in Zurich as follows: "The Catholics point out that preventing any manual exercise for the adolescent before the age of 15 risked taking away his taste for work and jeopardizing his professional training, and that the same prescription extended to agriculture would have practically reached the point of absurdity," *Sperimento sociale,* in DC III, 291.

12. *Sperimento sociale*, in DC III, 292.

13. Cf. ibid., 292–93.

14. Ibid., 294.

15. Ibid., 295.

16. Ibid., 296–99.

17. Ibid., 301–9.

18. Ibid., 309. On the topic of the work-family relationship, the debate still remains open, and new aspects are being grasped as, little by little, the female sensibility on equality develops together with the urgency that this not jeopardize family life. Finding the right balance is a challenge still open: cf. S. and V. Zamagni, *Famiglia e lavoro. Opposizione o armonia?* (Cinisello Balsamo: San Paolo, 2012).

19. The RISS, vol. XXIV, 493–521; now in DC III, 324–59, with an article signed T. A. (for G. Toniolo, I. Agliardi), reports on the Paris Congress of 1900, at which interesting convergences were reached on the limitation of the working day ("almost all of the speakers advocated the general introduction of a maximum day of 11 hours, with a prompt transition to a day of 10 hours," DC III, 349), on the limitation and prohibition of

nighttime work, on the inspectorate in factories, and on the establishment of an international association for the legal protection of workers. The statutes of the latter were approved. Toniolo, present at the congress, agreed to support the constitution of the Italian section (DC III, 358) and became its president by election (cf. memoranda of September 18, 1901, and November 20, 1901, published in RISS; now in DC III, 360–66).

20. *Sperimento sociale,* in DC III, 312.

21. Ibid., 322.

22. Ibid.

23. *Passato e futuro,* in DC II, 290.

24. Ibid., 292.

25. *Provvedimenti sociali,* in DC III, 182.

26. Cf. "*Precisazione sui contratti agrari. Osservazioni e discussioni durante il II Congresso cattolico italiano degli studiosi di scienze sociali*" (1896), in DC III, 381–88.

27. Ibid., 388.

28. Cf. Toniolo's review of P. G. Molteni's book *Gli affitti collettivi e la loro importanza sociale*, in RISS, 1905, vol. XXXIX, 134–36; now in DC III, 396–99; see also Toniolo's preface to A. Portaluppi, *L'affitto collettivo. Concetto e norme pratiche* (Treviglio: Tip. Messaggi, 1911; now in DC III, 418–20). Here he underlines that, of the two possible forms — united management system and divided management system — it is the latter that should be given preference, since it allows cooperative action by farmers that does not agglomerate them but rather unites them in an organic way, to the advantage of the family, of cultivation itself, lastingly binding the rural population to the soil.

29. He refers in this regard to the *Association internationale pour la protection légale des travailleurs: Provvedimenti sociali,* in DC III, 193.

30. *Provvedimenti sociali,* in DC III, 194.

31. *Passato e futuro,* in DC II, 295.

32. Ibid., 296.

33. Ibid.

34. *Provvedimenti sociali,* in DC III, 147.

35. As C. Vallauri notes, the corporate system of fascism, as established by the law and regulation of 1926 and by the Labor Charter (1927), takes a name dear to Catholics and tends toward the solidarity of the various factors of production, incorporating in this a principle of the Catholic social school, but "the organizational characteristics (binding), the nature (organs of the state), the ends (higher interests of production and of the nation) of the new institutions differ substantially from those indicated by the Church, as moreover from the positions of many exponents of fascism itself," *Alle radici del corporativismo* (Rome: Bulzoni, 1971), 146. I also refer on this topic to D. Sorrentino, *La conciliazione e il "fascismo cattolico." I tempi e la figura di Egilberto Martire,* preface by F. Malgeri (Brescia: Morcelliana, 1980), 131–37. See also F. Tamassia, "*La rappresentanza politica organica in Toniolo come momento del corporativismo cattolico,*" in M. L. Fornaciari Davoli, G. Russo (eds.), *Attualità del pensiero di Giuseppe Toniolo* (Milan: FrancoAngeli, 1982), 71–152.

36. *Provvedimenti sociali,* in DC III, 156. Cf. also "*I sindacati obbligatori,*" speech by Toniolo at the IVth International Scientific Congress in Fribourg, August 16–20, 1897; now in DC IV, 118–26; our author returns to the subject in a report to the scientific congress in Fribourg on October 20–22, 1903, published in installments in the RISS (1903, vol. XXXIII, 493–508; 1904, vol. XXXIV, 17–42 and 161–86); now in DC IV, 166–243: "*Problemi, discussioni, proposte intorno alla costituzione corporativa delle classi lavoratrici a proposito di recenti convegni sociali.*" On the topic of the obligatory character, see especially 210ff. Toniolo refers, on the problems of corporations, also from the point of view of a political structure of the state (proportional representation of corporations in the electoral and parliamentary body), to A. Boggiano, *L'organizzazione professionale e la rappresentanza di classe* (Turin: Bocca, 1903); A. M. Campeggi, *La costituzione del senato* (Rome: Desclée, Lefebvre & C., 1898). Toniolo also gave a summary on the theme of professional unions and corporate organization at the Social Week of Assisi (September 1911); now in DC IV, 256–61.

37. *Provvedimenti sociali,* in DC III, 158.

38. Ibid.

39. Toniolo uses this name by preference, but does not make an issue of the name. He also accepts the expressions "syndicate" and "corporation," as long as they express the same concept. Cf. "*Le unioni rurali cattoliche al Congresso di Pavia,*" published in RISS, 1894, vol. VI, 210–21; now in DC IV, 95–117. On the plurality of possible denominations, see ibid., 96, note 2.

40. "*Momento urgente e soluzione imperiosa. Lettera aperta al conte Stanislao Medolago Albani,*" in *La Patria,* August 19, 1901; now in DC IV, 142–55. Quote on page 149.

41. *Passato e futuro,* in DC II, 298–99.

42. *Provvedimenti sociali,* in DC III, 147–48.

43. *Criteri scientifici,* in TES V, 503.

44. Ibid.

45. Ibid., 503–4.

46. Ibid., 504.

47. Ibid., 505.

48. Ibid., 505–6.

49. Ibid., 506.

50. Ibid., 506–7.

51. Ibid., 507.

52. Ibid.

53. Ibid.

54. Ibid.

55. Ibid., 508.

56. Ibid.

57. Cf. the critical observations made in the letter of July 14, 1896, published as the preface to a book by one of his disciples, A. Farnocchia, *La banca unica di emissione e il monopolio del commercio bancario affidato allo Stato* (Lucca: Canovetti, 1896), v–vii; now

in TES V, 551–52.

58. Speaking at a conference at the Catholic University (*L'uomo come fine,* March 21–23, 2012), he says: "Toniolo's opposition to the central bank is probably explained in part by his distrust of large concentrations of capital, especially financial, partly with an unclear understanding of its functions at the heart of a modern banking system. It must also be traced back to the position of Toniolo and the Catholics on the role of the state in the economy. It is a position that Catholic thought subsequently revised, perhaps erring in the opposite direction, and that stems partly from the theoretical roots of Toniolo's thought (I would venture to say more liberal than is commonly said) and moreover from an opposition to *that* state rather than to the state *tout court*. This last reason, for example, most likely explains Toniolo's opposition to the Italian state's assuming full responsibility for the organization and management of the educational system, from primary school to university. Toniolo seems not to see the results obtained by the Italian state in the spread of literacy. … The nonrecognition of these results and the lukewarm support for the scholastic reforms of the Giolitti era by Italian Catholics were among the many fruits poisoned by the post-unification division of Italians," *L'uomo come fine*, 528.

59. Held in Fiesole from August 31 to September 4, 1896. Report published with the title "*Criteri direttivi sull'ordinamento degli istituti bancari esclusi i banchi di emissione*," in *Atti e documenti del XIV Congresso cattolico italiano* (Venice, 1897), pt. I, 186–94; now in TES V, 537–50.

60. "*Criteri direttivi*," in TES V, 542.

61. "*Riforme del sistema tributario*" [hereafter *Sistema tributario*], in *Atti del II Congresso cattolico italiano degli studiosi di scienze sociali* (Padua, August 26–28, 1896) (Padua: Tip del Seminario, 1898), 194–209; now in TES V, 524–36.

62. *Sistema tributario,* in TES V, 534–35.

63. Ibid., in 527.

64. Ibid., 528. I have not been able to identify the author Toniolo refers to here.

65. For this he refers to St. Thomas: In distributive justice it is not the principle of the equality of thing to thing that applies, but the proportion of things to people: *in iustitia distributiva non accipitur medium secundum aequalitatem rei ad rem, sed secundum proportionem rerum ad personas: Summa Theologiae,* II–II, q. LXI, a. 2; he also cites the concept of the Church as a body developed by St. Paul, extending it to the organic concept of society, to emphasize that, in the hierarchy of social classes, it is just that the one who is higher up and more powerful should help the one who is more in need (cf. *Sistema tributario,* in TES V, 529–30).

66. *Sistema tributario,* in TES V, 531. See also, on the topic, the letter of October 27, 1912, to Jacopo Tivaroni, in LL III, 315–19.

67. To L. Caissotti di Chiusano, March 1, 1897, in LL II, 52.

68. Ibid., 52–3.

69. Ibid., 53.

70. Ibid. Here Toniolo refers to P. Antoine, *Cours d'économie sociale* (*Corso di economia sociale*, Siena, 1901); V. Brants, *Compendio di economia sociale* (Siena, 1896).

71. Letter of September 28, 1903, to L. Caissotti di Chiusano, in LL II, 382–85.

72. Ibid., in LL II, 383. Toniolo compared English colonial policy with that of ancient imperial Rome, calling the English, following Cesare Balbo, the "new Romans" called to spread Christian civilization throughout the world. Cf. Letter of June 20 to L. Caissotti di Chiusano, in LL III, 10–11.

73. Letter of September 28, 1903, to L. Caissotti di Chiusano, in LL II, 383–84.

74. Ibid., 384.

75. Ibid. He invited the correspondent to write an article on these topics, and this was "*Imperialismo e riforma fiscale in Inghilterra*," in RISS, a. XII, installment 134, Feb. 1904, 187–212.

76. Letter to Marius Gonin dated August 12, 1914, in LL III, 375–78. Quote on page 376. He concluded the letter by expressing his conviction "that the Catholic Church, with the pontificate that embodies it, from which not a few governments boasted of having completed their separation, is the supreme organism of universal human society, indispensable for the balance and peaceable greatness of all nations, indeed the axle on which the social order of civilization perennially revolves" (ibid., 377–78).

Conclusion: Perspectives and Provocations

1. "*Discorso di apertura del II Congresso cattolico italiano degli studiosi di scienze sociali*" (Padua 1896), published in *Atti e documenti del II Congresso cattolico italiano degli studiosi di scienze sociali*, 114–21; now in DC I, 243–51. Quote on page 245.

2. "Another factual circumstance that may perplex those who are unaware of the inspiring criteria of Toniolo's scientific work is that, while he is generally considered a leader in the field of political economy, in reality nowhere in his writings on production or distribution or money or credit or foreign trade is there a body of doctrines that, in the context of theoretical economics or applied economics, marks a constructive contribution and links its name to the elaboration of this or that theory," Introduction to the *Trattato*, TES I, xii.

3. Cf. *Trattato*, TES III, 3–5.

4. *Profilo di storia*, vol. II, 187.

5. *Dum Romae consulitur Saguntum expugnatur*. A saying that summarizes Livy's comment on the fact that the Roman Senate got lost in consultations while Hannibal was conquering the city of Saguntum, whose ambassadors had gone to Rome for help (cf. Livy, *The History of Rome*, XXI, 7, 1).

6. T. Piketty, *Il capitale nel XXI secolo* (Florence-Milan: Giunti-Bompiani, 2019), 34.

7. A critical appraisal of the lights and shadows is in *Chiesa nella storia*, 251–80.

8. I refer to my contribution "*Santità laicale e questione sociale: la profezia di Giuseppe Toniolo*," in *Economia e società*, 3–24.

9. cf. Toniolo's reference to Le Play in note 23 of chapter VII.

10. Toniolo expands on the concept of economic "technique" or "technology" in the introductory volume of the *Trattato*: cf. TES II, 10–12.

11. Cf. chapter 2.

12. *Linee e quesiti*, in TES II, 367–91.

13. Cf. ibid., 374–75.

14. One authoritative expression of this ecclesial certainty is what Vatican II teaches in the constitution *Gaudium et Spes* regarding the changes that characterize current society: "The Church also maintains that beneath all changes there are many realities which do not change and which have their ultimate foundation in Christ, who is the same yesterday and today, yes and forever (Heb 13:8)" (10).

15. In the process of the journey toward civilization — "*incivilimento*" — Toniolo distinguishes three aspects, or possibilities: "progress, regression, renewal, which are inherent to the fact of civilization and make up its physiology, pathology, and therapy," *Socialismo*, in CS, 275.

16. According to Pareto: "The efficiency of an allocation is maximal when it is impossible to increase one economic dimension without decreasing another. In the specific case of social well-being, the Paretian criterion assumes the well-known formulation according to which a certain economic configuration is optimal when it is impossible to improve someone's well-being without worsening that of someone else," *Profilo di storia*, vol. I, 290–91.

17. *Trattato*, TES II, 18.

18. Cf. A. Kirman, "The Intrinsic Limits of Modern Economic Theory: The Emperor Has No Clothes," in *The Economic Journal*, 99 (1989), 395, 126–39.

19. On the Walrasian view of the economic system, cf. *Profilo di storia*, vol. I, 234–44.

20. In particular Kenneth Joseph Arrow and Gérard Debreu: cf. *Profilo di storia*, vol. II, 81–97.

21. Cf. ibid., 97.

22. Cf. ibid., 100–10.

23. "There is, in Marshall's view, unlike in that of Walras, an inextricable interweaving between the economic, social, and cultural spheres, a strong connection between the facts of the material sphere and those of the moral sphere, a connection that entails significant consequences on the manner of conceiving, for example, interventions in the economy by the state," *Profilo di storia*, vol. I, 261. On Toniolo's interest in Marshall, cf. A. Spicciani, "*Giuseppe Toniolo, un economista storico*," in *Contributi alla conoscenza*, 188. In effect, among the foreign treatise writers to whom he looked with interest in the introduction to his *Trattato*, starting with Schmoller of the *Grundriss der allgemeinen Volkswirtschaft*, there is Marshall, whom he considered "perhaps the most original of all" (*Trattato*, TES I, 3).

24. Elsewhere I developed this "ideal-type," playing on the Greek root of the term "economy." To distinguish the new approach, I used the form most in keeping with the Greek, *oikonomia*, to underline that precisely in the *oikos* (home, family) the human person finds the first plexus of his relationships, which multiply in the human-social (the universal human family) up to the environmental level (what *Laudato Si'* calls the "common home"), arriving at the transcendent *oikos* — that is, God, the root and

ultimate destination of the human, especially in the typically Christian vision of the "Trinitarian communion": cf. D. Sorrentino, "*Economia e nuovo umanesimo*," in F. Del Pizzo, A. Gargiulo (eds.), *Teologia, economia e lavoro. Per un umanesimo della fraternità* (Trapani: Il Pozzo di Giacobbe, 2020), 15–33 (the volume reproduces the proceedings of a conference organized by the Theological Faculty of Southern Italy, Naples, November 10–20, 2019). I took up the theme again in *Francesco d'Assisi e l'economia della fraternità. Per ripartire dagli ultimi (*Perugia: Edizioni francescane italiane, 2020), 69–78.

25. Encyclical *Populorum Progressio* (1967), par. 14 and 42.

26. Cf. the *Programma dei cattolici*, in DC I, 8–9. Toniolo called for a strong link between the lending capitalist (pushing him to take on responsibilities and not to want to profit in safety from the risks of industry) and the enterprising capitalist, who does business and produces, containing the speculative phenomenon by subjecting credit to rules and controls in its various forms.

27. Cf. V. Zamagni, *Perché l'Europa ha cambiato il mondo*, 326.

28. Cf. A. Picchiarelli, *Tra profilazione e discernimento. La teologia morale nel tempo dell'algoritmo* (Assisi: Cittadella Editrice, 2021), 152–54.

29. Cf. for example, L. Tomassini, *Il grande salto. L'uomo, il digitale e la più importante evoluzione della nostra storia*, preface by G. Riotta (Rome: Luiss University Press, 2020), 81–98.

30. Cf. S. Zuboff, *Il capitalismo della sorveglianza. Il futuro dell'umanità nell'era dei nuovi poteri* (Rome: Luiss University Press, 2019).

31. See the paragraph "*uomini e robot*" in P. Bianchi, 4.0. *La nuova rivoluzione industriale* (Bologna: il Mulino, 2018), 82–92. At the conclusion of a careful analysis of the foreseeable scenarios with the exponential growth of automation, the author wonders, "Should we be optimists or catastrophists, imagining a world in which, freed from work, we will carry out only works of art, or foreseeing brutalized societies of men without work, on the margins of production systems dominated by machines?" (ibid., 91). He maintains that it is probable that there will be a "coexistence" — certainly very precarious and with predictable tensions — between two types of people, depending on whether they find themselves at the levels of the automated economy or at those of the simpler economy with little added value. A "split" society.

32. The term "imo," now obsolete, was customary for Toniolo: cf. *Programma scientifico*, in IC, 130–31.

33. Cf. on this hypothesis F. Manzalini, "*Toniolo e la scienza economica del suo tempo*," in *Economia e società*, 54–57.

34. I would think of authors like John Galbraith, Warren Samuels, Marc Toll, Kenneth Boulding: cf. *Profilo di storia*, vol. II, 210–16.

35. Cf. E. Basile et al., *Istituzioni e sviluppo economico nel capitalismo contemporaneo. Il caso di Cina e India*, 30–42.

36. Cf. A. G. Gruchy, *Modern Economic Thought: The American Contribution* (New York: Prentice Hall, 1947).

37. Cf. V. Di Giovinazzo, "Shitowsky Tibor," in DEC, 719–25.

38. In addition to the introduction by S. Zamagni and L. Bruni to the DEC, cf. C. Montesi, *Il paradigma dell'economia civile. Radici storiche e nuovi orizzonti* (Terni: UVE 2016); S. Zamagni, *Economia ed etica. La crisi e la sfida dell'economia civile*, interview by N. Curci (Brescia: La Scuola, 2009); K. Raworth, *The Doughnut Economics: Seven Ways to Think Like a 21st-Century Economist* (London: Random House, 2017).

39. And so not through a voluntary yet precarious negotiation of the type proposed by Rousseau.

40. Cf. L. Dini, A. Marzano (eds.), Meno Stato più società. *Meno spesa pubblica, meno tasse, meno pubblico più privato* (Rome: Il periscopio delle idee, 2016), with contributions by L. Tivelli, S. Cuzzilla, A. Diotallevi, A. Malaschini, A. Monorchio, C. Malinconico, F. Giubilei, L. Mazzella.

41. Cf. A. Ardigò, *Toniolo il primato della riforma sociale. Per ripartire dalla società civile* (Bologna: Nuova Universale Cappelli, 1978).

42. V. Zamagni, *Perché l'Europa ha cambiato il mondo*, 263.

43. *Distribuzione*, in TES IV, 207.

44. *Trattato*, TES I, 22.

45. I developed this thought with the image of a triangle of the crisis in *Crisi come grazia. Per una nuova primavera della Chiesa* (Perugia: EFI, 2020). I drew some aspects of this diagnosis precisely from Toniolo's thoughts. On this, I refer to my contribution "*Santità laicale e questione sociale: la profezia di Giuseppe Toniolo*," in *Economia e società*, 3–24, especially on pages 14–17.

46. S. J. Gould, *I pilastri del tempo* (Milan: Il Saggiatore, 2000).

47. *Untersuchungen über die Methode der Sozialwissenschaften und der politischen Ökonomie insbesondere*, 237. Cf. *Profilo di storia*, vol. I, 247.

48. *An Essay on the Nature and Significance of Economic Science* (London: Macmillan, 1937): "The economist deals not with ends as such, but with the way in which their attainment is limited. The ends may be noble, or they may be base. They may be 'material' or 'immaterial' — if ends can be so described. But if the attainment of one set of ends involves the sacrifice of others, then it has an economic aspect" (25).

49. Cf. *Profilo di storia*, vol. II, 113–16.

50. S. Zamagni, *Economia e etica. Saggi sul fondamento etico del discorso* economico (Rome: AVE, 1994).

51. Ibid., 20.

52. As is well known, they are: (1) No Poverty, (2) Zero Hunger, (3) Good Health and Well-being, (4) Quality Education, (5) Gender Equality, (6) Clean Water and Sanitation, (7) Affordable and Clean Energy, (8) Decent Work and Economic Growth, (9) Industry, Innovation, and Infrastructure, (10) Reducing Inequality, (11) Sustainable Cities and Communities, (12) Responsible Consumption and Production, (13) Climate Action, (14) Life Below Water, (15) Life on Land, (16) Peace, Justice, and Strong Institutions, (17) Partnerships for the Goals.

53. Cf. S. Zamagni, *Economia ed etica*, 16–17.

54. Cf. L. Bruni, *Il capitalismo e il sacro* (Milan: Vita e Pensiero, 2019), 2–3.

55. Cf. V. Zamagni, *Perché l'Europa ha cambiato il mondo*, introducing her detailed demonstration. She writes, "There is in the volume a driving thesis that justifies its title, a thesis summarized as follows: the Industrial Revolution, with which the economic and social transformation of the world began, could only be born in that Europe imbued with a concept of man of Christian origin, which at the same time exalted his freedom but limited his power over other men through the practice of justice and brotherhood" (10).

56. Cf. E. Basile et al., *Istituzioni e sviluppo economico nel capitalismo contemporaneo. Il caso di Cina e India*, especially 72–93.

57. L. Bruni, *Il capitalismo e il sacro*, 33.

58. Cf. "*Applicazioni pratiche sociali della SS. Eucaristia*," in *Atti del Congresso eucaristico di Milano* (Milan, 1896, pt. II), 186–93; now in SS I, 62–71; "*L'Eucaristia e il risorgimento civile*," in *Atti del Congresso eucaristico ed esposizione di arte sacra di Orvieto* (5–8 settembre 1896) (Orvieto, 1897), 262–67; now in SS I, 72–8; "*L'Eucaristia e l'avvenire della società*," in *Atti del Congresso eucaristico di Venezia ed esposizione di arte sacra (3–12 agosto 1897)* (Venice, 1898), 259–66, now in SS I, 79–91.

59. Cf. V. Possenti, "*Maritain e il marxismo*," in *Aggiornamenti Sociali*, November 1977, 607–24.

60. Cf. chapters 5–7 of the Gospel of Matthew.

61. J. E. Stiglitz, *Invertire la rotta. Disuguaglianza e crescita economica* (Bari: Laterza, 2017).

62. Cf. F. Caffè, *L'economia senza profeti. Contributi di bibliografia economica* (Rome: Studium, 2013), 119.

63. L. Bruni, "*Giuseppe Toniolo e lo 'spirito del capitalismo'*," in *Economia e società*, 71.

Bibliography

Writings by Giuseppe Toniolo

(For brevity, we limit ourselves to the titles of the *Complete Works*. For a meticulous list of over 300 titles by Toniolo, in chronological order, one can consult F. Manzalini, *Elementi di economia politica in Giuseppe Toniolo* (Siena: Cantagalli, 2009, 167–203)).

Capitalismo e socialismo. Vatican City, 1947.

Dei remoti fattori della potenza economica di Firenze nel Medio Evo e scritti storici. Vatican City, 1952.

Democrazia cristiana. Concetti e indirizzi, I–II. Vatican City, 1949.

Democrazia cristiana. Istituti e forme, I-II. Vatican City, 1951.

Iniziative culturali e di azione cattolica. Vatican City, 1949.

L'odierno problema sociologico. Studio storico-critico. Vatican City, 1947.

Lettere, I (1871–1895), II (1896–1903), III (1904–1918). Vatican City, 1952–1953.

Scritti spirituali, religiosi, familiari e vari, I–II. Vatican City, 1952.

Storia dell'economia sociale in Toscana nel Medio Evo, I, *La vita civile-politica*, II, *La vita economica.* Vatican City, 1948.

Trattato di economia sociale e scritti economici, I–V. Vatican City, 1949–1952.

Writings on Giuseppe Toniolo

Various authors, "*Atti del Convegno 'Stato degli studi e prospettive di ricerca sulla figura e sull'opera di Giuseppe Toniolo*,'" in *Bollettino dell'Archivio per la storia del movimento sociale cattolico in Italia*, 20, 1985, 191–329.

Various authors, *Contributi alla conoscenza del pensiero di Giuseppe Toniolo*. Pisa: Pacini, 1984 (proceedings of the conference "Economia e società in the Crisis of the Modern State: The Thought of Giuseppe Toniolo" (Pisa, December 18–19, 1981)).

Arcidiocesi di Pisa Opera Giuseppe Toniolo. *Atti del Convegno di studi su Giuseppe Toniolo (Pisa 7–8 ottobre 1988)*. Pisa: ETS, 1990.

Ardigò, A. *Toniolo: il primato della riforma sociale. Per ripartire dalla società civile*, Bologna: Nuova Universale Cappelli, 1978.

Bazzichi, O. *Giuseppe Toniolo. Alle origini della dottrina sociale della Chiesa*, Turin: Lindau, 2012.

Bianchini, M. and Manzalini, R. *Economia sociale, diritti, cooperazione*. Pisa-Rome: Fabrizio Serra Editore, 2015.

Bodega, D. and Carera, A., eds. *Economia e società per il bene comune. La lezione di Giuseppe Toniolo (1918–2018)*. Milan: Vita e Pensiero, 2020 (conference proceedings, Catholic University of the Sacred Heart, November 24, 2018).

Burgalassi, S. *Alle origini della sociologia. G. Toniolo e la scuola pisana (1878–1915)*. Pisa: ETS, 1984.

Carera, A., ed. *Giuseppe Toniolo. L'uomo come fine. Con saggi sulla storia dell'Istituto Giuseppe Toniolo di Studi Superiori*. Milan: Vita e Pensiero, 2014 (conference proceedings, Catholic University of the Sacred Heart, March 21–23, 2012).

Cova A. "*Lavoro e capitale nel pensiero di Giuseppe Toniolo*," in Carera, A., ed. *Giuseppe Toniolo. L'uomo come fine*, op. cit., 111-138.

Fanfani, A. "*Il contributo di Giuseppe Toniolo agli studi di storia economica*," in Various authors, *La figura e l'opera di Giuseppe Toniolo*. Milan, 1968, 75–98.

Fornaciari Davoli, M. L. and Russo, G., eds. *Attualità del pensiero di Giu-*

seppe Toniolo. Milan: FrancoAngeli, 1982.

Manzalini, F., *Elementi di economia politica in Giuseppe Toniolo*. Siena: Cantagalli, 2009.

Manzalini, F. "Il credito e la circolazione della ricchezza," in Carera, A., ed. *Giuseppe Toniolo. L'uomo come fine*, op. cit., 139–172.

Manzalini, F. "*Giuseppe Toniolo e la scienza economica del suo tempo*" in Bodega, D. and Carera, A., eds. *Economia e società per il bene comune*, 43–58.

Molesti, R. "Il pensiero economico-sociale di Giuseppe Toniolo," in Molesti, R., ed. *Giuseppe Toniolo. Il pensiero e l'opera*, Milan: FrancoAngeli, 2005, 131–167.

Molesti, R. *Il pensiero economico e sociale di Giuseppe Toniolo*. Pisa: Ipemedizioni, 2017.

Pecorari, P., ed. *Ketteler e Toniolo. Tipologie sociali del movimento cattolico in Europa*. Rome: Città Nuova, 1977.

Pecorari, P. *Giuseppe Toniolo e il socialismo. Saggio sulla cultura cattolica tra '800 e '900*. Bologna: Pàtron, 1981.

Pecorari, P. *Economia e riformismo nell'Italia liberale. Studi su Giuseppe Toniolo e Luigi Luzzatti*. Milan, 1986.

Pecorari, P., ed. *Giuseppe Toniolo tra economia e società*. Udine: Del Bianco editore, 1990 (conference proceedings, Pieve di Soligo, October 28–29, 1988).

Pecorari, P. *Toniolo. Un economista per la democrazia*. Rome, 1991.

Pecorari, P. "*L'Unione cattolica per gli studi sociali in Italia dalle origini (1889) alla fine dell'Ottocento*," in *Associazionismo economico e diffusione dell'economia politica nell'Italia dell'Ottocento, vol. II*. Milan: FrancoAngeli, 2000.

Pecorari, P. *Alle origini dell'anticapitalismo cattolico. Due saggi e un bilancio storiografico su Giuseppe Toniolo*, Milan: Vita e Pensiero, 2010.

Pecorari, P. *Carteggio Giuseppe Toniolo-Luigi Luzzatti (1869–1918)*. Vatican City: Biblioteca Apostolica Vaticana, 2017.

Sorrentino, D. *Gli intellettuali cattolici e le origini della 'sociologia cristiana'. La Rivista internazionale di scienze sociali e discipline ausiliarie*, in Camadini, G., ed. *La 'Rerum novarum' e il movimento cattolico italiano*. Brescia: Morcelliana, 1995, 88–151.

Sorrentino, D. *Giuseppe Toniolo. Una Chiesa nella storia*, Milan: Vita e Pensiero, 2012.

Sorrentino, D. *L'economista di Dio. Giuseppe Toniolo*, Rome: AVE, 2012.

Sorrentino, D. "*Santità laicale e questione sociale: la profezia di Giuseppe Toniolo*," in Bodega, D. and Carera, A. *Economia e società per il bene comune*, 3–24.

Spicciani, A. "*Giuseppe Toniolo, uno storico fra economia e scienze umane*," in Fornaciari Davoli, M. L. and Russo, G., eds. *Attualità del pensiero di Giuseppe Toniolo*, op. cit., 181–206.

Spicciani, A., "*Giuseppe Toniolo, un economista storico*," in Various authors, *Contributi alla conoscenza del pensiero di Giuseppe Toniolo*, 155–202.

Spicciani, A. *Giuseppe Toniolo tra economia e storia*. Naples: Guida editore, 1990.

Tangheroni, M., "Toniolo storico della Toscana medievale," in Arcidiocesi di Pisa Opera Giuseppe Toniolo, *Atti del Convegno di studi su Giuseppe Toniolo*, 35–50.

Villani, U. "*Il progetto di un Istituto cattolico di diritto internazionale*," in Bodega, D. and A. Carera. *Economia e società per il bene comune*, 131–142.

Violante, C. "*Il significato dell'opera storiografica di Giuseppe Toniolo nell'età di Leone XIII*," in Rossini, G., ed. *Aspetti della cultura cattolica nell'età di Leone XIII*. Conference proceedings (Bologna, December 27–29, 1960). Rome: Cinque Lune, 1961, 707–67.

Vito, F. "*Giuseppe Toniolo e la cultura economica dei cattolici italiani*," in Rossini, G., ed. *Aspetti della cultura cattolica nell'età di Leone XIII*. Conference proceedings (Bologna December 27–29, 1960). Rome: Cinque Lune, 1961, 9–34.

Essential bibliography

Antoine, P. *Corso di economia* sociale. Siena 1901.

Basyle, E., et al. *Istituzioni e sviluppo economico nel capitalismo contemporaneo. Il caso di Cina e India*. Milan: FrancoAngeli, 2021.

Bazzichi, O. *Dall'economia civile francescana all'economia capitalistica moderna. Una via all'umano e al civile dell'economia*. Rome: Armando editore, 2015.

Bianchi, P. *4.0. La nuova rivoluzione industriale*. Bologna: il Mulino, 2018.

Bianchini, M. *La parola e la merce. Una guida al pensiero economico*. Reggio Emilia: Diabasis, 2005.

Boggiano, A. *L'organizzazione professionale e la rappresentanza di classe*. Turin: Bocca, 1903.

Brants, V. *Compendio di economia sociale*. Siena, 1896.

Bruni, L. *Il prezzo della gratuità*. Rome: Città Nuova, 2006.

Bruni L. and di Giovinazzo, V. "*Felicità*," in Bruni, L and Zamagni, S., eds. *Dizionario di economia civile*. 381–396.

Bruni, L. and Zamagni, S. *Civic Economics. Efficienza, equità e pubblica felicità*. Bologna: il Mulino, 2004.

Bruni L. and Zamagni, S., eds. *Dizionario di economia civile*. Rome: Città Nuova, 2009.

Campeggi, A. M. *La costituzione del senato*. Desclée, Rome: Lefebvre e C., 1898.

Cossa, L. *Introduzione allo studio dell'economia politica*. Milan: Hoepli, 1892 (entirely revised 3rd edition of the *Guida allo studio dell'economia politica*).

De Gasperi, A. *I tempi e gli uomini che prepararono la Rerum novarum*. Milan: Vita e Pensiero, 1945.

Demucci, F. *I molti e i pochi. La società 'sotto-sopra' dei diseguali*. Soveria Mannelli: Rubbettino, 2015.

Del Pizzo, F. *Salvatore Talamo e la rinascita moderna della dottrina sociale della Chiesa*. Soveria Mannelli: Rubbettino, 2018.

Drèze, J., Sen, A.K. *An Uncertain Glory. India and Its Contradictions*. Princeton: Princeton University Press, 2013.

Faucci, R. *L'economia politica in Italia. Dal Cinquecento ai nostri giorni*. Turin: UTET, 2000.

Gould, S. J. *I pilastri del tempo*. Milan: Il Saggiatore, 2000.

Graziani A. *Istituzioni di economia politica*. Turin: Fratelli Bocca editori, 1904.

Montesi, C. *Il paradigma dell'economia civile. Radici storiche e nuovi orizzonti*. Terni: UVE, 2016.

Picchiarelli, A. *Tra profilazione e discernimento. La teologia morale nel tempo dell'algoritmo*. Assisi: Cittadella, 2021.

Piketty, T. *Il capitale nel XXI secolo*. Florence-Milan: Giunti-Bompiani, 2019.

Screpanti, E. and Zamagni, S. *Profilo di storia del pensiero economico, I, Dalle origini a Keynes, II, Gli sviluppi contemporanei*. Rome: Carocci, 2004 (6th reprint 2017).

Sorrentino, D., *La conciliazione e il "fascismo cattolico". I tempi e la figura di Egilberto Martire*. Brescia: Morcelliana, 1980.

Sorrentino, D., "La 'democrazia' di Luigi Sturzo," in *Impegno e dialogo: incontri culturali 1985–1986*. Biblioteca diocesana S. Paolino-Seminario di Nola, 117–137.

Supino, C., *Principi di economia politica*. Naples: Luigi Pierro editore, 1904.

Stiglitz, J. E., *Invertire la rotta. Disuguaglianza e crescita economica*. Bari: Laterza, 2017.

Talamo, S. *Il concetto della schiavitù. Da Aristotele ai dottori scolastici*. Rome: Tipografia dell'Unione Cooperativa, 1908.

Todeschini, G. *Ricchezza francescana. Dalla povertà volontaria alla società di mercato*. Bologna: il Mulino, 2004.

Tomassini, L. *Il grande salto. L'uomo, il digitale e la più importante evoluzione della nostra storia*. Rome: Luiss University Press, 2020.

Toniolo, Gianni. *Storia economica dell'Italia liberale (1850–1918)*. Bologna: il Mulino, 1988.

Weiss, A. M. *La questione sociale*. Trento, 1897.

Zamagni, S. *Economia e etica. Saggi sul fondamento etico del discorso economico*. Rome: AVE, 1994.

Zamagni, S. *Prosperità inclusiva. Saggi di economia civile*. Rome: Studium, 2021.

Zamagni, S. and Zamagni, V. *Famiglia e lavoro. Opposizione o armonia?*. Cinisello Balsamo: San Paolo, 2012.

Index of Names